D1576714

*A Social History of the Diocese
of Newcastle*

A SOCIAL HISTORY OF THE DIOCESE OF NEWCASTLE 1882–1982

Edited by
W. S. F. Pickering

Foreword by
Alec Vidler

ORIEL PRESS

STOCKSFIELD
BOSTON   HENLEY   LONDON

First published in 1981 for the centenary of the Diocese
by Oriel Press Ltd (Routledge & Kegan Paul Ltd)
Stocksfield, Northumberland, England NE43 7NA

Photo-set in Plantin and
Printed in Great Britain by
Knight and Forster Limited, Leeds

ISBN 0 85362 189 6

346394

FOREWORD

AT THE END of the chapter on Northumberland in the 1811 edition of Thomas Fuller's *The Worthies of England* mention is made of some books that had by then been published on the subject; thus, 'Various Collections have been made towards a History of this County: and "A Description of the antient Kingdom of Northumberland", by Dr Nicolson, then Archdeacon (afterwards Bishop) of Carlisle, was announced by Bagford in 1695, as ready for the press, but then remaining in the Dean and Chapter's Library at Carlisle . . .' I am glad that the present collection of essays is not remaining in any library or libraries but is to be published at a most appropriate time, namely when the Diocese of Newcastle will be celebrating its centenary.

The Diocese is to be congratulated on having been able to produce from its own resources so comprehensive a survey of its own history (without help from Carlisle!). I spent two of the happiest years of my life in Newcastle and still, on the rare occasions when I am able to alight at the Central station, I am overwhelmed with sentiments of recollection and anticipation. But I realize now that, when I lived and worked on Tyneside, I knew very little about the story of the Diocese's inception and development. I have therefore found this volume to be full of interest and enlightenment. I am sure that many others who live and work, or who have lived and worked, or who will live and work in Northumberland will do so too.

At the same time, it will surely be of interest to a much wider circle of readers. So thorough a survey of a single diocese is an important contribution to the historiography of the Church of England as a whole, and dwellers in other parts of the country will derive instruction from comparing and contrasting what has happened in their dioceses with what has happened here.

Different readers will naturally relish some chapters more than others. Those concerned with the social history of the period will welcome the amount of precise factual and statistical information that is provided. Others will savour more the testimonies that are based on personal experience. And today's clerics should find engaging what is recorded about the achievements and goings-on of their predecessors. I myself was particularly taken with Chapter XIII, for the conditions there described, which may now seem to be exaggerated, correspond exactly to what I recall of the slum parish in central Newcastle in which I worked sixty years ago: I can vouch for the accuracy of the vivid picture that is given in this chapter.

A book such as this occasions many reflections, or provides much food for thought as the saying is. The Bishop in his *Concluding Remarks* picks out the most striking points. It is true that the general impression left by the essays is of the Church's declining influences of which realists have been long aware, though it has seldom been so usefully documented. I do not myself find the story depressing, perhaps because as an historian, I am too familiar with the many fluctuations in religion that have taken place in this and other parts of the world. Today what is happening in England is by no means characteristic of what is happening elsewhere, nor may it go on like this. A well-known and very shrewd commentator on the social scene said to me not long ago: 'My fear is that the Churches will not be ready for the great religious revival of the twenty-first century.' I am not myself enough of a prophet to endorse such a statement. All I can say is that I regard it as a singular honour to have been invited to introduce this notable symposium. I hope it will have very many readers.

ALEC VIDLER
(Honorary Fellow and former Dean of King's College, Cambridge)

Acknowledgements

In a book which has so many contributors who have worked in widely different areas, it is impossible to thank all those who have assisted in this venture. Some contributors have offered notes of thanks at the end of their essays. However, over and above the individuals so mentioned, the Editor would like to thank in particular the staffs of the Central Public Library, of the Library of the University, and of Church House, Newcastle upon Tyne. And those who have done so much of the typing, Annemarie Rule and Angela Ross, are warmly thanked for their endeavours.

I am very grateful to Mrs. Ward Davis, who has allowed us to use part of a manuscript written by her late husband, which constitutes Chapter XIII.

Gratitude is also expressed for financial help from the Haltwhistle Trust, the Joicey Trust, the William Leech Trust, the Rothley Trust, the Douglas Smith Trust and the Sponsorship Committee for Publications of the University of Newcastle upon Tyne.

We also wish to thank the Audio-Visual Department of the University of Newcastle upon Tyne for preparing the map of the Diocese.

But above all I extend deep appreciation to all of the contributors who have laboured so hard and who have endured so amiably my constant goading them. Without them there would indeed be no book at all!

W.S.F.P.

Editor's Preface

This volume of essays is very much a local product. Its concern is with a particular area of England designated by ecclesiastical boundaries. It is also local in so far as those who have contributed the essays have not only used home materials as it were, but are themselves with one exception,* local people. Few were born in the area but most of them have been resident in Northumberland or Durham for a considerable time. When the volume was first suggested in 1975 by the Bishop of Newcastle, the Right Reverend Ronald Bowlby, the idea was raised and quickly rejected that it should be written by specialists of national reputation, whether they resided locally or not. The policy decided on was to recruit people on the spot, mainly historians and sociologists, who would select for description and analysis some aspect of the development of the Diocese during the first hundred years of its existence. Even the publishers, it was hoped, would be local. For better or for worse these aims have been achieved.

We offer to readers the fruits of our labours in the hope that the contributions as a whole constitute a fair account of what has been happening in the Diocese during a particularly difficult period in the life of the Church at large.

To write a history of the Church, even with the boundaries we have set ourselves, raises a number of theoretical issues, such as the nature of the Church and the problems of being 'objective' about what some hold is a divine institution. We have deliberately avoided discussing these theoretical topics and have concentrated instead on dealing with the specific areas of church life as they have impinged on society as a whole in the area. This is what we imply in calling the book a social history.

Our wish is that what is recorded about the past hundred years of the Church in the most northern corner of England will sound a note of thankfulness for what has been achieved and perhaps act as a basis of discussion, as well as being a spur to action as the Diocese enters its second century.

---

*Peter J. Jagger, who has written Chapter II, The Formation of the Diocese of Newcastle.

ABBREVIATIONS

B.L.D.N.	*Bishop's Letter and the Diocesan Newsheet*
N.D.C.	*Newcastle Diocesan Calendar*
N.D.Ch.	*Newcastle Daily Chronicle*
N.D.G.	*Newcastle Diocesan Gazette*
N.D.Y.B.	*Newcastle Diocesan Year Book*

BIBLIOGRAPHY AND REFERENCES

Readers will find in the Appendix the bibliography which covers the references in all the chapters, except Chapter II and XIV. It includes books, articles, journals, newspapers, etc. in which the Diocese of Newcastle or people associated with it are specifically mentioned. Such items are marked with an asterisk. Others have been included which contain no such references but which are mentioned by the contributors.

Apart from the exceptions just noted, the method of reference is by the item's author and date of publication. For example, (Atlay 1912), means J. B. Atlay, *The Life of the Right Reverend Ernest Roland Wilberforce, First Bishop of Newcastle upon Tyne and afterwards Bishop of Chichester*, published in 1912. If the reference is (Atlay 1912:72), it means page 72 of that book.

CONTENTS

PART ONE

The Creation and Development of the Diocese

LIST OF PLATES
and Photographic Credits

The Editor and Publisher express their thanks to all who have helped in providing the illustrations.

A PRACTICAL NOTE ABOUT READING THIS BOOK

The essays vary a great deal in length and style. Some readers might, therefore, be advised not to begin at the beginning but to start with some of the more personal contributions, such as Chapters III, IV, XIII, and then turn to the more strictly historical and sociological chapters.

PART ONE

THE CREATION AND DEVELOPMENT OF THE DIOCESE

DIOCESE of
NEWCASTLE

o Berwick upon Tweed

Holy Island
(Lindisfarne)

o Ford

o Wooler

urban area

county boundary

The Cheviot
△

Archdeaconry
of
Lindisfarne

o Alnwick

Warkworth

o Rothbury

Ashington o

Bellingham
o

Morpeth o
Whalton o

Blyth

Archdeaconry
of
Northumberland

Corbridge o

NEWCASTLE
UPON TYNE
○

Tynemouth
River Tyne

Hexham o

Gateshead o

County
of
Durham

o Alston

*Note: Parts of the County of Northumberland and the County and City of
Newcastle upon Tyne were designated as parts of the County of Tyne
and Wear in the early 1970s*

Chapter I

THE SOCIAL AND ECONOMIC CHARACTERISTICS OF NORTHUMBERLAND IN THE 1880s

D. J. Rowe

THE KEY-WORD for this book might be considered to be 'change' —
the way in which the Diocese has changed and adapted to change in its
first century. But it is important to see that the Diocese was born out
of change and to a considerable extent the changes which it had to face
in the secular world resulted from those already taking place before
1882. It is obviously a truism that change speeds up, if not exponen-
tially at least noticeably, in each century and to each generation. In the
last quarter of the twentieth century change comes easily to us. It is
virtually all-pervasive — even in technology in remote rural areas —
and is, therefore, relatively easily assimilated. By comparison the last
quarter of the nineteenth century was less used to change and had
more change thrust upon it. As a result there were considerable
developments and problems in the economic and social organisation
of the area in 1882 — problems from which the Church neither could
nor wished to stand aside.

Some intimation of the changes, and of their particular influence on
Tyneside, may be obtained from William Glover's presidential
address to the Northern Architectural Association in 1900 (Rennison
1979:228).

> We are now drawing to the close of the century. On reviewing it we must feel
> that it is the greatest in the history of this Empire . . . it is associated with . . . the
> power of steam, hydraulics and electricity, the last of which, now only in its
> infancy, may be regarded as the future propellor, illuminator, and chemical
> agent. In my opinion the speculative builder has been the most important agent
> in providing suitable houses for the poor . . . [since 1875] within three miles
> radius of Newcastle, 2,492 acres have been laid out for building purposes, on
> about two thirds of which the following houses have been erected : 109 detached
> villas, 209 semi-detached villas, 1,960 superior self-contained houses, 1,184
> superior flats, 3,547 workmens' self-contained houses, 12,788 workmens'
> flats . . .

3

A purist may cavil at the writer's sudden switch from industrial change to the role of the speculative builder but there was a close link — industrial growth in the area brought a rapid expansion in jobs, population had expanded dramatically and there was heavy demand for accommodation. This was especially strong for working-class housing and the speculative builder put his finger unerringly on the rewarding financial spot and built for the working man (or rather for the landlord who would rent to the working man). Hence just over eight-tenths of the accommodation built between 1875 and 1900 was for working men (and about two-thirds in the form of Tyneside flats) with the resultant shortage of 'executive housing' so often bewailed in the later twentieth century.

Before looking in any depth at the changes to which Glover points, it is important to note that change was not new to the area in the second half of the nineteenth century and that it was less than all-pervasive throughout the Diocesan area. Newcastle had begun to experience changes from the late eighteenth century at the time of the classic industrial revolution period. The old town walls had begun to be cleared, the built-up area spread, old industries declined and new ones developed and urbanisation began to affect Tyneside. Population in the North-East expanded but the rate of growth was below the national average and did not exceed it until after 1821. It seems likely that in the late eighteenth century the North-East, although growing absolutely, was in economic terms in relative decline as compared with areas such as London, the West Midlands, Lancashire and Yorkshire (see Rowe 1977a), that the first half of the nineteenth century saw rates of growth in the North-East catching up with the rest of the country, and that it was not until the second half of the century that the North-East became an engine for growth in the country's economy. Nor were the changes which came only economic — the extension of steam power, the gradual introduction of iron which was to replace wood in shipbuilding by the 1870s, the rise of the chemical industry etc. — there were also changes in the Church itself. It might easily be argued that the insignificance of Newcastle within the Church of England was a reflexion of the enormous power of the Palatinate of Durham and its Prince Bishop, but Van Mildert was the last Prince Bishop and when he died in 1836 his staff of office was broken and laid to rest with him. The process had been begun by which a new see could be created.

That change is already occurring is one important qualification to any discussion of the area's economy and society in 1882, a second is the fact that change was not even throughout the area of the Diocese and its extent depended very much on the economic structure of different parts of the area. The contrasts between the Tyneside belt and the rest of the county of Northumberland were considerable. Even the south-east Northumberland coalfield was only gradually being exploited in the third quarter of the nineteenth century and Ashington did not become a major mining centre until later with its population expanding from 2,206 in 1881 to 14,138 in 1901. Apart from a small number of isolated industrial enterprises the rest of the county (together with the parish of Alston, which was also included in the new Diocese, whose lead mining activities were in decline by 1882) was almost entirely agricultural (see Ch. VI). Perhaps more important was the fact that Northumberland was the county with the highest proportion of its total acreage in large estates. While the Duke was responsible for a considerable part of this acreage (in 1873 he owned 181,616 acres) and also for much of the reputation of Northumberland as the most feudal county in the country, there were many other large landed estates and the continuing power and responsibility of the aristocracy, gentry and squirearchy in the county provided a considerable barrier to over-indulgence in change. While change inevitably came in agriculture and in rural towns and villages the presence of the large landed families maintained traditions which decayed and died in areas of non-resident landlords. Of this 'presence' and 'tradition' the Duke was, of course, a special case, whose significance, not just for Alnwick, was seen even in the Newcastle press.

> 'The Duke of Northumberland is dead', wrote the *Newcastle Journal* in 1865; 'it will spread a gloom and sorrow in the north whose dark shadow will fall upon a generation to come', and the entire issue of the paper was black-bordered. The dead duke was Algernon the Benevolent, 'the greatest of all the Percies', whose practical efforts for the poor and for the welfare of his county had earned him the love of the humblest cottagers, some 7,000 of whom filed past his coffin during the two days it lay in state at Alnwick. For his special train the platforms at Newcastle, Darlington and Durham were crowded, and the Minster bells tolled as it passed through York (Thompson 1963:81).

Some thirty years after the demise of the last Prince Bishop of Durham it is clear that the secular power of the Percies, added to by the genuine benevolence of a noted holder of the title of Duke, had not weakened. Indeed Professor Thompson (1963:291) went on to note that:

> The landed interest entered the late nineteenth century with its social position largely intact. The Percy dependants, at an annual dinner, could still state their

5

position with frankness and enthusiasm:
> '...Those relics of the feudal yoke
> Still in the north remain unbroke:
> That social yoke, with one accord,
> That binds the peasant to his Lord...
> And liberty, that idle vaunt,
> Is not the comfort that we want;
> It only serves to turn the head,
> But gives to none their daily bread.
> We want community of feeling,
> And landlords kindly in their dealing.'

It may thus be seen that change was taking place in the area of the new Diocese against a background of stability, and land ownership was certainly the backbone of that stability. The New Domesday survey of 1873 of landowning in the country and John Bateman's (1883) analysis of it show that fifty per cent of Northumberland was held in great estates (of more than 10,000 acres), which was the largest proportion of any county in the country, other than Rutland (a very special case of a tiny county largely owned by its eponymous Duke), followed by Nottinghamshire with 38 per cent in such estates. A further 35 per cent of Northumberland was owned in 'gentry' estates of one to ten thousand acres, which placed it in front of any other county for the proportion of land in estates of more than 1,000 acres. By contrast only 3 per cent of the county was owned in estates of one to 100 acres, only one-half of the 6 per cent of the next lowest county, Rutland (Thompson 1963:32, 113, 117). Many of these large estates had been in the hands of the same family for centuries and on those tradition was likely to be stronger. One such was Hesleyside, Bellingham, the 21,000 acre estate which the Charltons tried, unsuccessfully, to sell in 1887, when agricultural depression was severe, but which they still possess today. A few estates, such as that of the Culleys (Rowe 1971 and Macdonald 1979) had been built up by the enterprise of farmers who had made money in earlier periods of agricultural prosperity.

A considerable number of estates, however, reflected an aspect of change in rural society as industrialists bought into land for reasons of security but above all for social postion. Again this was nothing new; there was a long history of merchants and industrialists, especially coal owners, buying into landed estates. Of this class the Ridleys of Blagdon were pre-eminent (with an estate of 10,152 acres in 1873, with a gross annual rental of £12,189) but there were also the Taylors of Chipchase, the Cuthberts of Beaufront, Straker of Benwell Old

6

House and Stagshaw House, Corbridge, and the Cooksons of Meldon whose wealth was founded not only on coal but a melange of eighteenth and early nineteenth century Tyneside industries, including glass, iron and steel and lead. In the second half of the nineteenth century this tradition was continued and perhaps extended. The Joiceys were the prime example carrying on the coal-owners' tradition. By 1873 they were living at Newton Hall, Stocksfield, with the ownership of 5,816 acres in Durham and 2,038 in Northumberland and this was extended with the purchase of the Ulgham estate, near Morpeth, from the Earl of Carlisle in 1889. Other industrial sectors now provided sufficiently large fortunes to contemplate the purchase of a landed estate, especially shipbuilding and engineering. While C. M. Palmer decided on Yorkshire for his purchase of Grinkle Park, the other major industrialist in these fields W. G. (from 1859 Sir W. G. and from 1887 Lord) Armstrong remained true to Northumberland. By 1873 he owned Cragside with 2,265 acres and subsequent purchases in the Rothbury area (some of them from the Duke) meant that Armstrong had joined the ranks of the great landowners by the time of his death in 1900, with 16,000 acres in Northumberland.

Northumberland was already an area which contained some advanced farming, especially the Milfield Plain area in the north of the county, by the end of the eighteenth century. These advances became more widespread in the next sixty or seventy years, although much of the central part of the county remained backward. The old types of cattle and sheep gave way to new and improved breeds which fattened earlier and the old practice of fallowing land gave way to new crops and crop rotations, while feudal dues, such as those in existence in the 1780s at Melkridge, ceased. Although much of the reputation of the county's agriculture was based on turnip cultivation and sheep-rearing, there was a large output of grain crops and the still extant remains of the buildings which housed the power source (usually horse-wheels) for threshing machines testify to the extent of corn output in the mid-nineteenth century and to the high ground on which it was grown (Hellen 1972). The esteem in which local agriculture was held is suggested by a letter from a politican interested in agriculture to John Grey, a noted Northumberland farmer, in which he wrote, 'My farm is exactly 258 miles from Milfield Hill [in north Northumberland] — an appalling distance' (Butler 1869:110).

In the new technology that was affecting agriculture Northumberland was in the van. It was the earliest English county to be affected by the switch from the flail to the threshing machine and the reaping machine was invented by John Common, a Northumberland millwright. Technology and change also affected the Ducal estates, not known for their advanced farming habits, with the appointment of 'His Grace's Manager of the Steam Plough'. Even the agricultural labourers benefited from the changes, particularly in the northern part of the county where the hinds (labourers hired on an annual basis) had the reputation of being the best-off agricultural workers in the country. The major drawback to their prosperity, the appalling conditions of their cottages, to which Canon Gilly (1841) had drawn attention, had largely been removed through the work of Cottage Improvement Societies, which mushroomed in the 1840s, many of whose model cottages can still be seen. From the 1870s, however, agriculture was clearly experiencing difficulties and the acreage under grain was on the decline. The basic problem was increasing imports of grain, especially from North America, which were reducing prices. Most affected were the farmers whose output was entirely arable (in Northumberland chiefly the less advanced farmers in the centre and east of the county). Fortunately mixed farming (pasture and arable) was much more common in Northumberland and rising demand for meat and other pasture products led to reasonable prosperity in the last quarter of the century when cries of agricultural depression abounded in the country as a whole.

As with an earlier period of depression in agriculture, in the years after the Napoleonic Wars, Northumberland generally seems to have weathered the storm quite well, although the Charltons' inability to get a buyer for Hesleyside suggests that remote moorland estates were not profitable. A Royal Commission on Agriculture which reported in 1897 took evidence showing that on one large Northumberland estate the total rent income to the landowner fell by less than ten per cent in the twenty years after the early 1870s. While rents were falling by two and three times as much generally in agriculture and by much more in the corn-growing areas of the eastern counties and with the general price level in the country falling by one quarter or more, this was a reasonable sign that Northumberland tenant farmers were not too hard pressed. The Royal Commission also noted evidence for Northumberland that landlords were aiding tenants with a considerable increase in capital expenditure on farm improvements — new buildings, drainage, fencing, etc. — especially in the early 1880s. Moreover relative immunity to the problems was not confined to the traditionally well-farmed areas to the north of the county — although it was undoubtedly more marked there. Perry's study (1972) of the geography of agricultural bankruptcy in the last decades of the nineteenth century shows the county to have been among those with the lowest rates of bankruptcy. If tenants could pay increasing rents in real terms (i.e. the rent they paid fell more slowly than the general price level) but not go bankrupt and in the lack of any general outcry that their income was being squeezed, then we may conclude that the last decades of the century were not too bad a period for local agriculture.

The rural community was in decline, however, relative to the urban one and in some cases absolutely. To some extent the seeds of this decline were contained within agriculture itself; technological improvements reduced the demand for labour on farms, especially the introduction of reaping machines, which reduced the summer bulge in labour demand. But the decline came chiefly from pressure from outside the rural area, from the growing power of industry. From the late 1840s the railway improved communications enormously. Newcastle was linked to Carlisle in 1838 and to Berwick by 1847. These main lines were supplemented by a surprising number of rural routes, often as a result of attempts by other companies to obtain routes to Scotland independent of the North Eastern Railway (see Warn 1975). The Haltwhistle to Alston line was the first of these rural lines to open, in 1852, and the last to close, in 1976. In 1856 the first section of the Border Counties Railway was opened from Hexham via Bellingham to Plashetts and in 1862 it was extended to Riccarton to link with the west coast route to Scotland. In 1867 the Hexham and Allendale line was opened, three years after the Wansbeck Railway had provided a cross country link from Morpeth via Scots Gap to join the Border Counties at Redesmouth. In 1872 the first (and as it happened only completed) section of the Northumberland Central Railway was opened from Scots Gap to Rothbury. This was a proposal for an independent route to Scotland, which if completed might have had the impact of making the tiny and remote village of Scots Gap the railway hub of Northumberland. Finally in 1882 was authorised the last major route in the county (apart from light railways), the Alnwick — Cornhill (Coldstream) branch of the North Eastern Railway, opened in 1887.

These developments gave Northumberland one of the most complete railway networks of any largely rural county. As a result it became increasingly possible for cheaper town-made shoes, clothes and household goods to be sold in rural villages and local producers suffered. As well as pushing people out of rural villages by reducing the scope for their employment there, the towns also acted as positive attractions. Their streets may not have been paved with gold but there were expanding employment opportunities and wages were much higher than in agriculture. As a result, beginning in the 1840s but with a marked increase from the 1870s, migration from country to town increased and became more rapid than the rate of natural increase in rural areas with consequent falls in population. Indeed some villages, especially in the north and south-west of the county ended the nineteenth century with smaller populations than those with which they had begun it and this in itself led to a sense of depression as cottages were left uninhabited. The population of Ford was 1,903 in 1801 and only 1,140 in 1901, having fallen by more than one-half from its peak census year of 1851 when the population was 2,322. Even Belford, with the advantage of being on the main A1 road (which surely encouraged trade, although it may also have encouraged mobility away from the village) had a population fall from 902 inhabitants in 1801 (and a peak of 1,354 in 1831) to 782 in 1901. In the south-west Allendale's population dropped dramatically from a peak of 6,401 in 1861 to 2,763 in 1901 under the influence of the decline of lead mining, while the marginal nature of its agriculture on high ground meant that farming there suffered more heavily from the price fall.

Not all the rural parts of the county saw population decline in the later part of the century and obviously those close to Tyneside became engulfed in urban sprawl, although it is worth noting that much of this development is of our present century — Darras Hall, for instance, had 21 inhabitants in 1801 and 16 in 1901 not long before the railway was built to it (in 1913) and turned it into a commuter centre. Market towns such as Berwick, Hexham, Morpeth, Bellingham and Haltwhistle saw expansion. Berwick's population rose from 7,187 in 1801 to 8,277 in 1901 and Hexham's from 3,427 to 7,071. While this was slow as compared with the county as a whole, whose population rose from 168,000 to 603,000 it was fast enough to accommodate some change and modernisation as compared with villages whose population was stagnant. As a result the market towns saw new houses built, to an increasingly high standard as the century progressed, with more rooms and improved facilities, recognisably modern shops came in the last quarter of the century and municipal buildings could be justified with new town halls, libraries, etc. There was sufficient change both to maintain economic progress and, therefore, employment prospects, and also, psychologically, to prevent the feeling that the area was a backwater which would have driven the ambitious away. On the other hand change was insufficiently great to overwhelm and cause the break-up of well-knitted communities as was clearly to happen as a result of the population expansion of south-east Northumberland.

In 1801 the north Tyneside area (from Wylam to North Shields and extending north to include Throckley, Gosforth, Longbenton and Whitley Bay) had a population of 61,079, which meant that it was already the most significant centre of population, accounting for rather more than one-third of the county total. By 1851 the population of the same area was up to 141,250, or 47 per cent of the total for the county, and by 1901 it had reached 368,793, or 61 per cent of the county's total (see Rowe 1977b). To put it more simply, the population of the county increased by 435,420 during the century and slightly over 70 per cent of that increase lived in the narrow North Tyneside belt.

There is then a sense in which change in the Diocese is heavily and increasingly concentrated during the nineteenth century on Tyneside and especially on Newcastle itself, which, helped by the extension of its boundaries, increased its population by almost 200,000 during the century (from 34,092 in 1801 to 233,644 in 1901). From growing at a pace considerably below the national average in the eighteenth century, Northumberland's population growth was around the average for most of the nineteenth, growing at an average of about 13 per cent per decade from 1811 to 1881 and then rising above the national average with growth rates of 17 per cent in the 1880s and 19 per cent in the 1890s. This late upsurge in population growth appears to have been influenced chiefly by the expansion of coal-mining in south-east Northumberland and to have been brought about by a considerable increase in migration into the county rather than by natural increase. In 1881 there were 114,000 people resident in Northumberland who had been born in a different county but by 1901 this figure had risen to 179,000 and the proportion of 'incomers' to total population had risen from 26 per cent to 30 per cent. Many of these migrants would not have travelled far, a lot of them no doubt coming from County Durham where there had been a slowing down in population growth — but contemporary biographies and other accounts show that mining communities especially had heterogeneous populations with Scots, Cumbrians and natives of many other English counties. Noticeably in the last decades of the century there was a growing contingent of East Anglians driven from that area by depression in arable agriculture.

Given the heavy nature of many of the expanding industries it was inevitable that transport advantages would dominate locational factors and population growth was therefore along the banks of the Tyne and based on other coastal and riverside communities connected to the coalfield. Ashington has already been mentioned but Blyth's population grew from 1,170 in 1801 to 5,472 in 1901. Early in the

11

nineteenth century the pressure on the river banks for industrial use was limited and parts of the coalfield neglected, with the result that there were many small unconnected communities along the river and in south-east Northumberland. Near the coast, places like Monkseaton, Whitley Bay, Murton and Preston each had populations less than 1,000, while Heaton did not exceed 1,000 until 1881 and Benwell was only just over that figure until the 1860s. With the expansion of shipbuilding in iron from the 1850s with large yards employing many men, with big increases in coal shipped from the river, in chemical and engineering works, river frontages were at a premium. Cooksons rented a site from the Duke of Northumberland at Willington Quay during the 1850s and, not requiring it all immediately for their own purposes, found in the following decade that they could sub-let part of it to a shipbuilding firm for more than the rent they were paying for the whole site. Since there was no convenient and cheap form of transport for working men until the horse tram in the last couple of decades of the century, they wished to live near their work and gradually the small communities along the river, which had been so charmingly illustrated by J.W. Carmichael in the 1820s (see Middlebrook 1969), merged into the present urban corridor and largely lost their individuality.

This was a development which was most obvious on the outskirts of Newcastle, which had begun to break out of its old walls only in the later eighteenth century. The first serious expansion was to the west in the parish of Westgate, which had a little over 1,000 inhabitants in 1821, but 21,000 by 1861. From there the progression was further westwards into Elswick, along the Scotswood Road as Armstrong's engineering and armaments works expanded. In 1851 Elswick had three and a half thousand inhabitants, in 1861 14,000 and by 1881 34,000. But even to the west urban growth was slow by our modern standards. A map of 1874 shows no building beyond Bentinck Road to the west, little beyond Jesmond Road to the north, nothing beyond Sandyford towards Heaton and only a little into Byker, while a later guide book could comment on the area where the Bishop of Newcastle was living, 'Benwell is a small village about a mile and a half beyond the end of the tramway' (Snell 1884:36). To the east of Newcastle, with no such spur as that applied by Armstrong's, expansion came later and more leisurely. Byker reached a population of 7,000 by 1851, 21,000 in 1881 and 45,000 by the end of the century, while Heaton from rather over 1,000 in 1881 had reached 16,000 by 1901. Of the four parishes of the old town, All Saints to the west and St Andrew's to the north had the greatest scope for expansion but they were in decline

12

by the end of the century, while the central parishes of St. John and St. Nicholas saw large population losses from the 1860s as housing was demolished and replaced by commercial premises.

The steady expansion in population put pressure on accommodation and necessitated an extension of house-building. From the old tenement-type building of Newcastle centre and the small, one- or two-roomed cottage of the rural and mining areas, the style of building changed in the second half of the century, most noticeably to the Tyneside flat. The early development of the 1860s tended to be of small two- and three-roomed flats but by the 1880s three- and four-roomed were the norm. Some of these houses were built by employers for renting to their workmen. The Richardsons built a small terrace at Elswick for their leather workers, while Andrew Leslie built accommodation for his shipyard workers. While the evidence generally suggests that the quality of such housing was better than that produced by speculative builders to be sold for renting, there is no doubt that speculative building, as at Scotswood, was by far the most common form of housing provision. Nevertheless the standards of accommodation were being improved. Working men occupying Tyneside flats had more housing space than those who lived in older Newcastle housing, as may be seen from the article by Grace (1977). The front doors of Scotswood terraces may have opened straight onto the street and the back doors onto small yards but there were limited attempts at ornamentation and design of door and window lintels which show some slight concern for the aesthetic. Moreover interior accommodation improved and the regular incorporation of water closets and even baths in new housing was placing pressure on the supply of water to Newcastle by the 1880s (Rennison 1979:227). There was, however, much poor quality building, especially in mining areas, to meet the demands of rapidly expanding populations. In an article on 2 August 1873, in its series on the colliery villages, the *Newcastle Weekly Chronicle* noted at East Cramlington, Special Wood Row, 'a very sorry affair indeed, and its name is not easily accounted for, except by the supposition that it was built for little men with little wives and no families', and Double Wood Row, 'Two rows with distinct roofs have been built up against each other quite upon the mutual support principle, as though each were so narrow of itself that it might blow over were it not backed by the other'.

While there is clear evidence that the more rapid increase in population of the second half of the nineteenth century was more than met by an enormous expansion of house-building, this was insufficiently rapid to prevent the accumulation of the evils of over-crowding which were already apparent at the beginning of the century. For most of the nineteenth century figures for overcrowding, based on the number of persons per house shown by the Censuses of Population, are unreliable. Nevertheless the figures show that Newcastle was consistently more seriously overcrowded than other large towns in England and they were borne out by the more accurate figures available from the 1891 Census onwards. Moreover it now became clear that it was not just the large Tyneside towns in which overcrowding existed but that this was a typical feature of the whole of Northumberland and most of County Durham. In 1891 38 per cent of the population of Northumberland was living at a density of more than two persons per room and, with the exception of Durham, no other county had remotely comparable figures, while only 20 per cent of the population of London lived at such a density. Even so late as 1911, by which time some improvement had occurred, overcrowding was severe not only in large towns (Newcastle 32 per cent) but also in smaller urban centres (Morpeth 33 per cent) and in rural areas (Belford 31 per cent). These findings were subsequently confirmed by even more careful surveys and precise definitions of overcrowding and the towns of the North-East have had the dubious reputation of being at the top of this particular league into the second half of the twentieth century. The major reason for the high level of overcrowding was that house size was small. In 1891 two-thirds of the dwellings in Northumberland were of three rooms or less as compared with just over a quarter for England and Wales as a whole. It seems likely that the norm for working-class accommodation had been set in the region in the early nineteenth century or earlier with the single room, 15 feet square cottage with an unceiled sleeping apartment above, or the single room in a tenement and that expectations of housing accommodation were therefore low. Hence the move to two- or three-roomed dwellings would have been seen as an improvement, even though it was poor by national standards.

Closely linked to overcrowding was the question of public health which is discussed in an article by Smith (1977). Again it is clear that poor standards have existed on Tyneside for a long time and the sanitary enquiries of the 1840s and 1850s provide an appalling indictment of the area. That these were conditions not just related to heavily industrialised urban areas may be seen from the following comments on Hexham (quoted in McCord 1979:158):

> I enquired for the return of the mortality, and found that, for the last 7 years, it was actually some 27½ in the thousand, but with 'cooked' returns it was 24 in the thousand... I then traced disease to crowded room tenements, undrained

streets, lanes, courts, and crowded yards, foul middens, privies and cesspools. The water I found was deficient in quantity and most objectionable in quality, dead dogs being lifted out of the reservoir... I am staying at the best hotel in town, but there is no water closet, only a filthy privy at some distance.

But the worst conditions undoubtedly existed in Newcastle. The cholera epidemic of 1853 had caused enormous concern and some activity for improvement but, as so often happens, once the immediate cause was withdrawn little was done. The 1848 Public Health Act had set a death rate of 23 per 1000 as a level above which the central authorities could intervene in a town to impose the regulations of that Act. Although this death rate was exceeded in Newcastle nothing was done and it was not until 1873 that the town appointed a Medical Officer of Health. In that year the death rate was 30 per 1000 and although it fell from that high level, the average annual death rate was above 23 per 1000 throughout the 1870s and 1880s and did not fall consistently below 20 per 1000 until after 1901 (by comparison the present day figure is about 13 per 1000). For much of that period Newcastle's death rate was above the average for the large towns in the country. One of the major reasons for the high death rate was a high level of infant mortality which was around 160-170 per 1000 per annum in the last two decades of the century with no evidence of any decline. In other words about 17 per cent of babies born live would be dead before they reached the age of twelve months.

In many instances of contagious disease it is clear that there was an almost complete lack of public awareness of the dangers, and H. E. Armstrong, Newcastle's Medical Officer of Health from 1873, continually inveighed against this in his annual reports. In 1879 of a house in Hamilton Street, where a child had died of enteric fever, he noted, 'The Water Company's pipes are laid to the house, but, owing to frost, there had been no supply for seven weeks before the children took ill. The family used impure water from an open drain in a field, and shortly afterwards the children took ill...' (Armstrong 1879:31). Armstrong also felt that he was being deliberately obstructed in his attempts to improve public health and wrote (1880:33):

When the [infectious] disease breaks out in a household, those most endangered (to wit the healthy members of that household) instead of giving information to the authorities such as might lead to the discovery of its cause in defective structural sanitary arrangements, a polluted water, an infected milk supply, or the like, conceal the fact, as though the family affliction were some punishable offence; and the medical adviser, apparently with the same idea, declines to report it unless compelled to do so. There is something wrong in a condition of things such as this.

There were, however, improvements. In one report (1882:38) Armstrong was able to note that his department had commenced a 'systematic *house-to-house inspection* ... This inspection is intended to include the examination of every house in the City, and the compilation of details as to the sanitary condition of each under different heads.' This inspection made it clear that the worst aspects of slum property were concentrated in particular areas. Despite the great fire of 1854 which had destroyed many of the worst of the overcrowded properties on the Quayside and led to their replacement with offices and warehouses, the old centre of the town still contained many deplorable tenemented buildings. In 1880 the death rate in the parish of St. Nicholas at 37 per 1000 was almost twice that of St. Andrew's, further to the north, more recently built up and less enclosed. The infant mortality rate for St. Nicholas' was 258 per 1000 (i.e. more than one quarter of live births dying before reaching twelve months) in 1879 against 116 for Westgate. There were also very poor areas of housing on the edges of the city, where overcrowding was severe as people had been pushed out of the centre by re-building. One such area, just to the north of the cattle market and east of Rye Hill, was George Street (West) and Back George Street, on which the Health Department made a special report in 1884. The population density here was 638 per acre, not high when compared with modern multi-storey housing but these were two-storey, small houses, some with separately occupied cellars, averaging 13 persons per house. Special reports such as this and inspection of houses led to some improvements as the Medical Officer brought pressure to bear on landlords both directly and through the Council, but the latter was not always helpful. Armstrong had complained about the system of emptying middens and ashpits into the streets until the carts could come to collect their contents for delivery to local farmers as manure. Inevitably this encouraged flies to breed and led to the spread of disease, although contemporary knowledge was insufficient for Armstrong to know how this occurred and he was mainly concerned about the smell (a hangover from older miasmatic theories of disease transference) — 'On two occasions recently the smell from midden-refuse emptied on front streets has been offensive at a distance of about a hundred yards.' A debate was initiated in Council but the financial return from selling the manure was presumably too great to lose, for it was decided to continue the system, although the decision was taken to burn the remainder of the town's refuse and 'An experimental furnace will shortly be constructed for the purpose by the Borough Engineer' (1878:29-30, 37).

The improvements which did take place were insufficient to the minds of 54 clergymen, who, on 4 December 1889, signed a memorial to the Council complaining about the high death rate in the town. This brought forth a defence from the Sanitary Committee which expressed great confidence in the measures currently being taken and also one from the City Engineer, W. G. Laws. A sentence from his report (1890:3) shows the contemporary feeling, from within the local authority, of confidence in improvement; 'To allow panic so caused as to influence the steady course of sanitary effort would be like being alarmed at the bogle for which we had ourselves furnished the broomstick and white sheet, and helped to set it up.'

This is merely one symptom of the general aura of confidence which the town appeared to exude in the 1880s. To some extent this was a renewal of an earlier confidence and pride in the town's achievements, especially in the rebuilding of the 1830s which had produced Grey and Grainger Streets, the Theatre Royal, Eldon Square and the Royal Arcade. In a splendidly perceptive article, W. L. Burn (1956), commenting on the town at the time of the cholera epidemic of 1853 and the fire of 1854, wrote:

> One finds Newcastle writers of that period very much on the defensive, anxious to clear the town from the reputation for bad luck or bad management which they felt it had acquired. What we casually describe as mid-Victorian complacency was not, in fact, the most obvious characteristic of Newcastle a century ago. I leave with you a picture of a generation anxious, to some extent disillusioned, certainly stripped of much of the febrile optimism of the 'thirties; but self-reliant, trusting in life and its capacity to manage life, filled with a sturdy hopefulness which the next half-century was largely to justify.

Even at the time of which Burn was writing there were developments and events which boosted the confidence of the area, such as the official opening, on 29 August 1850 by Queen Victoria, of the High Level Bridge and Central Station (giving Newcastle the advantage possessed by no other major town of a single railway station shared by all the area's railway companies). But in the 1880s the aura of confidence is unmistakable. One expects town guides to exaggerate but those of that decade do so with panache. Thus Snell (1884 : 1) (with some disregard for the niceties of the truth to be expected from a cleric) wrote:

> It is not necessary to impress the reader with a sense of the importance of our subject; if he is a resident, he is already convinced of it, and if he is a visitor, his visit is a guarantee that he has recognised the interest attaching to our 'Metropolis of the North.' Indeed it would be difficult to name a town in Britain with more attractive points in itself... .

17

One of the more attractive points was that the town had achieved commercial and industrial notability without having extended so much geographically as to destroy its immediate links with the countryside. Maps attached to guide books of the late nineteenth century show the town as a very compact area and the country within easy walking distance from the centre. Armstrong (1880:35) commented in one report, 'Newcastle-upon-Tyne stands *first* of the large towns of the United Kingdom in regard of amount of public exercise ground provided, both in proportion to area of the Borough and to population.' This was chiefly a result of the continued existence of the Town Moor (owing a lot to the obduracy of the freemen of the town in seeking to maintain their grazing rights) which accounted for one-fifth of the acreage of the entire borough. But it was increasingly the result of the availability of public parks, Elswick Park, Heaton Park, Armstrong Park, often the gifts of landowners and topped in 1884 by the addition to Armstrong Park of Jesmond Dene and the Banqueting Hall by Sir William Armstrong.

This resulted from Armstrong's abandoning his house in the Dene and residing permanently at Cragside. It was the most conspicuous example of the industrialists, commercial and professional men moving away from the area in which they made their money to live in more secluded and sylvan surroundings. In the mid-century a Newcastle guide book could describe Barras Bridge and Brandling Park — little more than a mile north of the Quayside — as 'the pleasure abodes of the affluent', and a house in Jesmond provided a comfortable country life-style for the successful, a move away from the old town houses of the rich (which had often been cheek-by-jowl with those of the poor) which themselves now became tenemented for the poor. A further result of the increasing affluence which these moves reflected was a weakening of the link betweeen industrialists and their businesses. In the early nineteenth century the Parker who was managing partner of Walkers, Parker & Co. of the Elswick Lead Works lived in some style in Low Elswick House (now the successor company's offices) actually within the works. He had a 'Georgian residence with all the appurtenances appropriate for a gentleman's family', as a late Victorian sale catalogue might have put it, with an ice house, fernery, peach house and several greenhouses in the grounds. By mid-century the Parkers were living at Whickham and then at Scot's House, West Boldon. This kind of movement was common and led to a decline in the level of interest shown in the town by industrialists. At the highest levels it took the form of becoming a landed gentleman, such as Armstrong, or the coal-owning Joiceys, who first built Whinney House, Gateshead

18

and then moved on to the greater splendours of Newton Hall, Stocksfield, and Blenkinsopp Hall, Haltwhistle. At rather lower levels of fortune it meant the purchase of a pleasant country house and small estate, a large villa in Jesmond, Gosforth or Low Fell in Gateshead and for the limitedly successful industrialist or professional man, one of the large terraced houses of Jesmond. Thus a trip through Ward's *Directory of Newcastle* for 1879-80 shows all the Cooksons living in the country. John at Meldon Park, G. J. at Newbrough Hall, and Norman at Oakwood, Wylam; T. E. Smith (of Smith's Dock) at Gosforth House : Charles Mitchell at Jesmond Towers; G.W. Rendel at Condercum House, Benwell, leafy enough but still very convenient for the Elswick Works where he was a director, while Andrew Leslie was in similar position in Wallsend House; of the Priestman Brothers, coalowners, H.B. lived at Benwell House and Jonathan at Derwent Lodge, Shotley Bridge. C. M. Palmer presents something of a surprise, living, when in Newcastle, in Jesmond High Terrace; R. Hood Haggie lived in Haldane Terrace, C.T. Maling, of the Ford Pottery, in Ellison Place and Victoria Square was popular, housing John Philipson of the coach builders and W. Allhusen of Newcastle Chemical Works Co. Many other examples could be given but, almost without exception, the business leaders of the community now lived outside the old town, in premises which reflected their rising prosperity and whose design frequently showed levels of conspicuous consumption born out of the consciousness of that prosperity.

Also out of that prosperity came new symbols of Newcastle's progress. Nothing certainly so impressive as the Grainger re-building of the 1830s but certainly steadily rising above the disillusion of the early 1850s which produced the rather mean town hall in the Bigg Market. By the 1880s it was being criticised by guide books. Roberts (1887:75) wrote, 'The front to the square [St. Nicholas'] is imposing, but the buildings, from their having to be adapted to a site narrowing to its upper end, are very ungraceful and inconvenient' and another guide expressed the hope, not to be fulfilled until 1968, that Newcastle should have 'a Town Hall more worthy of her'. Building the Town Hall in the Bigg Market, a cramped site, was obviously an attempt to obtain a central and imposing position near the later Cathedral and 1855 was perhaps a little early to be influenced by the exuberance of later Victorian town hall building in other towns. The new public library of 1880 in New Bridge Street showed not only the willingness to spend money on large and expensive buildings but the growing interest in education, as had the Bath Lane Schools of 1871. In 1884 the Natural History Museum was moved from its cramped quarters to the new Hancock Museum, built to the memory of the local naturalists Albany and John Hancock, with money contributed largely by local industrialists. Further development of the town's social amenities came with the building of the Fleming Hospital in 1887 as a memorial to his wife by John Fleming, a local solicitor. In the same year came, perhaps, the most self-conscious expression of the town's pride and late Victorian exuberance with the buildings of the 'Newcastle upon Tyne Mining, Engineering, and Industrial Exhibition' of 1887 (The Royal Jubilee Exhibition) in Exhibition Park. With its massive pavilion and its smaller scale but still very impressive facsimile of the medieval Tyne Bridge built across the lake in the park, the Exhibition aimed at showing off the area's achievements to the many visitors of that year, for whom a large crop of guides to the town was produced, and to mark which the *Newcastle Daily Chronicle* of 10 May produced a detailed account of the area's industrial progress in the preceeding fifty years.

For those who were residents Newcastle society was offering an increasing range of facilities. In 1867 the Tyne Theatre in Westgate Road (now The Stoll) extended the dramatic provision, while on 3 November 1880 the Newcastle Chamber Music Society began, at the Assembly Rooms (themselves then over 100 years old), the series of evening concerts which still continue today. In the sporting field in 1882 the first Northumberland County Lawn Tennis Tournament was held (not long after the first lawn tennis court had been laid out at Whitburn in County Durham in 1873 for Sir Hedworth Williamson). In the 1880s, also, association football began to become popular — Newcastle United being formed in 1895 from an amalgamation of two earlier clubs — while several current cricket clubs were already then in existence. In more esoteric fields amateur and professional alike met in the learned societies which sprang up. The Natural History Society of Northumberland and Durham, founded in 1829, started publishing its *Transactions* from 1831 and its northern neighbour, the Berwickshire Naturalists' Club, published its proceedings from the following year, while a more mundane interest in country matters was served by the Newcastle Farmers' Club (and, of course, many others in the county) which was founded in 1846 and published its *Journal* from 1879. In the scientific field the importance of the chemical industry on the Tyne had led to the setting up of the Newcastle Chemical Society, whose *Transactions* were published from 1868-1882, and if that Society was on the wane by the early 'eighties it is appropriate that the North East Coast Institution of Engineers and Shipbuilders was founded in 1884 and has published its *Transactions* since that date, while the North East Institute of Mining and Mechanical Engineers had been founded in 1852.

In the cases of the last three societies it is noticeable that while they were learned bodies, publishing the papers read to them, they were largely composed of practical men working in industry and the chief subject matter of their discussions was the problems and practice of the major industries on which the local economy was based. Coal mining and the coal trade were obviously the base of the area's economy, although, as has already been suggested, agriculture remained the dominant industry for most of the county. Newcastle had grown to commercial importance on the base of the coal trade and, although in the 1880s there were still relics of earlier industry, such as the Locke Blackett lead works in Gallowgate, it was largely a commercial and professional centre (the occupational distribution of population is discussed in Rowe 1973). On Tyneside industrial change during the nineteenth century had been considerable. Some old established industries, such as the manufacture of salt, had withered completely as a result of competition from salt more cheaply produced elsewhere. Others expanded, such as the manufacture of glass, which had been of significance since the seventeenth century, in which the Tyne held a dominating position in national production in the 1830s and 1840s. In the second half of the century the glass industry locally had gone into serious decline, mainly as a result of the more effective development of productive methods on the Mersey but also as a result of competition from Belgian manufacturers.

Much the same was true of the heavy chemical industry producing alkalis, which had been responsible for about one-half of U.K. production in the middle of the century. In 1862 the output of heavy chemicals on the Tyne was 115,000 tons valued at £800,000, while by 1873, at the peak of the trade cycle boom, it had reached 223,000 tons worth £2m. Already, however, the seeds of destruction had been sown. In 1873 Brunner Mond had been set up at Winnington in Cheshire to exploit a new and cheaper method of manufacturing soda than that used by the Tyneside manufacturers who, committed to their existing investment in plant, did not adapt to technical progress and gradually closed. A hand-book to the district (Bruce 1889:136-7) noted 'Since the year 1875 the number of chemical works has been gradually decreasing...' as with glass where 'Matters are very different now. There are only seven glass works on the Tyne'. It is unlikely that the similarities in the decline of the once dominant glass and chemical industries, especially the failure to adopt new technology, were the result of chance. It is possible that the development of the railways may have given locational advantages to other parts of the country but it seems much more likely that the cause of decline was a local one, since it was possible for C.T. Maling to build up the Ford Pottery at Newcastle to a position among the largest U.K. manufacturers in the 1880s without any obvious locational advantages. It may be that both the financial and entrepreneurial capacities of the area were so stretched in the second half of the century by the enormous expansion of the coal-mining, engineering and shipbuilding industries that other industries failed to attract capital and talent.

In employment terms these three industries expanded dramatically; coal-mining increased its share of total employment in the county from 9 per cent in 1851 to 19 per cent in 1911; shipbuilding from 2 to 5 per cent and metal-working from 6 per cent to 9 per cent. Shipments of coal from the Tyne rose from about 3.6m. tons in 1848 to 12.2m. in 1894, with a steadily increasing proportion going to export markets, while under the impact of the opening out of the Ashington pits shipments from Blyth rose from 235,000 tons in 1880 to over four million by 1914. Engineering and shipbuilding output followed the same path, exemplified by Armstrongs, amalgamated in 1882 with Charles Mitchell's Walker shipyard to form Sir W.G. Armstrong, Mitchell & Co., with an eventual employment level of over 10,000 on the Tyne, in the early twentieth century. The firm produced warships for many of the navies of the world and built an international reputation in the armaments field. Much of the expansion along the Tyne was a result of considerable improvement to the river after the formation of the Tyne Improvement Commission in 1850. Over the previous half century there had been considerable complaint about the deterioration of the navigability of the river and loss of trade to the Wear. In 1856 the entrance piers to the river were begun; in the following year Northumberland Dock was opened, to be followed by the Albert Edward Dock in 1884; massive dredging of the river channel was undertaken from 1860; and in 1876 the Swing Bridge (powered by Armstrong hydraulics) was opened to replace the old Tyne Bridge, thus enabling ships to be built at the Elswick Works. By the 1880s the Tyne had been improved dramatically and was the third port of the country behind London and Liverpool for total tonnage entering and leaving. In many industrial fields there was much of which Tynesiders could be proud, not only in the sheer volume of production but also in inventiveness and entrepreneurial drive. In 1879 J. W. Swan had invented the incandescent electric lamp and Tyneside was set on the path to become a major centre of electrical engineering, while in 1884 C. A. Parsons constructed the world's first turbine which was later to have dramatic impacts on the shipbuilding and electricity generating industries.

In the 1880s, in spite of a period of depression which reduced profits and increased unemployment levels across the country as a whole, the situation in Newcastle and on Tyneside was promising. Although the size of population had never been the only factor in determining whether a town should have a bishopric, Newcastle could increasingly point to the fact that its growth of population and industry made it difficult for the old Bishopric at Durham to maintain contact with the new society, a problem being experienced in many parts of the country. Manchester had become a separate diocese in 1848 and Liverpool in the same group of creations as Newcastle, while Birmingham had to wait until 1905, Sheffield 1914 and Bradford, Coventry, Derby and Leicester until after the First World War. Together with the grant of city status, which came, formally, only a few weeks after the diocese was created, the appointment of a bishop could be seen as marking the town's and region's recent achievements. Those achievements brought problems, such as dramatic population growth, which placed responsibilities upon the Church, but there is a sense in which the achievements contained the seeds of self-destruction. The growth process itself, with the North-East catering for the capital goods demands of wider markets, national and then international, was something the region could not control and resources became locked into a narrow industrial grouping for whose products demand fell as other countries began to produce them or substitutes effectively. In the new conditions then created change came too slowly, both in the region's economy, and, perhaps, in the Church's response to the problems, although one recent change, the re-opening of the Bishop's first residence, Benwell Tower, renamed 'The Mitre', as the region's latest 'real ale pub', may be of significance.

Chapter II

THE FORMATION OF THE DIOCESE OF NEWCASTLE

Peter J. Jagger

BEHIND the Bishopric Act of 1878, which ultimately led to the formation of the Diocese of Newcastle, lay numerous attempts to increase the episcopate. Mounting pressure in both Church and Parliament for the establishment of more English sees can be traced back to the early part of the nineteenth century, but in the case of Newcastle upon Tyne the first move to set up a new diocese was made in the sixteenth century. When Tunstall, Bishop of Durham, was imprisoned in the Tower of London in 1552, accused of treason, Dudley, Duke of Northumberland, immediately put forward a proposal to divide the see of Durham and create a new see at Newcastle. To implement these proposals a Bill was drawn up 'For the Dissolution of the Bishopric of Durham' (7. Edward. VI[1]). The integrity of the Bill is very much open to question. It was argued that the Diocese of Durham was too large and could not be served by one bishop. The King desired to have: 'God's most holy and sacred word in those parts adjoining to the borders of Scotland being now wild and barbarous ... taught and preached and set forth amongst his loving subjects.' Newcastle was to be raised from town to city status and a suitable church there to be called the cathedral. Durham was to provide funds to endow the new see. The Bill had its first reading on 20 March, 1553, and in just over a week passed through both Houses and received Royal assent. The premature death of King Edward thwarted the instigators of the Bill, and another one to re-erect and establish the bishopric of Durham and to restore Tunstall was placed before Parliament on 27 November, 1553. Opposition to this reversal came from the burgesses of Newcastle and others with vested interests in the dissolution of the see of Durham and in the annexing of Gateshead to Newcastle, which was one of the objects of the original Bill. Victory went to Durham which returned to its former state when the second Bill was passed in 1554.

Three hundred years later there was another attempt to establish a diocese of Newcastle. Here also the motives seem to have been mixed and earthly. High sounding ideals were confused with secular aggrandizement. The ambitions of a duke were replaced by dreams of a group of town councillors, prompted by the good intentions of Sir John Fife, an alderman of Newcastle upon Tyne who, on Wednesday, 14 June, 1854, submitted the following motion to a meeting of Newcastle Town Council:

> That this Council adopts a memorial to the Ecclesiastical Commissioners, and to the Secretary of State for the Home Department, showing that the Diocese of Durham is too extensive for its proper administration, that it is expedient to institute a Diocese of Northumberland, to purchase the Vicarage of Newcastle from the Bishop of Carlisle, to make St Nicholas' Church in Newcastle the Cathedral, the Vicar a Dean, four of the senior clergy Canons, and to raise Newcastle upon Tyne to the dignity of a metropolitan City.

In the debate which followed, the mixed motives of at least some of the councillors and the sincere opposition of others indicates that little had changed since the sixteenth century. The opposition left the advocates of the new diocese in no doubt that the task was not to be accomplished without a fight, and this attempt was to be abortive largely because there was no legislation to enable a new see to be created along the lines put forward.

Introducing the motion Sir John said that he intended to treat it solely as a local question, his object in presenting the motion being to promote the aggrandizement, wealth and prosperity of Newcastle by obtaining a more equal distribution of Church revenues. 'Whether Churchman or Dissenter', he declared, 'no man possessing property in Newcastle, or carrying on trade or business, or desirous of seeing it flourish and grow both in rank and wealth, has otherwise than an interest in determining that about £10,000 or £15,000 a year taken out of Church property in Northumberland and Newcastle, should be kept in Northumberland and Newcastle, instead of part of it going into the principality of Wales, and part of it going to the county of Cornwall.'

Anticipating a strong reaction against his motion from both anti-Establishment and zealous Dissentient councillors, Sir John explained that if it had involved the question of Church reform he should scarcely have thought himself sufficiently orthodox to have introduced it to the Council, for he was opposed to sinecures, pluralities, and to seats being held in the House of Lords by the bench of bishops. He treated this question only with reference to its secularity. He pressed the point that the subject was of equal importance to both Churchmen and Dissenters. After all: 'Every Dissenter in the room represents a large number of Churchmen and every Churchman here is the constitutional guardian of the rights and privileges of Dissenters.'

When he went on to speak of the spiritual destitution of Newcastle and the paltry sum paid to the established clergy in the town, one of his fellow councillors exclaimed: 'What does that signify to a Dissenter?' At that point the motion was attacked from many sides.

Councillor Newton, an outspoken Dissenter, said he was sorry that the subject had been introduced into a Council meeting. What good could be done for the locality by having a bishop? The question they ought to be considering was whether there should be a Church establishment at all and if so, what its form should be. They would not, he believed, advance the interests of religion by importing into the Council questions that belonged exclusively to a sect that wished to promote its own ends. It would have been a more legitimate course of action for Sir John Fife to have convened a public meeting to consider the motion he had brought before them. As a councillor and a Dissenter, Newton felt that he should not be called upon to further the interests of the Established Church.

Other councillors supported Newton, and Mr. Longridge thought that Sir John might have put the subject upon higher grounds than the commercial. To this Sir John replied that he had taken the secular ground because he thought that was the ground on which they could all meet. Then, speaking on the proposal that Newcastle be made into a metropolitan city, he said that while some cities had greater populations, none was of greater importance, not only from a commercial point of view, but in the organisation of the country; it was the centre of the northern railway system; the Assizes were held there, and it was the second port in the Empire, being above Liverpool in the amount of tonnage handled.

Mr. L. Laycock, who led the opposition, fervently attacked all that Sir John Fife had to say. To the suggestion that a bishop of Newcastle would bring prosperity to the town, he said that, if they looked around they would see that towns where they had bishops were never prosperous. He proposed an amendment to the motion, that the surplus income of the see of Durham be used to increase church accommodation and the improvement of the incomes of the vicars and clergy of the borough. The amendment was seconded by Mr. Gregson, who vehemently argued that the bishops were both overpaid and useless in enforcing the discipline and doctrine of the church, and that the conduct of too many of the bishops tended to weaken the church and bring it into disrepute. He was not alone in holding and expressing such derogatory views concerning the bishops of the day. However, while Mr. Laycock and his supporters were opposed to any suggestion of creating a new bishopric, even if it be called the bishopric of Newcastle, they were certainly not opposed to finding some means whereby the surplus money from the see of Durham could be spent in Newcastle rather than in other places.

Even the good Sir John had not overlooked the great wealth attached to the ancient see of Durham. With any division of the diocese there must, he said, be a corresponding distribution of the wealth of the Church. He was under the impression that when a new diocese was created it would be endowed by the original diocese. During the debate, which centred upon the wealth of the see of Durham, the view was expressed that unless they had a bishop of Newcastle they could get no portion of the surplus episcopal funds drawn from Durham and held by the Ecclesiastical Commissioners. Some councillors said that if this were true it would influence their vote. If the only way to get the money was to have a bishop then a bishop they would have.

Alderman Hodgson asked the Town Clerk to clarify this point, that the surplus income from the diocese of Durham in the Episcopal Fund held by the Ecclesiastical Commissioners must be appropriated to the formation of another see. Having consulted the Act of Parliament bearing on this point the Clerk said that this appeared to be correct. With this assurance the original motion was put and carried with only two dissentients.

The Council's Memorial, written in fine copper-plate, and signed by the Mayor, Ralph Dodds, was presented to both the Ecclesiastical Commissioners and Lord Palmerston; it began by quoting the 1851 Census figures for the diocese of Durham.

> Having regard to the extent of the population of these Counties, and the large amount of episcopal property within them, your Memorialists respectfully but earnestly submit that the circumstances of the case demand the establishment of a separate bishopric of Northumberland, which shall include that County and the County of the Town of Newcastle-upon-Tyne — that the Seat of such bishopric shall be the town of Newcastle-upon-Tyne — and that a portion of the surplus revenue arising from the property of the See will be properly applied in the support of such bishopric.

It claimed: 'That the spacious and beautiful Church of Saint Nicholas in this Town will supply to the new Diocese a fit Cathedral ...'[2] The revenue of the see of Durham was thought to be in the region of £30,000 per annum. Unfortunately what was proposed was not so simple. Many of the points raised in the Memorial were to be debated at great length in the years which followed and thus helped to prepare the way for the Bishopric Bill of 1878.

In a letter to Lord Palmerston, on 7 July 1854, the Ecclesiastical Commissioners made it clear that they would not agree to the endowment of the proposed new bishopric from their Common Fund. The Secretary informed Palmerston that the Commissioners had applications for the augmentation or endowment of more than fifteen hundred benefices and churches which stood in need of financial assistance. Voices in Parliament in the ensuing years advocated that the surplus income held by the Commissioners should be used to improve the lot of the parish clergy and for the extension of the Church at local level rather than for the setting up of new sees.

Among the letters to the press prompted by the Memorial was one to the *Guardian* on 1 July 1854, in which the writer urged that Parliament should give immediate effect to the request of the Memorial by passing a measure before the close of the present session. There would, he wrote, be objections in Parliament from certain quarters: 'Dissenters, especially political Dissenters, will oppose every attempt to extend the English episcopate, and thereby strengthen the national Church.'

Letters to the press and opposition from Dissenters were not the only things provoked by the Memorial. In March 1855, prompted by local rivalry, John Forster, member of Parliament for Berwick until 1857, presented the Ecclesiastical Commissioners with a Memorial from 'the Ancient Vestry and other inhabitants of the County of the Borough and Town of Berwick upon Tweed.' Apart from inserting four references to Berwick-upon-Tweed its contents are very similar to those of the Newcastle Memorial. The great distance of the Borough of Berwick and the Border District from the Bishop's residence at Bishop Auckland and the large amount of episcopal property derived from the northern portion of the diocese were put forward as sufficient reason to support their demand for a separate bishopric of Northumberland. Forster, in his letter accompanying the Memorial, stressed that the new bishopric ought to be 'supported out of the very large Ecclesiastical revenue drawn from that part of the present Bishopric.' Most of the leading inhabitants of Berwick-upon-Tweed who were members of the Church of England had signed the Memorial and this, said Forster, 'can bear testimony to their title to represent the wishes and opinions of the residents of that persuasion.' The secretary of the Ecclesiastical Commissioners sent a standard reply on 10 March: 'The Commissioners have no power or authority under the Acts regulating their proceedings to found or endow new Bishopricks, and ... they cannot therefore take any steps with reference to the prayer of the Memorial.'

For the Ecclesiastical Commissioners their letter to the Berwick Memorialists on 10 March brought the subject to a close. But the people of Northumberland were not so easily dissuaded by the dogmatic pronouncements of the comparatively new Ecclesiastical Commissioners, founded in 1835. The facts of history, they believed, supported their reasonable claim, for the see of Northumberland was established at Hexham in 678 A.D. It was from Hexham that the next appeal came. At twelve noon on 10 January 1856, Sir Edward Blackett chaired a public meeting there. Five resolutions were passed and presented to the Ecclesiastical Commissioners. The first two are of particular interest. The first stated: 'That an additional See is loudly called for in order that the Episcopal functions, forming as they do an essential element in the constitution and adminstration of the Church of England, should be frequently and effectively discharged throughout the County of Northumberland.'

The Memorial referred to the Cathedral Commission (1855) which left undecided whether the new see would be more advantageously erected at Newcastle or Hexham. The Meeting obviously favoured Hexham. It was more central and offered greater facilities to a bishop for personally superintending his clergy and discharging the duties of his office. Then there was the existence in Hexham of the magnificent and 'venerable monument of ancient piety in the conventual Church ... which at no great expense might be repaired and embellished so as to vie with the most admired of our Cathedrals'. There was also the fact that for nearly two hundred years Hexham had flourished as an episcopal see under twelve successive bishops. The final argument put forward in support of their claim was:

> The situation of Hexham is more conducive to the contemplative and serious habits as well as to the independent action of a Bishop than the impure atmosphere and the various distractions of a crowded manufacturing and commercial Town, so that whether the decision turns upon antecedent associations and privileges or on the salubrity of climate or adaptation of locality to a Bishop's occupation, or on facility of intercourse and supervision, the advantages are decidedly in favour of Hexham.[3]

These arguments, however, received the same negative reply as the Ancient Vestry of Berwick-upon-Tweed.

The claims of Hexham were to continue, but they came to nothing. Years later, when the Increase of the Episcopate Bill was being debated in Parliament, a writer on the subject in the *Church Quarterly Review*, 1876, had some scathing things to say about proud Hexham:

> It is true that the old-fashioned stagnant market town of Hexham, the seat of a bishopric in pre-Norman days, still contains a stately minster ... But, with Hexham vegetating on the verge of the county, and with such a town as Newcastle, containing a population which the Registrar-General in 1875 computed at 137,665, standing on the main north line, and an excellent railway centre, there can be little doubt as to the claim. Fortunately this growing place contains the Church of St Nicholas, well worthy by its size and character to become a cathedral.

During the ensuing years other places were also put forward as offering a suitable title for the new see, or the ideal cathedral, or the most desirable episcopal residence, including Lindisfarne, Alnwick and Bamburgh.

Without the necessary Parliamentary legislation the Church of England and the now powerful Ecclesiastical Commissioners were unable to respond to the many earnest pleas to create new sees to enable the Established Church to meet the needs of the new society which had emerged as a result of the industrial revolution. The carefully kept file of the Ecclesiastical Commissioners for the Diocese of Newcastle contains no correspondence on the subject of the bishopric of Newcastle after January 1856 until they received a letter and press cutting from Bishop Charles Baring of Durham in February 1878. This lack of information in the files of the Commissioners does not mean that Churchmen were disheartened, for there had been some success in the past with the creation of the sees of Ripon (1836) and Manchester (1847). There was a growing awareness that pastoral reforms were necessary if the Church of England were to minister effectively to a nation where widespread spiritual destitution was recognised and where indifference, and even hostility, towards the Church were on the increase.

The formation of the Newcastle Diocese can only be understood against the background of national demand which began with the Established Church Act of 1836, which gave new power to the Church to reform itself. Ten years later, when Lord John Russell became Prime Minister, the desirability of increasing the episcopate was an issue which exercised his mind. On 9 December 1846 he wrote to the Archbishop of Canterbury:

Regarding the great increase of the population since the Reformation, and the heavy burden of duties which presses upon some of the bishops, the Queen's Ministers are of the opinion that four new bishoprics ought to be founded. One of these would be Manchester; another might comprehend Nottinghamshire and part of Yorkshire; a third by a better division of diocese, might relieve the Bishops of London and Norwhich of some part of their labours; the fourth would probably comprehend Cornwall . . .[4]

Others were not so enthusiastic about such increases. Edward Maltby, Bishop of Durham, wrote to Edward Harcourt, Archbishop of York, on 29 October 1847, expressing the opinion that funds for establishing three new bishoprics, including Manchester, would be better distributed among the parochial clergy, many of whom were in financial difficulties.[5] In the same year Robert Issac Wilberforce in his Archidiaconal Charge spoke of the need of an increased number of bishops which arose not only from the vast growth of population, but because their present number fell short of what was found needful both at the time of the Reformation and before it. Walter Farquhar Hook, Vicar of Leeds, also argued that the sub-division of parishes was of little benefit to the Church unless there was a corresponding sub-division of dioceses.

On November 10 1852 a Royal Commission was set up by Lord Derby to inquire into the state and condition of the Cathedral and Collegiate Churches in England and Wales. In the first report of this Commission, published in 1854, consideration was given to the possibility of Cathedral and Collegiate Church revenues being made available for the erection of new sees. No decision was reached but the possibility was left open for future consideration. The third and final report was published on 25 May, 1855.[6] It was to provide the guidelines for the debate over the next twenty years. Among its recommendations were, first, that a permissive Bill should be formed and introduced into Parliament to permit the division of any diocese under certain conditions of territory and population and with the consent of the bishop whose diocese was to be divided; secondly, that in no case should a new see be erected unless sufficient income and a suitable residence could be provided; thirdly, that funds for these purposes might be provided partly by local contributions or out of episcopal property now in the hands of the Ecclesiastical Commissioners. A list of those places offering special claims and facilities for the creation of additional bishoprics was given: Newcastle was not included, but the Report did go on to state: 'We also record our opinion: That there are other places in which it is desirable that new Sees should be founded.'

The 'Schedule of Additional Sees' attached to the Report, includes Durham, giving the following information:

> Population 701,381, with nearly two million acres. Benefices 242. It has been proposed that it should be divided into two Dioceses; one containing the county of Durham, with a population of more than 390,000; the other, to consist of the county of Northumberland, with a population of 391,000, and a new See at Newcastle or Hexham.

This Report not only provoked the people of Hexham to present their own Memorial to the Ecclesiastical Commissioners; it also prompted an article in the July-December 1855 issue of the *Christian Remembrancer* entitled 'The Future of English Cathedrals' in which the writer, referring to the proposed Northumberland see, wrote: 'The see shall be, it is proposed, either at Hexham, with its Saxon tradition, and its noble minster; or else at Newcastle, with its teeming population and its fine Church of St Nicholas. Tradition in this case must, we think, yield to existing needs, and Hexham give place to Newcastle.'

From the publication of the Cathedral Commission's Reports in the early 1850s to the early 1870s opinion was growing within the Church of England that the shortage of bishops was seriously hindering the work and extension of the Church. There was no common agreement about how many bishops were required. Some pressed for four new sees, with the appointment of suffragan bishops where required. Others said they would settle for nothing less than 50-60 additional bishops. Not a few argued that before there was any increase in the episcopate there must be episcopal reform, including a change in their social position and their ecclesiastical status. Then there was the question of salary; some felt £750 per annum was sufficient while others believed that even £4,000 per annum would not enable a bishop to exercise his ministry adequately without unnecessary concern about his income.

Samuel Wilberforce, Bishop of Oxford, in October 1858, presented the Upper House of the Canterbury Convocation with a petition pressing for an increase in the episcopate. It was the beginning of a Convocation debate which was to go on for many years. Once again the vast increase in the population was put forward as a sufficient cause to justify this move. Population growth was to be a recurring argument used by most of those who pressed for the formation of new sees. Effectiveness was also emphasised in Wilberforce's petition: 'Your petitioners ... feel that the opportunity of more frequent personal intercourse between a Bishop and the clergy and laity of his diocese would tend to infuse new life and vigour into the Church, and promote unity, consistency and efficiency in the labours of those who are working for the salvation of souls.' Bishop Wilberforce urged that Parliament be asked to approve a Bill which would enable the number of bishops to be increased as the need emerged.

The strong views of the English Church Union, under the leadership of the Hon. Colin Lindsay, were made known in a petition presented to the House of Lords in July 1862. It asked the Lords to sanction any well considered scheme for the increase of the episcopate. Earlier that same year Canon Wordsworth presented the Canterbury Convocation with the Report of the Committee on the 'Increase of the Episcopate', based on the assumption that the need for such an increase was generally admitted and that the shortage of bishops debarred many English people from certain spiritual privileges. Two methods of meeting the urgent need were recommended: first, the sub-division or re-arrangement of existing dioceses and secondly, the appointment of suffragan bishops. Division was thought applicable where a diocese was too populous or too extensive for one person. Any considerable reduction in the income of any of the present bishoprics was rejected by the Committee, with the exception of Durham, concerning which the Report stated: 'The existing endowments of the see afford the means of providing for a second bishop without diverting the revenues from the district to which they belong.' Differences emerged over the income thought necessary for the new bishops. It was argued that it should be sufficient to keep them on a par with the gentry, for the dignity of the office had to be maintained, and if the incomes were too low those appointed would always be looking out for a better paid see. The Archdeacon of Taunton, George Anthony Denison, felt that on moral grounds £2,000 per annum was too much and proposed £1,500.

When the debate on this subject was resumed at the 1863 Convocation the Archbishop of Canterbury, Charles Thomas Longley, argued that that portion of the Common Fund which is derived from the Episcopal Estate, should be appropriated in part toward the foundation and endowment of any new see. Six years later, on 5 October 1869, Longley's successor, Archibald Campbell Tait, wrote a private letter to W. E. Gladstone: 'My opinion is (and therein I agree I believe with all the Bishops and with both Houses of the Convocations of Canterbury) that three new Sees ought to be erected' (Newcastle was not among them). The income of the new bishops should be sufficient to keep them free from anxiety and enable them to do their work. Tait told Gladstone that he did not feel that the possession of private wealth was a qualification for the episcopal office. The existence of private means, said Tait, was to be disregarded: 'If the office of Bishop is to exist it ought to be capable of being conferred simply on the fittest man.' Tait had no inhibitions about pressing his point with Gladstone and went on to write: 'I am strongly of the opinion that there is a great opportunity at present for a moderate and yet sufficient increase of the Episcopate. The thing can only be done by a powerful Ministry and will only be done by Ministers who like yourself (and the Lord Chancellor) have a real understanding of what is needed in such a matter and a real desire to improve the machinery through which the Church acts.' Tait told Gladstone that if the scheme he had outlined was not approved he had an alternative, but did not think it as good as the scheme he had presented. Gladstone was assured that if he took up the matter he could rely on the co-operation of the existing bench.[7]

Just over three weeks later Gladstone replied to the Archbishop stating that he had discussed the subject with his colleagues and he suggested that Tait and two or three of the Episcopal Body should meet three to five members of the Government at Downing Street to discuss the issue at greater depth. After the meeting Gladstone wrote to the Archbishop that he and his colleagues recommended that an application be made to Parliament for the creation of three new sees. For some reason, however, Tait had now changed his mind and informed Gladstone, on 6 November 1869, that the bishops who had been present at their joint meeting agreed that 'such application ought not under present circumstances to be made.' It was felt, wrote Tait, that the consecration of suffragan bishops would be beneficial and that the Act of Henry VIII allowing for such consecrations should be put into force.[8] With this the matter was dropped, at least for the time being.

The solution of suffragan bishops may have satisfied some of the bench but did not satisfy many of the clergy and laity whose views were made known in a resolution presented to the Upper House of Canterbury Convocation on February 11th 1873:

> This House earnestly and respectfully commends the memorial of the Society for the Increase of the Home Episcopate to the attention of their lordships of the Upper House; more especially it requests their lordships to use their influence in their places in Parliament to support any well-considered measure which may be proposed for the sub-division of some of the large dioceses of England.

Little did they realise that some of the bishops in 1869 had already turned down Gladstone's recommendation to bring the matter before Parliament. Samuel Wilberforce, now Bishop of Winchester, introducing the Report to the Upper House at the February Convocation, referred to the consecration of suffragan bishops, which Tait had recommended: 'We cannot', said Wilberforce, 'regard them as meeting the wants of the Church.' The Report stated that the erection of the new sees must depend upon local circumstances. What was required was a general enabling Act of Legislature which would allow for the formation of a new see by the division of any existing see whenever such a division was seen as necessary. Existing legislation required a separate Act of Parliament for the creation of each new see. Any suggestion that the Common Fund of the Ecclesiastical Commissioners should be used to endow new sees was rejected by the Report, which went on to state: 'We cannot . . . find in the present revenues of the Church the means of providing the necessary endowments for new Episcopal Sees . . .' The Committee felt that because of the increasing wealth of the country the sons of the Church of England would provide the necessary money. The Report was accepted by both Houses.

One of the great advocates of an increase of the Home Episcopate was Lord Lyttelton who, towards the end of 1872, sent out a questionnaire to the 740 rural deaneries in England and Wales, enquiring whether they supported the proposal to increase the episcopate. Of the 477 replies received, 468 were, for the most part, unanimously in favour of the division of the larger sees.[9] A short time after the Canterbury Convocation of February 1873 Lyttelton had a private meeting with Archbishop Tait and eight bishops. The bishops assured Lord Lyttelton that they would support a Parliamentary Bill for an increase of the episcopate if the Bill was constructed along the lines of the resolutions recently approved by Convocation and provided that:

1. It did not mention the source of the endowment.
2. It continued the existing mode of succession to seats in Parliament.
3. It did not contain any mention of minimum income for the new bishoprics.[10]

Armed with the assured support of the bishops and the knowledge that at least 468 rural deaneries supported the idea, Lord Lyttelton was now prepared to present a Bill for the Increase of the Home Episcopate, and did so on 8 February 1875.

Funds for an increased episcopate were seen as the greatest problem. Frederick Temple, Bishop of Exeter, was not alone in saying that raising the money from voluntary subscriptions would not be easy. He suggested that a large living would provide the new bishop with both an income and a residence, while his chaplains could discharge the necessary parochial duties. This suggestion provoked indignant replies from both Lord Lyttelton and the Lord Chancellor: no man, they felt, could discharge the duties of a bishop and do the work of a parish priest; the appropriation of a living or a Cathedral Canonry was the worst possible 'misappropriation of trust funds'.[11]

Numerous objections were raised in the Lords to Lord Lyttelton's Bill but he maintained that it was not a Bill for increasing the episcopate but for enabling persons who wished to increase it to do so on certain conditions. Those who desired to see a new bishopric established and were able to provide funds would go to the Commissioners and express their wishes — the Commissioners' duty was to prepare the scheme to meet the request.[12] An amendment at the third reading limited the Bill to the establishment of five new sees, which did not include Newcastle. Fortunately for Newcastle the amendment was rejected, although the Lords passed the Bill and sent it to the Commons. Opposition in the Commons led to its withdrawal on 11 August 1875. The following February it came before the Commons for its Second Reading, and again in July when the debate was adjourned. It was now becoming clear that it was to have no easy passage.

At the request of the Home Secretary the Archbishop of York called together the bishops of the Northern Province. They were to meet in London on 3 May 1876 to consider whether there was need for an increase in the episcopate in the Province of York. Bishop Baring of Durham was unable to attend and wrote a long letter to Archbishop Thomson on 24 April which was published in the *Guardian* on 6 September. He admitted 'I have never been an advocate for any large increase of the Episcopate, nor do I believe it is desired by the majority of sober-minded churchmen. But there can be no doubt that in some Dioceses the area is so extensive, or the population has so largely increased, that a sub-division is urgently required.'

He claimed that he had not found the demands of his own diocese so numerous or onerous that he could not discharge his duties. But in making this claim he did not mention that in May 1874 he had commissioned the Rt. Reverend David Anderson, sometime Bishop of Rupert's Land, and in August Vincent William Ryan, sometime Bishop of Mauritius, to exercise and perform episcopal functions in the Diocese of Durham. While making it quite clear that he could fulfil his episcopal duties he reminded Thomson that between 1861 and 1871 the population of Durham had increased more rapidly than that of any other English county and that during his episcopate ninety-one new parishes had been formed. 'And if the iron and coal trade should revive, the increase of population and the formation of new districts will probably proceed at the same rapid rate as it has done in the last few years . . . I have therefore no hesitation in expressing my conviction that it would be of much benefit to the interests of the Church of England in these parts, if the County of Northumberland with a population of 386,959 and with 154 benefices were formed into a separate Diocese.' Turning to the necessary income for a new see, he wrote:

> I should hope that difficulties in finding an adequate endowment for the new Diocese would not be great. I think that £1,000 or even £1,500 per annum of the present endowment of the See of Durham might be applied to this object . . . I think also that on the first vacancy one of the two canonries, of the value of £1,000 per annum, which are not attached to an Archdeaconry or Professorship might form part of the endowment of a new see . . . I do not think it unreasonable to expect that the Laity of this wealthy Diocese would be ready to contribute a capital sum sufficient to yield an income of £1,000 per annum to effect so good an object, and thus an endowment of £3,500 might ere long be obtained.

Ending this long and interesting letter Baring admitted that as the Archbishop had asked for his views without delay he had not been able to consult with others. If he had he would have found that not all agreed with him. For instance, about this time George Hans Hamilton, Archdeacon of Lindisfarne, received two letters on the subject, one from the Duke of Northumberland who wrote that he did not think it the proper time for launching the project in view of the poor conditions of the commercial state of the county, and another from Mr. Watson Askew saying:

> I have of course foreseen the division of this Diocese must take place sooner or later, and can quite believe it will be for the benefit of the church – at the same time in common with many other conservatives, I shall be very sorry sentimentally that '*the Bishopric*' has to be broken up – and that our connection with it must be severed.

He then went on to raise a number of questions which he felt must be answered before he could take part in any venture to raise the necessary funds.[13]

That autumn Bishop Baring referred the question of the expediency of forming a see of Northumberland to the ruridecanal chapters. Replies to the enquiry showed a wide difference of opinion about the source of the endowment and the amount required, but they were almost unanimous about the desirability of creating the new see. Baring now actively supported the inclusion of Newcastle in any Act for the formation of new sees. Six years later, looking back to Bishop Baring and very mindful of J. B. Lightfoot, the writer of an article on the division of the Diocese of Durham in *The Durham County Advertiser* of July 1882, expressed the opinion that it was: 'A decided triumph of modern enlightenment and religious zeal.' In the palmy days of the bishopric the prince prelates who held almost imperial sway within its boundaries would have resisted to the death any innovation which threatened either their power or their revenue. 'It was reserved for this age, however, to see the spectacle of a Prelate unselfishly promoting the division of his see and the diminution of his revenue, because he feels that he cannot successfully minister to the wants of the souls entrusted to his charge.'

Herbert S. Hicks, Vicar of St Peter's, Tynemouth, wrote a letter of well over 1,000 words to the *Guardian* in October 1876. He clearly recognised and brought to the surface a number of very human elements which were to influence the situation in the days ahead.

> Locality, he wrote, seems to colour the opinions of both clergy and laity with respect to the best title for the new bishopric and the most fitting position for his seat. Those who reside in the east, north and west of the county have their 'most suitable title and seat' somewhere near themselves. Hexham, Alnwick, Lindisfarne and Bamburgh, all have their ardent supporters.

But all these suggestions were found wanting. Of Newcastle he said that although it was situated in the extreme south of the proposed new see, it was the most suitable because more than half the population of Northumberland lived within a few miles radius of it; it was also the most accessible, and the title 'Bishop of Newcastle' was one which commended itself. Finally, the strongest argument in favour of Newcastle was, said Hicks, the likely availability of funds: 'Where shall we look for the bulk of this sum if not to Newcastle? And is it likely that Hexham, Alnwick, Lindisfarne and Bamborough will commend themselves so strongly to Newcastle men as their own town? Newcastle is not insensible of the advantages or the honour of having a Bishop, and I am sure the success of the project depends greatly upon the settlement of title and residence in favour of the county town.'

Unfortunately, however, in spite of the increasing recognition by the people of the north that the Diocese of Durham would have to be divided, for the good of the Church, and the mounting support for the projected division, two years were to elapse before a Bill passed through Parliament and six before the new see was formed.

In July 1876 a report entitled *Deficiencies of Spiritual Ministration* was presented to the Canterbury Convocation; here it was stated:'We have given . . . great prominence to an increase of the Episcopate because, in our opinion, a large portion of the difficulties which have to be faced cannot be satisfactorily removed until such an addition has been made.' While there was no mention of Newcastle, a Supplementary Report in 1877 heartily approved of the proposal made by the Additional Home Bishopric Endowment Fund: 'That the Diocese of Durham should be divided and the County of Northumberland formed into an independent diocese, having the seat of its bishop at Newcastle-on-Tyne . . .'

Despite the support of Convocation, the House of Commons was still unable to agree on the need for new sees. Behind the scenes Sir Richard A. Cross, the Home Secretary, and an Ecclesiastical Commissioner, wrote a very confidential letter to Archbishop Tait on 25 November 1876, informing him that he was prepared to bring a Bill for the Establishment of four new sees before Parliament, but he stressed the need that 'Churchmen be first agreed upon it. If we are to face our enemies we must at all events be united among ourselves.' He included Newcastle in his list and considered that the income for the new sees should be between £3,500 and £4,000 per annum.[14] Tait acknowledged in his reply that there was a strong feeling in favour of a new see somewhere about Bradford and Newcastle.

Cross introduced a new Bishopric Bill in 1877 which recommended the provision of four new sees, including Newcastle, with a minimum income of £3,500 per annum. This new Bill was to have its ardent supporters and its scathing opponents, and much was to be both said and written before it finally emerged as the Bishopric Act of 1878 (41 and 42 Vict. Ch. 68).

Earl Beauchamp presented it for its first reading in the House of Lords on 18 March 1878. Referring to Newcastle he mentioned the £1,000 per annum which would be contributed from the see of Durham and the possibility of the Hedley bequest estimated at £25,000, and ended on the optimistic note: 'There is therefore every possibility that a sufficient endowment of the see of Newcastle will be provided at a not distant date.'

At the second reading in the Lords on 26 March Lord Houghton expressed his disapproval of the proposed separation of Northumberland from the large and important see of Durham, The people of the north, he said, had a pride and affection for the old see — there was no portion of England in which episcopal remembrance and tradition were more cherished than in Durham. The inhabitants of Teeside spoke of the district as 'the Bishopric'.

Bishop Baring made his own contribution to the debate, pointing out that if the bishops were increased in the same proportion as the population then 100 bishops would be required. Although population was not the only factor, it was significant that its increase in Durham had been more rapid than in any other county since the last Census, while in the last 50 years the number of benefices had doubled and the number of clergymen had more than doubled. All this placed a greater amount of work on the bishops. He regretted that the salaries of the new bishops would be only £3,500 a year. Such a small income would limit their opportunities of doing good. Rejecting Lord Houghton's views Baring said that he should himself feel keenly the separation from Northumberland, where he had met with so much kind and hearty support, but there was a strong feeling in the county that the separation was of such importance and of such lasting benefit to the Church of England that churchmen there had unwillingly consented to it. An article in the *Guardian* on 27 March 1878, reporting on the Bishopric Bill before the Lords, mentioned the Bishop of Durham's offer of £1,000 a year and the Hedley bequest, and went on to state: 'We need not doubt that with such a start the very modest effort still required will be made at once, and a Bishop of Newcastle-upon-Tyne consecrated within a few months.'

This was not to be. Even with the support of the Bishop of Durham and the offer of £1,000 per annum from his own income, strong opposition continued to demand a hearing. The Duke of Cleveland in the Lords debate of 4 April said that in Durham, Northumberland and Cumberland very strong objection was felt to the division of the see of Durham. Although he admitted that once it was determined that there should be an additional bishopric, the people of the new diocese would come forward with their usual liberality to find the funds, personally he did not see any necessity for dividing the present diocese and hoped that no immediate steps would be taken in that direction. Whatever the decision he did not see why the funds of the present bishopric should be reduced by £1,000 a year.

Among the many and various objections to the Bill the most violent were expressed by the Liberal M.P. for Newcastle, Joseph Cowen. On 31 July 1878 he delivered a speech in the Commons which covers almost 14 columns of Hansard.[15]

He made no attempt to hide his antagonism towards the Church of England or his open rejection of her doctrines and ministry. Perhaps it was his lack of sympathy towards the Established Church which blurred his thinking and resulted in a number of inaccurate statements. At the very beginning of this speech he declared his strong opposition to both the 'rule' and doctrine of the Church of England, and then went on to say that: 'If they took State pay, they must submit to State control.' Had it not been for the fact that the district in which he lived was directly affected by the Bill he would, he said, have abstained from interfering in the discussion on it, but as it proposed to fasten a bishop on the borough he represented he could not remain silent on the issue. His first objection to the proposal was that there was no popular demand for it. The number of petitions that had been presented in its favour, and the number of meetings that had been held in its support were insignificant. As far as he knew the only people in favour of the Bill were women, clergymen 'and that small but intelligent section of laymen who took an aesthetic and architectural interest in ecclesiastical matters.'

From every conceivable angle Cowen launched a vitriolic attack on the Church. Parliament, he said, was unable to deal with the numerous Bills and resolutions before it which were for the general good of the people and were having to spend their valuable time debating a Bill of interest to only a fraction of the public, and only a fraction of that fraction were anxious about the enactment of the Bill. Throughout the speech he continued to emphasise its limited appeal. Referring to the prelates of the ancient see of Lindisfarne he said: 'Those men were really pastors of their flocks. They interested themselves in the material and moral, as well as in the spiritual welfare of those amongst whom their lot was cast . . . But they lived before the time when Bishops had begun to raise their mitred fronts in Courts and Parliaments. There was not one attribute in common between the ancient and apostolic Bishops and the modern ecclesiastical creations. None would object to an increase of bishops such as those who had once lived at Lindisfarne but they did resent an increase of State officials such as the Bill sought to establish.'

The people of Newcastle, Cowen said, required many things, including a purer atmosphere and a higher culture – but they did not want a bishopric. There was a bishopric at Durham and that was near enough. Quoting the findings of the Religious Census of 1851 in support of his opposition to the Bill, he said that on Census Sunday there were 66,000 worshippers in the Church of England in the Diocese of Durham and in the same area Nonconformist and Roman Catholic worshippers numbered 130,000 (see Ch. V). But even this did not give a true picture . He accused the Church of England of augmenting those counted in their numbers by drumming up the

41

children of the National Schools and Sunday Schools, the inmates of the hospitals and the asylums and the poor people of the workhouses. If deductions were made for these then the strength of Nonconformity would be seen to be even stronger than the Census figures suggested. Cowen admitted that the Church of England, which he referred to as 'that sect', had spent £509,239 building new churches and schools during the period 1863-76. However, in the past twenty -five years the Nonconformists and the Roman Catholics had not stood still; they had spent half as much again as the Established Church on building chapels and schools. Episcopacy, according to Cowen, was autocracy and had never been popular in the north of England. There was, he insisted, no demand for a bishop of Northumberland, therefore there was no need to supply one.

Commenting on Cowen's objections Bishop Baring said he was sorry that Dissenters were objecting on a question which did not concern them, viz., refusing to allow an increase in the episcopate which would improve the efficiency of the Church of England. In spite of all the opposition the Bill had its third reading on 14 August and received Royal Assent the following day.

The Bishopric Act, 1878 (41 and 42 Vict. Ch. 68) offered the Church of England a new approach and opportunity for the creation of new dioceses in those areas believed to be most in need. The Schedule attached to the Act listed the new bishoprics to be established: Liverpool, Newcastle, Southwell and Wakefield. Contributions towards the endowment of these sees were to be deposited with the Ecclesiastical Commissioners who would issue certificate for the formation of the see once the minimum amount had been raised. Existing bishoprics from which the new sees were to be created would make a contribution from their income towards the endowment of the new see. The endowment fund would have to produce an income of not less than £3,500 a year and not more than £4,200. If a fitting episcopal residence was provided this would be reckoned as equal to £500 per annum. The Act made it clear that in founding these new sees there was to be no increase in the number of seats held by the bishops in the House of Lords.

Concerning Newcastle, the Schedule states: that the Bishop was to be Bishop of Newcastle; the diocese would consist of the county of Northumberland, and the counties of the towns of Newcastle upon Tyne and Berwick-upon-Tweed. St Nicholas Church Newcastle upon Tyne was to be the Cathedral.

In theory there was now nothing to prevent the formation of the Diocese of Newcastle. But the prediction of the *Guardian* that, once the Act had been passed, it would be only a matter of months before the see was established, was not to be fulfilled.

Speaking at a luncheon following the re-opening of one of his churches Baring remarked on the Bishopric Bill that for himself, and as far as the diocese was concerned, the provision of the Bill would work for the benefit of the Church.

Sometime later and shortly after the Bishopric Act had received Royal Assent, Baring delivered his last Charge to his diocese. While impressing on the diocese the need to complete the task he also acknowledged that while 'trade remained in its present depressed position, it would be useless to form any committee.' Commenting on the Charge the *Guardian* of 20 November, stated: 'There does not seem from the Bishop's account any immediate hope of a division of the diocese . . . the prospect of accomplishing this good work is remote.' Whatever the local problems, the *Guardian* believed that the situation was urgent and that the scheme ought to be put into effect without delay.

Bishop Baring was not alone in thinking that the time was not ripe. Earl Percy wrote to Hamilton, the Archdeacon of Lindisfarne, on 26 November 1878. They had discussed the need to form a Committee to carry the Bishopric Act into effect in Northumberland but, he commented:

> It must be remembered that an appeal of this kind will be made at this moment under the most adverse circumstances. With the Nonconformists it will of course be most unpopular. And even amongst members of the Established Church a demand upon their pockets is not likely to meet with much favour at a time of extreme commercial and almost equal agricultural depression. I fear that any move of this kind just now might be disastrous both from an ecclesiastical and a political point of view.

He admitted these were very much his own views and suggested that before a decision was made they ought to consult the principal landowners and capitalists. There was, he suggested, a middle course, which was to form a committee and announce a willingness to receive any contributions, or promises of contributions, while at the same time abstaining from bringing any pressure to bear on the public for the present. But he felt the real question was whether it was opportune at this time to launch such an appeal.[16]

When Baring announced his resignation on 3 December 1878 yet another reason was found for postponing any attempt to create the new diocese, although his successor, Joseph Barber Lightfoot, consecrated Bishop of Durham in Westminster Abbey on 25 April 1879, came to Durham pledged to carry out without delay the division of the diocese. Even as bishop-elect, and within a few days of Baring's resignation taking effect, Lightfoot visited the Ecclesiastical Commissioners on 15 February 1879, to discuss the proposed bishopric of Newcastle and particularly the Hedley legacy, about which there was a considerable uncertainty.

Bishop Baring had written about it to the Ecclesiastical Commissioners on 27 February 1878, enclosing with his letter a press cutting from the *Standard*. Was the statement in the cutting correct? asked Baring. It stated that the brother of the late Thomas Hedley was willing to hand over the residue of the estate, about £38,000, to the Commissioners as soon as they were prepared to receive it. Baring commented that he had expected only £25,000. The Commissioners replied that they had no information relating to the Hedley bequest in favour of the bishopric of Northumberland. On 10 March 1879 Lightfoot, still at Trinity College Cambridge, wrote as bishop-elect to Earl Stanhope: 'So long as the present uncertainty with regard to Mr. Hedley's bequest remains it is impossible for me to solicit contributions towards the establishment of the Bishopric with any effect as I am met with a question which I cannot answer but on which eventually the amount to be raised very materially depends . . . a great point will be gained if the value of the bequest can be ascertained.'[17]

Because of the continued uncertainty the 'Newcastle Bishopric Hedley Bequest Case' was presented to Judge Francis H. Jeune who gave his opinion on 21 July 1879. William Hedley, to whom Thomas Hedley his brother had left the estate, offered a settlement to the Commissioners of £18,000, provided they paid the legacy duty and costs. Francis Jeune advised acceptance, if the Commissioners were satisfied with the amount offered. It was accepted and after costs resulted in £16,200 being added to the Newcastle Endowment Fund (see Ch. IX).

Looking to the future endowment of the new see Bishop Lightfoot wrote to the Ecclesiastical Commissioners on 23 June 1879. His letter prompted the Commissioners to instruct their surveyors to prepare a schedule of property in Northumberland calculated to secure the sum of £1,000 per annum which was eventually to form part of the income of the diocese of Newcastle.

Lightfoot's early enthusiasm to implement the division of the Diocese along the lines of the Bishopric Act was to be thwarted, and even he had to concede that delay, while much regretted, was inevitable. At a later date he had to admit to the Diocese:

When I accepted the see of Durham, it was represented to me that the formation of the new see was imminent; and this expectation weighed greatly with me. When therefore I entered the diocese, I seized the first opportunity to emphasise this measure as one which should engage our immediate attention. But the moment was represented to me as inopportune. Everything was against us. Agriculture was in a deplorable condition. Commerce was at its lowest ebb. The mineral trade more especially, on which the diocese is largely dependent was fearfully depressed. Moreover, the evil resulting from the state of the market was aggravated beyond measure by chronic strikes, which not only inflicted heavy losses in themselves, but paralysed industry and enterprise by creating a general sense of insecurity. I do not know whether I acted rightly. Perhaps a bolder venture of faith would have been better. But I was afraid to endanger a measure of so great importance by a false start. I deferred to these representations, and held my hands for the time. But I have never wavered in my own mind as to the importance of the measure in itself.

There were also personal reasons for the delay:

My own position was a serious impediment in the way of active measures at first. My hands were too full to give much time and attention to the matter, while I was still learning the work of the diocese. Where localities are unfamiliar and men are unknown, a very small matter of business, which might otherwise have been transacted in five minutes, may involve much correspondence and take up some hours, if it is properly done. Moreover, the vacancy of the see had left arrears of work. Thus, within seven months I had to hold confirmations for two years ... This was an additional reason for delay.[18]

As soon as the situation improved Lightfoot quickly seized the opportunity. At the Diocesan Conference of September 1880 he pressed for the immediate creation of the new see. From that Conference efforts to obtain the required income began in earnest. Lightfoot set about drawing together a Committee to undertake the necessary fund raising. On November 18 1880 he wrote to Albert H. G. Grey, M.P. for South Northumberland, asking if he would serve on the Committee. In this letter Lightfoot wrote: 'I am more and more impressed daily with the urgent need of the new See.' Writing to those whom he felt ought to serve on the Committee, Lightfoot asked them if they were not able to be present at the first meeting, to be held at Durham Castle on 23 December 1880, to let him know how much they would contribute to the fund. What the Bishop had to say at the meeting made it clear that despite the commercial difficulties which had delayed their action and his own personal problems he had, nevertheless, been quietly working and making personal appeals for contributions towards the Endowment Fund.

45

On 12 February 1881 he issued a Report for private circulation. A capital sum of roughly £63,000 was required, the Hedley bequest of £16,000 reduced this total to £47,000. In order to meet all contingencies Lightfoot suggested they aimed for £50,000, of which he was able to report that nearly £32,000 had already been promised. Therefore, less than £19,000 had yet to be found: 'It ought not to be difficult', wrote Lightfoot, 'to raise this sum in the two wealthy counties of Northumberland and Durham, for Durham is almost equally interested with Northumberland in the division of the Diocese, and should bear its proper share of the burden.' No one could doubt that Lightfoot had done more than his share in personally raising nearly £32,000; of this, £20,000 came from seven gifts including £10,000 from the Duke of Northumberland and Lightfoot's own magnificent gift of £3,000. In March 1881 Bishop Lightfoot sent a letter to the daily press, headed 'To the Clergy and Laity of the Diocese of Durham.' It began:'The time has now arrived when a general appeal should be made to complete the Endowment Fund of the Bishopric of Newcastle . . . at the recent Diocesan Congress I ventured to dwell on the subject at some length, and since then I have devoted all the time that I could spare to the prosecution of the work.' He went on to say something of the encouraging response he had received to his personal appeal for donations and how the subscription list indicated that Durham had borne its full share of the burden. He concluded:'It remains for me now to hand over the work of collecting the remainder to the clergy and laity of the diocese, more especially to the laity.'

This letter brought the subject before the Diocese more prominently than ever before. A Committee was formed with ninety-four members under the chairmanship of Earl Percy and an Executive Committee of twenty-nine. Meetings were held in all the large towns of the two counties and in these Bishop Lightfoot, despite his decision to hand the matter over to others, played a prominent part. He attended most of the public meetings and personally urged the importance of the scheme.

Some were critical about the way the new see was to be endowed and felt that the Ecclesiastical Commissioners ought to do more. Some said that more than £1,000 per annum ought to be contributed from the Diocese of Durham. Lightfoot pointed out that the Diocese of Durham would still remain twice the size of the new Diocese and that the estates of the Bishop of Durham were entirely within the county of Durham. Any real criticism on this matter was silenced when Bishop Lightfoot publicly announced that every penny, and more than every penny, of his official income was spent in and on the diocese and that he had become poorer since he came to Auckland Castle, and would be poorer still when he had paid his promised subscription. He contradicted the foolish rumour that the Ecclesiastical Commissioners had promised to make up anything he gave to the new see.

In a letter, written from Auckland Castle on 18 July 1881, to the Ecclesiastical Commissioners Lightfoot complained that local attempts to raise funds for the new see were being hampered by the restrictions imposed by the Act. 'I shall be obliged to hear if the Commissioners would consider the propriety of providing a house for the Bishop of Newcastle out of the resources of the Durham Bishopric Estate . . . When I have been soliciting contributions for the Newcastle bishopric I have constantly met with the objection that the Commissioners deducted a very large revenue from the estates of the Durham bishopric, and that as a matter of equity, these resources should be employed first of all to secure sufficient episcopal supervision by the erection of the new see. Many have given with reluctance and many have refused to give at all, on this ground.' His reply to the objectors was that the Commissioners were forbidden by Act of Parliament from endowing new sees out of the Common Fund. If a house could be made available in the way he suggested this would be highly acceptable throughout the Diocese and would help to remove the frequent complaint that the Commissioners drew far more from Durham than they returned to it. On 3 August the Commissioners replied that what he proposed was impossible according to the Act. The provision of the episcopal residence could only be made out of the Newcastle Endowment Fund.

At this moment of keen disappointment an unexpected gift, from an even more unexpected quarter, changed the situation. John William Pease, a member of the Society of Friends and a partner in the banking firm of Messrs Hodgkin, Barnett, Pease, Spense & Co., wrote to Bishop Lightfoot in November 1881:'I have notice that funds for the endowment of the new See of Newcastle have come in rather slowly of late, and the purchase of a house large enough to meet the requirements of a Bishop must therefore be a difficulty. Having an unoccupied house which is considered the most suitable place in the neighbourhood for your purposes I have decided to hand it over to you.' In addition to the house, Benwell Tower, Pease offered to hand over the gardens and the Lodge and as many cottages as required. Immediately Lightfoot wrote to the Commissioners informing them of his good fortune. He told them:'I had already fixed on Benwell Tower, as the most suitable house for this purpose, before I had any idea that it could be provided otherwise than by purchase; and it was therefore with extreme satisfaction that I received the munificent offer of Mr. Pease.' Lightfoot enclosed with his letter a highly satisfactory architect's report.

Benwell Tower was situated about two and a half miles west of Newcastle, a short distance north of the Tyne. At that time tram cars ran from Grainger Street near the North Eastern Railway Station to within about half a mile of the Lodge. It had been erected in the late eighteenth century on the site of a mediaeval house. It contained eighteen bedrooms, one of which it was suggested was of sufficient size to be divided into five excellent single rooms for ordination candidates. The architect summed up his report:'On the whole, notwithstanding certain deficiencies, there can be no doubt that the house is a substantial and excellent residence. For the purposes of a Bishop it would probably require a few alterations and additional fittings . . . though to complete it properly a Chapel would probably be deemed a necessary adjunct.' A chapel was in fact added by Wilberforce in 1887, towards which he personally provided £500, and raised a mortgage from the Commissioners of £1,500 to complete the building.

The Report went on to observe:'As it stands, however, unless a liberal endowment be provided for the new see, a house of this magnitude might prove to be a severe strain on ordinary resources, if it is to be thoroughly well maintained as the episcopal residence of an important Diocese.[19]

The Archbishop of York wrote to Pease on 24 November 1881: 'The Commissioners whilst thanking you for your munificent offer and accepting the same, desire to express their high sense of your great and well-timed liberality which will speedily remove all obstacles to the formation of the new see.' In correspondence with Pease the question of mineral rights and previous coal-mining under the house and its adjoining buildings had been raised. Pease wrote to the Commissioners on 3 January 1882 and referred to reports he had received on the state of the coal under the property:'I gather that Benwell Tower and its gardens are the only pieces of property near Newcastle resting on a really solid foundation.' In March that year the Benwell Tower Estate was conveyed to the Ecclesiastical Commissioners as a free gift.

The Northern Echo on 26 July 1882, reported:'The value of the munificent gift is about £30,000, and thus the largest contribution to the new bishopric comes from a Dissenter — a singular instance of the interest with which the movement has been regarded by those outside the pale of the Church.'

During the months in which the offer of Benwell Tower was being negotiated fund-raising continued in an all-out attempt to reach the required sum. When the Church Congress met in Newcastle in October 1881 Bishop Lightfoot acted as President. In his Inaugural Address he spoke of the Increase of the Episcopate: 'Here is a question of living and lively interest – never more lively than in this huge overgrown northern diocese.' What he had to say resulted in a collection of £2,734 towards the Newcastle Endowment Fund.

John J. Hunter, Honorary Secretary of the Executive Committee of the Newcastle Endowment Fund wrote to the Ecclesiastical Commissioners on 29 December 1881, requesting them to take the necessary steps for the speedy formation of the bishopric. Hunter reported that when the final investments had been made, the income, including the house, would be £3,750 per annum. Included with his letter was a statement of the capital raised, which amounted to £46,354, in addition to the £1,000 a year from the diocese of Durham and the £605 a year from the investment of the Hedley legacy and the £500 a year value of Benwell Tower. Success did not bring an immediate cessation either to the attempts to raise money or to the generosity of donors. Several months later the Bishop of Durham announced a £10,000 donation from Thomas Spencer. With this the minimum amount was well exceeded, indeed the final accounts showed that £75,166.12s. 9d was raised, not to mention £1,200 provided by the ladies of Newcastle and neighbourhood towards the furnishing of Benwell Tower.

Convinced that nothing should now delay the formation of the new see, Bishop Lightfoot wrote to the Commissioners on 5 January informing them that he had requested those responsible to transfer all securities and funds to the Commissioners so that the final arrangements could go ahead. Events did not move as quickly as Lightfoot expected and he found it necessary to write again to the Commissioners on 8 April 'I should be obliged if you could let me know whether there is likely to be any delay in the creation of the bishopric.' They replied that they were not aware of any, and then on 4 May they wrote to the Secretary of State providing the required certificate indicating that the annual value of the Newcastle Endowment Fund was not less than the required £3,500 per annum. A similar communication was sent that same day to the Queen. *The London Gazette* on 23 May 1882 announced: 'Her Majesty is pleased, by and with the advice of her Most Honourable Privy Council, to order and declare as follows: The Bishopric of Newcastle is hereby founded . . .'

Speculations about the appointment of the first bishop began to occupy the minds of those who had worked to raise the income for the new diocese. Not a few in the Diocese of Durham felt that the ideal person would be the Archdeacon of Northumberland, Henry William Watkins. His work in the Diocese and the fact that he was widely known suggested that his name ought at least to be given serious consideration. Churchmen, including those of Northumberland, generally felt that Gladstone would appoint the man most fitted for the new see. His choice fell on Canon Ernest Roland Wilberforce, son of Samuel Wilberforce, reformer of the episcopate, and grandson of William W. Wilberforce the evangelical philanthropic member of Parliament and advocate of the abolition of the slave trade. Gladstone wrote to offer him the bishopric of Newcastle in a letter which reached him on 21 May, two days before the formation of the see was Gazetted. Gladstone wrote: 'I have to propose to you that you should now become the first incumbent of the new see of Newcastle. In making this grave request, I bear in mind all that it involves. But I earnestly hope that your acceptance of it may, if it please God, carry far onwards into a second century the unbroken association of your honoured name with the history of the Church of England, and that you may add largely to the records of the noble service of your father and your grandfather.' Wilberforce asked the Prime Minister to allow him a few days before replying.

Obviously the success of his father and grandfather whom all highly esteemed made his situation difficult. He wrote to his wife:

> I do not feel in the least the man for the office, and how awful would be failure: (and then to Gladstone): Knowing well, as I do, the awful responsibility of a Bishop's office, and my own deep lack of many of the most important qualifications for such a post . . . I have felt an almost overwhelming shrinking from the post which you have been led to offer me. But after much prayer and thought, and consultation with my most intimate friends, I have come to the conclusion that I dare not refuse a work to which I may humbly hope my Master is calling me . . .

Wilberforce's reluctance to accept the appointment and the deep sense of his own inability to fulfil the office of bishop makes a striking contrast with an article in *The Hampshire Chronicle* which spoke in glowing terms of his experience and suitability, and commended the wisdom of those in authority in making the appointment. The *Chronicle* recognised that it was not to be an easy appointment: 'For the Bishop of Newcastle is not to be called to a life of easy dignity, nor is it every learned theologian or every gifted preacher who would discharge the duties of that bishopric satisfactorily. A man is wanted there in the full burst of vivid manhood . . . he must be ready to endure hardship and to give himself, mind and body, to genuine toil amongst the rougher elements of our social system.' Wilberforce, at forty-three, was felt to be the man for the job.

He was consecrated first bishop of Newcastle at Durham Cathedral on Tuesday, 25 July 1882, and enthroned in the new Cathedral of St Nicholas on Thursday, 3 August. Welcoming the bishop on behalf of the laity the Duke of Northumberland spoke of how the increasing opulence and commercial activity which had raised the city and surrounding neighbourhood to a high level of prosperity had brought with them 'the dark shadows of demoralisation and vice which follow in the train of wealth and luxury.' In combating these evils the Duke assured the bishop that he would have the full support of the laity of the Church and of men of all religious opinions. The vicar of Newcastle also spoke and ended his address by assuring the bishop that in the work that lay ahead he would also have the full support of the clergy. Bishop Wilberforce responded to both addresses:'In these days the Bishop's hands are weak unless they are strengthened by the co-operation both of the clergy and laity.' He asked for their prayers, advice, counsel and encouragement that together they might work for God in the diocese.

Wilberforce then preached his first sermon in his new Cathedral. He recognised that the separation of Newcastle from Durham was not acceptable to everyone and that for some it was still a cause for deep sorrow; and yet for others it was a reason for thankfulness and jubilation. He concluded with the words: 'I venture, my brethren, to beseech you to carry out completely the purpose of God . . . rendering this old diocese, now made new by God, a centre of life, of prayer, of work for the Master, in fuller measure than ever before . . . The work that lies before us as a diocese is difficult, and will require many years for even its partial completion . . . We must have in this work lay people acting side by side with clergy, as God's new work goes onward to its appointed end . . . '

NOTES
1. A fine hand-written copy of 7. Edward VI. *For the Dissolution of Durham* is held in the Record Office of the House of Lords. See also (William Cobbett) *The Parliamentary History of England, from the Earliest Period to the Year 1803*, Vol. i., A.D. 1066–1625 1806, pp.601–2.
2. The original manuscript: 'To the Ecclesiastical Commissioners for England: The Memorial of the Mayor, Aldermen and Councillors of the Borough of Newcastle-upon-Tyne', is in the Ecclesiastical Commissioners File 8627.
3. The Hexham Memorial is in the Ecclesiastical Commissioners File 8627.
4. Walpole Spencer, *The Life of Lord John Russell*, 1889, Vol. i., p. 474.
5. Lambeth Palace Library MS. 2172 f. 37.

6. *First Report of Her Majesty's Commissioners appointed November 10, A.D. 1852, to Inquire into the State and Condition of the Cathedral and Collegiate Churches in England and Wales,* 1854, and *Third and Final Report of Her Majesty's Commissioners appointed . . . to Inquire . . . with an Appendix,* 1855.
7. Lambeth Palace Library – Tait Papers, 86, f. 284.
8. *Ibid.,* ff. 307, 324, 326.
9. See *Hansard,* 3rd Series, CCXXII., (1875), 724.
10. Lambeth Palace Library – Tait Papers, 188, ff. 337–8.
11. *Hansard,* 3rd Series, CCXXII (1875), 1476–7.
12. *Ibid.,* 1472.
13. Durham, Lightfoot Papers – Newcastle File – dated 23 August, 1876.
14. Lambeth Palace Library – Tait Papers, 96, F. 256.
15. *Hansard,* 3rd Series, CCXCII, (1878), 829–842.
16. Durham, – Lightfoot Papers – Newcastle File – dated 26 November, 1878.
17. Ecclesiastical Commissioners, File 8627, dated 10 March, 1879
18. *Durham Diocesan Calendar 1881,* pp. 99–100.
19. A copy of the Architect's Report has been preserved in the Ecclesiastical Commissioners' File 8627.

Acknowledgements
The Author wishes to thank the following for their permission to reproduce manuscript material for which they hold the copyright:
Durham University Department of Palaeography and Diplomatic; Lambeth Palace Library; Sir William Gladstone; the Church Commissioners; the Dean and Chapter Library, Durham: Lightfoot Trustees.

Chapter III

A PERSONAL ACCOUNT OF THE DIOCESE OF NEWCASTLE

Malcolm Nicholson

1. THE DIOCESE AND ITS BISHOPS

> I should have been happy to spend the rest of my working life on Tyneside and in Northumberland, where there was a more friendly atmosphere throughout the Church than I have found anywhere else... Shocking as were the housing conditions, I found the people uniformly friendly and lovable... I rapidly lost my heart to Tyneside and have had a painful nostalgia for it ever since. (*Scenes from a Clerical Life,* by Alec R. Vidler, 1977 pp.55 and 44)

YET IT IS fifty years since Dr. Vidler served in Newcastle, and then in one of its worst slums, at the Mission of the Holy Spirit, and in the depths of the Depression. Since then he has served with distinction and in delightful settings such as St. Deiniol's Library Hawarden, Windsor Castle as Canon of Windsor, King's College Cambridge as Fellow and Dean – fair places indeed. These fifty years of congenial academic and personal work have not quenched the nostalgia for Tyneside.

Dr. Vidler is not alone in this. Mandell Creighton, when Bishop of London, speaks of his persistent longing for Northumberland: his early days as vicar of Embleton were the happiest days of his life. Roger Lloyd, Canon of Winchester, though he never served here, underlines this fact in his history of the *Church of England in the Twentieth Century* (1950:196):

> It (Newcastle) is therefore one of the happiest places for a priest to work .... It is noticeable that a priest who has once worked in Newcastle for a time and then left it to go elsewhere, often likes to get back there if he can.

One cannot begin to understand the Diocese of Newcastle unless one notes first this element of deep and persisting affection engendered.

A hundred years is not a long time, three generations encompass it. Edward Barry Hicks was the first man to be ordained deacon in the Diocese, in 1882. He was still an honoured figure when I was ordained in 1932 – the exact middle of the centenary period. His sons, Walter and Barry, were already ordained in the Diocese; his grandson, Richard, is today vicar of Prudhoe. Their years of steady and loyal service tie the Diocese together historically and indeed geographically – for between them they have served in Newcastle, Ainwick, Killingworth, Haltwhistle, Berwick, Alston, Warkworth, Monkseaton, Lucker, Cornhill, Wallsend, North Shields, Percy Main and Prudhoe. This clerical dynasty underlines the closeknit family nature of the Diocese which derived from its identification with the County of Northumberland, apart from a few acres from Durham and Cumberland. Northumberland was a proud, self-conscious county, fostering strong county loyalty – neighbourhood meant more then than today. To the rest of England, Northumberland seemed remote – for the Northumbrian, foreigners began at Gateshead.

This separateness begat clannishness in both county and Diocese; in the latter it gave birth to a strong sense of being a family.

Before considering the bishops, it is salutary to take note of the sobering fact that the health of the Diocese depends first and foremost upon the quality of the parish clergy. A parish seldom flourishes if it receives a priest who is not up to his task. In justice, one must add that some parishes will not respond even to faithful and good priests – such men, for no fault of their own, receive little reward for their faithfulness. It is a fearful thing to become a parish priest – or it should be. In early days this excessive dependence of the parish upon the quality of its priest was mitigated by two things – first, the wide though far from universal acceptance of the duty of worship and, second, the existence of the Book of Common Prayer as the sole and unrivalled pattern of authoritative worship.

Bishops are different. The outstandingly great bishop, a rare person indeed, can elevate the tone of the whole diocese but a bishop who proves to be inadequate for his high calling may do little harm to the diocese, as we shall see later. To write of the early bishops and of the condition of the Diocese is a frustrating task. The monthly *Newcastle Diocesan Gazette* maintained a bland tone with little hint of dissension. Yet the 1880s were a time of controversy in matters of faith, fierce quarrels arose from the linguistic studies of the Biblical texts and the recent archaeological discoveries – it was only twenty years since the clash over evolution between Huxley and Bishop Samuel Wilberforce of Oxford. The Diocese must have contained disturbed minds among clergy and laity but the *Gazette* reveals little of this. At this time it was called *The Diocesan Magazine, A Chronicle of Church Work in Town and Country*, though it tells little of either town or country parishes. It plays for safety with articles on, for instance, 'A tour among the Normans and Bretons', 'A visit of the British Association to America', a heavy series on the Apostles Creed, a serial story. No reference of course to that glorious Northumbrian, Josephine Butler, then reaching the climax of her campaign – no word indeed that could disturb or challenge (see Chapter XV).

The Bishops

E. R. Wilberforce	1882-1896	E. Jacob	1896-1903
A. T. Lloyd	1903-1907	N. D. J. Straton	1907-1915
H. L. Wild	1915-1927	H. E. Bilbrough	1927-1941
N. B. Hudson	1941-1957	H. E. Ashdown	1957-1973
R. O. Bowlby	1973-1980		

Ernest Wilberforce, the first bishop, stayed fourteen years before being moved to the Diocese of Chichester. In many ways he resembled a later bishop, Noel Hudson – he 'revolutionised the ideals of churchmanship in Northumberland', he stressed the primacy of prayer and action over talk, he took infinite pains to care for those whom he had ordained. The *Times* foolishly regretted that 'he was not so affable and hearty as he might have been' – he was in fact an honest and direct man, not inclined towards smooth affability, the shallow smile worn in public. The fourteen years spent here, about the right period for a founding bishop, were very good years, laying a sound foundation (see Chapters IX and X). His successor, Edgar Jacob, was an able man too but was snatched away too soon, going after five years to the see of St. Alban's. Dr. Lloyd who took his place had been a much loved vicar of Newcastle, some years before, but was already a sick man when he returned and was dead within four years. His burial elicited a demonstration of affection seldom equalled for a cleric. His death led to the appointment of Dr. Straton, the odd man out among our bishops, his singular distinction being that he created and nurtured dissension among brethren. No doubt he held his views sincerely but they were so narrow and exclusive that they sat ill in a Church which accepted the fact that good men could differ widely in many matters yet live side by side in tolerance. He sought to use the letter of the law to drive out men who were devoted pastors but did not share his own views on permissible patterns of worship. It was not only the extremists, whose practices were indubitably at variance with the laws on worship, that he persecuted. A plea from a large body of clergy, including moderate men like E.B. Hicks, that he should be ready to accept that in the Church of England there were views other than his own narrowly Protestant ones was received with anger. Straton declared that none of these men who were pleading for gentle tolerance could expect his favour again. He continued to persecute, refusing to visit certain parishes or to send curates to parishes which did not conform to his own brand of Anglicanism. Many of these were slum parishes where heroic work was being done by dedicated priests, such as the Mission of the Holy Spirit. It was a sad episcopate. It is significant that when Straton's successor, Dr. Wild, was announced, the *Newcastle Daily Chronicle* in its welcome to the new Bishop revealed what the *Diocesan Gazette* had kept hidden: 'It is to be anticipated that Bishop Wild will make *harmony and co-operation* the keynotes of his administration'. And that is exactly what Dr. Wild did. He did it so well that in a very short time the old wounds were healed. It is possible that Bishop Straton's bigotry had even strengthened the church life in most of the parishes that he had banned. A touch of persecution can be stimulating and to be banned by some bishops is not without its compensations.

The Straton years and their aftermath revealed the resilience of the Church: where there is a happy relationship between parish and parish priest little can do serious damage.

Herbert Louis Wild, 1915-1927, was a scholarly man; he had been a don at Durham and at Oxford, where he became Vice-Principal of St. Edmund Hall at an early age. Then to parish life for 12 years and thus to Newcastle, to be bishop, in January 1915. He had not only the normal discomforts of the War but for his first three years he had no telephone, no electricity, no car, and, as was the custom then, he had to surrender a third of his income to his retired predecessor. Most of his travelling round the Diocese was by train, he would get back late at night to the Central Station, catch the tram to Benwell church, walk the rest, carrying a case with his robes in one hand, with his pastoral staff in the other. To assist him, he had one archdeacon who was 75 and bed-ridden, another who had been a bishop 22 years previously, a vicar of Newcastle on the verge of retirement. Their senescence however carried seeds of hope – before long he was able to bring in new men, among them Leslie Hunter (later a distinguished Bishop of Sheffield, see Chapter XVI.), Oliver Quick (later Professor at Oxford and at Durham), George Newsom (formerly a Professor at King's College London, later Master of Selwyn College, Cambridge). Benwell Tower played a great part – the Bishop and Mrs Wild abounded in hospitality despite the fact that entertainment and all expenses came out of the Bishop's pocket, and their five children added to the attraction of the place. One hears of a Diocesan meeting being enlivened by the arrival of a pet monkey pursued by its young owner, a welcome and ice-breaking diversion. Perhaps every episcopal home should have a monkey? One of Mrs. Wild's many wise and kindly acts was to remove from the dining room a glowering portrait of Straton – it had a dispiriting effect upon nervous guests. Wild was a peace-maker certainly; 'he brought peace in place of heartburning and dissension' said his successor. But he was far more – he had quality and he attracted and encouraged talent. Perhaps the best tribute came when he died, from a priest who would have made Straton's blood boil, Brock Richards. 'Although he was not an Anglo-Catholic, he always showed us sympathy, he trusted us. In him we had a real Father-in-God. A man of great learning, great spiritual power, one who lived very near to God.'

Of Dr. Wild's successor, Dr. Bilbrough (1927-1941) it is difficult to write, for the general verdict among those of us who remember him is that one remembers very little about him. He had had a reputation for good parochial work in his early days, he came to Newcastle from being Suffragan Bishop of Dover where he had made himself useful and acceptable to the Archbishop of Canterbury, but in Newcastle he seemed a spent force. Having considerable private means, he was able to give a few thousands to this and that, which concealed the absence of those endowments which one expects from a bishop. His easy bonhomie, his genial smile, combined with the fact that those who initiate nothing make no enemies, made him a popular figure, as contrasted with Bishop Wilberforce or Bishop Hudson. He exemp-lifies the fact that a bishop who is not up to the job need do no great harm. He was glad to leave the real leadership to Archdeacon Hunter, and the Diocese had a number of very good parish priests and some excellent laypeople, who enabled the Church to do a good job amidst the Depression. Roger Lloyd (1950:194-208) speaks with admiration of the Diocese of Newcastle in this period. He makes no reference to its Bishop.

It is worth recording that Newcastle Diocese was a breeding ground for clergy who called themselves 'Socialists' or maybe 'Christian Socialists' in those days (see Chapters XII and XVII). Back in 1908, the Diocesan conference had chosen socialism as the subject for one of its main discussions and the report now makes strange reading. On the whole, the clergy who spoke were for and the laity against it. The clergy had experience of the shocking social conditions: they had personal affection for many who lived in disgusting slums, their 'socialism' came from the heart. This was still true in the thirties. Socialists had achieved little power. We had seen the 'hard-faced men who had done well out of the War' but not yet had we seen the men who had done well out of the socialist movement. We were starry-eyed about it, as starry-eyed as the miners with whom I stood and chatted when the coal mines were nationalised, not many years later. Dear good men they were, old miners who had been through the worst and remained strangely free from bitterness. Now they rejoiced — the mines belonged to the people, all would be well, no more argument over wages!

The report of the 1908 Conference reveals a certain naivete among the clergy who were not moved by economic or political theories but rather by anger at the distress around them and pity for the distressed. Anger and pity are unreliable counsellors and in the 30s and 40s we were still underestimating the ubiquity and power of original sin. Yet our emotions did convey to many of our poor parishioners that we were on their side. Moreover this slant was at the time necessary to redress the balance; the Church of England is dogged, and not without reason, by the suspicion that it tends to favour the *status quo*, to be blind to the injustices that cripple the lives of many. It is worth remembering that throughout the Depression, many clergy, and their wives, were ready to serve amidst scenes of sad poverty and to bring up their children there. They could do little to help their people materially yet in many ways they comforted them and they played an honourable part in the life of the poor (see Chapters XII and XIII).

Bishop Bilbrough was succeeded by Noel Baring Hudson, in 1941, having had him in the Diocese for five inspired years as vicar of St. John's, Newcastle (1926-31). When Hudson came to St. John's he came trailing clouds of worldly glory (see Nicholson 1970). He had gone to the Western Front as a subaltern in September 1914; he spent the War there, emerging as Colonel of the 8th Berks and Acting-Brigadier at the age of twenty-four. On the way he had won two D.S.O.s and two M.C.s, and been wounded thirteen times. As one of his sergeants said: 'The Colonel was a real gentleman and a fine soldier, even if he was religious'. His letters from the Front to his mother reveal how he agonised over his men, whom he admired and loved. The Army sought to retain him after the War – he would have reached high distinction – but he remained faithful to his priestly vocation. After his ordination preparation (when he captained the Harlequins R.F.C.) he went to Leeds as a curate (when he played for

58

Headingly and Yorkshire) and after two years became vicar of the parish. Four years later to Newcastle, where his five years as vicar are inseparable from his sixteen years from 1941 as bishop. Under Bilbrough he was a key man, making great impact on the Diocese. Thus he served this Diocese for 21 years, for over a fifth of its story. I stayed with him at the vicarage frequently at that time, corresponded with him when he was in Borneo and after, was too much his disciple to judge him dispassionately, so turn to the man chosen to give his funeral oration in Newcastle Cathedral. Canon Gordon Ireson was well placed to do this. As Canon Missioner for 10 years he worked intimately with him yet the fact that he spent three-quarters of his ministry in other dioceses gives him detachment. In his oration he has this passage:

> When we first met we did not seem to have a single natural common interest, we did not delight in the same things or read the same books. Yet I saw him in action a few days later, at an Institution at Sugley, and came away with a glad heart. Here was *a man born to be a bishop*, everything he said and did rang a bell. He did not like preaching in general, especially on formal occasions, but when he found himself among one of his artisan congregations at the Parish Communion, his shyness fell away, he spake with simplicity and power. That which was to become the most significant movement in the Church of England in our time had been anticipated by Hudson as Vicar of St. John's many years before. I refer to the Parish Communion, and all that stemmed from it, which spread from St. John's back in the Thirties throughout this Diocese. Because his teaching was essentially Biblical, closely linked with the Book of Common Prayer, it was acceptable both to the 'Evangelical' school and to the 'Catholics'. Old suspicions began to wither, church people were drawn together. Later, as Bishop he remained a parish priest at heart — he needed the affection which parish life gave him to overcome his inhibiting shyness. He cared deeply for the clergy — *it was the job of the parish priest to know and to care for his people.*

Why did Ireson refer to the Parish Communion as 'the most significant movement in the Church of England in our time'? The answer is seen in Hudson's short period at St. John's. In 1926 he came to a successful and well-attended church but one which veiled the reality, especially the unity, of the Body of Christ. There were five services each Sunday, the worshippers chose the service they liked the best; one might say there were groups of worshippers but nothing you could point to as being the Body of Christ united in common worship. St. John's had its slum parish and also a host of people from other parts of Newcastle — amidst this varied band of worshippers there was a challenging opportunity for bringing this variety into one offering of family worship. But in fact nothing had been made of this;

C*   59

the worshippers hived off into separate compartments based on likes and dislikes. Noel's aim then was to seek to build up one central act of worship in which rich and poor, young and old, should share at one time each Sunday and this became known as the Parish Communion. Though a man with authority, he was also gentle and patient, and did not cut off other services, but set out by teaching and pastoral strategy to build up this family gathering, which was not an easy feat. People at first clung to the old ways, for example the 11 o'clock congregation did not really want the boys and girls from the parish disturbing their peace, but the message was pressed home that our oneness in Christ was vastly more significant than our worldly differences. Inevitably the people would be separated in their everyday life, split up by living in different areas, by social educational financial status: for them to capture and retain the sense of belonging to one another, because they were baptised into Christ, they must at least worship as one. Little Gracie English, in her first year at Rutherford College, Newcastle, having worshipped alongside her redoubtable headmistress would exchange a word and a smile with her, though at school next morning she would not presume upon this.

Most important of all was the fact that the Parish Communion was not just a fellowship meal, a jolly get-together (though it was that), it was primarily and through and through an act of worship, *directed towards Almighty God*. It was a response to the First and Great Commandment, Thou shalt love the Lord thy God; it was an act of obedience. The growth in brotherly feelings was but a by-product of a common surrender towards the Father. In the event, St. John's developed a sense both of family feeling among the worshippers and of service to those outside that I have never seen bettered yet this was not despite, but because of, its primary focussing on the sheer worship of God. This emphasis is not natural to English religion – which prefers the second to the first of Our Lord's Commandments – but it was the heart of Noel's message, first to St. John's and later to the Diocese. He came to a flock which was complacent and at ease in Zion and, so to say, took it firmly by the scruff of the neck and brought it face to face with God, and to our common need for redemption and mercy, so that we might surrender ourselves to him, in penitence and thanksgiving, growing in love for him and, for his sake, with our neighbour, not least when he is a wriggly urchin from St. John's slum parish. From this worship came all the other things. In the mid-twenties he was instilling the idea of stewardship — the essential duty of giving thoughtfully, prayerfully and sacrificially to the Church. To rub in this duty, he got the P.C.C. to give up diocesan grants, that the faithful might have the privilege of giving all from their own pockets. Furthermore, it was accepted by the people, with misgivings no doubt, that all 'efforts' such as bazaars must be used to provide more money to give away — never used to bolster the parish finances. This was strong meat. Tyneside was in the depths of the Depression, and the fact that it was accepted, that the people learned to be proud of these demands, was clear proof of Noel's charismatic leadership. Fruits of the power of stewardship springing from worship were such things as the Mothers' Camp — groups of mothers from the parish were taken to hutted accommodation by the sea, cossetted by the Church Rangers, who looked after their young children — the camp being paid for, staffed by, members of the worshipping community. The strong Scouts, Guides, Cubs and Brownies were all led by St. John's worshippers, similarly the Soup Kitchen each weekday. Another aspect of this caring spirit was the great support given, alongside other parishes, to the Church Housing Improvement Trust, which bought up decaying property, renovated it and let it out at modest rentals, a long time before local authorities woke up to the renewal of the inner city (see Chapter XII). To go on with the manifold services done to the needy would be wearisome and one must remind the reader that every facet of Christian service radiated from the central theme which the people were never allowed to forget — the total priority of the glory of God and the duty and joy of worshipping him amidst the brethren. When, a mere ten years after leaving St. John's, he returned as bishop this was his message still but it is in the parish we see the vision take shape. It never changed but in the Diocese he had to work through other men.

'A man born to be a bishop' was Ireson's judgment. A true judgment but it raises a doubt today. It all depends upon what you expect from a bishop. To Noel it meant first of all that the bishop of a diocese was the Father-in-God but in a traditional understanding of the word 'father'. The Father-in-God had not only to love his family, the diocese, deeply, and above all others, but in the last resort he was a man with authority, he had to lead and he had to command, and on all relevant and important matters he had the last word. In 1941 this was accepted but how would a man born to be that sort of bishop fare today? The modern notion which imports democratic processes from worldly practice into such realms as the declaration of theological doctrines and the ordering of divine worship erodes the authority of the bishop and indeed eventually that of Holy Writ, of the original Gospel and of Catholic tradition. In this field the modern Church has softly adapted its thinking and practice to the mood in society. Things have changed so rapidly and widely since the sixties that it requires an effort to realise and evaluate the authority wielded by a bishop such as Bishop Hudson in 1941. Words from an autobiography he began to write clarify his attitude: 'The War taught me to accept authority and responsibility and to associate the privilege of command with the call to pastoral care'. He might appear now to be a dictator, an unrestrained autocrat, but this would be a gross caricature. For one thing it is impossible in a church like our own — people can and will vote with their feet, withdraw their labour. His authority was twofold — he not only commanded, he obeyed — he obeyed the Prayer Book, three times he accepted jobs against his wishes but in obedience to others. He accepted that his authority was indivisible from his responsibility, and that the two were subject to the overriding call to pastoral love. Though free from the restraint of synodical votes, he was sensitive to the need to win the support of the consensus of opinion. He accepted moreover a subtler restraint which few understood. As bishop he had to do without that which had been his main comfort, the unrestrained affection of his parish, the people whom he really knew, with whom he was really at ease. He was not at his best in casual encounters, he might seem brusque, almost cold; partly this was through his deep shyness, hard to realise of so distinguished a man. Partly it was through deliberate policy — having acted his sacramental part in a confirmation, he did not wish to linger in the parish hall and upstage the parish priest. In the parish it was vital that the respect and the love should go to the parish priest. He accepted that one of the inevitable parts of the price that a bishop must pay was loneliness — the one source of affection and warmth was in the vicarages. Hence his perpetual ramblings around the Diocese from vicarage to vicarage where he found comfort in the homes of clergy, their wives and their children, but such visitations were not just for pleasure, they were the essential core of the episcopal role. The bishop does not function chiefly by taking a line in diocesan gatherings or committees, he functions through the parish priests. If he was conscious that he had accepted the duty of command and responsibility and that this meant he must speak out clearly and give a definite lead, he then left it to the clergy and their faithful to implement the strategy, without interference. His visits not only were a pleasure to the clergy, and their wives, but they left the priests stimulated, more ready to carry out their own responsibilities. The battle ground was the parish and the parish clergy were the key men — the role of the Father-in-God was to know them intimately, one by one, to sustain them and then above all to trust them. Despite his pre-eminent gifts of leadership and his natural authority, he was in fact the least autocratic of men.

Seeing his office as primarily *pastor pastorum* he could never use suffragan or assistant bishops — if the work-load threatened to become too heavy then other things must be shed, the personal care of the clergy was the first care and joy of the Father-in-God. He remained united with the parish priests — knew that neither he nor they could ever be successful — that they must be content to be faithful to the Gospel. He was as Evangelical as he was Catholic — fully aware that a message rooted in such concepts as original sin and the universal need for redemption was never likely to be popular.

I doubt whether he was widely popular in the parishes: he could not escape from his self-consciousness and go round with a genial smile or show any of the marks of an election candidate. As the *Times* had said of Bishop Wilberforce — 'he was not as hearty and affable as he might have been' — the parishes would not know that the impetus that brought new vigour to the Diocese in the 40s and 50s derived from the Bishop. Two things separate him from the Church of today. First he was surely and serenely rooted in the apostolic tradition, in that Gospel which derived from the scriptures and came down essentially undiluted through the creeds, and was enshrined in the Book of Common Prayer. He was intensely interested in political developments in the world but saw no call for radical change in the ordering and worship within the Church. Secondly, recognising the need for a solid framework in the life of the Church militant here on earth, he accepted the episcopate as the God-given means of conveying this, recognising that a bishopric was not a prize to be coveted but a burdensome role to be endured. The better the bishop, the heavier the price he pays: he must be misunderstood by the populace and is frequently lonely. I apply to Noel words spoken at Churchill's funeral describing the 'Valiant Man' —

> He commands without tyranny and imperiousness; obeys without servility. He floats steadily in the midst of all tempests. Deliberate in his purposes; firm in resolution; bold in enterprising; unwearied in achieving; happy in success; and, if ever he be overcome, his heart yields last.

He moved in 1957 from the bishopric of Newcastle to that of Ely, unhappily, but in obedience to the urging of the two archbishops who wanted him in that honoured diocese — readiness to obey he saw as the corollary of readiness to command. But not only was he sixty-four but the wounds inflicted in the trenches to body and to nerves, combined with growing deafness and the pain of losing his old friends, were too much. He was not sorry to resign six years later, thus escaping the liturgical disturbances of the following decade.

As a footnote to his episcopate in Newcastle one must note that in 1947 his old friends, Mr. and Mrs. Stirling Newall gave their home Shepherds Dene to the Diocese, a munificent gift which continues to be a great blessing. It was given to be (1) a place of recreation and refreshment for the clergy and their families and (2) a retreat and conference house for the parishes of Newcastle Diocese. One can never sufficiently praise the part played by Canon Ireson in nourishing the work of the House. Few men, if any, have been as widely trusted and loved as he throughout the Diocese. He shared the outlook of Bishop Hudson and was trusted by him implicitly and possessed a gift which the Bishop lacked, the ability to establish immediate rapport with all sorts of people. He could bring out the shy, bring the tongue-tied to speech — any mixed gathering soon became a band of brethren and friends.

The year 1957, when Bishop Hudson left and Bishop Ashdown arrived (see Chapter XVI), was the 75th year of the Diocese and these first three-quarters of the story of the Diocese, though they contained variations in mood and policy, shared the general tradition of the Church of England of which the Book of Common Prayer is the main symbol. The final quarter is quite other; no longer could one say with John Selden, that staunch Anglican, 'if you would know how the Church of England serves God, go to the Common Prayer Book, Consult not this man or that'. The Prayer Book still stands indeed but is widely ignored, elbowed away from the centre of the stage by the various alternative and experimental services. A number of these have been put together in one volume, due for publication in 1980 — an *alternative* Prayer Book but one doomed to be called popularly the *new* Prayer Book. It is not expected that this collection of services will stand their ground for long. Uncertainty will continue and uncertainty in the liturgy of the Church spawns general uncertainty in belief. The source of this confusion lies in the fact that when the Church quite rightly decided it should take a look at the Prayer Book to see where it might be improved, it did so in the worst of all times for such an exercise — the sixties — of which Mr. Levin wrote — 'It was a credulous age ... Never was it easier to gain a reputation as a seer, never was a following so rapidly acquired ... Fashions changed, faster and still faster ... Certainty vanished, conviction was vanishing ... There was a restlessness which communicated itself everywhere." (*The Pendulum Age*, Levin, Cape, 1970.)

A bad time to consider thoughtfully the liturgy of a church which derived its faith from events which occurred, words which were spoken, two thousand years before. The difference between the first period (1882–1957) and the second is that the first was a time of growth and development of an historic tradition, the second a time of radical change. The radical explosion still rumbles on and I do not think we have reached a stage where an assessment may be made. At any rate I have no stomach for such a task and take comfort from the fact that this chapter is entitled a *personal* account and other writers will present their verdicts. Radical changes are made rapidly and tend to breed unexpected children. Who can say how we shall worship in 1982 or what notions will be presented to us? Shall we be taught still that the Church of England 'has been led by the Holy Spirit to bear a *witness of her own to Christian truth in her historic formularies*. Now as before she has responsibility to maintain this witness through her preaching and worship, the writings of her saints and confessors, and the utterances of her councils.' These words were written some ten years ago by one of our liveliest men, Dr. Ian Ramsey of Durham, but already have an old-fashioned ring in many ears.

Chapter IV

A PERSONAL ACCOUNT OF THE DIOCESE OF NEWCASTLE

Malcolm Nicholson

2 THE PARISHES – URBAN AND RURAL

The Urban Parishes

AT THE START of the 1939 War, a Welfare Officer addressed the incumbents of the City of Newcastle about the Rest Centres to be set up to cope with victims of air raids. No one, he said, could foresee what would happen, what needs would have to be met in a specific incident. The man in charge would have to be ready for anything without direction from above, acting off his own bat. 'That is why,' he continued, 'I want you to take charge of the Centre in your parish, for I have observed that the parish clergy are wont to go their own way, regardless of authority.' This individualistic, almost anarchical, trait was more common then than now; it has meant that no two parishes are exactly the same and that a parish under one vicar may be quite different under his successor. A large volume therefore would be insufficient to chronicle the story of the parishes, to attempt to cover the scene in a chapter would be absurd. I am forced to be selective, picking out one or two aspects characteristic in the Diocese, and two or three parishes. I shall not cover the whole period, I write of what I know at first or second hand, nor can I claim to be detached; I write from within the Diocese which I have loved since first I met it fifty years ago. The Diocese is part of the Church militant here on earth, it displays the warts that disfigure the Church militant. But I shall not dwell on them, they are blatant and widely remarked, they need no further publicity from me.

As a young man at Cuddesdon Theological College, Oxford, in 1931, I found that it gave me a certain cachet to be going off to serve in Newcastle, for it was known in the lush pastures of Oxfordshire that Newcastle was a notoriously Depressed area. True, there were prosperous areas on the Tyne but it was not to them that one was going.

One was going to live and work amidst poverty — that was the lure — and if the vision contained an element of false romanticism it was not dishonourable. One did not know that in fact there are more deadly circumstances than that of material poverty, one did not know that ministry (*for a priest*) in a prosperous parish is more exacting than in a poor one. All one knew was that the background of one's life was to be drab streets where two or three or more families shared one house, wherein one family kept their rooms sweet and clean, plagued by another family across the passage whose dwelling was carelessly sordid. Above praise were those mothers who, against heavy odds, kept their families well fed and well behaved. Even in a 'deprived area' no child is fatally deprived unless he lacks a loving mother. From our 'faithful' we found nothing but affection and hospitality, the latter could not rise above a cup of tea, richly brewed and stewed, but to refuse this was impossible. One of the qualifications for a priest, unmentioned by the ordination service, was a strong bladder. Outside the faithful, people were still friendly, a residue of religious feeling survived in unexpected quarters in those days. I sat with a young couple whose church links were invisible, the baby was dying. The man sat silent, apparently sullen, averting his eyes from me, embarrassed by my presence. Yet as I rose to go, he got up and came to me, clutched me by the shoulder and said urgently — 'You will *pray* for the little bugger, father?'

The men were in a worse plight than the women. Back in the shipyards or the pit, many had cursed their work but, getting home at night, they were treated as heroes, waited upon. Now, however, having sat around idle and morose, getting in the way of the housewife, they were no longer heroes. The wife still had her role, the man none, he had lost status, in the world and at home. In work he had belonged to a famous work force, he belonged to a man's world, was united to his mates, united by the very harshness of the yard, he worked hard, he often drank hard. He came home exhausted, often scarred, he had earned cossetting by his wife, respect from his children. But now the stuffing had been knocked out of him. Poverty was not new — it had dominated Tyneside for much of the century. Those who can speak of the days before 1914 tell of a world where those who were laid off work were plunged into destitution. In those days, in many places, the Church was practically the only source of welfare (see Chs. XII and XV). The clergy could dispense food vouchers, letters for medical treatment and the like, but it was a source of danger for the Church, since it could attract the scrounger, stir up bad feeling for there was never enough to go round. What should one do confronted by the ailing child whose need arose from a father who was earning good money but squandering it on drink? The Church in those days seems to us to have been obsessed with Temperance, reference to a Band of Hope can today raise a derisive titter, but drunkenness is not funny. One remembers the women and children waiting in fear for the return home of a father violent in drink (see Ch.XV). The slum priest may have been using methods wholly inadequate to deal with the problem but at least he was there, facing the drunkard, comforting his family — he did more than the World did. The burden for the priest was that he was fighting on two levels, he witnessed against wordly injustice but also he recognised and sought to resist the element of sin. For him, it was sin that was the primary evil. In the parish all might be caught up in the suffering that comes from unemployment and poverty yet, while some were overcome, others were triumphant; they refused to be beaten, they did not yield to bitterness, and it was these whom we tended to find within the worshipping family of the Church. In that family they found the dignity that the world denied to them, they were welcomed and honoured. Their faith underpinned their natural goodness, their homes were different from those of their neighbours. They had higher standards — their small sons, for instance, would get grubby during the day like all small boys but they went to bed clean and they went to school next morning clean.

I draw the attention of the reader to the memoirs of one parish priest who worked amongst the poor of Newcastle in a chapter ahead (Ch.XIII). Another type of parish is that of All Saints Gosforth which was cut out of the old parish of Gosforth, St. Nicholas, a huge parish, largely empty when the Diocese started but destined to fill up with the expansion of Newcastle. A Mr. Bindley came as vicar of Gosforth in 1882, saw and faced the situation and began the plans for a new church on the west side of the Great North Road. A layman, William Cochran, was his right hand man, and a gifted architect was chosen, Robert J. Johnson. The building was to seat 500, the first stage would cost £4,500! Of this sum, £3,500 was quickly given largely from substantial gifts but Bindley, a good priest, wanted the giving to be shared by all. 'The way to build churches is by small sums collected each month.' The corner-stone was laid in 1886 but money came in slowly. Bishop Wilberforce was a bold man — he gave the parishioners a jolt by telling them that he would not in fact consecrate the building till they had given enough money to pay for another curate to serve that area. No building was much use without a pastor. Despite Bindley, the lay people, alas, adopted the method of charging pew rents though Bindley withstood them, saying this method must be no more than temporary. The church of All Saints was consecrated in 1887 — Bindley died six years later at the age of fifty-one. He had built well for the future, showing foresight and determination. The next vicar of Gosforth, Maddison, was quick to face the fact that the parish must be divided into two; not a welcome proposition, one wonders whether the worshippers at the old parish church of St. Nicholas, Gosforth, guessed that the new parish would eventually outstrip the old. Maddison, wanting the people of the parish to commit themselves, held a poll but with discouraging results — only 77 troubled to vote, which revealed an endemic disease within the Church of England, people prefer to leave decision and responsibility to the vicar and the small band of enthusiasts. Maddison would have none of this; he told them that the decision would be postponed till the parish was out of debt. The new parish of All Saints was founded in 1906, the first vicar being Walter H. Ainger, a splendid man who thirty years later was still regaling us with startling stories of the early days. One finds phrases with a familiar ring in the church minutes of those days (1910) 'considering the state of trade and the local strikes the accounts are satisfactory', while next year it was noted 'that collections have suffered in the summer owing to so many of the congregation being away at weekends'. A church hall was built in 1908, used by such groups as the Church Lads Brigade, Men's Society, Mothers' Meetings, Girls' Friendly Society and the like. In those days the church set great store by societies. Mission churches had been set up at Kenton and Coxlodge — the latter being 'to look after the spiritual welfare of the navvies employed on the construction of the Gosforth and Ponteland Railway'. The railway completed, the navvies moved on and the curate, the Rev. A. P. B. Barker, used the timber from their huts to build a new church. From his stipend of £150, this admirable young man gave up £50 a year — 'that the work might go forward'.

After ten faithful years Ainger was succeeded by W. A. Studdert Kennedy who stayed from 1916 to 1947, during which time the Diocese was transformed in ethos and policy. Kennedy belonged to the older world — he worked hard but as an autocrat, delegating a share of power to few beyond the wardens. When parochial church councils were set up early in this period, Kennedy made it clear that to him the P.C.C. was not what William Temple envisaged, for Kennedy it was merely 'an advisory council, a body of gentlemen, to whom he and the wardens could go for help and advice, *should the necessity arise*'. He himself would guarantee the council freedom from financial worry, provided that finances were left solely to him; half an

69

hour on the telephone to the right people could at any time bring him in some £200. Financially the Kennedy method did work in that place and at that time, *provided that* the parochial sights were not raised too high — no chance under Kennedy of building new churches in the parish which would rival All Saints. I have no doubt that many in the parish loved the Kennedy way, it saved them from worry or any disturbing challenge. But it carried within it the seeds of decay and left his successor a formidable task but, by the grace of God and good sense of the bishop, that successor was John Turnbull. Turnbull was in the Noel Hudson mould, clear-minded, persuasive, pastorally minded — of great courage. He inherited a church where the paid choir delighted the congregation and the heart of the parish was the matins congregation, 40 to 60 in numbers and largely comfortably off. Pew rents still survived. They would be ready to answer an occasional appeal for the funds of the Church Lads Brigade or Hospital Sunday, even readier for a choirboys treat, but the essential vision of the whole Church as the worshipping Body of Christ, bound together as one by a common faith and sacrament, was missing. As soon as he felt he knew his congregation through visiting, he called a Parish Meeting to which they came in good numbers and there, without delay, Turnbull put all his cards on the table. Much that he said was uncongenial at first to many of the people but he spoke clearly and with authority. Five more similar meetings were held, the promise was made that matins would not be discontinued without their consent, opposition was diminished and the Parish Communion was launched. At first the congregation stayed at sixty or seventy but this embraced most of the P.C.C. and officials. It grew after each Confirmation till it settled at about 250-300 communicants — later it grew again.

Turnbull also implanted in All Saints the principles and practice of Christian stewardship, thoughtful planned sacrificial giving, in money and in time, which meant a vast amount of organisation and visiting by both clergy and laity. This was reinforced by the setting up of some thirty house groups, each of 10 or 12 people who thrashed things out together. All of this prepared the parish for the next big challenge — the building of proper churches at Kenton, Fawdon and Regent Farm — a formidable task made possible only by the co-operation of the whole congregation at All Saints. Not only were these churches to serve adequately the needs of an ever growing parish but the effort deepened the commitment of the All Saints' people, it made them outward-looking and preserved them from the danger of complacency. As each church was built, the next testing step was taken; Turnbull encouraged the people in that area to transfer their allegiance to the new church. Many would not wish to do this for natural reasons but when John Turnbull encouraged you to do something you usually ended by doing it. Only thus could the church grow. Perhaps one more thing should be said to clarify the picture. One was tempted to write off All Saints as a congregation of well-off people for whom life was easy. But in fact by the time that Turnbull had been there for some time, the congregation was far more varied than that. A considerable proportion it is true of the professional and executive classes, unknown in some parishes, but also a fair proportion of people in more modest circumstances, to use a wordly phrase — clerks, artisans, poor people — all welded into the family and treated with equal honour. If the financial resources were still well above the average, so were the challenges they accepted and successfully accomplished. Much similar work was being done elsewhere to which one would eagerly pay tribute if space were adequate but nowhere was so large an area covered in so deeprooted a manner — it was a golden chapter in parochial history.

All Saints was the sort of parish whose light could hardly be hid under a bushel. I turn now to the ministry of one whose life was spent away from the limelight. He spent forty-six years of exemplary pastoral service within this Diocese yet was never asked to serve on any important committee, received no honorary canonry. His name was Charles Frederick Medd. Born in 1876, the son of a London barrister, he was educated at Winchester, Oxford (where he took a good degree) and Cuddesdon. The Victorian age, despite its blemishes, had among its glories the spate of young men who were content to go from privileged homes and education to serve among great discomfort and for modest reward, either in the jungles of the Empire or in the slums of England. Medd came first to be a curate at Berwick, moving four years later (1904) to a second curacy at St. Gabriel's, Heaton. He stayed a further thirteen years there as a curate, a victim of the vendetta waged by Bishop Straton against parishes whose worship displeased him. Medd's only chance of moving was into a new diocese but, if he had, Straton would have allowed no replacement to go to the large parish of St. Gabriel's. Loyalty kept him where he was — a curate for eighteen years, though he had married in 1911 to his lasting joy. In 1918 — Straton having been removed by a merciful Providence — Bishop Wild sent him to be vicar of St. Mary's, Blyth. He was forty-two, had three children, there he served for eighteen years. The parish had a population of 15,000, was just about to move into the great Depression — the people were poor in the parish and in the vicarage — yet depression did not mark the congregation or the vicarage where 'cheerfulness kept breaking through'. One heard, and can still read, of the 'tremendous fun we had then' and of 'the great affection between the vicarage family and the parishioners'. Charles Medd was an absent-minded man — so much so that, called upon to judge an ankle-competition at a vicarage garden party, he innocently awarded 1st prize to his wife, 2nd to a daughter. I should not question his taste in ankles but it was the sort of thing that might take some explaining away in the parish had not the parishioners loved him well. There he was then for just under twenty years, wholly content with his parish and his family. In 1936, when he was sixty he was moved to the parish of Woodhorn and Newbiggin — a curious call for a man of his age; two villages, two churches, 12,000 parishioners, no curate for much of the time and he did not drive a car. On a Sunday, he would celebrate the Holy Communion at Woodhorn at 8.0, rush to Newbiggin for 9.0 with Merbecke and sermon, back to Woodhorn for a service at 11.0. In the evening, he took the bulk of evensong and preached at Woodhorn, leaving a reader to finish off as he made for Newbiggin where a reader had started the service, there he preached again. In those days readers seldom preached. Conditions at the vicarage were primitive — he did not press for money to be spent on this — I fear that it was his wife and daughters who suffered in consequence. Cooking done mainly on a huge coal range, oil for light and heat. 'There is absolutely nothing I don't know about painting large vicarages, with no grant, and black-leading vast kitchen ranges' — reports one of his daughters. No words are adequate to praise many of the vicarage wives and daughters in those days. They wrestled with a house that had once known two or three maids — having toiled in the morning like kitchen maids they were expected to appear in the afternoon poised and gracious. For much of his time at Woodhorn, Medd was plagued by osteo-arthritis and a chronic bronchial condition, but it was no time for a priest to retire because of the War. So he went on, stumbling around his people, devoted to his flock and to the priestly calling. War ended, in 1946 he resigned, he was seventy. From his ministry over the years came six priests and three missionary workers.

A concrete illustration of the pre-eminent qualities of Charles Medd, his humility and his love, is revealed in the following incident. When curate at St. Gabriel's, during the 1914 War, it was his wont to meet trains bringing men back on leave from the Western Front. One night he met a man who after an exhausting journey, straight from the trenches, arrived wearing boots unfit for use. Medd gave him his own boots and arrived home at midnight, having walked from the Central

Station to Heaton in stockinged feet.

The essential diocese, like the essential Church, is impossible to assess. One can only assess certain manifestations, certain actions or pronouncements, of the Church — the heart of the matter is hid with God. Thus the onlooker sees an institution which its own members are the first to confess fails, yet it persists for two millenia, and the onlooker wonders why it does so. He is then confronted with the fact that he must first accept the lordship of the Christ before he can begin to learn his secret. This seems unreasonable and yet the Church continues to nag at men's thoughts, it will not go away — it reminds one of the old Geordie saying, 'it's dead but it won't lie down.'

The Rural Parishes

> My husband and I felt that our years spent at Embleton must remain the happiest of our life. They had been full of work and of opportunities for gaining varied experience by coming into close contact with the realities of life. The strange charm of Northumberland had won us all, and no other part of the world could hold our affection in the same way.

The writer's husband was later Professor at Cambridge, Canon of Worcester, Bishop of Peterborough, Bishop of London — his name Mandell Creighton, the historian, the greatest of the clergy of this Diocese. When he died, Rosebery said of him, 'He was perhaps the most alert and universal intelligence that existed in this island at the time of his death'. He came to Embleton in 1875 from a Fellowship at Oxford, purposing to study church history, with a curate to care for the parish. Having arrived, he fell in love with the parish and became an absorbed and exemplary pastor, yet devoted his mind sufficiently to his studies to be elected Professor of Ecclesiastical History at Cambridge nine years later. His mornings were in the main devoted to his studies, his afternoons to visiting, he, his wife and the curate setting off together to some corner of the parish on foot, they would split up and then all meet for a farmhouse tea. His evenings he devoted to his family and then turned to his studies again until 11 o'clock.

It might be noted that Embleton parish lay alongside the North Sea, seven miles long by five miles wide, a few miles from Alnwick, and was sparsely populated.

Having a curate, Mandell Creighton could, despite his scholarly work, make time to go into Alnwick and work for better sanitary conditions throughout the area, help set up a Provident Dispensary, stimulate the improvement of the water supply — at that time Emble-ton village had only one pump, supplied by a well. There was a strong desire among the thoughtful members of the parish for education — he was kept busy on such things as Penny Readings, Shakespeare recitals and the like. The people needed diversions, especially in the winter — he stimulated concerts and dances — the vicarage became a centre of fun, lively with children and with the young men who came from time to time to study there. He and his wife visited the neigh-bouring clergy, in an open pony carriage, and entertained them — his contacts with them suggest a higher standard among the clergy of the area than one might perhaps have feared. He was specially lucky in the quality of his squires, good men with cultivated minds, Craster of Craster, Grey of Fallodon, Forster of Newton, and Lord Grey at Howick and Bosanquet at Rock. It is good to record the intimate friendship that grew among them; they were men of rank and distinc-tion, he was the grandson of a joiner, brought up over his father's shop, and this was the age of the Duke of Omnium, of the tightly graded world of social rank. Perhaps it was because of the magic of Northumberland.

Looking back, Owen Chadwick in his work, *The Victorian Church* (1970:335) places Creighton among the three Anglican bishops who were among 'the leaders of European scholarship' — at Embleton he pursued learning indeed but more than anything he learnt about 'human life as it really is'. This he learnt by accepting his flock as they were and loving them. When he left for the academic world he said — 'I thought there was plenty of zeal and of practical capacity applied to the work of the Church but I scarcely think there is enough learning'. Years later as a bishop he was to say — 'I have been alarmed at the want of wisdom among the bishops. There is zeal, earnestness, practi-cal ability, eloquence – but wisdom? Creighton had high regard for Ernest Wilberforce and wrote thus to his bishop when he was leaving:

> I have learnt much from you and have looked with admiration on qualities which I lack. You have shown me above all things how great a thing it is to *speak out straightforwardly* even when it may not be pleasing at the time. People are saying – The Bishop knows his own mind, and we know what he means.

This was not an invitation to dictatorship but a call to the bishop of all men to clarify his mind and declare his convictions, accepting that he may eventually be proved wrong, thus Creighton adds elsewhere — 'we must not unchurch or condemn those who do not share our convictions'.

Fifty years after Creighton left Embleton, in 1934 Walter Hicks went to Lucker — his notes on the scene show how little the background had changed, though in fact things were just starting to do so. He found poor housing, no proper sanitation, a communal tap. Mechanisation was beginning, thus fewer people needed on a farm, older people moved elsewhere to retire, casuals moved in. Congregations were small but faithful. Later, moving to Cornhill on Tweed he found that Presbyterians outnumbered the Anglicans. Church congregation was very small. The numbers in the school had dropped from 100 to 24. The ministry of Walter Hicks illustrates an abiding feature in country parishes. He had done well in the suburban parish of St. Mary, Monkseaton, and been happy — he was not an easy mixer but there he had found sufficient friends, not least in the church tennis club. Then he was moved to Lucker and Cornhill, thirty years in remote country vicarages, a bachelor and a lonely man — though one never heard him complain. It was not the rural bliss that it might appear to the townsman out for the day in his car — not for the priest who comes in from afar, with no family around, no car, little money, little encouragement in his work. He was good and faithful but lacked those personal gifts which enable a man to break the ice, to get through the reserve of the older country folk. Creighton spoke of this barrier in his day but he had got through it, partly through the charm of his wife. Today it would be easier as most country parishes now have a sprinkling of people who have retired from the town to the country, who have indeed rather taken over the country parishes, not wholly yet largely, to their advantage. The only excitement for Walter Hicks was his monthly expedition by bus to Newcastle to join his brethren of the Society of St. Jerome to study the New Testament in Greek — there he was at his ease, full of talk. In those days there were a number of priests in the country who were really awaiting a re-call to the town. However faithful to his flock he may be, a man needs a few friends who are on his own wave-length, with whom he can relax, among whom he can safely speak his mind. Loneliness was and still is a serious problem for many rural clergy. Leslie Hunter (see Chapter XVI) writes in 1969, having retired from the bishopric of Sheffield:

> We drove through Northumberland recently and I felt again what an attractive county it was to live and work in. The present failure of the Church in the rural areas is distressing. Bishops and archdeacons, instead of attending more and more committees and giving endless addresses, should be giving their minds to this and be spending hours with rural incumbents, sitting and listening and helping and encouraging.

Wisdom indeed but gained after retirement — it was not a conspicuous feature of his own episcopate though he was a particularly able and good man. Nor is it fair to pick out the *rural* areas above the urban areas, neither is the failure especially a failure by the clergy. Many a parson is a clear presenter of the Gospel and a good pastor yet wins little response from his people. It should not be so but the Church is restricted, in its impact, by the mood of the world in any particular generation. Nor is the Church of England alone in its impotence — the faithful Methodist preacher finds few to listen to his message — the same message which once drew men and women in their thousands to Jesus. But we do well to remember that it is not only the Christian who fails, nor is it only today — the great voices from the humanist world, from Socrates to Russell, have had scant success in drawing mankind into the paths of righteousness and peace.

I suspect that it is to the countryside that the Church should today turn its attention more seriously than it does. I believe that the very change which many greeted with dismay, and as a sign of decline, the enforced joining together of small parishes into bigger units, has in it potential seeds of revival. I think of one such new unit, formed out of four parishes, each with one village and one church, which has now been vastly stimulated in its church life and worship. Their method is to have one church on one Sunday in each month to be the rallying point for worshippers from the whole area — thus they have a lively service of about eighty every week, providing unity among the parishes and a widening of horizons. All that was needed was for the people to accept the new situation, with its exciting possibilities, for car owners to be happy to transport others if they had spare seats. A congregation of 80 is sufficient to be encouraging, it has in it the seeds of growth; one can take children to it with confidence which one could seldom do in the old pattern. The church relying on its one village, in a non-churchgoing age, could often expect no more than a dozen regulars — splendidly faithful people indeed but one could hardly encourage a young person, or some adult contemplating a return to worship, to venture into what seemed to them somewhat pathetic.

The country parson, like many of his people, has a car and a telephone and his people are no longer tied to their village, either physically or mentally — the country atmosphere has changed far more than that of the town. No longer are there Two Nations — the townsman and the countryman — the gathering in the Jolly Fisherman in the fishing village of Craster is on the same wavelength as that of the local in virtually urban Monkseaton. The country parson is free from the personal insecurity of his predecessor, whose income fluctuated with the price of cattle and corn, and he receives far more help in the care of his vicarage, quite rightly. But to use the opportunity offered by the new situation certain things are essential. The country parson must not be a man who in his declining years has been sent out to grass, nor must he be a younger man who has been sent out for a few years and is longing to get back into the town. In the country vicarage, isolation is not what it used to be but it is still a threat to the parson, and even more his wife, they can still feel cut off. It would do no harm for the clergy to meet almost monthly in chapter even when there is no 'business' to be done, however much kindness a man may receive from his flock the priest's life is a lonely one. A fruitful injection of spiritual life and vision would be provided if the Church could encourage its younger theologians to spend some of their intellectually formative years in a country cure. People like Creighton, Stubbs and Dean Church did this in the previous century and they were exemplary pastors to their rural parishes and at the same time, and with that pastoral background, pursued their studies and grew in wisdom. All did a good stint — Creighton 9 years, Stubbs 16, Church 19 years — all became very great scholars. A better use of their growing years than that of the modern theologian who has seldom known anything but the faculty in a modern university. The theologian after a brief two years in a parish, and often not even that, spends his life in a faculty and becomes a career academic, and his faculty is one that ranks low now in the university pecking order. It is the scientist, the economist, the psychologist who win the limelight, gone are the days when the theologian became a head of a college. The stumbling block between the theologian and the rest is the supernatural, the fact that Christian theology is rooted in revelation — thus the theologian is tempted to edge away from his loneliness towards the other disciplines. He would grow better in the formative years in the milieu of a parish, under the discipline of parish life.

A problem which beset the writing of this chapter and which will be apparent to the reader is the lack of material concerning the life of a parish in the past century. A parish may well have fascinating evidence regarding early centuries — safeguarded one hopes in the County Archivists — but scarcely a line about the parish when grandfather was a boy. Parish leaflets abound which tell of the building, 'the South Aisle was added in 1746', and so on, the parish registers record baptisms, marriages, deaths, the service books record numbers of communicants and the amount of collections. Surviving parish magazines are few, the minutes of the P.C.C. are discreet, and there is nothing else. A parish needs a log book such as have been kept by the heads of church schools and, which when well kept, have been invaluable records. A vicar could do good service for the future by setting down such a chronicle of parish life. For we need to know more about the actual happenings of the Church militant in the parishes — at present we tend to cling to tales handed down as true. When and where were churches full in the olden days? And why? How, and by what means, did the parishes accept the abandonment of the services on which everyone had been brought up and their replacement by Series III? Was it a matter of swift conversion or was it a matter of clerical sleight of hand? And, most importantly, is the Church any the stronger? Most Anglicans are quiet silent people in church matters, anxious not to rock the boat, willing to support the vicar, we hear little of what they really think. With the new extended parishes, with the diminution in the numbers of clergy, it is high time that more of the laity in the parishes accepted responsibility, plucked up their courage, learnt the difficult art of speaking out, of speaking what they believe to be the truth in love.

To sum up the position of the Church in this Diocese in the 1970s I would claim that the division into town and country parishes has become meaningless. The people gathered for a Harvest Supper in the country look, think and talk just like the people in an urban church hall. Outside the worshipping body, the world offers the same picture in town and country. It is a world where the old widespread feeling that a person really *ought* to go to church, and where people felt the need to invent excuses for not doing so, has now largely gone.

Let the Church be the Church — content to be the salt, challenging the wisdom and the might of the world, never accommodating its message to the world, or indeed its vocabulary. 'Ye are an elect race, a royal priesthood, a holy nation, a people for God's own possession, that ye may show forth the excellencies of Him who called you out of darkness into His marvellous light'. It is no service to the world for the Church to cloak its faith in the saving Gospel of Christ, to wrap it up in a concordat with the contemporary wisdom. The Gospel is what the Diocese stands for. 'Take no thought for the harvest, but only of proper sowing' (T. S. Eliot, *The Rock*, Faber, 1934).

Chapter V

CHURCH-GOING IN NORTHUMBERLAND IN THE PERIOD JUST PRIOR TO THE FOUNDATION OF THE DIOCESE

G. E. Milburn

HOW WAS the Church of England faring in Northumberland in the years prior to the creation of the Diocese of Newcastle in 1882? This chapter seeks to throw some light on the answer to that question by an examination of the evidence provided by the Census of Worship of 1851 together with other materials which can help to amplify and explain the Census statistics.[1] It goes without saying that the heart of religion cannot be expressed by statistics. All they can measure is the outward manifestation of belief, not the nature of that belief nor the sincerity with which it is held. Yet there is real value in attempting an objective study of the role of religion in society by measuring those things which can be measured. This is the reason for the interest and importance attaching to the Census. True, it measures outward things: the provision of places of worship and the number of those attending them on Sunday, 30 March 1851. Yet the facts it offers are of great usefulness in building a framework of knowledge about the strength and distribution of the various religious bodies in mid-nineteenth century England. The framework may be skeletal but it can be clothed with flesh and blood by the use of other sources of information in conjunction with that of the Census itself. It is hoped that those who read this chapter may gain some insight as to how this might be done and may even be encouraged to undertake their own researches, pursuing the enquiry further and more deeply into aspects of the whole topic than has been possible here within the confines of one chapter.

There is obviously a 'generation gap' between the holding of the Census in 1851 (it was never repeated) and the founding of the Diocese over thirty years later. Neither the churches nor the society of which they were a part stood still in that period, as a section at the end of this chapter and other chapters in the book will testify. Is the

Census therefore relevant to the main theme of this centenary volume? Obviously one would have much preferred to work on a census nearer in time to the founding of the Diocese than 1851 but, apart from a local count for Newcastle churches on a Sunday in 1881 (see pages ahead), we have no such source. Yet it would be a pity to overlook the 1851 Census which provides such a large and potentially valuable body of evidence about all the denominations, Anglican, Nonconformist and Roman Catholic, which have made so interesting a contribution to the religious and social life of the county of Northumberland. And used with care and imagination its findings can illuminate for us not only the mid-century scene but also some of the long-term trends and deep-rooted influences and attitudes which affected religious developments in the North-East certainly up to the foundation of the Newcastle Diocese and indeed beyond it.

The Provision of Churches
The Census showed 154 places of worship belonging to the Church of England in the county of Northumberland, including parish churches, chapels-of-ease, licensed rooms and privately owned chapels. These constituted rather less than half the number of Anglican places of worship in the Diocese of Durham as a whole (327). There was, on average, a Church of England church or chapel for approximately every 2,000 persons in the county of Northumberland as a whole. It is instructive to compare this with the situation in some other dioceses:

York	1 : 1,150
Carlisle	1 : 1,053
Salisbury	1 : 682
Manchester	1 : 3,964

But this neat average conceals widely varying situations within different census districts;[2] for example in Bellingham there was, on average, one Anglican church for each 546 persons, while in the Tynemouth and Newcastle districts the proportions were 1 : 5,334 and 1 : 7,430 respectively. However while the provision of churches relative to population appears much more adequate in the rural districts it is important not to overlook the vast size of some of the ancient country parishes which made attendance at church a major undertaking especially when the weather was inclement. At least fourteen parishes were above 20,000 acres (31 square miles) in extent and of these half a dozen were 35,000 acres (54 square miles) or more, Elsdon topping the table with 75,000 acres (117 square miles) (see Ch. VI). We find echoes of this kind of situation in the rather plaintive comments

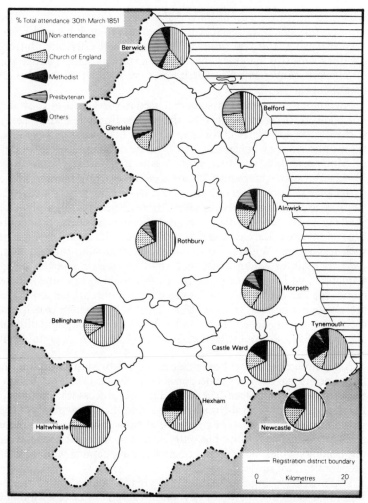

% Total attendance 30th March 1851

- Non-attendance
- Church of England
- Methodist
- Presbyterian
- Others

Berwick

Belford

Glendale

Alnwick

Rothbury

Morpeth

Bellingham

Tynemouth

Castle Ward

Hexham

Haltwhistle

Newcastle

Registration district boundary

0   Kilometres   20

The Religious Census in Northumberland 1851, showing the patterns of attendance and non-attendance for each of the twelve registration districts. The percentages are based on the total attendances at all services throughout Census Sunday, and therefore tend to exaggerate the actual strength of the denominations and to diminish the true extent of non-attendance (see text).

(Map drawn by the cartographic staff of the Geography and History Department, Sunderland Polytechnic.)

which some rural incumbents added to their Census returns. The vicar of Eglingham for instance remarked that though his parish was very extensive (thirteen miles in length) it had only one church, together with two daughter churches in a ruinous state. Here it was often more convenient for worshippers to attend the churches of neighbouring parishes.

No doubt determined parishioners, used to rural hardships, would not allow difficulties to prevent their attending when they really wished to do so. We read for instance of a marriage party walking three miles from a Cheviot shepherd's house on a cold December day to Alnham church and then home again afterwards (Dixon 1895: 51–52). But such feats demanded some sacrifice. And not only was the parishioners' duty to attend church, but also the pastor's responsibilities to care for his flock, rendered more difficult by these physical challenges of distance and weather. A dedicated and energetic incumbent might rise to the challenge. A mid-nineteenth century example of such was Robert William Goodenough, vicar of Whittingham from 1835 to 1880, of whom it was said that 'he made a point of being acquainted with everyone in his parish and could at any time tell the name, age and circumstances of even the most obscure person in the most outlying hamlet' (Dixon 1895 : 285). Whittingham parish was then some twenty seven square miles in extent with a population of 1,905 in 1851, so Robert Goodenough's achievement was no mean one.

A beginning had in fact been made in the subdivision of some of the large ancient parishes in the decades before the Census, as at Simonburn in the early nineteenth century. But this process was costly and involved all kinds of problems with regard to the endowments of the newly-created parishes. The provision of chapels-of-ease was a more straightforward possibility but once again had financial and staffing implications which not all incumbents or parishioners were able or prepared to face up to.

Peel's 'district churches' Act of 1843 greatly facilitates the foundation of parishes and a crop of new ones, carved out of older mother parishes, appeared in various parts of Northumberland in the years immediately following[3].

But despite what was done in the 1840s, the provision and accessibility of places of worship of the Church of England in 1851 left much to be desired. The more energetic incumbents might tackle the problem by licensing a room or school to serve as an extra place of worship and the Census reveals several such as at Gosforth, Broomhaugh, Belsay, Etal, Capheaton and Lillswood near Whitley; but this could be regarded as no more than a temporary solution.

Related to the provision of churches was the number of sittings available within them. Over the whole county there was room, according to the Census, for 52,405 worshippers in all the Anglican places of worship. (If allowances are made for incomplete returns this figure may be as high as 55,000 but the lower figure is used here). Thus the Church of England had seats for just slightly more than 17 per cent of the county population and a very similar situation prevailed in the county of Durham, giving the Durham diocese the lowest figures for Anglican accommodation in all the English dioceses, worse even than Manchester (18 per cent).

The figures for the Northumberland districts show, as would be expected, the lowest percentages of accommodation in Newcastle and Tynemouth (12 per cent and 11 per cent respectively). Elsewhere the figures range from 18 per cent to 34 per cent.

In the whole county just over one third of all Anglican sittings in churches were free, as distinct from those which had been appropriated (rented, owned or allocated) for the sole use of particular families or individuals. The practice of renting pews was generally accepted by all denominations in the mid-nineteenth century as a regular means of income at a time when weekly collections were not customary. In Anglican churches appropriation did not always imply the payment of rent. At Carham in the Glendale district for instance the incumbent remarked on his census return that the sittings in his church were all appropriated to the various landed proprietors and their tenants but the latter were principally dissenters and did not occupy the seats appropriated to them. It was unlikely that they would pay for seats they had no intention of filling.

Whether payment was made or not the disadvantages of appropriated pews are obvious, particularly in towns and developing industrial areas where the expansion of population put pressure on church accommodation, and would-be attenders either could not find a free seat or, if a rented one were available, might not be able to afford the charge expected. By 1851 many churches including some belonging to the Church of England were making an increasing number of seats freely available, mostly for the poor. This was often done by building galleries, an arrangement which also allowed for what some Victorians would consider an appropriate segregation of the classes. The addition of galleries to existing buildings had been fairly widespread in the Diocese in the eighteenth century under the impetus given by Thomas and John Sharp (Shuler 1975: 461 ff.). The policy was continued in the early and mid-nineteenth century. For example at

Whittingham a large gallery was provided in 1840 to provide sittings for the townships of Harbottle and Glanton as well as a home for the barrel organ which replaced the old church band at that time (Dixon 1895: 208). In the church of Bywell St. Peter an old painted board informs us that, as the result of alterations done in 1849, eighty-four extra sittings were provided 'to be free and for the use of the poor for ever.' (This enlargement was one of the first acts of the vicar, Brereton Dwarris, who served this parish from 1845 to 1901.)

The varying policy with regard to pew appropriations may be illustrated by the Newcastle churches (information from the census returns.) There were no free seats at all in the fashionable churches of St. Paul and St. Thomas and only a small proportion at St. Andrew (150 out of 1,150) though here the practice of declaring all seats free in the evening was being pursued. St. John's had 1,700 sittings of which only 150 were free but another 400 were set aside for children (and presumably also free). However in the new 'district' church of St. James, Benwell, 350 of the 560 seats were free, an indication of the new policy with regard to church accommodation. But as we have seen the majority of pews were still appropriated in one form or another. There was however a considerable degree of variation in the percentage of free sittings found in the various districts ranging from 17 per cent in Alnwick to as high as 48 per cent in Bellingham and 50 per cent in Berwick.

Church Attendance

Without allowing for the handful of incomplete returns, the Census showed a grand total of 47,395 attendances at all services in Anglican places of worship within the county of Northumberland, which constituted (in round figures) 37 per cent of all attendances (Anglican and non-Anglican) and 16 per cent of the population (Table I). Let it be stressed that these figures relate to total attendances and not to individual worshippers. Nevertheless, the broad proportions which the attendance figures reveal are instructive. The map, which is based on them, gives the relevant figures for the various districts in graphic form. The actual total attendance (maximum) figures on which the map is based are shown in Table II where, in addition, the minimum figures based on the best attended services are also shown.

Table I

The Religious Census of 1851 in Northumberland

Morning, Afternoon and Evening Attendances by the Main Denominational Groupings

Denomination	Number of Places	Morning		Afternoon		Evening		Totals	
Church of England	154	27,978	41%	11,047	43%	8,370	24%	47,395	37%
Nonconformist	304	33,679	49%	12,782	50%	24,804	73%	71,265	55%
Roman Catholics	20	6,994	10%	1,781	7%	732	2%	9,507	7%
Other	10	168	—	128	1%	332	1%	628	1%
TOTALS:	488	68,819	100%	25,738	100%	34,238	100%	128,795	100%

Table II

The religious Census of 1851 in Northumberland

A comparison of Anglican and non-Anglican strength by districts, showing maximum and minimum numbers of worshippers

1 District	2 Places	3 Sittings	4 Sittings as % of pop	5 Maximum No. of worshippers (Total attendance)	6 Max. as % pop	7 Max. as % of total max. worshippers (Ang & N. Ang)	8 Minimum No. of worshippers (Best attended services)	9 Min. as % pop	10 Min. as % of total min. worshippers (Ang and Non-Ang)
NEWCASTLE (89,156)									
(i) Anglican	12	10,488	12	15,417	17	43	7,599	9	38
(ii) Non-Anglican	42	19,016	21	20,590	23	57	12,155	14	62
TYNEMOUTH (64,248)									
(i) Anglican	12	6,965	11	6,960	11	24	3,706	6	25
(ii) Non-Anglican	75	20,004	31	21,604	34	76	11,253	16	75
CASTLE WARD (13,897)									
(i) Anglican	17	3,521	25	2,293	16	50	1,443	10	57
(ii) Non-Anglican	26	3,379	24	2,263	16	50	1,106	8	43
HEXHAM (30,436)									
(i) Anglican	28	6,773	22	4,262	14	36	2,655	9	41
(ii) Non-Anglican	74	9,117	30	7,545	25	64	3,816	12	59
HALTWHISTLE (7,286)									
(i) Anglican	8	1,532	21	511	7	29	277	4	28
(ii) Non-Anglican	19	1,626	22	1,249	17	71	722	10	72
BELLINGHAM (6,553)									
(i) Anglican	12	2,248	34	816	12	36	633	10	32
(ii) Non-Anglican	10	2,447	37	1,474	22	64	1,438	22	68

1 District	2 Places	3 Sittings	4 Sittings as % of pop	5 Maximum No. of worshippers (Total attendance)	6 Max. as % pop	7 Max. as % of total max. worshippers (Ang & N. Ang)	8 Minimum No. of worshippers (Best attended services)	9 Min. as % pop	10 Min. as % of total min. worshippers (Ang and Non-Ang)
MORPETH (18,127)									
(i) Anglican	17	5,347	29	3,838	21	51	2,274	12	51
(ii) Non-Anglican	19	3,909	21	3,678	20	49	2,173	12	49
ALNWICK (21,122)									
(i) Anglican	13	4,375	21	4,075	19	45	2,772	13	48
(ii) Non-Anglican	19	5,755	27	4,990	24	55	3,046	14	52
BELFORD (6,871)									
(i) Anglican	6	1,920	28	1,790	26	49	1,460	21	49
(ii) Non-Anglican	7	2,327	34	1,856	27	51	1,542	22	51
BERWICK (24,093)									
(i) Anglican	10	4,363	18	4,077	17	28	2,728	11	32
(ii) Non-Anglican	22	8,137	34	10,548	44	72	5,906	24	68
GLENDALE (14,348)									
(i) Anglican	12	2,843	20	1,996	14	30	1,420	10	28
(ii) Non-Anglican	14	6,431	45	4,623	32	70	3,710	26	72
ROTHBURY (7,431)									
(i) Anglican	7	2,030	27	1,360	18	58	981	13	53
(ii) Non-Anglican	7	1,513	20	971	13	42	868	12	47
TOTALS (303,568)									
(i) Anglican	154	52,405	17	47,395	16	37	27,978	9	37
(ii) Non-Anglican	334	83,661	27	81,400	27	63	47,745	16	63
	488	136,066	45	128,795	42	100%	75,713	25	100%

By far the greatest number of Anglican worshippers was found at morning service when 129 churches were open for worship attended by nearly 28,000 men, women and children (9 per cent of the population). The figures for afternoon and evening respectively were 11,000 worshippers (4 per cent of the population) in 85 churches, and 8,400 (3 per cent) in 25 churches.

Not without interest are returns from particular parish churches which may be well known to some readers. (The numbers in brackets are for Sunday school scholars and are included in the overall figures beside them.)

CHURCHES		ATTENDANCES		
	Morning	*Afternoon*	*Evening*	*Total*
Newcastle				
St. Nicholas	1510 (510)	900 (510)	1500	3910
St. John	1390 (290)	500 (200)	600	2490
St. Andrew	1120 (320)	500 (300)	900	2520
St. Thomas	1272 (314)	623 (318)	441	2336
Hexham (Priory)	552 (112)	267 (124)	282	1101
Whalton	73 (7)	68 (10)		141
Thockrington	6	–	–	6
Rothbury	299 (56)	269 (49)	–	568
Berwick	770 (20)	520 (20)	–	1290

Table II and the map together show how the Anglican patterns of church-going varied throughout the county. On the basis of maximum figures (i.e. total attendances) it would seem that 16 persons in every 100 (over the whole country) attended church on Census Sunday; the minimum figures based on the best-attended services indicate a proportion of 9 per cent. As said earlier the truth will be between these two and probably nearer to the 9 than the 16, although the latter figure may well be an acceptable, if approximate, indication of the proportion of active Anglican support among those who *could* attend church, rather than of the total population.

It is obvious that, as with other statistics, the county averages conceal quite marked regional variations. In sheer numbers Anglican strength was greatest in the two urban districts of the south-east corner of the county (Tynemouth and Newcastle) where over 47 per cent of all Anglican attendances were registered, worshipping (it may be noted) in 24 churches constituting only 16 per cent of the total number of places of worship belonging to the Church of England.

However in proportion to population these two districts were among the weakest areas of Anglican strength, especially if the minimum figures are used when only Haltwhistle shows a lower percentage.

It was in fact in the five southern districts (running along the Tyne Valley) that Anglican strength in proportion to population is seen to have been weakest, with minimum ratios between 4 per cent and 10 per cent and an average of 8 per cent. In the remaining districts minimum ratios ranged from 10 per cent to 21 per cent, with an average 13 per cent. It appears that the Church of England was proportionately weakest where population growth had been rapid. However, it was not rapid population growth alone which put the church at a disadvantage (though that obviously is one factor); the economic nature of the area must also be borne in mind. The four districts of Newcastle, Tynemouth, Hexham and Haltwhistle were those which were most affected by urban growth and by the unsettling consequences of coal and lead mining, with the accompanying frequent migrations of workers due to strikes, booms and slumps, the opening of new coal mines, the decline of lead mining, and so forth. Some northern districts though having a higher population growth than Hexham, were not subjected to these same social dislocations and it may be that this explains in part why the Church in these areas was less adversely affected in its attendances than in Hexham.

Church of England Schools

The educational activities of the Church in general in Northumberland are dealt with in another chapter in this volume, but it may be useful to comment briefly on this matter with regard to the year 1851. We are helped here by a Parliamentary Report on Education drawn up as part of the findings of the Census of that year, and published in 1854. The compiler was Horace Mann who was responsible also for the Report on the Census of Worship. Table III is based on some of the evidence provided by this Report (Census 1851:Education 195-197). Obviously what such statistical information can tell us is limited to quantifiable factors.

We find that over the whole county there were 131 Anglican Sunday Schools, which was rather more than one third of the total number belonging to all denominations (Table III). The 9,069 recorded Sunday scholars in Church Schools comprised 3 per cent of the total population of the County, but local percentages varied widely between a minimum of 0.5 per cent and a maximum of 6 per cent. It is notable that the three districts which had the most marked population growth in the period 1801-1851 are those with the lowest percentages -

Newcastle 2, Tynemouth 0.5 and Haltwhistle 2. These figures help to confirm the generally poor showing of the Church in all respects in these areas. However in Hexham, where the Church attendance percentage was among the lowest, the Church Sunday schools were apparently relatively successful with 5 per cent of the population attending them, which is the third highest figure for the twelve districts of the county. Outside the three weakest districts the percentage of attendance of scholars ranges from 3 per cent to 6 per cent, with an average of 5 per cent which represents a quite considerable achievement based on voluntary effort throughout the parishes.

The pattern of day school provision (which in the table includes schools supported by the National Society, as well as other Church of England schools) does not differ very markedly from that of Sunday schools, though Tynemouth and Haltwhistle (as well as Glendale and Rothbury) show a better record in this respect.

Table III

Church of England Schools in Northumberland 1851

District	Number of C. of E. Churches recorded in the Census	Number of C. of E. Sunday Schools	Total No. of Sunday Schools including C. of E.	Scholars in C. of E. Sunday Schools	Sunday Scholars as percentage of total population	Number of C. of E. Day Schools	Scholars in C. of E. Day Schools
Newcastle	12	8	41	1956	2	8	1805
Tynemouth	12	5	63	334	0.5	9	622
Castle Ward	17	14	27	593	4	10	580
Hexham	28	23	58	1524	5	18	1121
Haltwhistle	8	4	10	138	2	7	238
Bellingham	12	6	15	195	3	5	181
Morpeth	17	13	23	853	5	13	958
Alnwick	13	19	37	1339	6	10	999
Belford	6	6	13	356	5	4	304
Berwick	10	12	34	870	4	9	848
Glendale	12	12	26	585	4	15	994
Rothbury	7	9	12	326	4	8	458
County Totals	154	131	359	9069	3.0	116	9108

Anglicanism in Relation to Other Denominations

The patterns of Anglican church provision and church-going, considered so far in isolation, ought to be seen also in relation to the other denominations, and the question asked whether non-Anglican strength and distribution can (if only inversely) throw light on the position of the Church of England itself.

There were more than twice as many non-Anglican places of worship as Anglican in Northumberland in 1851, 334 as against 154, or, on average, a chapel for every 900 people compared with the Anglican ratio of 1 to 2,000 in round figures. Of the districts only Bellingham had more Anglican churches than non-Anglican; elsewhere the Church was outnumbered and in some districts very considerably so, as for instance in Hexham, Newcastle and Tynemouth, which were the three most populous. The proliferation of non-Anglican chapels was of course due in part to the divided nature of Nonconformity, and the relative ease with which the Nonconformists could undertake the building of new places of worship where they were needed, compared with the legal processes facing the Church in the foundation and endowment of new parishes (see Chs. IX and X). It is true that the average size of churches was larger than that of chapels (using these terms as useful labels for Anglican and Nonconformists places respectively) but on the other hand the greater number of chapels meant that they could be more accessible. However, it was only the five southern districts and Berwick where the Nonconformist advantage in chapel provision was sufficiently large to make a real difference in this respect.

The Nonconformists with most chapels to their names were the Methodists though they were not a single movement by 1851 because of the divisions and secessions which had occured between Wesley's death (1791) and the Census. After the Methodists, with their 198 chapels, came the Presbyterians (of various denominations) with 68, spread over the whole county but with a heavier concentration in the seven northern and central districts. The other dissenters followed with a total of 38 chapels in all and the Roman Catholics with 20.

The map indicates the attendance patterns of the various non-Anglican denominations. What broad conclusions can be drawn from them, and in particular what relevance have they for the Church of England?

Compared with the Anglican attendance ratios (attendance expressed as a percentage of population) of 16 per cent (maximum) and 9 per cent (minimum) the total non-Anglican equivalents were 27 per cent and 16 per cent. Of the total number of attendances at all churches and chapels the non-Anglicans commanded 63 per cent as against 37 per cent for the Church of England. The broad fact of Anglican weakness in comparison to the other denominations is clear enough. It is true that Nonconformity was much divided and that Anglicanism was stronger than any other individual denomination. For example the Methodists and Presbyterians, the two strongest Nonconformist bodies, mustered overall 11 per cent and 9 per cent attendances (maximum figures), both well below the Anglican figure. However the main point from the Anglican view was not so much that the non-Anglicans were divided among their own denominations as that they did not worship at the Church of England. Or at least, we assume that they did not. There may in fact have been a certain amount of crossing of denominational boundaries. We know that some Presbyterians, especially in the remoter parts of the county, attended Church if that was more convenient. (This is specifically mentioned on the Return for Carham.) Some Methodists (especially the more conservative Wesleyans with a lingering love of the Church of England) may have attended matins or evensong at the parish church before going on to their own preaching service at night. And how many evangelical Anglicans (most churches being closed in the evening) were included among those 25,000 evening worshippers at Nonconformist chapels? The Census unfortunately cannot provide answers to these questions but it may be that detailed research in localities would do so.

A more detailed examination by districts of the attendance figures for Nonconformity shows considerable variety, from a ratio of 13 per cent (maximum) in the Rothbury district to one of 44 per cent in Berwick. In two districts the Anglican attendances outnumbered the non-Anglican (Rothbury and Morpeth) and in another two they were virtually balanced (Castle Ward and Belford). Elsewhere Nonconformity (with which we may for our purposes include Roman Catholicism) was dominant and in most cases its stronger position was very evident. The patterns of strength of Methodism and Presbyterianism are complex, but it seemed to be the case that where the Presbyterians were strong, as in the north, Methodists were weak and Methodist following was much firmer in the south of the county (see Horner 1971:42-53).

Patterns of Non-Attendance at Worship
Amongst all the calculations and interpretations which the Religious Census figures for Northumberland have given rise to in this chapter, one very clear fact cannot have been overlooked, namely that a

majority of the population attended no place of worship at all. Such a state of affairs would excite no special comment in modern society but to discover that it was true of the Victorian 'age of faith' may come as a surprise. Over the whole country, according to the calculations of Horace Mann, the numbers of individual worshippers on Census Sunday probably were in the region of 7.3 million, or just over 40 per cent of the population of England and Wales. This is a high ratio compared with the situation today but to Mann and many other earnest Christians of the mid-nineteenth century the revelation of the apparent widespread neglect of public worship was viewed with grave concern and was seen as a real challenge to the churches. Of course not all people were able to attend. Mann calculated that at any one service 58 per cent of the population should have been able to do, and throughout the whole of Sunday, perhaps 70 per cent. But even with this allowance there was a deficiency of considerable proportions, which was most marked in certain highly urbanised areas.

In response to this challenge all the denominations were to undertake much noble and sacrificial effort in the decades following the Religious Census, building new churches and enlarging old ones, founding parishes, organising all kinds of evangelistic endeavours, and reorganising their machinery. For the Church of England in Northumberland the episcopate of Bishop Charles Baring (1861-1879) was to be outstanding in this respect.

The statistics of non-attendance in 1851 in Northumberland, especially when viewed in the light of the presuppositions of Victorian churchmen, had little comfort to offer to the churches. The table shows the situation.

Table IV

Percentages of the population not attending a place of Worship on 30th March 1851 in the twelve Northumberland registration districts (in round figures).

District	Percentage of non-attendance	
	Minimum (a)	Maximum (b)
Newcastle	60	78
Tynemouth	55	78
Castle Ward	68	82
Hexham	61	79
Haltwhistle	76	86
Bellingham	66	68
Morpeth	59	75
Alnwick	57	72
Belford	47	56
Berwick	39	64
Glendale	54	64
Rothbury	69	75
County	58	75

(a) The minimum non-attendance percentage is based on the difference between population and the total attendances at all services.

(b) The maximum non-attendance percentage is based on the difference between population and the attendances at the best attended services.

The minimum non-attendance figures are not really satisfactory since they are calculated from the figures of attendances at worship throughout Census Sunday not upon the numbers of individuals. The maximum non-attendances (based upon minimum numbers of worshippers) are more concrete and meaningful, but are presumably too high in most cases. The truth will lie somewhere in between, and one might not be very far wide of the mark by concluding that in the county as a whole two-thirds of the population (about 202,000) did not attend church or chapel on Census Sunday. Of that proportion some could not attend by reason of age, occupation or infirmity. If we accept Horace Mann's conclusion that 70 per cent of the population could have attended at one service or another on Sunday, this leaves some 92,000 (30 per cent) in Northumberland who could not attend, and 110,000 (37 per cent) who might have done so but were absent, with 101,000 (33 per cent) actually attending.

The absences were most marked in the five southern districts of the county, but were less so in the remaining seven, and here again we are obliged to conclude that the areas which had seen the most pronounced economic and demographic upheavals were those in which organised religious life would appear to have been most dislocated.

From 1851 to 1882

The three decades between the 1851 Census of Worship and the formation of the Diocese of Newcastle saw very considerable changes in Northumbrian economy and society (Middlebrook 1950:Chs. 19-22; McCord 1979). There was a vast expansion in these years in the mining and export of coal, and in shipbuilding and engineering, all of which brought very considerable social consequences especially with regard to population growth and the extension of urbanised and industrial areas (see Chapter I).

It was the south-eastern part of the county of Northumberland which was affected by these changes. Elsewhere there was a different story to tell. The continuing decline of the English lead industry, and the agricultural depression beginning in the 1870s cast a shadow over the economic life of large parts of rural Northumberland. The population figures of 1881 are very revealing when compared with those of 1851. In the county as a whole there was a net increase of 130,000 people in these thirty years, an overall growth rate of 43 per cent. But this growth was virtually confined to the six districts in the south and south-east of the county, especially Newcastle, Tynemouth, Castle Ward and Morpeth which had growth rates of 68 per cent, 78 per cent, 41 per cent and 99 per cent respectively. Elsewhere population was either static (as at Alnwick) or actually declining as a consequence of rural depression and the migration of working men and their families in search of employment wherever it was to be found, whether on Tyneside or more distant parts of the country or in the colonies. Three districts (Glendale, Rothbury and Bellingham) had in fact less people living in them in 1881 than when the nineteenth century began.

What did all this mean for the Church of England and for church-going? Obviously the demographic and social changes posed challenges to add to those already revealed by the 1851 Census of Worship. Rural impoverishment meant that there was less money and less potential support for the country churches, though the need for pastoral care remained as real as ever and as difficult to fulfil in the widely scattered communities of the central and northern parts. On the other hand those southern districts where the Church was already most straitened were those where population growth always threatened to swamp its efforts no matter how energetic they might be. The heart of the problem lay in the three districts of Newcastle, Tynemouth and Morpeth where 129,000 more people lived in 1881 compared with thirty years earlier. 61,000 of the additional 129,000 were to be found in the Newcastle district.

Sadly we have no official census of worship to test in a detailed way the strength of organised religion in Northumberland in 1882 as we have for 1851. In the later nineteenth century however a number of local surveys of church accommodation and attendance were organised by provincial newspapers, usually by those whose proprietors had Liberal and Nonconformist sympathies, and the findings of two of these counts throw some light on the work of the Church of England in Newcastle in the period just before the formation of the new Diocese.

In 1871 the *Nonconformist* (a national journal of fervent dissenting outlook, dedicated to the cause of disestablishment) made a survey of church and chapel accommodation in a number of towns throughout the country. The aim was to discover what increases had been made since 1851 and in particular to throw light on the relative improvement between the establishment and Nonconformity. There was a definite air of competition about the enterprise. 'The *Nonconformist* newspaper, as champion of the Free Churches, came forward and, picking up the gage of combat on the point of its practised lance, made ready for the statistical tournament, and now appears in the lists to test the pretensions of State-Churchism' (*Newcastle Daily Chronicle* 26 Oct. 1872). This does not mean that the census was loaded, or its findings dubious, but it does show the confidence felt by militant Nonconformists that, despite the great efforts by the Church since 1851, they had nothing to fear from its challenge. This confidence was in fact borne out by the results of the survey. Of the fourteen largest towns (excluding London) with populations over 100,000 six did show the Church to have had a higher percentage of increased accommodation than Nonconformity in the period 1851-1871. But in five of the six so great was the Church's deficit prior to 1851 that it was still a long way behind the other churches in the number of actual sittings it provided by the latter date. In Leeds for instance the Church had increased its sittings by 44 per cent as against 22 per cent for the Nonconformists, but it was still 31,000 sittings behind by 1871. In the other eight towns the increases all favoured the Nonconformists. Among them was Newcastle with percentage increases of 46 per cent for the Church and 76 per cent for the Nonconformists. These figures admittedly look impressive and together constitute an increase in accommodation at a rate well ahead of population growth in Newcastle. But when the percentages are translated into actual numbers of sittings a different state of affairs is revealed. The Nonconformist increase was around 14,500 and that of Anglicans 4,500, in a period in which the population of the town rose by almost 40,000. It is in the light of discrepancies of this magnitude that the efforts of the Church of England in the decades after 1851 have to be judged. As Professor W. R. Ward has written : 'The Religious Census of 1851 was to drive home how much furious running churchmen needed to do simply to stand still in relation to social development' (in *Davies et al.* 1978:79). The trouble was that the Church was attempting its recovery from a situation which was already weak owing to its inertia in the eighteenth and early nineteenth centuries. Dr. Gilbert's comment with regard to Anglicanism in general is very relevant to the Church in Newcastle : 'It is a measure of the gravity of the Anglican failure in early industrial society that the substantial recovery of the Victorian era was too little and too late to reverse the tendency towards institutional decline in Anglicanism' (Gilbert 1976:29). The *Newcastle Daily Chronicle* (whose proprietor was the Liberal Nonconformist Joseph Cowen) drew its own moral from the 1871 census findings: 'In spite of all her laudable activity for two decades the Protestant Episcopal Church is less truly the Church of the Nation than it was in 1851'.

The 1871 surveys were concerned with accommodation only. Ten years later there appeared a crop of local counts of attendance at worship beginning with one in Newcastle where the *Newcastle Daily Chronicle* 'decided to greet the delegates to the Church Congress then meeting in the city by counting attendances at morning worship in the Tyneside boroughs' (McLeod 1973:43). *The Liverpool Daily Post* followed suit and there ensued a nation-wide movement covering most of the provincial towns and cities, in each case the census being conducted voluntarily, but with (on the whole) conspicuous carefulness, by a local newspaper. Most of these counts were conducted in the autumn of 1881 but in the case of Birmingham not until 1892. Before looking at the Newcastle results it is worth setting them in some kind of context by considering very briefly the situation in two other cities, Sheffield and Birmingham (Wickham 1957:147-150, 275-280. Bryman 1976:12-28). Each of these had seen massive population growth since 1851, in Sheffield's case an increase of 110 per cent by 1881 and in Birmingham's 135 per cent by 1892. Total Anglican attendances in these two cities had increased since 1851 at the rates of 127 per cent (Sheffield) and 75 per cent (Birmingham) without counting Sunday Scholars who were however included in the 1851 calculations. If scholars are allowed for the Birmingham increase by 1892 was 125 per cent; a comparable figure for Sheffield is not possible since scholars were not counted there in 1881. In both cases these remark-able increases in active Anglican support had been won in the face of strong Nonconformist competition and, in Birmingham's case at any rate, without any encouragement or leadership from the bishop, at least until Bishop Perowne was appointed to the Diocese of Worcester in 1891. (Readers are referred to a helpful section dealing in general with the religious censuses of 1881, and related matters, in Chadwick, 1970, Ch. V.)

The figures for Newcastle however were far from encouraging for church people. Organised religion as a whole was shown to be rela-tively weaker in 1881 than it had been in 1851, with only 15 per cent of the population of Newcastle at morning worship compared with 21 per cent at the earlier census (afternoon and evening services were not enumerated, see Table V). In this period the population of Newcastle had increased by 70 per cent, the number of morning worshippers by 20 per cent. Indeed the only denomination to register any significant increase of strength in relation to population was that of the Wesleyan Methodists, who demonstrated a remarkable recovery from their secessionist troubles of the mid-century. Elsewhere the story is of standstill or decline. This is true even of the Roman Catholics and Presbyterians, despite continued immigration into the city of Irish and Scots workers and their families. It might be of course that if the census had been continued to cover the afternoon and evening ser-vices the Presbyterians, and indeed all the Nonconformists, would have appeared in a better light, but the same can hardly be said of the Catholics.

As far as the Established Church was concerned this Newcastle census showed, on the face of things, a pretty disastrous state of affairs. Apart from three of the smaller dissenting causes in the city it was the only denomination to register a decline in the actual number of morning worshippers over the thirty year period, and its percentage index was almost halved. This is extraordinary, especially in view of the fact that there was a number of distinguished preachers (represen-tatives of the Church Congress) in Anglican pulpits on that particular Sunday morning of October 2, 1881, and that one would therefore expect the attendances to be better than normal.

Can anything be said in mitigation of the Church's very poor showing in this census? It may be that its relative strength would have been seen in a better light if the afternoon and evening attendances had also been counted. This would only be the case if the balance of church-going had swung since 1851 in favour of evening attendance. The *Chronicle* assumed that this was not so and that a morning count

Table V

Attendance at morning worship in Newcastle 1851 and 1881 (1)

Denomination	30 March 1851 (Popn. 87,784)	Percentage of popm.	2 Oct 1881 (Popn. 149,549)	Percentage of Popm.	Increase	Decrease
Church of England	7,202	8.2	6,441	4.3		761
Presbyterian	2,499	2.8	3,053	2.0	556	
Roman Catholic	3,389	3.9	3,845	2.6	456	
Baptist	1,072	1.2	805	0.5		267
Congregational	826	0.9	1,290	0.9	464	
Quaker	217	0.2	124	0.08		93
Unitarian	461	0.5	220	0.1		241
Wesleyan Methodist	1,270	1.4	3,345	2.2	2,075	
Primitive Methodist	806	0.9	977	0.6	171	
United Meth. Free Ch. (2)	630	0.7	1,145	0.8	515	
Meth. New Connexion	210	0.2	369	0.2	159	
Bible Christians	–	–	200	0.1	200	
Catholic Apostolic	–	–	150	0.1	150	
Danish Church	–	–	70	0.04	70	
Jews	50	0.05	255	0.17	205	
Undenominational	8	0.01	245	0.17	237	
TOTALS	18,640	20.96	22,534	14.86	5,258	1,362

Notes: (1) Table based on *Newcastle Daily Chronicle*, 5 Oct. 1881, page 5. The figures for 1851 are from the Religious Census Report 1851, p. cclxv. The figures refer to the city of Newcastle not the Newcastle Census district which was slightly larger.

(2) The United Methodist Free Churches were formed in 1857 from a union of the Wesleyan Association and the Wesleyan Reformers who seceded in the mid 1830s and c.1849 - 1850 respectively.

100

would in fact favour the Church and be detrimental to Nonconformity, a surprisingly altruistic attitude. And yet the evidence of other places shows that this in fact was not always so by 1881. Sheffield for instance had 13,000 attendances in Anglican churches in the morning and 19,000 at night, whereas in 1851 the balance had been in the other direction. If this trend were true also of Newcastle a count of evening worshippers plus those meeting in Sunday schools and bible classes in the afternoon would have shown a very different state of affairs than is revealed from the morning figures alone. It is worth emphasising that even in 1851 the Anglican attendances in Newcastle in the afternoon and evening together exceeded those of the morning. Moreover the Newcastle Anglican index of morning attendance of 4 per cent in October 1881 was very little below that of Sheffield (5 per cent) where as we have seen the Church was managing to keep abreast of demographic change. The great advance in Sheffield had been in the size of evening congregations which more than trebled between 1851 and 1881. One can therefore only repeat the regret that a lack of evening figures for Newcastle in 1881 makes it impossible for us to assess the position of the Church of England as accurately as one would wish to do.

There is also the question of whether Sunday scholars were counted in 1881. If they were not some calculation ought to be made in order to make a more meaningful comparison with 1851. In that year scholars made up something like one quarter of morning attendances, and if this kind of allowance is made the 1881 attendances should be more like 8,500 with an index of rather less than 6 per cent.

Despite these qualifications (which are anyway somewhat hypothetical) there is still no doubt that the 1881 census reveals the very serious weakness of the Church of England in Newcastle in the later nineteenth century. Though it remained the largest single denomination its support (as measured by the *Chronicle* count) was only 29 per cent of all attendances on the Sunday morning in question (the comparable figure for Gateshead was 32 per cent). And it appears to have attracted only four (or possibly at the most, six) out of every hundred people in the city into its services, even on the morning when its pulpits were occupied by noted clerics (the figure for Gateshead was three in every hundred). These figures of course tell us little or nothing of the *quality* of the Church's life and work, nor of the sincere devotion and endeavour which certainly characterised much of it, and which may well have been stronger in 1851 than in 1881. But what they do show is that institutional Anglicanism was under severe pressure in urban Northumberland on the eve of the formation of the new Diocese, and that the work of that Diocese would have to be carried out in a society whose values and outlook were increasingly dominated by secular considerations.

NOTES

1. The Census of Worship of 30 March 1851 represents the only occasion when an official national survey of religious allegiance (measured by attendance at worship was attempted in this country. Though not legally enforceable, the coverage was remarkably thorough. The two major sources of evidence produced by the Census are the published Report of 1853, and the original Returns and associated papers preserved at Public Record Office. It is upon the latter that the Report is based and its many tables present a remarkable body of statistical evidence regarding organised religion in the mid-nineteenth century. These tables refer to a variety of geographical units — the country as a whole (i.e. England and Wales -Scotland was dealt with separately), dioceses, counties, large towns, and registration districts (see note 2). There is also an extended introduction by the chief organiser of the Census, Horace Mann, which is interesting for revealing the response of earnest Victorians to the major findings of the Census. These were, over the national as a whole, that:

    (a) 60 per cent (10.6 millions) had attended no church or chapel on Census Sunday, though it was accepted that many of these (perhaps one half) could not have done so; (b) the Church of England commanded the allegiance of only half the worshippers; (c) in some areas the Church was heavily outnumbered by Nonconformity; (d) organised religion of any sort was patently weak in some heavily urbanised and industrial areas and (e) the provision of places of worship had fallen far behind population growth.

    The Census Returns are important for the vivid detail regarding individual churches and chapels which can be gleaned from them. They offer a unique entry into the study of religion in specific localities in the Victorian period.

    The Census is not without its problems. Was it accurate and complete? Was it affected by the weather or other circumstances connected with the chosen day 30 March 1851 (it was Mothering Sunday)? Was it honest? The conclusion of many modern historians is that the Census *is* valuable (a) for its broad indications of religious strength and (b) for the detailed local insight offered by the Returns, but that it has to be used with care and informed awareness. In particular it has to be remembered that the Census counted *attendances* not *attenders* and there is no certain way of converting the figures of attendance into numbers of individual worshippers. One way of attempting to resolve this problem is by considering the figures of the *best-attended* services in order to reach a solid minimum number of individual worshippers to compare with the total attendances (which offer a hypothetical maximum assuming that no-one worshipped more than once, which obviously was not the case). This 'maximum-minimum' approach has been employed in one of the tables in this chapter. It is not perfect but has some advantages when assessing denominational patterns over reasonably large geographical areas.

    For further detailed consideration of this Census of Worship readers are referred to Gay (1971), Inglis (1960), Milburn (1977), Pickering (1967) and Thompson (1967).

2. The Census was organised locally within the Registration Districts of each county, which were equivalent to the recently created Poor Law Union areas. There were twelve registration districts or unions in the county of Northumberland and their names and positions are shown on the map accompanying this chapter. Their size, population density, and socio-economic features varied considerably and these facts need to be borne in mind when considering the religious patterns in the county. In 1851 Newcastle district had a population density of 1,257 per 100 acres, Tynemouth 165, Berwick 45 and all the rest were below 20 with Bellingham at the bottom with 3 people per 100 acres.

3. Parishes in Northumberland which were created in the 1840s, mostly under the terms of Peel's 'district churches' Act, included the following:

New Parish	Date of Creation	Mother Parish
Newcastle, St. Ann's	1842	All Saints
Benwell	1842	Newcastle, St. John's
N. Sunderland	1843	Bamburgh
Byker	1844	Byker, All Saints
Cambo	1844	Hartburn
Newcastle, St. Peter's	1844	Newcastle, St. Andrew
Scremerston	1844	Ancroft & Tweedmouth
Alnwick, St. Paul	1846	Alnwick
Elswick	1846	Newcastle, St. John
Matfen	1846	Stamfordham
Seghill	1846	Earsdon
Walker	1846	Longbenton

Chapter VI

THE DEVELOPMENT OF THE DIOCESE OF NEWCASTLE

W. S. F. Pickering

1 AN OVERALL VIEW

IN CONSIDERING the development of the Diocese of Newcastle, it is necessary at the beginning to present a number of basic facts. This exercise has an immediate value to the reader because it is believed that little is known about the Diocese, even amongst Anglicans who have lived within its borders all their lives. Here is an opportunity for them to be better acquainted with what has gone on in the past and what is happening in the Diocese today. But such material will also be illuminating to those readers who have little knowledge of the Church and its milieu in the far north-east corner of England, especially those who are geographically far removed from it. The data, however, have not been selected at random. They have been collected in most cases according to some pattern based on time-periods, which it is hoped will lead to generalizations about the development of the Diocese. One wants to be able to scan the whole period of the hundred years of its existence and to draw conclusions about the directions in which it has moved and the trends which have beset it.

When the Diocese came into existence in the 1880s, institutional religion in England could be seen to be more or less at its height — judged at least by certain criteria such as absolute figures relating to church attendance. The country was the most prosperous of all western nations, there was every hope of continued expansion and growth, which would bring even more prosperity and wealth to the nation, and it was a time of peace, with no glimmer of the two world wars which were to face the people of Great Britain. The churches were still forces that had to be reckoned with. At the level of ordinary people they had, compared with today, a strong following with every indication that numbers would grow as the population was expanding. Further, in the corridors of power the leaders of the churches, particularly Anglican bishops, had a place of privilege and respect. Very shortly the tide was destined to change. Everyone is now aware of the fact that over the past hundred years or so — the life-time of the Diocese — the churches have lost considerable following and status within the general community. This process of decline is frequently referred to as the secularization of society. There are great problems in the use of the term and where it is employed here it refers only to the decline of the institutional churches over the past century. Since the history of the Diocese corresponds to this period of extensive change, it seems only right that one should attempt to examine in detail what has been going on in the Diocese against the general trends within society itself. It will be interesting to know, for example, whether Newcastle has weathered the processes of erosion and decline as much as other areas, or whether, as one might guess, it has suffered even more in the light of continued industrialization along the Tyne; for it is commonly said, rightly or wrongly, that the forces of modern economic production are responsible for the dechristianization of the west and the demise of religion in its institutional forms.

Certain presuppositions therefore emerge at the very outset. The focus of this essay — and one might add, of all the essays in this volume — is the Church seen as an institution — a social body in society. There can be no escape from such an assumption since the book is about the Diocese: and what can be more institutional than that! Unashamedly and without hesitation, the concern has to be with the organization of the Church and the physical and social channels through which it claims to receive and dispense the grace of God, that is, through the sacraments, public worship, the common life of its members, and the various bodies associated with its government. Therefore, what is taken to be religious is located precisely here. It is assumed that the Church has of necessity to maintain visible, concrete, institutional structures. However, no one should deduce that the writer holds to the position that religion is to be found solely within the institutional church. Very far from it. Religious virtue and grace are to be found not only in and through institutional channels. Isolated individuals, whose faith and practice is highly privatized and concealed within themselves, can indeed be called religious and, if one may make the judgement, are just as much 'religious' as those never-failing attenders at Anglican or other churches. Religion in this wide sense is not the subject at issue. It is something more specific, it is the Diocese, seen as an organization with clear-cut boundaries, and examined as far as is possible objectively and impartially.

And so to particular facts before an attempt is made to return to these wider and more general issues.

105

The Area of the Diocese

The Diocese roughly covers the county of Northumberland, as it was before the boundaries were changed in 1974, when Tyne and Wear came into existence. It includes the old city and former county of Newcastle to the south; the town and county of Berwick-upon-Tweed to the north; and the parish of Alston, in Cumbria, the highest town in England, situated in hills to the west.

Two archdeaconaries divide the Diocese: Northumberland (of early origins) and Lindisfarne (created in 1842). In all there are 12 rural deaneries, which despite their name cover urban areas of the Diocese as well.

The land embraced by the Diocese extends to 2,077.5 square miles or 1,290,312 acres. By the criterion of area it is the seventh largest diocese in England, being smaller than Lincoln (the largest), Exeter, Oxford, Salisbury, York, and Carlisle.

Like the North-East itself, the Diocese has geographical features and a settlement of population that make it a clearly defined area. The only urban 'fuzziness' is to the south, into the 'foreign' Gateshead and Co. Durham, but even here, the river Tyne, which largely constitutes the southern boundary of the Diocese, not only acts as a physical divide but a sociological one as well.

TABLE 1

Population of Diocese[1]

Year	All ages	Aged 15 and over (000s)	% of population aged 15 and over
1882	438,704 (1885)	296 (1885)	67 (1885)
1891	509,414	332	65
1901	606,253	410	68
1911	699,968	487	70
1921	749,640	543	72
1931	759,668	580	76
1941	793,000 (1940 est.)	636 (1940 est.)	80
1951	800,924 (1950)	626 (1950)	78
1961	823,890 (1960)	627	76
1971	823,160 (1970)	636	77
1976	787,750 (est.)	613 (est.)	78 (est.)
1978	777,798 (est.)	605 (est.)	78 (est.)

[1] The author wishes to thank Victor Janes of the Central Board of Finance of the Church of England, Church House, Westminster, and David Hide of the Diocesan Office, Grainger Park Road, Newcastle upon Tyne, for help in compiling these and other Tables, and statistics used in the text.

TABLE 2
Number of Full-Time Clergy (as at July 1979)

		Total Numbers
Clergy with parish responsibility Rectors and vicars	119	
Clergy with incumbent status	20	139
Curates Others	30 9	39
Bishops, cathedral clergy, chaplains	8	8
Total		186

TABLE 3
Members on Electoral Rolls

Year	Number on electoral rolls	Percentage of population aged 15 and over on electoral rolls
1931	83,164 (1930)	14.3
1941	68,046 (1940)	10.7
1951	54,635 (1950)	8.9
1961	41,673 (1962)	6.6
1971	40,557 (1970)	6.4
1976	27,321	4.7
1978	21,842	3.6

TABLE 4
Infant Baptisms

Year	Number	Percentage of live births[1]
1921	13,215	
1931	9,197	
1941	7,990 (1940)	
1951	9,200 (1950)	
1961	7,893 (1960)	54.9
1971	5,984 (1970)	51.4
1976	3,974	45.4
1978	3,802	44.0

[1] Where no percentage is given, the reason is because it has been impossible to obtain the relevant number of live births.

TABLE 5

Confirmations

Year	Number of Confirmations
1882	5,186 (1883)
1891	3,075
1901	3,204
1911	3,366
1921	3,724
1931	3,945
1941	2,604
1951	2,738
1961	3,708
1971	2,249
1979	1,305

TABLE 6

Easter and Christmas Communicants
(Easter, for the years 1885-1921, Easter Day only; for subsequent years, Easter Day and Easter Week added together.)

Year	Easter Communicants		Christmas Communicants	
	Number	% of population aged 15 and over	Number	% of population aged 15 and over
1882	20,770 (1885)	7.0		
1891	21,216	6.4		
1901	27,784	6.8		
1911	29,652	6.1		
1921	32,169	5.9		
1931	38,000	6.6		
1941	35,360 (1940)	5.6		
1951	30,970 (1950)	4.9		
1961	39,977 (1960)	6.4	37,607 (1960)	6.0
1971	34,269 (1970)	5.4	33,186 (1970)	5.2
1976	28,550	4.7	26,254	4.3
1978	28,020	4.6	24,880	4.1

The Population of the Diocese

Since the Diocese was established in 1882, the population has almost doubled. In 1881 it was 438,000; in 1978 it was estimated to be 778,000. From the statistics given in Table 1, the peak was around 1961 with a population of 824,000. The general growth of population has been very slightly faster than that of the country as a whole. The most rapid expansion occurred between about 1880 and the time of the First World War; during these 30 years or so, it grew by a factor of about 1.6. After that War the growth continued but at a much slower pace. As indicated, since the 1960s there has been a slight decline. The predicted figure for 1981 is 771,000.

This is not the occasion to consider in detail the age structure of the population, but one crude indicator of this is given in the accompanying Table by showing the numbers of people aged 15 years and over. In the early 1880s, 67 per cent of the population was 'adult'; today it is 78 per cent. Such changes are a reflection of what is happening everywhere in the country, namely, the emergence of an ageing population. Over the years the level of young people in the Diocese has approximately corresponded to that of the country at large.

In terms of sheer population, Newcastle is a relatively small diocese. The Northern Province — dioceses grouped around the Archbishopric of York — has only four dioceses of smaller population (Bradford, Carlisle, Ripon, Sodor and Man).

Number of Churches and Seating Accommodation

Anglican churches, which are independent of adjoining local churches and which have their own parish and rector or vicar, are called benefices or livings. When the Diocese came into existence the number of benefices was 162. Today (1976), by a strange coincidence, the number is the same. But this is hardly a fact that should give rise to self-congratulation because, as has already been mentioned, this constant level in benefices must be seen against a population that has virtually doubled. There was a time when the figure for livings was somewhat higher — 182 — roughly in the period, 1920-50. In 1961 it dropped to 175 and since then has fallen to the present level.

A relatively sharp increase in the number of benefices occurred shortly after the creation of the Diocese and this growth is dealt with in detail in a chapter ahead, as is the closure of certain churches. Suffice it to say here that the demise of churches and the elimination of benefices is nearly always due to the poor support given to the churches, which in turn may reflect a declining population. In the main, though not entirely, the closure and reorganization of churches and parishes has occurred in rural rather than urban areas. The scaling down of benefices may occur in a number of ways. Sometimes the parish and its church are merged into adjoining units; on the other hand the parish may be allowed to continue independently but is linked with an adjacent parish and the one priest runs both churches as independent units. In the countryside he may well have several such small parishes. It is not surprising that for these reasons as well as others, the number of parishes exceeds the number of benefices. In

1961 in the Diocese there were, as has been stated, 175 benefices, but the number of parishes was 19 more. By 1976 the number of parishes had declined from 194 to 188, which would indicate not just a decline in the population but a deliberate policy on the part of the Diocese in closing or amalgamating parishes.

The number of places of worship — churches and chapels — is generally greater than the number of parishes. They include daughter churches, chapels in hospitals, in prisons, in religious houses for monks and nuns, and so on. They can be quite numerous. For example, in 1963 they were as many as 82, over and above parish churches which were estimated to be 174. Livings in that year amounted to 166.

Church leaders in the nineteenth century, faced with the rising population in part brought about by the growth of industrialization, were concerned not only to supply an adequate number of churches but to ensure that the churches were large enough to seat a goodly proportion of the population. It was often alleged, and perhaps erroneously argued, that people in the nineteenth century did not attend church because there was inadequate seating, especially in urban parishes. In the middle of the century the Nonconformists — Congregationalists, Baptists, and with them the Methodists who were not strictly Nonconformists — vied as a whole with the Church of England to produce a good deal of accommodation, and indeed tried to show that they had outstripped the Established Church (see Pickering 1967). Today, in the face of declining congregations, that competitive struggle is ironic and was totally misjudged. In 1921 in the Diocese there was seating accommodation in the churches which amounted to just under 73,000, representing just less than a tenth of the total population. In church halls a further 20,000 could be seated. Not surprisingly these figures have declined. In 1965, which seems to have been the last time such estimates were made, seating in churches and chapels amounted to 68,000, plus a further 9,000 for extra seats to be brought into the churches if necessary. For the year in question this meant that in the Diocese there were 9.3 seats for every 100 of the population. The figure was below the national average of 12.5. For the country as a whole, there were only nine dioceses which had 'worse' ratios than Newcastle's.

Number of Clergy and other Workers

Perhaps some readers will be surprised to learn that at first sight the number of full-time clergy within the Diocese has only slightly declined over the past hundred years. Today (1979) there are about

190 clergy, which includes beneficed clergy, curates, chaplains, cathedral staff, and bishop (Table 2). In 1882, according to the *Diocesan Calendar*, there were 228 clergy. Then almost twenty years later it was reported by the Bishop that the number had risen to 324 — an increase of just over a third (Jacob 1900:33). Statistics about the number of clergy are difficult to come by but it would seem that over the years there has been a gradual rise and decline, but the changes have not been as severe as might be thought. However, lest a spirit of complacency emerge when the figure in 1882 is compared with that of almost a hundred years later, it should be noted once again that the constancy must be viewed against a growing population. On average over the years parish ministers have had to be responsible for an increasing number of people. For each ordained minister (rector, vicar, curate, chaplain, etc.) in the early 1880s, there were on average 1,900 people; today the comparable figure is about 5,000. This fact means that heavier duties in terms of responsibility for the general population now fall on the shoulders of the clergy compared with a century ago. However, the load is very unequally distributed and this has been so ever since the industrial revolution. In one sense, the average figure does not have much meaning, in so far as great extremities existed in the past and still exist today. A country priest can be responsible for a population of a few hundred, for example, the parish of Simonburn by the North Tyne (250); and an urban incumbent, single-handed, can be responsible for many thousand people, as in the case of Walker Gate in the Tyneside area (20,000 people). Attempts on the part of church authorities to produce a more equitable situation over the years have met with very little success.

In many ways the easy method of overcoming the challenge of parishes with a large population is to give to the parish one or several curates. This has always been the traditional solution and is invariably tried first rather than the more complicated, difficult and expensive (legally) procedure of dividing the parishes into one or more other parishes. For a number of reasons the supply of curates is now falling and this, together with the problems of having to raise salaries, means that vicars and rectors can no longer rely on such help. Men are now being ordained in their 30s and 40s, and even older — this was scarcely known a hundred years ago — and it means that their maturity encourages a quicker move to becoming a rector or vicar than was formerly the case with curates. The meagre statistics which are available point to the marked decline in the number of curates with the passing years. In 1900 it was said there were 135 curates in the Diocese (Henderson 1900:61) which represented 42 per cent of all clergy. In 1931 the number had fallen to 69; and today (1979) that figure is more than halved to 30, or 16 per cent of the Diocesan clergy. In the light of the virtually constant number of parishes, any alleged decline of the clergy over the past century is to be seen in terms of curates rather than rectors and vicars. The position in earlier times has been described by William Wand, who later became Bishop of London. He wrote that in the period just before World War I there were seven clergy at Benwell Parish Church when he was a curate there (1965:46). Benwell is a working-class area in the west end of Newcastle. Admittedly the parish then had five churches, including mission churches, to look after. Nevertheless, no church in the Diocese today can claim a staff of such a size, despite the fact that the population of some of the parishes has remained very high. It is rare these days to find a curate! (*Punch* is quite right in abandoning jokes about them!) However, it is true to say that the Diocese has always been able to recruit an adequate supply of clergy to work in the City of Newcastle and in rural Northumberland.

Clergy working or residing within the Diocese are rather more numerous than the number included in the statistics that have been given. Quite apart from retired clergy living in the area, who have not been taken into consideration, there are a number of ordained men who are licensed to officiate but who do not work full-time for the Church and whose salaries come from 'secular' sources. These men go under the general title of the Auxiliary Pastoral or non-stipendiary ministry. In the main, they are of two types. Those who were trained as clergy, were ordained, and worked for some time in the parish ministry or in a chaplaincy but who later withdrew and took up another occupation, such as teaching or social work, but who continue to help in the parish on a part-time basis. And there are also those whose occupation may not have changed with the course of time but who have studied for the ordained ministry in their spare moments and after ordination help in a parish as they are able. From diocesan statistics it is difficult to separate these two categories. However, one thing is quite clear. It is that in recent years the number of those involved in the Auxiliary Pastoral ministry has grown considerably. The reasons for this are complex but it is plain to see that some clergy feel more fulfilled in an occupation other than that to which they were ordained. At the same time there are those who do not want to relinquish their present work but who wish to function liturgically and pastorally as priests on Sundays and at other times. In the past this second group was never given a place in the church and the nearest that could be achieved was to work as a lay reader. No official statistics are kept of those in the non-stipendiary ministry, but it was found that in 1978 there were four men in established posts (priests-in-charge, vicars) and eight in non-established posts (honorary assistants). There were also three men, ordained, who had retired from their secular occupations, who were working full-time in the church. This makes a total of 15, to whom might be added a woman worker, also non-stipendiary. Until comparatively recently the North-East lagged behind other areas in the training of men who wish to continue in their occupations but be ordained and help in parishes on a part-time basis.

And in connection with part-time clergy, we must not overlook other workers in parishes who, paid by the church, have done faithful service all down the years — deaconesses, parish workers, and in earlier times, paid lay readers or scripture readers, and lay mission workers, including officers of the Church Army. Their numbers in the past are difficult to discover but it is safe to say that they have seriously declined as other forms of ministry have emerged, but the new forms, as has just been noted, are mainly on a part-time basis. Thus, with the decline in the number of curates and the number of paid lay workers, the 'professional' work force of the church has also declined. As a consequence, one fact must be faced, truism though it may be. It is that the amount of work a full-time worker can give to the parish far exceeds that which can be given by those who work on a part-time basis.

As has also been noted, local ministries have been helped in the past, and are still being helped by voluntary lay readers, now known as readers, who take services, preach, and generally assist the clergy in public worship. Numbers once again are not easy to obtain, but it seems that the figure has remained fairly steady with the passing of the years. In 1956 there were 49 parochial readers (working only in one parish) and 35 diocesan readers (helping in any parish in the Diocese). Today (1979) the total number of readers has slightly grown to 99. There are thus sure signs of overall increase, certainly compared with an earlier period, 1900, when it was reported there were only 62 readers (Henderson 1900:60).

For those who would like to know about the marital status of the clergy, it should be said that in 1956 in the Diocese, 18 per cent were single; 80 per cent married; 3 per cent widowed. The figures for English dioceses as a whole were very much the same — 15, 82, 3 respectively. A slight tendency to the unmarried in the Diocese then! And today? The proportions are probably much the same, although some parishes which once wanted only unmarried clergy have had to settle for married men, be they curates or vicars. As in the population at large, so amongst the clergy, marriage shows signs of a growth in popularity. It might also be noted that the age-structure of the clergy in the Diocese is marginally younger than that for Anglican clergy in the country as a whole.[1]

Despite the fact that in recent years the parish ministry, viewed as an occupation or profession, has received considerable study at the hands of sociologists, virtually no material directly derived from the Diocese has come to light which might make some contribution to the subject. Two personal observations, however, might be made. The first is that the clergy once they come to the Diocese tend to stay in it, and if they move, do so to another parish within the Diocese rather than venture into another part of the country. (For example, from mid-1978 to mid-1979, only 2 clergy moved from the Diocese to other dioceses — the lowest figure for any diocese.) The other, that an examination of the Diocesan Yearbooks would appear to show that a comparatively high number of local clergy went to the University of Durham, including King's College, Newcastle upon Tyne, formerly part of the University of Durham, now an independent university. When Durham University came into existence in 1836 it was intended to provide local people, geographically removed from Oxford and Cambridge, with an education of similar stamp as that available at those universities. The growth of railways actually beginning in the Durham area at precisely that time, together with other forms of transport, undermined the purposes of Durham University. Just because universities in England attract only a very small percentage of local students, it is interesting that so many ex-Durham graduates have taken up appointments in the Newcastle Diocese. It seems most likely that many clergy from outside the area wish to work in it as a result of taking their higher education in the North-East.

The sociologist, H. A. Mess, writing in the 1920s about the social conditions along the Tyne, held that the churches were on the whole failing to keep pace with the growth in population and indeed in many cases were falling behind. The buildings were too large, discouragingly empty and were costly to maintain (1928:138). He advocated that a better use of human resources could be made by encouraging ministers to work in a team with specialised functions (ibid:140). He saw no signs of such changes occurring, for to bring them about needed a spiritual revival. Though not precisely as he thought, there are signs of team ministries emerging, employing a group of clergy, whose work covers several parishes and who join forces in some corporate way. In the Diocese at the present time there exist about eight such team ministries. The cynic might be inclined to comment

114

that these ministries have come into existence, not as a result of a spiritual awakening as Mess thought necessary, but rather through economic necessity. Economic arguments, not theological ones, are the only arguments the Church understands! And such has been the slowness of the Church to act that something like forty years had to elapse before the first team ministries began to emerge in the Diocese.

Membership by Electoral Roll, Baptism, and Confirmation

Largely because the Church of England is the Established Church, and assumes that everyone who is not a member of another denomination is potentially if not actually Anglican, it has never evolved a comprehensive method for determining membership. There was in the nineteenth century and later a strong resistance to such a move, not least because it would give rise to a counting of heads. However, an attempt was made to correct what was seen to be an anomaly just after World War I with the Enabling Act of 1919 and the Parochial Church Councils (Powers) Measure which followed in 1921. By this legislation, every Anglican who wished to register his membership was and is still invited to put his name on the electoral roll of the church where he worships. The requirements are that he or she has been confirmed and must be, until recently, 18 years of age and over, now reduced to 17. Membership carries with it certain privileges, such as being elected onto the parochial church council and the right to vote. Membership of the electoral roll has never really gained a central part of the life of the church, as has membership in the Free churches. The laity as a whole and perhaps some of the clergy still think in terms of an assumed membership of the Established Church and therefore do not place a great deal of importance on declared membership. Further, recruiting to the electoral roll has really always rested with the initiative of the parish minister and some clergy have in the past and still today shown indifference about keeping rolls up-to-date. The General Synod now requires new rolls to be prepared every six years. Having one's name put on the roll and taken off is a nominal act without ritual procedure and with little consequence one way or another, except the possibility of service on the parochial church council.

In 1931 there were about 83,000 electoral roll members in the Diocese, representing 14 per cent of the population aged 15 years and over (see Table 3). (Mess put the proportion at 9 per cent of the population over 18 years of age for Tyneside in the 1920s (Mess 1928:131).) By 1961 the number and percentage of electoral roll members had halved — a serious drop indeed. A further serious decline was recorded in the 1976 returns when there was a fall of a third on the 1961 figures. Today (1978) the number stands at 22,000, or only 4 per cent of the population aged 15 years and over. But it should be noted that the calculated percentages are in fact slightly smaller than they are in reality, since the age group taken for calculation is 15 years of age and over, whilst membership was for some time 18 years and above although it was lowered in 1957 to 17 years and over.

Electoral roll membership has little meaning theologically: baptism has. Baptism, as the initiation rite into membership of the church, is one of the chief sacraments. It is biblical and nearly every Christian denomination accepts it. For this reason, some clergy see baptism as a more serious indicator of membership than that of the electoral roll. In the light of recent liturgical revival and historical research, baptism is now being given a much more carefully considered place within the life of the Church than it was in previous decades, when it was taken very much for granted. Further, baptism continues to be a popular rite amongst people at large, although care has to be taken in examining the statistics in the local situation. Absolute figures may not be a good indicator of the level of baptisms, since the number of live births in a given area may vary considerably from year to year. Unfortunately baptismal statistics for Newcastle are not available for years before World War I, although they have been computed subsequently. Nor has it been possible to obtain the number of live births for the area of the Diocese until more recent periods. As might be expected, the number of baptisms in 1921 was high – 13,000 (see Table 4). Ten years later it had fallen to 9,000 and the same figure was recorded for 1950. In 1978 the number had dropped to 3,800. Mess calculated that for Tyneside as a whole in the 1920s, seventy per cent of children born were baptised in the Church of England. It has been calculated that for 1956 in the Diocese, 60 per cent of all live births were baptised in Anglican churches. By 1970 it had dropped to 51 per cent and today (1978) it is 44 per cent. Such percentages as are available for the Diocese approximate to those for England as a whole. One can therefore hazard a guess that in the past and perhaps still today what happens in the country probably occurs also in Newcastle. In order therefore to show something of the fluctuations in the level of baptisms we give the following percentages which are for England:

Year	Percentage of baptisms compared with live births
1885	62
1891	60
1901	65

Year	Percentage of baptisms compared with live births
1911	68
1921	70
1931	70
1940	64
1950	67

It may be thought to be somewhat extraordinary that the level of baptisms in 1885 in the Anglican Church was lower than it was in 1950. An interpretation of the statistics is complicated and the variations have never been adequately explained. One thing that has to be taken into account is the actual registering of baptisms and it could well be argued that clergy in the past were not altogether careful in writing up the baptismal registers, especially in towns and there is the whole problem of baptisms in the home which were carried out in the face of a relatively high infant mortality rate. But all those facts apart, one thing does emerge and that is that the level of baptisms has remained relatively high throughout the period, at least until recent years. The reasons why baptism and other rites such as marriage and burial have persisted so strongly is a highly complex and conjectural subject which cannot be entertained here (see Pickering 1974).

One thing is becoming increasingly clear and that is that within the last ten or fifteen years, or perhaps a little longer, there has emerged a somewhat significant decline in the level of baptisms in the Anglican Church. One knows little about the reason for this. It could be due to the extension of secularizing attitudes in which people are openly rejecting the opportunity of having their children baptised. On the other hand, it could be argued that the Church has in some way encouraged this by the fact that certain clergy who for some time have been opposed to the 'lax attitude' of people towards baptism want to lay down conditions, such as parents attending preparation classes or being required to attend public worship. In the face of these formidable obstacles, parents have not persisted in their intention of having their children baptised. In some cases they go to other parish churches or churches of other denomonations.

Confirmation is best viewed as a rite which is an extension of baptism — some see it as a completion of baptism, although certain theologians would deny this and hold that baptism is a rite that is complete in itself. In practice in the Church of England confirmation is a mark of full membership of the church, admitting the person to receive Communion at the other great sacrament of the church, the Eucharist. Up to the time of the Second World War it used to be administered in the main to boys and girls in their middle and late teens. Since then, the age has gradually been lowered and today children are frequently confirmed at twelve or thirteen. It is difficult to know how to present confirmation statistics other than to present absolute numbers. Against what does one judge them? The general population? Hardly. The numbers baptised in previous years? But in the light of the discrepancies of the age of confirmees, how far back? Because of these difficulties, all that can be done here is to present absolute figures (see Table 5). Excluding 1883, the figures show remarkable stability until perhaps the mid-sixties – a figure of about 3,000. In 1883 the number was high, 5,200, due to the drive of the new bishop to have people confirmed, but during the first eight years of Bishop Wilberforce's episcopate the annual number on average was about 3,500. Mess calculated that in the 1920s in Tyneside, confirmations represented 20 per cent of the adolescents of the area.

Since 1971 Diocesan returns have shown a very serious – almost dramatic – fall. Between 1971 and 1979 there has been a decline of 42 per cent. The numbers are as follows:

1971	2249
1972	1909
1973	1683
1974	1281
1975	1597
1976	1386
1977	1413
1978	1511
1979	1305

These falls are more marked in this Diocese than in any other in the Northern Province. The figure for 1974 was the lowest of all the Northern figures. It should be noted, however, that confirmation statistics are subject to considerable fluctuation.

And of course it is more girls who get confirmed than boys. It was true according to the returns in the early days of the Diocese: it is also true today — the ratio is about two girls to every boy. It is also probably the case that the population of adults being confirmed at the present time is greater than it was a few decades ago.

Religious Practice: Attendance at Church
It has been a long-standing practice to estimate the level of minimum commitment in terms of attendance at church by the numbers receiving Communion at Easter. The 1662 Prayer Book states that all members of the Church of England are to receive Communion three times a year, of which Easter shall be one. It is difficult to know how far those

who today call themselves Anglicans still accept the exhortation. Nevertheless, the numbers of those who communicate at Easter Day services remains one of the most reliable and best indicators of church attendance that is available. The Anglican Church has for the past century or so kept accurate statistics for this kind of activity. In some of the returns, additional numbers, which are usually small, are added to those given for Easter Day and represent the number of communions made during the week following.

In 1885 in the Diocese there were about 21,000 communions made on Easter Day, which represented 7.0 per cent of the population 15 years of age and over (see Table 6). This was the highest percentage to be recorded in the years that followed, although the level was as much as 6.6 per cent in 1931. In that year and the following years included communions made during Easter week. Recently there has been a falling off, but it has not been as marked as for other indicators of church life. Today (1978) the number of communions stands at about 28,000, representing 4.6 per cent of the 'adult' population. Up to the 1960s the differences in percentage-level between the Diocese of Newcastle and England as a whole was about 2 or 3 per cent higher for England. Subsequently the two levels have been much the same. Thus, it can be argued that over the past hundred years or so, the slow decline in the percentage of communions at Easter compared with the 'adult' population has been marginally less marked in Newcastle than for the country.

Christmas does not carry with it the official ecclesiastical constraint to attend church that is associated with Easter. Yet it has become, in terms of receiving Communion, as popular a festival as Easter. Statistics have only been available since 1960 when the numbers were virtually the same — indeed, if the Easter week communions are deducted from the total, Christmas Day communions were slightly larger than those for Easter Day. In 1960 Christmas communions were 38,000: in 1978 25,000. As with Easter communions, there has been a marked decline in numbers during the last decade or so. The levels in the Diocese are very much the same as those for the country as a whole.

Figures for festivals are no indication of numbers on an ordinary Sunday. Attendances for an 'average' Sunday are difficult to obtain and have seldom been asked for in returns sent to the clergy for diocesan or national bodies. In recent years, however, questions have been put in the hope that the clergy will produce perhaps well informed guesses or better, carefully calculated averages. There can of course be no guarantee of the accuracy of the figures given. In 1978 for the Diocese of Newcastle, the total average church attendance was about 17,887 or 2.3 per cent of the total population, or again, 3.0 per cent of those 15 years of age and over. Five years earlier, the figure was slightly higher at 19,000, but the corresponding percentages were almost exactly the same. In 1968, earlier still, the figure was 26,000 or 3.5 per cent of the total population, or 4.1 per cent of the 'adult' population. If the returns can be relied upon, there is a clear falling away of numbers attending church on average — a decline of 36 per cent over eight years, which must be seen as a serious erosion of practice.

In 1976 for the first time, parochial returns asked for the average number of communions or communions on a normal Sunday. In the Diocese these amounted to just under 12,000 — that is, 5,000 below that of the average attendances. Total communions on an average Sunday thus represent 2.0 per cent of the population aged 15 years and over. In 1978 the number had increased to just under 12,500 but there was no significant change in the percentage level.

Once again for purposes of comparison, the findings of H. A. Mess are given, this time in connection with a very limited church attendance survey that was carried out on 28 February 1928. In Wallsend he found that total attendances made by members of all denominations amounted to 20 per cent of the population, 14 years of age and over (Mess 1928:137). Sunday school attendances were included. We have calculated that the Anglican figure was 3.0 per cent of the 'adult' population, that for Roman Catholics 8.4 per cent, and that for the Free churches 8.6 per cent.

Marriages and Burials

Unfortunately no statistics are available for the Diocese which indicate the number of marriages clergy have performed in the past, as well as the number they perform today. In the light of such a deficiency, all that can be done is to look at the country as a whole and assume that what is seen to occur there in the matter of marriages is also reflected in the Diocese. Set out below are certain statistics relating to marriages contracted in England and Wales:

Year	Percentage performed in Anglican churches	Total number of marriages (1,000's)
1879	72.3	182
1889	69.8	214
1899	67.8	262
1909	61.4	261
1919	59.7	369

Year	Percentage performed in Anglican churches	Total number of marriages (1,000's)
1929	56.2	313
1952	49.6	349
1962	47.4	348
1972	36.5	426
1976	35.0	358

There are thus marked signs of a decline in the proportion of marriages solemnized in Anglican churches throughout the period. The proportion is roughly half today what it was in the early 1880s. However, the position is somewhat more complex than the figures give us to understand (see Pickering 1974). It seems fairly true to say that until recently – the last ten to fifteen years – the population as a whole tended to get married in churches of one denomination or another, unless the partners were divorced. The rigidity of the Anglican Church remains until today, although there are signs that the clergy legally entitled to marry divorced people are now prepared to do so. As the number of divorces has risen in society, so the proportion of those getting married in church would appear to have declined. But the register office is not only a popular place for the marriage of those who themselves or their partners have been divorced, it seems that it is also being frequented by those who are getting married for the first time. This has happened in the past, especially when economic circumstances were difficult and civil weddings were much cheaper than church weddings. It is also apparent in the findings of Mess. For 1908 he calculated that of all marriages 31 per cent were civil marriages; in 1912 28 per cent; in 1924 27 per cent (Mess 1928:138). Incidentally these percentages were slightly higher than those for Co. Durham.

If there are indications that the population at large shows signs of opting for civil marriage, there is no parallel movement towards a civil burial (Pickering 1974). Undertakers and registrars frequently assert that 99.9 per cent of burials are conducted by a priest, minister, or someone deputed to perform a religious ceremony. Anglican clergy are involved in the burial of the dead to a far greater extent than clergy of other denominations. As ministers of the Free churches are declining in numbers, it seems likely that the task of burying people at large falls increasingly on the shoulders of Anglican parsons. Probably something like three-quarters or more of all burials are conducted by them.

Training the Young

No set of statistics has shown a more devastating and decisive decline than those relating to Sunday school members, members of bible classes (senior Sunday schools), and Sunday school teachers. Such is the general attitude towards these groups — it seems to be an attitude of despair — that church authorities no longer ask for statistics of this kind. Although Sunday schools were relatively well attended in the nineteenth century, no statistics have been found about them which relate to the Diocese as a whole. For more recent years we quote the following:

Year	Sunday school scholars	Bible class members	Sunday school teachers
1921	36,421	5,766	2,689
1931	33,551	5,602	2,917
1961	15,904 (1960)	–	1,284

In the forty years (1921–1961) numbers have been more than halved. And that was up to 1961! How many children attend Sunday school now is not known with accuracy. In a newspaper report in 1970, the Diocesan Secretary of Education put the figure at less than 5,000 (*Journal* 7 October 1977). Mess calculated that in the Tyneside area in 1925 there were 36,363 Sunday school scholars, or 20 per cent of all children between 4 and 14 years of age. Hardly a proportion to be found in Newcastle today!

It would seem that after the Second World War a serious decline set in, perhaps due in part to external factors such as the increased number of cars and the growth of television. But other reasons can be found within the churches themselves. The post-war generation of clergy appeared to have relatively little time for Sunday schools and directed their attention towards a changed pattern in adult services, especially in the introduction of Parish Communion, which was held during the early part of Sunday morning.[2] Whole families were encouraged to attend this service, thus avoiding the old pattern of adults worshipping at the main services and children at Sunday schools and Bible classes. Hence the schools not only lost status, they also lost members, as some of the children whose parents were already worshipping members, attended the Parish Communion. Whether this Parish and People Movement, as it came to be known, has been successful in theological and sociological terms cannot be debated here. But there is one thing that is clear and that is it has helped to undermine Sunday schools.

The demise of Sunday schools raises the whole problem of recruitment to the church. We have no statistics which show the age-structure of church membership and attendance at worship. Evidence from data elsewhere and from personal observation suggests that the young in most churches are a relatively weak force and this implies the inadequacies of training, or to use a more technical word, the socialization of the young. Fifty years ago it was thought to be serious enough: it can hardly be more serious now. The problem of course is a universal one, not just confined to Newcastle.

In looking at the statistics for the 1950s, the most popular age group of Sunday school members was that of 7-10 years of age. There were twice as many girls as boys and amongst Sunday school teachers the ratio was something like 5 to 1 women to men.

Newcastle Compared with other Dioceses

It has already been noted that in terms of total population, the Diocese is relatively small compared with other dioceses. In this respect, it stands eleventh out of fourteen dioceses in the Northern Province.

Amongst the dioceses of the province, and judged by other factors, it is very much in the middle of the ranking order, not that dioceses deliberately vie with one another for superiority! Such ranking however allows one to make generalizations about the Diocese and to see that according to several indicators of church life, it is not to be found at the extreme ends of the spectrum. For example in 1973 it was:

> 6th in the percentage of Easter communicants compared with the population, aged 15 years and over
> 8th in average Sunday attendances compared with the population, aged 15 years and over
> 9th in infant baptisms compared with live births.

The best diocese in the north for 'piety' was Carlisle with a level of Easter communicants of 9.6 per cent (Newcastle 4.7 per cent) and in England as a whole the 'best' diocese was Hereford with 12.0 per cent. The dioceses of Hereford and Carlisle tend to be strongly rural and in many respects so is Newcastle. It is to this characteristic that we now turn.

The Mix: a Rural-Urban Diocese

We have already observed that the area of the Diocese is 2,077.5 square miles. Of this, it was estimated in the mid-1950s that 1928.5

square miles covered rural districts and therefore only 149.0 square miles were designated as urban districts. This means that by land area 93 per cent is rural and only 7 per cent urban. By land area alone, Newcastle is the seventh largest diocese in England. But if one observes other criteria than just land area the position is very different. For example, take the crude indicator of the number of parochial churches compared with the total area. When this is done, Newcastle is the most rural of all dioceses in the country, for it has only one church per 10 square miles. There were five dioceses in the mid-1950s which had two churches per 10 square miles (Ely, Truro, Bradford, Carlisle, Ripon, Sodor and Man). Thus, whilst Newcastle is not the most rural diocese in terms of land area, it is the most rural in terms of its few churches situated in the rural areas. This is reflected in the way in which the population is located outside the towns — the moors and villages are very sparsely peopled indeed.

The Diocese as a whole is fairly thickly populated – 396 persons per square mile, calculated in 1961. This means that it has much the same population density as for example the Diocese of Peterborough, and there are eleven other dioceses in England with fewer people per square mile. But once again average figures are misleading. From personal experience everyone knows that Northumberland is very rural and this is demonstrated when a more careful statistical analysis is made. Once again according to the 1961 figures, which are the latest available for urban and rural populations in the Diocese, computed by the Registrar General, we have the following:

Urban areas	713,392 people	(86.6 per cent)
Rural areas	110,040 people	(13.4 per cent)
Total population	823,432	(100.0 per cent)

Thus for the Diocese a little under 90 per cent of the population is found in urban areas. It might be noted that in the Diocese of Durham it is 80 per cent and in Manchester and London 100 per cent! Within the urban areas themselves the number of people per square mile was, in 1961, 4,788, and in this respect Newcastle was the ninth most densely populated diocese in the country. It is however an examination of the rural areas that makes Newcastle virtually unique. In the countryside of Northumberland, in terms defined by the Registrar General, there were on average 57 persons per square mile. This figure makes Newcastle the most rural diocese of the country, just above the dioceses of Bradford and Carlisle. Some of its parishes are surely amongst the largest and most thinly populated of all parishes in England, for example Elsdon with 76,000 acres, which is not the most extensive in the Diocese!

These contrasts are to be seen in the size of the parishes. In 1961 the Diocese had 15 parishes with under 199 people, which constituted 8 per cent of all parishes. (Lincoln has many more such microscopic parishes – 245 out of a total of 653.) At the other end of the scale Newcastle has 6 parishes with a population of over 20,000, that is 3 per cent of its parishes which is a slightly higher proportion than for the Diocese of London! For parishes between 10,000 and 19,999 people Newcastle has 26, or 14 per cent of all its parishes – the proportion in London is just under twice that.

These facts make Newcastle unique amongst the English dioceses. None has such vast and sparsely populated rural areas, which surround an area of high-density population. It is a diocese of extremes. But also what is most interesting is that the two contrasting zones are clearly differentiated. As soon as the traveller leaves the urban belt which hugs the Tyne, he enters into what seems an unending rural area extending some 70 miles north to the Scottish border and to the Pennine hills in the west.

With such demographic contrasts, it is tempting to compare the levels of institutional church life in rural and urban areas. Such a comparison would help to confirm or challenge a common assertion – perhaps not made so much nowadays, but still one worth considering – that rural folk are more 'religious' than those who dwell in large towns and cities. We can of course use only those indicators connected with church life which we have used already. Because of this no conclusion can be drawn as to whether country dwellers are more 'religious' than town dwellers because they have a more acute sense of God, since, it is alleged, they live close to nature and to the soil.

For technical reasons it has not been possible to calculate accurately urban-rural figures for the general population of the Diocese according to the returns of the Registrar General and relate them to the ecclesiastical returns for religious practice, say for 1976. However, some kind of approximate calculations have been made. The deaneries of Newcastle, West, Central, and East, together with the deanery of Tynemouth, have been grouped together. They constitute what might be called urban Newcastle. The rest of the Diocese which covers most of Northumberland is called rural Newcastle. On this basis, 63 per cent of the population can be called urban and 37 per cent rural. Against these two basic percentages the corresponding proportions for different aspects of religious practice were calculated as follows for 1976:

	Percentage urban	Percentage rural
Population	63	37
of all baptisms	53	47
of all Easter communions	50	50
of all Christmas communions	48	52
of all communions on a normal Sunday	59	41
of all church attendances on a normal Sunday	54	46
of all electoral roll members	44	56

It is to be seen that in every one of these indicators, proportionally fewer people per head of the population in urban areas participate in them than the proportions of people in rural areas. On the other hand, it could not be said that the imbalance was excessively great. Comparitively speaking the urban areas are weakest in terms of electoral roll membership, Christmas communions, and Easter communions. They tend to hold their own in the matter of communions on a normal Sunday, church attendances on a normal Sunday, and baptisms. The conclusion would seem to be that, according to these criteria, rural practice is proportionally higher than in urban areas but that the differences are not very marked. If modern secularization is defined in these terms, then it is quite clear that religious life in the country has been affected almost as much as it has in towns and cities.

Even in terms of the institutional church it might be argued that the comparison is unfair. The reason is simply that in urban areas there is a service in each church every Sunday. In the countryside this is not so. The large number of small churches means that it is often impossible to have services every Sunday, and certainly the Eucharist is not celebrated weekly on Sundays. But over and against this consideration it should be noted that those in rural areas have more clergy per head of population than those in urban areas. Of all diocesan clergy, including curates, cathedral staff and chaplains, 56 per cent were located in rural areas, in which the corresponding figure for the population is 38 per cent. Put the other way round it means that in urban areas 44 per cent of the clergy look after 62 per cent of the people.

A General Assessment
We have shown as simply as possible the various changes that have

occurred in a number of indicators relating to church membership and religious practice in the Diocese over the past hundred years. Admittedly such indicators are limited but use has been made of all that is available. What does it all add up to? Can any generalizations be drawn? Do the statistics indicate a hundred years of growth, of decline, or of little change?

About the Church of England generally on Tyneside, Mess observed in 1928 that it was not as strong as it was in other parts of the country (1928:131). This was not true, he observed, of the Roman Catholic Church and the Free churches, which were relatively well entrenched both in comparison with the Anglican Church, and also in relation to the distrubution of each within the country as a whole. We are not in a position to comment on these last observations since we have made no attempt to compare the Church of England with other denominations either in the past or the present. Suffice it to say that it is generally held that Roman Catholicism and Nonconformity used to have a good following in the North-East. Such soundings as have been taken indicate that in the main, compared with other dioceses in England, Newcastle in matters of religious membership and practice stands very much in the middle of the spectrum. There are some dioceses where there are slightly higher rates of conformity and other sees where membership and practice per capita are not as strong as they are in Newcastle. Some might be tempted to account for this middle position by referring to the extraordinary mix of city and countryside, to which reference was made in the last section. At best, all we can say is that there might be something in this combination of demographic factors, but how much it is difficult to say.

Compare the position in 1882 with that of today (1976), we set out below the direction in which the indicators have moved:

Growth	Little or no change	Decline
	Absolute number of benefices	
	Absolute number of clergy	Since 1890 a serious decline in the number of curates
		Benefices/population
		Clergy/population
		*Curate/population
		*Since 1922, electoral roll/ population
		Baptism/live births
		*steep decline

127

Growth	Little or no change	Decline
	Absolute number of those confirmed	Confirmation/population(?)
		*Sunday school members
		Church marriages/total marriages
	Easter Communions/ population	
✓		*steep decline

From the above it can be seen that no indicator shows a growth, four point to little or no change and nine indicators signify a decline.

Thus the verdict is overwhelming. Despite an optimistic burst which occurred during the first decades after the Diocese was formed, it has suffered continuous diminution from what might be called a combination of forces, which have undermined the relative strength and status of the Church as an institutional body within society. The first century therefore of the history of the Diocese has been a century marked by declining numbers and diminished allegiance. But having said that, it should be noted that the Diocese has not been alone in facing such diminution: other dioceses, some much older in history, have also experienced similar changes during this same period.

NOTES
1. Compare, for example, the following statistics for the year 1979 of the age-cohorts of clergy.

Age groups	Percentage of clergy in Diocese of Newcastle	Percentage of clergy in all dioceses
Under 40	26.6	24.7
40–49	28.2	28.0
50–59	21.3	24.1
60–64	14.4	13.0
over 65	9.5	10.5
Total	100.0	100.0

Source: *Church of England Yearbook 1980 Statistical Supplement:* Table 4.)

2. For example, H. de Candole, vicar of St. John's, Grainger Street, who was largely responsible for Parish Communion, felt that Sunday schools, Mothers Union meetings, and men's meetings were outdated (see Jagger 1975:133; also 1978).

128

Chapter VII

THE DEVELOPMENT OF THE DIOCESE OF NEWCASTLE

W. S. F. Pickering

2 BATTLING WITH THREATENING FORCES

IT MIGHT well be said that a relatively careful examination of trends within the hundred years' existence of the Diocese of Newcastle, which leads to the conclusion that the Diocese has experienced a weakening of its institutional components, is precisely what was to be expected. If sociologists constantly do battle over the notion of the secularization of contemporary society, whether there has been a decline in religion in general and what are the causes, there is one thing on which they are all agreed, as indeed are historians. It is that the Church defined institutionally, and certainly the Church of England, has suffered great losses over recent years in terms of loyalty, membership, and practice. Such losses have naturally been accompanied by a diminution of that power and control the Church once exercised over society.

The material that has come to light in taking a close look at the Diocese over the past century does not in itself make a great contribution to a fresh understanding of the complex process or processes of church decline. The trends merely confirm what has been occurring in the country as a whole. There is, however, one aspect of the subject which is often overlooked and which is apposite to examine in the context of the history of the Diocese. This is the attempt that was made by the Anglican Church during the past century to combat those forces which have threatened its institutional life. When sociologists and sometimes historians have attempted to deal with the question of secularization, they have frequently done so without reference to a careful acknowledgement of the fact that those who presumably felt the icy blasts of hostility and indifference the most keenly, because they were within the Church itself, endeavoured to oppose them vigorously and so preserve the institutional state and status of the Church. The fight against decline and then for self-preservation roused the Church to determined counteraction and with this it was revealed that, at various levels of the institution, the Church possessed an understanding of what was occurring, though often in a very simple way. What follows is an attempt to look at these counteractions, and this means that in the first place the approach once more is historical.

The Period 1880-1914 — One of Optimism

The period between 1880 and the outbreak of the First World War is one of considerable importance in analysing the place of the Church in society. Part of the importance arises from the fact that the situation was full of ambivalences, for on the one hand the Church seemed to be in an optimistic mood about its present and future, and on the other, there existed a number of Church leaders who were worried about the shadows cast by what they saw as impending decline or secularisation.

The note of optimism was clearly echoed in the Church Congresses which were held in Newcastle in 1881 and 1900. These national gatherings, held on an annual basis in various dioceses in turn, usually in their chief cities, were intended to involve the laity by giving them a voice in the affairs of the Established Church (see Chadwick 1970:359ff.). They began in 1861 in Cambridge and were held regularly up until the time of World War I. It is reported that on occasions they involved as many as 5,000 people and were organised very much along the lines of the British Association meetings with formal papers and replies. The topics that were covered were extensive but the focus was on the well-being of the Church of England at home and abroad. Supporters upheld the notion that the Established Church was the recognised Christian body in English society, and in this context they were as much concerned about the challenge of Darwinianism to Christianity, as the well-being and spiritual life of parishes up and down the countryside.

The second Church Congress to be held in Newcastle took place eighteen years after the foundation of the Diocese. During those years under the leadership of Bishop Wilberforce, the Diocese had experienced a wave of enthusiasm which pointed to new life and vigour. A great amount of church building had taken place and the number of clergy had been considerably augmented (see Chapters VI and X). The future was one that churchmen were keen to anticipate in hope and triumph. Welcoming the Congress, the Mayor, Sir Riley Lord, evidently an Anglican, said:

> The future of the Church of England here in the north probably was never brighter or better than it was at the present time (Dunkley (ed.) 1900:2)

And Canon Henderson, rector of Wallsend, speaking about the achievements of the Church in Newcastle and praising the remarkable building expansion within the Diocese proudly commented:

> The progress to which we believe we are justified in pointing has come in its true healthy natural order, and may, therefore, be expected to be permanent (Dunkley (ed.) 1900:61).

This optimism about the Anglican Church, apparent at the end of the nineteenth century and continuing up to the time of World War I, was to be seen in the country as a whole. At an earlier period people had become conscious of the fact that the Church of England, at a period of great industrial and urban growth, was drowsing, if not soundly asleep. Churches were not built in sufficient numbers and locally critics were not slow in pointing to inadequate facilities. In 1856 it was reported that there were two ecclesiastical districts in Newcastle with over 10,000 people and no church, parsonage or school, and there were three perpetual curacies in which one man on average had charge of 16,000 people (ibid:61). At a national level Methodism was a response to the early threats facing institutional religion and in the light of its successes, the Established Church was forced to arouse itself. Also, in the early nineteenth century, in the realm of intellectual ideas, rationalism and other anti-religious forces, often originating from the Continent, threatened the Church's flabby theology. The clergy were complacent and lackadaisical. Indolent and knocked about in these ways, the Church slowly became alive, became conscious of itself, of the problems that faced it, and was able to meet them with its hidden treasures and regained energies. Churches were built and repaired: more clergy were recruited (see Chadwick 1970:238ff.). It was able to break out of being, as it were, a weak, trampled-on, department of the state and attempted to gain its own autonomy. Within such an overall new consciousness, and indeed in part giving rise to that consciousness, was the Oxford Movement, which had not only given to the Church some theological impetus by infusing a new interest in the history of the early Church and its Catholic heritage, but later was instrumental in producing the Anglo-Catholic movement which was able to bring new vigour to the priesthood and encourage the clergy to work in a spirit of hope in the slums, particularly those of the east end of London. It was thus common enough for leaders at the end of the nineteenth century to speak of 'the progress of the Church'. This and similar terms were used by the Right Reverend W. Boyd Carpenter, Bishop of Ripon, in his address to the Church Congress of 1900 when he was talking about the state of the Church of England at home and abroad (Dunkley (ed.) 1900:42). He referred triumphantly to the growth in the number of dioceses in England during the recent past decades and also to the rapid development of bishoprics overseas. Between 1872 and 1900, 39 sees had been created in the Anglican Church around the world. It was this enormous expansion of the Church abroad, almost entirely confined to the British Empire, which involved large numbers of clergy and a great deal of money, which in part gave buoyancy to the ecclesiastical optimism of the day. Boyd Carpenter was doubtless not alone in seeing the whole world becoming Christian, he proudly presented statistics to undergird his unshakable hope.

Edgar Jacob, the second bishop of Newcastle, in his inaugural address to the Church Congress of 1900 also had no hesitation in speaking of the revival of the Church (ibid:30-42). He focussed his remarks on the fact that within a large part of the revival there was 'a recognition that religion cannot be severed from life but must consecrate and permeate every department of life'. Men were coming to a new realization of the Kingdom of God, which meant that the Church as a divine society, was bound to affect all areas of social life. A fresh awareness of Christian social ethics, as distinct from ethics that related to the individual, was emerging and in this way Christians were in a position to establish a social conscience in society.

But the optimism visible amongst Church leaders was not only founded on evidence from within the ecclesiastical body. This was the heyday of that hopefulness that was associated with the upsurge of democratic liberalism, not confined to any one political party. There was an overarching sense that all was going well with the world. Again, and despite the unhappy interlude of the Boer War, the extensive British Empire was part of the awareness that 'all was well' and was proving to be a great success in maintaining itself peacefully and profitably. At the turn of the century there was also the Diamond Jubilee which proclaimed a sense of destiny for the British people in their being a world power, indeed the foremost world power. At home, free education had become a fact and there were signs that the source of so much internal wealth centred on the productivity of the working classes themselves — that they were enjoying improved conditions at work and in their homes. Sentiments along these and other lines were freely expressed at the Newcastle Church Congress of 1900 (ibid:42-7).

Those of an optimistic frame of mind about the Church thus hastened to indicate the latter half of the nineteenth century had been one of a magnificent response to changes emerging in society in previous decades which appeared to challenge the Church when it was at a low point in its history. If the Church had responded in such a splendid way in the past, then there was every reason to believe that it would continue to do so in the future.

The period 1880-1914 — One of Alarm

'It was the best of all worlds: it was also the worst of all worlds'. There were spokesmen in the Church as well as outside it, who did not share such blatant optimism about the future as has just been described. They discerned the writing on the wall which indicated to them that the Church, especially the Anglican Church, was, despite the achievements of the nineteenth century, facing a severe crisis. They called upon people not to be blinded by the spectacular building programme that had taken place at various times during that century (Gray (ed.) 1911:14; and see Chapters IX, X and XI).The Church of England was failing to be the Church of the nation. And the failure was all too evident. It rested on the fact that only a proportion of society owed its allegiance to the Church judged by confession and practice (see Chapter VI). If one added the following of other churches to that of the Established Church, the position was little improved. The alarm over the inability of the Church to deal with a new situation was voiced in particular by those who were concerned about its poor showing in working-class areas. Admittedly such a cry was to be found at various times throughout the century, but the position seemed to be more critical as the results of censuses of church attendances in the 1880s and following years demonstrated a falling away from the churches, not only amongst the working class, but just as alarmingly, amongst the middle class itself (see Chapter V). No evidence of this kind of alarm seems to have been aired at the two Church Congresses held in Newcastle, except a passing reference to the breaking up of Christian morality, mentioned in a session on the problems of the spiritual life exercised in a world of activity and busy-ness (Swaby (ed.) 1882:438). There can be little doubt, however, that the Diocese was fully conscious of the problem — hence its building programme, which was coupled with an increase in the number of clergy, especially curates and lay missionaries of various kinds (see Chapter X).

One notable response to the awareness of the weakened state of the Church in the area came in 1912, when the Church of England Men's Society in Newcastle organised with the full support of the Diocese what by today's standards would be a gigantic mission. It was specifically for men and was said to be the first of its kind in the country. It employed as missioners twenty clergy, specially selected from outside the Diocese, who together with local clergy gave numberless sermons and talks. Addresses and services were held in the churches of the city and its suburbs, on the quayside, in the barracks, the gaol, shops, a picture hall (cinema), and on a boat. They were also given outside the works gates and in tram car sheds at midnight. There was a torch procession which accompanied a packed service at the Cathedral to initiate the mission and 1,500 men were said to be at the concluding service just under a fortnight later, when the *Te Deum* was solemnly sung. For the city as a whole, and on one weekday, twenty-eight meetings were held. Incidentally it was reported that when the clergy visited the quayside on a Sunday morning, their appearance brought forth many remarks from auctioneers, who found their audiences dwindling away and for an hour the missioners performed their tasks. This great mission was extensively reported in the press (see local newspapers, especially the *North Mail*, for February 1912). Just before the venture was launched it was said that if the mission failed it would not have been due to a 'want of organisation or sincerity'. At the beginning the local clergy were asked why people, especially men, rejected the claims and precepts of the Church of England and failed to attend public worship.

Local information about the alleged reasons for the weakness of the Church, with the exception of this 1912 mission, has been difficult to discover. Because of such a dearth of information, we turn to a book, published a year before, which was perhaps read by clergy and laity alike in the Diocese and which dealt specifically and systematically with the issue of what was called the alienation of the masses from the Church. It was entitled *Non-Church-Going. Its Reasons and Remedies*, edited by W. Forbes Gray and was one of several books of its genre to be published during the period. It consisted of a series of essays, including a good number by laymen such as Sir Oliver Lodge, and the future Labour Prime Minister, J. Ramsay Macdonald. Despite a sense of alarm, it also betrayed an overall optimistic note, since it was written very much from a liberal standpoint with an emphasis on a humanistic gospel of love and concern for man, coupled with socialist or Labour interpolations, such as Christ 'the simple carpenter', 'the poor man', 'the first socialist'. The book portrayed an overriding hope on a number of other counts. For example, the social change of the past hundred years was seen as 'the evolution of mankind into the Kingdom of God', which was proceeding 'with extraordinary rapidity' (ibid:83). Further, England was a country which had Christian ideals and 'is, so far as legend is concerned, more attached to the

Christian faith than any other. Probably also it is the most Christian country in the world' (ibid:128). There were of course the frivolities of the day seen in the mad chase after pleasure and amusement. But one author at least felt that this attitude of the British would never triumph because

> In time the native good sense and solidity of the nation will recover itself; possibly under the sobering effect of some great national disaster (may God avert it); or mere weariness and satiety may drive home the lesson that life is no life which is destitute of a spiritual element (ibid:51).

Little did the writer suspect that the holocaust of the First World War was but three years away and its results hardly checked what he feared!

The contributors were non-establishment men — no bishops were amongst their company — and they tended to be marginally anti-clerical in outlook. Not surprisingly there was no representative of the High Church or Anglo-Catholic wings. There were some Scottish writers and when the liberal-humanist element gave way to another, it was an evangelical note which was sounded, as by one author whose basic premise was that a conviction of sin and a need of a Saviour was never out of date. Consensus indicated that the English populace was not indifferent or hostile to Christ and what He stood for. The difficulty was in the churches themselves and the atmosphere they created. Therefore it was to be concluded that the people had not lost their inner faith but their allegiance to the institution (ibid:62). Three-quarters of the adult population was estimated to be permanently out of touch with organized religion.

As many reasons were offered for non-church-going as there were contributors — indeed more so, because each writer proceeded to trot out a number of reasons for the masses keeping aloof from the churches. (This was also true of the opinions of clergy in the 1912 Newcastle mission.) Such a multiplicity of causes underlines a weakness, namely, that there is no overall conclusion about the cause or even the causes of the alienation. The book however is useful in the study of the problem, not least because of the remedies that were put forward to improve the situation, which in turn reflected the reasons for the alleged weaknesses of the churches. Part of the optimism that the book displayed was that the situation could be righted in favour of the churches by a relatively simple manipulation of one or several of the components of institutional religion.

In summary-form a selection of the remedies is presented below under grouped headings.

a. *Intellectual Issues*. The Church needed to refute the current ideas which were said to be undermining Christian doctrine, notably the writings which stemmed from such evolutionist thinkers as Huxley, Darwin and Haeckel. At a more popular level attacks against Christianity which came from the Rationalist Press had also to be defeated. (Not a great deal of attention, however, was given to these points in the book.)

b. *Social Issues*. These received considerable prominence, since the alienation of the working classes from the Church was of particular concern to the authors. Poverty and the fear of poverty were seen to be crucial.[1] It was held that to ensure the well-being of society there should be adequate work available for all but it should not be 'dulling toil'. One of the reasons for the condemnation of excessively hard work was that people did not have time and energy outside their working hours to attend church. The remedy seemed to appear in a general support for an improvement in social conditions to be brought about by political intervention, such as that proposed by the Labour Party. On the other hand, the working classes and upper classes were obsessed in their different ways by material betterment — either by relentlessly seeking it or being seduced by it once it had been secured. The answer here seemed to be that the clergy should study economic problems and indeed sociology, but they were not to preach these social sciences from the pulpit. Dr. T. Chalmers, the Scottish theologian and social reformer, was seen by many as the hero to be emulated. The Church itself was the real source of alienation since it appeared to the working classes to be allied to capitalism and the Church itself showed a patronising attitude towards the labouring classes. A caste system operated which proclaimed to the working classes that they were, in the eyes of the establishment, outside the fold. Democracy was the political doctrine that appealed to the working classes but it was absent in the Church. Therefore the remedy was that the Church must itself take up democratic principles. Some Newcastle clergy in 1912 took the opposite view: for them socialism and strikes had discouraged men from attending church.

c. *Ecclesiastical Issues*. Many of these were associated with social issues. There was considerable consensus that Anglican services as generally conducted were totally inadequate and failed to meet the values of the day. Solemn matins and ante-communion had no appeal, most certainly amongst the working classes. Prebendary Carlile, the founder of the Church Army, felt that a more edifying service should take place each Sunday, namely the Holy Communion, celebrated early in the morning with simple music and a short address. (Here there is an early indication of what was to become Parish Communion, so popular in the Diocese since World War II. See below.) Many of the contributors, not with Carlile's Anglican background, pleaded for freer, easier services of the mission type, in the hope of appealing to those who rejected the formal services of all denominations. What was so highly commended were the Pleasant Sunday Afternoons which were for men only and which were found in the Free churches, especially the Methodist Church. When the book was written the P.S.A.s were at their zenith. They consisted of 'bright' services, coupled with educational components and often bordering on entertainment. It was estimated that they then drew a quarter of a million men in Britain each Sunday. Needless to say it was held that they attracted those who never attended the normal church service. Another type of criticism, strong in its thrust, was directed against sermons. They were dull. They were boring. They relied too much on morals. They were intellectually sterile and failed to employ the findings of science and philosophy. Remedies often stood in opposition to one another. There was a need of a simple, biblical instruction on the one hand — so said some Newcastle clergy in 1912 — yet on the other sermons should use a well grounded theology. Who can win against such diverse criticism? At another practical level, there was a firm and universal call for the abolition of pew rents — a call that can be traced back to the middle of the nineteenth century.

It might be noted that in connection with the Newcastle mission, the causes of the weakness of the Church, in addition to those already mentioned, focussed on the growth of science, which it was said absorbed men's attentions and made them indifferent to life after death and God's judgement. Also, the newspapers encouraged great diversity of opinion and so diverted believers from the truth, for truth and opinion were given equal weight. As well, sacredotalism kept men from church. But above all, local people were seen to be given not so much to infidelity as to succumbing to the attractions of the motor car, weekend trips, Sunday dinner parties, summed up in the phrase 'pleasure, leisure and treasure' (see *N.D.C.* 1893:lxxxix ff.; also Pickering 1968).

The Response of the Church
As the evidence of the book just referred to suggests, the Church, or to be more specific the Anglican and Free churches, were very much aware of what might be called their failure to deal with the changing situation which emerged in the nineteenth century and their failure to exercise power and authority over the populace. Deeply conscious of

their responsibility, especially from the middle of the nineteenth century onwards, Anglican leaders launched campaigns to right the situation — money was raised, land was purchased, many churches were built and thousands were repaired and renovated. There were large-scale missions. Also, as we have had occasion to note, increasing numbers of men offered themselves for ordination and were prepared to work in what was for them socially impoverished situations. At the same time, the Church attempted to adjust itself internally, and here one might compare what actually happened with the suggested remedies in the book mentioned above. It is probably no exaggeration to say that public worship was made more ritually attractive, simpler services were often introduced, preaching greatly improved. Clubs and societies which were meant to attract and hold members of the working classes both within the Church and also on its periphery, mushroomed overnight. The clergy attempted to live alongside the people. Democratic ideals were slowly introduced into the Church of England and were legally implemented in the early 1920s. Pew rents quickly disappeared. And if one looks at the changes in society itself, then it is clear that the extremes of poverty experienced in the middle of the nineteenth century began to disappear around the time of World War I. Labour or socialist policies in the re-distribution of wealth were put into practice. In more recent decades, the Welfare State has gradually come into existence. In another direction, the Rationalist Press no longer creates the stir and antagonism it once did.

It is probably not an exaggeration to say that nearly everything that was advocated in the book *Non-Church-Going* has been tried and most of the social and ecclesiastical improvements hinted at have either been put into practice or else serious efforts have been made to introduce them. Yet, despite the devotion and energy of the clergy and the deep consciousness of the situation, all their valiant efforts have met with singularly unsuccessful results. Decline and alienation have proceeded unchecked. Their labours seem to have been in vain. The rise and fall of the Pleasant Sunday Afternoons provide a symbolic comment. Admittedly they were found in the Free churches and had no place in Anglicanism. At the turn of the century their following, as has been noted, was very considerable. Nearly every contributor to *Non-Church-Going* found in them hope for the future. But come the years that followed the First World War and the P.S.A.s were dead and buried (see Pickering 1968). And again in another field, probably one of the most disappointing results relates to the role of lay people and the greater involvement of the man in the pew in the life of the Church. This emphasis on the layman was also widely advocated in the book, and the Church of England has gradually given him a much greater place in public worship, in pastoral work, and church government, and so placed great responsibility on his shoulders. Despite such changes, the alienation of the masses from the Church has persisted unabated. The greater use of the layman has not produced the hoped-for results. And it is hardly necessary to add that in the matter of missions, they seldom if ever doubled, let alone trebled or quadrupled local congregations.

Our immediate attention has been focussed on the country at large, but it seems safe to conclude that with the likelihood of local variations, what has happened in the country as a whole has also occurred in the Diocese itself. Against indicators which have registered decline and which we have mentioned, the Church has responded, as we have also seen, by increasing the number of parishes to deal with the growing population (see Chapter VI), the number of clergy, especially curates, and the number of lay workers. All these efforts have entailed the raising of large sums of money. Pew rents died a natural death.[2] The Church has also attempted to provide facilities of many kinds within the Church — libraries, clubs, societies, of every shape and kind. And more specifically within the Diocese it should be noted that in the 1930s the Parish Communion movement, which advocated a celebration of the Eucharist as the chief service on a Sunday morning with simple music and a short sermon, held between the hours of 9 o'clock and 10 o'clock, started in the Diocese (see Chapter III). By the 1950s the movement had spread all over the country but perhaps nowhere has it gained greater following than in this Diocese, where almost every parish today, rural or urban, has Parish Commuion, and if it is not called by that name, it has a service which possesses most of the characteristics of it (see Jagger 1978).

One might also point to a particular institution in Newcastle which exemplifies the efforts of the Church locally to deal with a changing situation. The Newcastle upon Tyne Church of England Institute was founded in 1853 and incorporated in 1893. Its membership was open only to Anglicans and the purpose of the Institute was categorically to strengthen the life of the Church in the area. During its history it has had a newspaper room, a gymnasium, a games room, a billiard room, and a café. It boasted of football and cricket teams. Lectures were organized covering all kinds of subjects, scientific, historical, theological. It offered prizes for essays submitted in competitions. In its heyday in the mid-1890s, its membership was as great as 1,500; and despite fluctuations that followed, it was still in the 1000 mark in the mid-1920s. The latter date is significant in the light of the then current unemployment. Today the Institute still exists but in very much reduced circumstances with a membership of around 200, and since 1972 it has been available not just to Anglicans but 'to all practising Christians'. Here was a more sober — should one say middle class? — answer to the problem which called forth the Nonconformist P.S.A.s, not organized at a parish level but for the Diocese as a whole. The Institute's rise and fall have similarities with those of the P.S.A.s. The expenditure of a great amount of effort in terms of time and money in order to strengthen the allegiance of those, either within or on the borders of the Church, by offering educational and social facilities, has parallels in both the Institute and the P.S.A.s.

Of course it is impossible to prove that the introduction of ecclesiastical reforms, of institutes, of liturgical changes, of more 'relevant' sermons, of democratisation, of a sense of community within the Church has had no lasting effect on the life of the institution. Clearly these movements and reforms have. But the argument put forward is this. The efforts which made such great demands upon their organisers and defenders have not turned the ebb tide of alienation and decline. The hopes of their architects have never been fulfilled. The remedies were put into action but the decline has persisted. One cannot say what the position of the Church would be today if the reforms and changes and movements had not been introduced. It could well be, though conclusive proof is impossible, that if such movements had not materialized the position of the Church would be considerably worse today than in fact it is. Conversely, conservative minded people, recording more recent changes, as for example the introduction of Series II and III of the Anglican liturgy, might wish to argue that some of the reforms have weakened rather than strengthened the Church. Once again, proof is out of the question. We reiterate our position: the decline of the institutional Church has proceeded unchecked, and perhaps has recently accelerated, despite the enormous efforts and thought and man-power and money which have been thrown into the 'battle' by church leaders.

The Argument Pressed Further

With the advantage of hindsight, we can look back to the remedies which were intended to overcome the alienation of people from the churches and be amazed at the naivety and multiplicity of the suggestions. We have the advantage of knowing the state of the Church now and seeing more objectively the enthusiasm and devotion of church leaders at that time, their analysis of the situation, as well as the extraordinary optimism, even of the pessimists! The editor of *Non-*

Church-Going was probably nearer the truth than he realized when he wrote of the Church in 1911: 'It is no more fit to do the work that is expected of it than the Spanish Armada would have been to cope with a modern fleet' (Gray (ed.) 1911:38). Could people seriously think that a more direct form of preaching, the introduction of a beautiful liturgy, informality in services, a greater use of the laity, the clergy trained in economics and sociology, Christian socialism, or any single item or simple combination of them would do the trick? Quite obviously people at the turn of the century did and they were keen to try everything. Perhaps this spirit is still to be found in the Church today.

Some might wish to argue that in introducing reforms over the past century, it was not the avowed intention of church leaders merely to counteract indifference, or even hostility to religion. The reforms and changes were and still are brought into being, not for the utilitarian reason of stemming the tide of decline but are introduced for their own sake as attempts to improve the life and witness of the Church. For example, the abortive revision of the Prayer Book in 1928, or the later legally established Series II Communion service, introduced in the 1960s, were not meant to be instruments to bring back the masses but to give the Church what was thought to be a better liturgy based on internal criteria. The same kind of argument about church government could also be said to be behind the introduction of parochial church councils in 1921. Many reforms were aimed just at improving the quality of life in the Church, without any regard to their effect on outsiders, positively or negatively. Yet it cannot be denied that the hope of most reformers *in the long run* was and is that changes will help to bring about a greater loyalty to the Church expressed by higher attendance at worship. Behind reforms and most ecclesiastical movements is the fact that the Church is a body deeply aware of its *raison d'être*, which is to bring all men to a knowledge and experience of Jesus Christ, lived out in some form of community. Thus the Church is for all men, at all times, in all places. Such is its claim to universality. Conscious of its mission, therefore, the Church must always hold up before itself the implementation of its basic aims. Institutional reforms cannot be for self-glorification but for the fulfilment of its universality. This striving should be, and in all probability is deeply entrenched in the conscious and unconscious thinking of church leaders and indeed many lay people. The writers of *Non-Church-Going* had no hesitation in openly expressing the object of their suggested reforms, which was to redress the alienation of the majority of people from the Church.

Yet, as we have suggested, all the reforms, the movements, the devotion to duty, the raising of money, the heroism of priests, the expenditure of sheer physical energy, all these and much more seem to have been a failure. Certainly the ends anticipated by reformers, by priests, by enthusiastic lay leaders, have not been acheived. Alienation has proceeded — perhaps halted now and then — but none the less has proceeded.

If the argument be accepted thus far, then certain questions of both a sociological and theological nature arise. We set out some of them below.

> Is it the case that the institutional Church over the past decades has been caught in a social situation over which it has exerted little or no control and therefore its efforts at reform and internal change have had no effect? Put another way, this means that whilst it might have tried to do some fine tuning from within, the forces of society have been and are of such a kind that continuous alienation is the inevitable outcome? And, is it not that the social forces operating in western society are such that the Christian churches are going to be pushed more and more to the periphery of life so that they will very shortly become marginal institutions to a greater extent than they are at present?

> Again, is it that the Church has never really understood the social forces of society in which it finds itself both in times of growth and decline?

> The apparent failure of the churches to overcome the alienation of the masses raises an acute issue for the theologian. How can he square such historical facts with the hope of realizable universality for the Gospel and the Church? Surely for the present moment and for years to come, such universality cannot be taken seriously?

> Does the theologian have anything to offer by way of consolation to those who devote themselves to the institutional Church but whose efforts seem to produce so little good in the face of continuing alienation?

It is hoped that these questions and others like them will give rise to thought and discussion, for there is no attempt here to answer them. However, the first one does prompt some exploration, especially as sociologists have contributed to it, and we conclude by presenting their arguments in a simplified form.

The Dilemma: The Church a Voluntary Society
Sociologists point to the fact that the Church has for the past century

existed in a social milieu that is markedly different from that in which it found itself from say the time of the Middle Ages up until perhaps the eighteenth century. The change is highlighted in the fact that the Church is now a completely voluntary society. At one time there were 'external pressures' to make people conform in matters of belief and practice, such as community ostracism, economic deprivation, legal sanctions, or even persecution. These have now completely disappeared in Europe. And even an 'internal pressure' like the fear of suffering in hell in life after death has all but entirely gone, due to changes in theology and in human values, which themselves have been reflected in theology. With the demise of these obvious components of force and fear, man now stands completely free *vis-à-vis* religion. He acts as a rational being, who knows the consequences of various alternative courses of action that he may take, and chooses those most profitable or pleasurable to himself or to people. He calculates which course of action, or which combination of actions, gives him the most satisfaction in the light of his basic needs or desires. He therefore weighs up costs and sets them against benefits. The costs can be expressed in terms of time, money, or the dissipation of energy, necessary for the achievement of any course of action. Benefits come with some sense of inner satisfaction — physical pleasure, increase in wealth, possessions or status for oneself or for the family. This model of decision-making does not necessarily mean that in any one given case the answer is simple. Far from it, the way in which a man comes to a decision is often very complex and he may not fully understand the process or the nature of the actions on which he embarks. The point is that he does make a fairly free choice between one course of action and another which are seen to be alternatives. When one examines the institutional Church today, it is necessary to place it against such a background. The man in the street will in all probability calculate for himself the gains and advantages over and against the costs in being a member of a church and in regularly practising religious precepts. Certainly the gains are no longer seen in avoiding negative sanctions, such as those imposed in the past. Advantages are therefore to be gauged in terms of pleasure and psychological or spiritual satisfaction, which are set over against the costs of time, energy, money, and perhaps boredom! One contributor to *Non-Church-Going* applies this kind of thinking to a particular example.

> Take the case of a working man. The strain of his labour is removed at the end of the week. He is free, or at least his chains are relaxed. To that man in his leisure

143

has come a choice. On the one side of the street is the club, on the other side of the street is the chapel. The chapel presents the higher call, and the loftier effort. But the man is so worn out that he has not the energy to pursue any line save the line of least resistance. Let us put it another way. Suppose he does work reasonable hours. He finds that the club affords him a chance of conversation and brotherly intercourse. At the club he can speak his mind; at the church he must sit silent, without the slightest opportunity for self-expression. He chooses the club (Gray (ed.) 1911:208).

With changes in detail the case can also be said to apply as much to a member of the middle class today as to someone in the working class, and indeed to a member of any class. The point is that the Church now has to enter the market for people's allegiance, and is forced to set up a stall alongside other stalls from which people can freely choose to buy or reject what is offered (see Berger 1967). Further, the stalls are numerous. Religion no longer has the privilege of being the manager of the market, of standing over and above the vendors. It has had to become one of the vendors, competing on equal terms for man's allegiance.

And who are the many rivals in the market? They are leisure-time pursuits which have become in recent times so many and varied (see Pickering 1968). Man makes his rational calculations in the face of costs and benefits relating to sport, gardening, T.V. watching, Do It Yourself mania, extended travel, membership of a political party, and so on. These possibilities are embraced on a voluntary basis, they are legal, pleasure-giving, although all of them call for costs of various kinds. The Church has to join them in vying for man's patronage and therefore has to demonstrate to him the benefits he will derive from religious activity which outweigh the costs. The trouble is that the Church is really not quite sure what the benefits are it wants to advertise and if it makes too much of the benefits, particularly if they are related to this life, then it will be seen to be little more than an avowed leisure-time pursuit (ibid). In this way it finds itself caught in a trap. It is forced to declare itself to be one amongst other leisure-time pursuits, yet if it shouts that chorus too loudly, it will be totally untrue to itself for it will be denying the essential message of the Gospel it proclaims. Pleasant Sunday Afternoons went about quietly killing themselves just because they attempted to be obviously restrained, leisure-time pursuits within the orbit of the Free churches. Seeing that the P.S.A.s were vehicles of entertainment and education, the members found they could get better services elsewhere and so turned to secular lectures, the gramophone, the cinema, cycling, a day out on the railways, and so on.

The Church still faces the same dilemma as a consequence of it being in a market situation. If it plays the market game it may well gain some success and be able to counteract the forces of indifference and alienation. If it disregards the market, however, it may remain true to what it sees as its Gospel, its mission, its essence, but then it seems destined to be weakened yet further.

Yet, having said all that, is it not the case that the local churches — the local congregations — where over a length of time the Gospel is clearly preached and the sacraments faithfully administered, do more for the dissemination of Christianity in society than the policies and speeches of its higher leaders — the diocesan bishops and the spokesmen of national fame?

NOTES
1. It was often alleged, and with good justification, that the working classes were prevented from regular church-going by not having good enough clothing. They were ashamed to come in their working clothes. Owen Chadwick in his recent Gifford Lectures, referred to the vicar of All Saints, Newcastle, which is an oval church famous for its architecture, situated in the centre of the city on the bank of the Tyne (see Ch.XI). In 1882 — and the date is to be noted — the vicar had a considerable success. 'He persuaded the parish to come "as they were", and all the women came with their heads in shawls. Five years later all the same women were wearing bonnets in church. The churchwarden said "they can afford bonnets now, but they are the same heads" ' (1975:101).
2. As a point of interest about the charges of pew rents, it might be noted that in St. Paul's, Elswick — formerly a middle class parish, now a blighted area — the cost was 8/– or 10/– per seat per annum in the 1870s. Rents brought in £150 per annum which was used as part of the vicar's stipend. In 1905 a quarter of his stipend was raised in this way. The rents were stopped around the time of World War II (Henderson 1978:111, 127, 156).

Chapter VIII

PRIEST AND PATRON IN A NORTHUMBERLAND PARISH

Robin Gill

THE HISTORY of the Diocese of Newcastle can in part, as previous chapters have shown, be depicted as the history of a church in decline. By 1882 the Victorian 'religious boom' in England had begun to lose momentum: by the end of the First World War membership of the Church of England had gone into serious decline: and throughout this century its membership has continued to decline, sometimes very rapidly. It is still very much an open question whether it will continue declining in the next one hundred years or whether it will increase again as it has done in other countries and in other centuries in this country.

In this chapter I intend to study a rather unusual attempt to halt this decline in a rural parish in north Northumberland. My excuse for focussing on this parish rather than on any number of other similar Northumbrian parishes is only in part because its patron was an unusual person in the short history of the Diocese. Mainly it is simply because the detailed study of any single parish is able to reveal things which a more diffuse study of parishes in general might overlook. Besides there are features of Ford parish which might well apply to other rural Northumbrian parishes.

Accordingly, I will examine and then attempt to evaluate three specific ways in which a Victorian patron attempted to change the social context of her parishioners, all with the general aim of encouraging them to become members of the Church. The period under review involves the time both immediately before and immediately after the creation of the new Diocese.

Lady Waterford

Louisa, Marchioness of Waterford, first came to live at Ford on the death of her husband Henry, the third Marquis, in 1859. Married in

1842, she had no children and was forty-one when she came to this isolated country parish, 12 miles from Berwick-upon-Tweed and all but touching the Scottish Border.

She was the second daughter of Lord Stuart de Rothesay, an Ambassador at Paris and St. Petersburg, and sister of Charlotte, wife of Viscount Canning, the first Viceroy of India. She spent her early life in Paris and then as a teenager at Highcliffe, a magnificent mansion built by her father at great expense and shipped in part over from Normandy, facing the Isle of Wight. She spent the sixteen years of her married life on her husband's estate at Curraghmore in Ireland, making only occasional visits to his other property, Ford castle. Undoubtedly she liked the place immensely. On her first visit she wrote: 'I must tell you how *delighted* I am with this place', but she added; 'but pray do not think that I shall ever like it better than Curraghmore' (Hare 1893, 1:234).

Lord Waterford clearly preferred his native Curraghmore too. He was a keen huntsman, with a reputation for being somewhat wild. Indeed, he died from a hunting accident, leaving Curraghmore to his brother who succeeded him and leaving Ford to his wife for her life-time, with its annual income of £10,000 (it reverted to the Waterfords on her death). With the death of her sister, without children, and then her mother in 1867, she became the outright owner of Highcliffe, and from that moment divided her time between the two places, spending the summer at the latter and the winter, somewhat curiously, at Ford. She finally died and was buried at Ford in 1891. Torn between the two places, she eventually conceded in 1881: 'I think there is nothing nicer than Highcliffe. I like it, alas! better than Ford' (Hare 1893, 3:413).

When she arrived at Ford in 1859 Thomas Knight had already been rector for 40 years. He was given the living in 1819 when he was only twenty-five. His predecessor, the unfortunate John James, had to agree on his appointment in 1811 to resign the living on the request of the then patron, Lady Delaval, if either Thomas or his brother John Knight required it. Knight remained as rector of Ford until his death in 1872, having held the living for 53 years.

The fact that he was himself related to the Delavals through his mother, and thus to the Waterfords themselves, did not prevent him from carrying out and winning a very protracted legal action against his patron. What came later to be celebrated as the Ford Tithe Case ended in 1841 after 11 years with Thomas Knight being eventually awarded £10,000 from the third Marquis of Waterford. The latter seldom visited Ford before his marriage to Louisa in the following year, but the settlement could hardly have helped his relations with the rector. Louisa herself never refers to it in any of her known writings.

The judgement of 1841 was really the culmination of a succession of legal actions between priest and patron in the parish — almost all of them to do with payment and tithes. Indeed, Vickers writes that 'the ecclesiastical history of Ford centres round the relations of the incumbents and the patrons, relations which from time to time were far from cordial, due to disputes about the emoluments and rights of the Rector' (1922:350). Of the instances he cites, the pluralist Robert Heron brought three separate suits against his patron Gilbert Heron in 1291, Robert Rotheram sued his patron Thomas Carr in the early seventeenth century, Alexander Davison sued the Blakes in 1678, and in 1760 George Marsh began legal action against his patron. Thomas Knight's successful verdict in the court of exchequer in 1841 and again at the Northumberland assizes in 1846 and the eventual out-of-court settlement of 1847 (made just before the Marquis of Waterford's appeal was called in the House of Lords), can thus be seen as the culmination of a series of acrimonious relations between priest and patron in the parish over a number of centuries. Indeed, writing in 1725, a Mr. Drake of Norham stated that 'this living has been so unfortunate as to have from time to time for incumbents men of so much condescension and for patrons men of such power and injustice, as that the church cannot come at her right without the ruin of her minister ... if justice were done this living, it would be the most eligible in the northern part of the diocese (Durham), both in respect of its value and the smallness of the cure' (Vickers 1922:356). Thanks to the 1847 settlement and the considerable de-population of the parish throughout the century folowing it, that is precisely what the living became. By any standards, by the time Lady Waterford came to live at Ford it was a rich and comfortable living — and remained so until fairly recently.

Re-organising the Parish

Lady Waterford seldom mentioned Thomas Knight in her letters. In itself this may be an indication of her intention to re-organise the parish, whilst ignoring the old and long-established rector. On the few occasions that she does refer to him she expresses anxiety about what she regarded as his Tractarian position. Only three months after her husband's death she wrote, very significantly: 'At Ford I shall be within a hundred yards of the church, and the very highest of High Church doctrines. I know our Rector will expect to find me a zealous advocate on his side, but I shall consider it right to tell him what a change has come over my opinions of late, that I may not appear under false colours to him. Whatever is my future, I can only pray it may always be firmly built on the only true foundation, and strengthened by the assistance of the Holy Spirit and the teaching of the Word of God' (Hare 1893,3:43). Like quite a number of aristocrats at this time she had evidently come under the strong influence of the evangelical movement (see further, Bradley 1976:34ff.). Again, writing to a Canon Parker in the same year, she suggested, even more critically, that 'the people here ... are more Presbyterians than members of the Church of England, and the ultra-Tractarian views of the clergy have, I think, driven a good many over to that side' (Hare 1893,3:43).

It is difficult to establish now just how 'ultra-Tractarian' Thomas Knight really was. Certainly Lady Augusta Fitz-Clarence, the widow of one of the sons of William IV and Mrs. Jordan, was inclined towards the high church. On the death of her husband and daughter she built an Anglican chapel within a parish at Etal, with the dedication of the long-vanished Etal Chantry, St. Mary the Virgin. Knight's successor, himself much nearer to Lady Waterford's evangelical position, wrote that 'Lady Augusta had so great a love for the Church of England, which to her was a true branch of the Catholic Church, and so reverent a belief in the Apostolic succession of the Ministry, that her treatment of the clergy was kind even to indulgence' (Neville 1897:322). There can be little doubt, then, that she was high church herself. However, the fact that Thomas Knight's son, Delaval, was appointed by her as the first chaplain at Etal church might also indicate that the Knights did indeed share some of her Tractarian views. More importantly, the fact that Etal church was completed in the very year in which Lady Waterford first came to live at Ford might well have served to confirm her suspicions of the Knights. When this is coupled with the fact of the long legal battles between Thomas Knight and her husband, it would have been surprising had she not found her relationship with him difficult.

It is, I believe, in this context that one must understand Lady Waterford's attempt to re-organise the parish. She did so in three specific, though inter-related, ways.

Her first method was the most typically Victorian. She altered the social context of her parishioners by a radical programme of re-building. At Ford, the castle and the church sit near the top of a hill over-looking the Milfield Plain and beyond it the Cheviots. The old village stretched down the west side of this hill towards the Till and Ford Bridge. Within a few years Lady Waterford had made fairly

149

extensive alterations to the castle, almost entirely re-built the church and had moved the village completely to the east side of the hill, leaving only the rectory on the west side. Once Thomas Knight died she demolished that too, leaving only the ruined remains of the old Pele Tower and housing the new rector, Hastings Neville, and his family in the enormous building that is now the school. Once this was completed in 1877 she reported that 'I think the happiest people here now are the Nevilles. They are quite delighted with their new house' (Hare 1893,3:376).

Like her father this extensive re-building caused her financial problems. Highcliffe, with its imported stones and perpetually crumbling cliff which needed shoring up, had very nearly ruined him. She was for a while forced to take out a mortgage on it to pay for Ford. Unlike him, though, more of her energies seem to have gone into 'improving' the village than in re-building her own home.

In all three places that she lived as an adult, Highcliffe, Ford and Curraghmore, she spent a good deal of time and money on the churches. At Ford, mid-nineteenth century paintings show the church to have been in a poor state of repair. Like many other Victorian patrons she decided that it should be radically re-built — preserving only a few of its thirteenth century features. Accordingly she employed the locally famous architect John Dobson to carry out the task and provide an extra aisle to accommodate the community of miners up on Ford Moss. There is no evidence in fact to show that it was ever needed. A good indication of her priorities is that this re-building of the church took place at the very start of her programme.

Another indication that her overall re-building plan was part and parcel of her evangelical mission is provided by her attempt to exlude public houses. As she grew older she became increasingly committed to the Temperance Movement (see Chapter XV). By 1885 she had monthly temperance meetings in both Ford and Highcliffe. At Ford she specifically excluded a pub, so that one was built to serve local needs just 200 yards into Lowick parish. At Highcliffe she even introduced a milk-bar, though it was apparently not supported much by the parishioners there. Again, at an afternoon service at Etal church which she attended with Lady Fitz-Clarence, Neville reports that a rather daring chaplain ticked her off in his sermon for 'the dreadful condition of the cottages, and the sin of their owners for not repairing them' (Neville 1897:325). As a result, according to Neville, from this time she 'gave increased attention to the farm hamlets on her estate, and left some of them models of what labourers dwellings ought to be' (ibid). If this story is to be trusted it does indicate again the importance of the Church to her role as a landowner.

The second way in which she sought to change the social context of her parishioners was somewhat more unusual. Like other evangelical landowners she took her role as ecclesiastical patron very seriously. When Knight died in 1872 she went to considerable trouble to find a new rector for this now desirable living. The man she eventually chose, Hastings Neville, provided a long account of his first interview with her. In characteristically eulogistic terms he later wrote that 'well did I know how the spiritual good of her people was uppermost in her mind, and the immense responsibility she felt it to have to select a clergyman to fill the vacant rectory at Ford, and I can never think without the greatest respect of her conscientious character, of the searching enquiries she made of the nature of my views in the summer-house by the sea at Highcliffe' (1897:139). He preached a sermon in the morning and evening at Highcliffe and between them the interview took place. She apparently told him that the morning sermon was 'a purely moral discourse' and then proceeded to ask him his views on the F. D. Maurice theological controversy, expressing the view that 'if the idea of the *endlessness* of (eternal) punishment were given up, the religious system which appeared so much based upon it, would suffer harm' (ibid:140). Fortunately for him he gave the correct reply to this question and preached a more acceptable sermon in the evening. With commendable honesty he commented later that 'it was some relief to be told that it had more of the Gospel than the sermon I had preached in the morning, and this was quite true, but I fear it was accidental' (ibid).

However, it was not really in her earnestness as a patron, or even in her knowledge of contemporary theological debates, that she was unusual. Rather, one of the distinctive things about her was that she attempted to be a patron *and* took on what might be seen as some of the work of a minister. Clearly she had decided theological views, which in the case of Knight may have caused friction, but in the case of Neville led her to prefer him over others — perhaps less because of his strong evangelical convictions (which are certainly not apparent in his books) than because of his willingness to blend his to hers. More specifically, though, she carried out an actual pastoral role in the parish. Her temperance work has already been mentioned. In addition, for may years she taught in the Sunday school and took classes for older girls in the castle on a Sunday afternoon. Like other Victorian ladies she held weekly meetings on an afternoon for the women of the parish and in 1885 organised revival-meetings in the schoolroom. In the 1870s she raised money for a new church at Duddo and again in 1885 she helped to establish a mission at Seaton Sluice. Her priestly activities even extended to taking services. Like other Victorians she read from the Bible at the daily services for the servants at the castle, but in addition she went around the parish reading the Bible and singing hymns to the old and infirm in the parish. Neville wrote:

> In her society you were always impressed with the idea that she was filled with a sense of the importance of life and opportunity, and the value of time. She had work to do which she felt to be a joy and an honour. She realized the true nobility of spending herself for the good of others, and took this for her mission. To visit sick and the poor was not with her a mere pastime; she rejoiced in it, but at the same time she made a real business of it, and did it as a duty of the first and most pressing importance. Everything else had to give place to this; it mattered not what visitors were in her house, she must make her usual round of visits to her humble friends (1897:100).

Even allowing for Neville's devotion to her, it is clear that she took this pastoral role very seriously. Possibly she began it because she felt that the 'ultra-Tractarian' clergy were out-of-touch with the parishioners when she first arrived. But by Neville's time it had become an established part of her role in Ford. Certainly some of this had carried over into her life at Highcliffe as well. On the evening when Neville preached his 'better' sermon there in 1872 she sang the anthem at the service.

The third and by far the most novel means by which she sought to evangelise her parishioners at Ford was through her art. She is remembered today in the North-East chiefly because of her talent as an artist, albeit as an artist of mainly religious themes. This I believe to be a mistaken understanding of her life and work. If my interpretation is correct she should be remembered instead as an evangelist, albeit as one with real artistic talent, but who used this talent primarily to further her work of evangelism.

Certainly she took her art seriously and this may have encouraged the idea that she was primarily an artist. In 1860 she went to Italy for six months with her mother, collecting things for Ford and studying Italian art. Both she and her sister were keen artists and she early expressed an interest in the Pre-Raphaelites. In 1842 she wrote: 'I hope to be in London in June, and have especial curiosity to see what the Pre-Raphaelites have done this year, whether they are beginning to allow themselves a little beauty in moderate quantities. I respect them for abstaining from the *pretty*, and am sure theirs is the only school which will come at real beauty at last, so we must be content to let them pass through all their phases of ugliness first' (Hare 1893,1:247-8). She corresponded with both Rossetti and Holman Hunt. In reply to a letter from Neville the latter wrote that 'it is a pleasure to me to assure you of my great admiration of the late Louisa Marchioness of Waterford's art' — although he then went on to make a number of criticisms of it (Neville 1897:81). However her main correspondence as it survives today is with Ruskin. In 1863 she described him as 'the reverse of the man I like, and yet his intellectual part is quite my ideal' (Hare 1893,3:240). His criticisms of her work were extraordinarily meticulous. So in 1858 he wrote:

> You had several bad habits to cure yourself of — leaving the colour in blotches with sharp edges for instance . . . but two years work will do it, and then you will be able really to paint — and that is what very few people in the world can do (Surtees 1972:26).

However, the essentially religious purpose of her art is never too far away in her correspondence. In 1851, in reply to criticism that she was spending too long on her art, she replied:

> The love of art must not be treated as a sin. All that is great and beautiful comes from God, and to God it should return. It is the misuse of great gifts which is the sin, not the gifts themselves . . . Oh never say the best parts of humanity are not gifts of God. *That* is wrong. If used for badness they may be turned to sin, but that would be by man's free-will; the gifts, in their goodness and purity, are God's (Hare 1893,1:347).

In 1875 she rejected the idea that she should be included in a volume on 'Lady Artists', claiming that she was just an amateur and in 1879, having just been to an exhibition in London, she wrote that 'these exhibitions are the best levellers I know; one has no more illusions about oneself, and no flatterers are of avail. I see myself just an amateur and no more — not altogether bad, but not good — no, not good at all; and it is the same with all amateurs — *there* is the difference' (Hare 1893,3:91-2). Her correspondence with Ruskin had finished in the early 1870s and whatever pretensions about her being an artist *qua* artist she might once have had, had by now certainly gone. Instead, she saw her art as a means of communicating the Gospel to those around her.

This is most evident in the 'frescoes' she painted for her new school in the middle of the re-built Ford village. For nearly twenty-two years she painted Biblical scenes in water-colour on paper which was laid on canvas and then stretched on frames to cover entirely the upper parts of the walls of the school-room. Since the room measures 63 feet x 20 feet this was no small undertaking. The long sides contain a series of panels depicting mainly Old Testament scenes, whereas the shorter west and east walls show first Christ blessing the little children and second the boy Jesus in the midst of the Doctors of the Law. In the middle of the long south wall is a striking picture of the child Jesus. Without doubt this was the most ambitious artistic enterprise that she ever attempted and still receives many visitors today.

Ruskin saw some of the early panels in 1864 and was most uncomplimentary. At the time she wrote that 'he condemned (very justly) my frescoes, and has certainly spirited me up to do better' (ibid:254). By 1875 much more was completed, but by now she could write (admittedly as part of her attempt not to be included in the book on artists) that, 'the work of the school has no art in it, and is even done in the commonest water-colours' (ibid:362). Even allowing for inevitable modesty here, her claim may in fact be correct. Ruskin had disliked the art in the school, but more significantly he was perhaps much more out of sympathy with the object of the art. She had deliberately chosen to carry out this work as part of the religious education of the Ford children. Whilst she undoubtedly took his criticisms seriously they did not deflect her from *this* task.

In this respect Hastings Neville's account of the 'frescoes' seems to be accurate. Elsewhere he is keen to stress their artistic merit (hence his letters to Holman Hunt and others soliciting their views). Significantly, though, he prefaces his description of the 'frescoes' with these words:

> The idea of this wonderful wall decoration is, of course, the instruction of the children and the elevation and refinement of their minds, and above all to produce a feeling of reverence and mindfulness of duty, by surrounding them with scenes of childhood taken from the Bible, showing them that the children of the Old and New Testament of whom they read in words, were real children like themselves — and that Christ himself, who sits enthroned to bless the little ones, was once a little one like those He blesses (Neville 1897:44-5).

This I believe to be an entirely correct interpretation of her work. Further, it is re-inforced by the fact that she used local people as her models for the pictures. The figure of Christ blessing the children was that of the curate, the figure of one of the Doctors was the schoolmaster's and that of the child Jesus was that of a miner's child. It is particularly significant that she chose the last to depict the central figure in the whole series of frescoes. The church had been deliberately extended to accommodate the mining community at Ford Moss. Although mining has been there since medieval times, a great flood occurred in 1777 which had put the mines out of action for some 30 years. By the time she came to Ford, however, the mines at Ford Moss (only about a mile from Ford village) were fully operational, and remained so until the opening of the Alnwick-Cornhill railway in 1887 brought better coal from the south. The religious needs of these miners were one of her main concerns. By depicting the child of one of them as the child Jesus she appears to have been attempting to encourage them to take the Gospel seriously.

An Assessment
So far, I have suggested three ways in which Lady Waterford sought to alter the social context of her parishioners. Each of these can be identified as methods in religious socialisation, since each was designed to recruit and maintain the parishioners as members of the Church. Each is related in varying degrees to her position as patron and landowner of Ford. The first method depicted, that of creating Ford as a model village, with a re-built church and school and no pub, was clearly only possible because she was both patron and landowner. The second method, choosing a theologically acceptable priest and herself taking on some of the functions of a minister, was again in part only possible because she was the patron. The third method, that of evangelising through art, was perhaps less dependent on her position in the parish than the other methods, but it too was given considerable scope by the fact that she was free to adorn the school that she had built. In so far as all of this is true, the particular pattern of religious socialisation belongs more to previous centuries than to the present one. Nonetheless something can still be learned from it.

The question I have yet to face is how far the combination of these three approaches inspired by such an unusual woman were effective. That is to say, did she really succeed in recruiting new members into Ford church or in retaining existing members? In the light of the study by Currie and others (1977) this question has taken on fresh significance today, since they maintain that church membership patterns show a greater response to external, social factors than to specifically internal, religious ones. Thus, political, economic and social factors are for them more significant in determining levels of church membership than internal attempts at evangelism or church policy-making.

It is, of course, notoriously difficult to establish the effectiveness of something so elusive as a particular pattern of religious socialisation.

Inevitably one has to rely upon external clues, since there can be no really hard evidence available about whether or not individuals' religious orientation was actually changed through Lady Waterford's efforts. It is difficult, if not actually impossible to establish this in a contemporary situation, let alone an historical one (see Gill 1975:89ff.). Even a seemingly straightforward category such as 'church membership' presents the researcher with problems. There were after all two Presbyterian churches in the parish at the time and it is conceivable that individuals may have become, or been retained as, members of them as a result of her evangelism. Again, it is really not possible to establish accurate statistics on membership in the Church of England at this time. There were records of baptisms, confirmations and communicants, but not of attendances at matins and evensong and as yet there were no electoral rolls. Inevitably this leaves gaps.

Nevertheless, the external clues that do survive do not encourage the view that her methods of evangelism were particularly effective. In a telling letter she wrote to a friend in 1883 of a revival meeting she was planning:

> I feel a little anxious about how it is all to go off. The children of the school have learnt a number of Sankey hymns to help others. I hear of crowds coming. I wish and hope it may be a sort of revival in the place, for there are many who are careless, and never care to go to church — men who stay at home all Sunday (Hare 1893,3:423).

By now she was no longer blaming the 'ultra-Tractarian' rector, since it was the man of her choosing who had been rector for eleven years. Nor was she suggesting that people were going to the Presbyterian churches instead. Indeed, Neville recorded that she would go about the parish urging people to go to church and, 'when in her pew she would cast many an anxious look around her to see who had come according to her advice' (1897:127).

Further, the statistics that can be gathered from the Ford church records (see Tables 1-3) do not seem to indicate that her methods were very effective. Hastings Neville's arrival in the parish in 1872 is actually marked by a drop in the proportion of babies brought for baptism at Ford compared with the total population (the population of the parish rose from 1807, in 1821, to 2322, in 1851, and fell to 1584, in 1881: by 1971 it was only 662). More importantly, the miners of Ford Moss, about whom Lady Waterford worried so much, brought their babies for baptism significantly more in the pre-

Waterford/Knight years than in the Waterford/Hastings years. The great decline at Ford Moss of the mines was not until 1887. Interestingly the current level of baptisms at Ford is very comparable to that in Neville's times.

Illegitimacy appears to have been a feature of the parish (and perhaps the whole area) throughout the period studied. Indeed, it can be seen that it still is a feature today (though this figure should be seen in relation to the national average for 1971 of 8 per cent of live births being illegitimate). It seemed to fluctuate independently of Lady Waterford's evangelism.

Again, the communicant figures that are available do not seem to readily indicate any clear pattern of religious socialisation. They refer, of course, only to Neville's ministry as there are no extant statistics for that of Knight. Although there is a slight rise in the average Easter communicant figures between the two nineteenth century decades studied, they compare very unfavourably with the most recent twentieth century decade (Christmas statistics would compare even less favourably, but this is confused by the recent introduction of Midnight Communion).

Indeed, if the time of Neville's ministry is compared with the parish today, it is only in the figures for confirmation that the former represents a greater proportion of the population. So, between 1883 and 1892 there were 135 confirmees (about 10 per cent total population), whereas between 1969 and 1978 there were only 38 (about 5 per cent total population — though it should be stressed that this comparison is very crude since it is unrelated to age differences between the two populations).

It should be emphasised that these are only external clues. They may or may not give an accurate impression of the involvement of the Ford parishioners in their church. Of themselves, though, they do not support the suggestion that Lady Waterford's evangelical methods were particularly effective. Indeed, it would seem that here at least the evangelical movement may not have had a discernible effect upon the rural working-class (see Bradley 1976), despite all the efforts of this and other evangelical patrons. It remains to be demonstrated whether other methods would have been more successful.

Table 1

BAPTISMS AT FORD CHURCH, NORTHUMBERLAND, 1842-91

Date	Overall Number	approx % population	Ford Moss Baptisms (% decade total)	Illegitimate Baptisms (% decade total)
1842-51	237	10%	96 (41%)	10 (4%)
1852-61	215	9%	67 (31%)	25 (12%)
1862-71	193	10%	36 (19%)	18 (9%)
1872-81	109	7%	7 (6%)	4 (4%)
1882-91	93	7%	5 (5%)	7 (8%)
1968-77	45	7%	–	3 (7%)

Table 2

COMMUNICANTS AT FORD CHURCH, NORTHUMBERLAND, 1873-91

Date	Easter Communicants	Christmas Communicants
1873	66	31
1874	48	23
1875	37	18
1876	49	–
1877	37	18
1878	66	18
1879	42	26
1880	57	32
1881	58	44
1882	76	29
1883	55	26
1884	63	32
1885	60	28
1886	53	22
1887	80	35
1888	54	–
1889	64	30
1890	65	23
1891	44	18

Table 3

AVERAGE EASTER COMMUNICANTS, FORD CHURCH, NORTHUMBERLAND

Date	Easter Average	% approx. Total Population
1873-82	54	3%
1883-92	58	4%
1969-78	65	9%

Chapter IX

THE FINANCIAL FOUNDATIONS OF THE
DIOCESE OF NEWCASTLE

Martin Bass

SINCE a diocese is an ecclesiastical area with conveniently drawn geographical lines, the creation of a new diocese out of an old one does not, in itself, seem to call for the raising of money. Why should money be necessary with all the physical amenities of churches, vicarages, and parish halls already there, and with clergy and lay workers continuing their duties? The answer to a justifiable lay question is that new salaries have to be found which would not come from existing livings: salaries for the bishop and his secretary, for the dean of the cathedral and the paid canons of the cathedral. A bishop's house (in the old days a palace) must be provided, and a cathedral church built or an existing church suitably adapted to act as the spiritual centre of the diocese. Further, there must be some kind of central bureaucracy, some official administrative centre of the diocese.

Salaries for all these posts have to be derived from the income from capital investment or from land; at the present time, usually the former. As well as the new facilities and offices which are needed on the actual creation of the new diocese, there are special needs within the designated area which, in part at least, provide the justification for the division of a see into two smaller and more manageable areas. Locally the major need, particularly in the North Tyneside area, was for the creation of new parishes, the building of new churches and the funding of salaries for additional clergy to minister to the increasing urban population. The complex procedures and efforts necessary to find the money to finance these objectives are set out below.

The Diocese of Newcastle was carved out of the Diocese of Durham. In 1876 Bishop Baring of Durham referred the question of the proposed Newcastle Diocese to rural deanary chapters. It was reported that 'while there was much difference of opinion expressed as to the source from which the endowment should be obtained, and the amount of the endowment, the judgement was almost unanimous

160

as to the desirableness of the creation of the new see.' Bishop Baring's initiative and the strong favourable reaction of the rural deanery chapters resulted in the passing of the Bishoprics Act of 1878 which provided not only for the creation of an independent see at Newcastle, but also for the establishment of the bishoprics of Liverpool, Southwell and Wakefield. The Act empowered the Ecclesiastical Commissioners, a national body concerned with administration and finance, to receive contributions to an endowment fund for each bishop, and also provided for a contribution from the endowment funds of the dioceses out of which the new sees were formed. As soon as the Commissioners were able to certify that the annual value of the endowment was not less than £3,500 (including the annual value of the bishop's residence, which was to be reckoned as £500) the foundation of the new bishopric could actually take place, by means of an Order in Council (for further details, see Ch.II).

In terms of the contribution required under the Act from the dioceses out of which the new sees were formed, Newcastle fared rather better than the other proposed bishoprics. Durham's annual contribution (either by annual payment or the transfer of a portion of the endowment) to the income of the bishopric at Newcastle was set at £1,000, whereas Liverpool received only £300 per annum from Chester; Wakefield £300 per annum from Ripon and Southwell, £500 per annum from Lincoln, and £300 per annum from Lichfield. The intention was that these contributions should eventually cease, or that the endowment from which the income was derived should be returned to the contributing bishoprics as soon as the endowment funds of the new sees could provide a sufficient annual income without this assistance. The first call on the endowment fund of each new bishopric, held by the Ecclesiastical Commissioners was to provide a net annual income not exceeding £4,200, plus a suitable residence for the holder of the office. When this had been provided, the Act directed that the Commissioners were then to make good to the contributing bishopric the portion of the endowment or income of that bishopric which had been transferred under the terms of the act to the new bishopric, and finally to endow the foundation of a dean and chapter for the new bishopric.

On the passing of the Act in 1878 to create new dioceses, the general depression in trade and agriculture was felt to be a serious impediment to the proposed dioceses in their efforts to provide the necessary endowment. Newcastle had an additional difficulty in that the see at Durham was vacant as a result of the death in 1879 of Bishop Baring and until the appointment of his successor relatively little was done to raise funds. However, the one advantage which Newcastle had over the other new sees was the size of the contribution from Durham which reduced the capital sum to be raised to one which would produce an annual income of £2,500. At the contemporary rate of expected return (about 4%) this implied a capital sum needed for the endowment of about £63,000. Between the passing of the Act and the commencement of serious fund raising efforts the Ecclesiastical Commissioners received a bequest from the estate of the late Thomas Hedley which, together with interest accrued, was expected to amount to £16,000 by the end of 1881. This further reduced the sum required by voluntary subscription to about £47,000, but in order to make due allowance for contingencies the target for the appeal was set at £50,000. The Liverpool bishopric had already raised about twice this sum by subscription and so it was with a degree of optimism that the new Bishop of Durham (Bishop Lightfoot) commenced actual operations.

His own anxiety for the formation of the see was proved by a personal capital contribution of £3,000 to the endowment fund: this in addition to the required contribution of £1,000 per annum from the income of the Durham see. At the Diocesan Conference of 1880 the Bishop of Durham initiated the appeal with a powerful speech and in succeeding months backed up the initial effort by canvassing for subscriptions from local landed families. The Duke of Northumberland headed the list of contributors with a generous promise of £10,000, and other influential residents of the Diocese pledged their support for the Endowment Fund. With such promises of assistance arising from the single handed efforts of Bishop Lightfoot, the next step was to form an appeal committee to spread the burden of the work which had had such a successful beginning. In late December 1880 the General Committee for the Formation and Endowment of the Diocese at Newcastle was formed under the chairmanship of Earl Percy. The first meeting was held on 23 December 1880 at Durham Castle and in the absence of Earl Percy, the Duke of Northumberland took the chair. Bishop Lightfoot gave an account of launching the appeal and detailed the promises of support which he had received to date saying that although hitherto he had kept matters in his own hands, he now felt that the fund had been placed on such a footing that he could, with confidence in its success, commend it to the laity of the proposed new Diocese of Newcastle. At this first meeting Sir Charles Trevelyan and James Laing were appointed honorary treasurers and John J. Hunter as the first honorary secretary. The second meeting of the Committee took place early in 1881 and fund raising from individual donations, large and small, and from church collections proceeded apace. At the Church Congress, held in Newcastle in October 1881, Bishop Fraser of Manchester suggested that the members of the congress should raise a special fund in aid of the bishopric and this resulted in the contribution of about £2,734 (see Chapter VII).

The next major contribution to the successful outcome of the appeal came in November 1881, when Mr. J.W. Pease, a Quaker, offered to present Benwell Tower to the Diocese as a residence for the Bishop of Newcastle. The property was valued at £12,500 and the gift virtually ensured that the minimum endowment would be available. The ladies of Newcastle and the surrounding area then concentrated on raising money to furnish Benwell Tower and their efforts resulted in £1,200 being made available for the partial furnishing of the Bishop's residence.   On 29 December 1881, with the minimum endowment ensured, application was made to the Ecclesiastical Commissioners for the appointment of a bishop to fill the new see. The fund for the endowment of the see was thus raised in a single year, with the application to the Ecclesiastical Commissioners being made within a week of the first anniversary of the committee's initial meeting. In the economic conditions of the time, this was undoubtedly a great achievement. After the application had been made a contribution of £10,000 was received from Mr. Thomas Spencer of Ryton thus providing a comfortable excess over the minimum endowment required. The sustaining force for the rapid and successful conclusion to the appeal undoubtedly came from Bishop Lightfoot, with able and active assistance from the officers of the Appeals Committee. The treasurer, James Laing, was responsible for the considerable task of maintaining the voluminous subscription list and the gratitude of the committee was expressed for his devotion to this extensive labour of love.

The total raised as a result of the appeal can be summarized as follows:-

Newcastle Bishopric Fund	£
Subscriptions	51,567
Bequest (Thomas Hedley)	16,200
Church Collections	1,871
Newcastle Church Congress	2,734
Interest	2,795
	£75,167
(Bishop's Residence – Benwell Tower,	£12,500)

The expenses of the Committee, including £1,000 for repairs to Benwell Tower, amounted to £1,506, leaving some £73,660 to be invested. The income from these investments, plus the annual income from Durham of £1,000, amounted to about £3,700.

Even before the Appeals Committee set about its task of providing the endowment for the see, efforts were being made to raise money for the refurbishing and renovation of the parish church of St. Nicholas. In 1876 a subscription list was opened to provide funds for repairs to the church. As a result of this effort funds were provided for the alterations to and renovation of the interior as well as for the restoration of the steeple under the direction of Sir G. Scott, the famous architect. A new organ was also installed during this period and when it became clear that St. Nicholas was to become the cathedral church a bishop's throne was provided. On 17 May 1882, the parish church of St Nicholas was designated the Cathedral Church of the Diocese by Order in Council.

The new diocese was thus founded with the necessary endowment for the bishopric, a cathedral church and a bishop's residence, but there were remaining many physical shortcomings in the provision of pastoral care for the still increasing population of the new see. Within as short a time as six months of his consecration and enthronement Bishop Wilberforce set up a commission to examine the spiritual wants and requirements of certain parishes in the Diocese of Newcastle on the north side of the River Tyne.[1] It thus concerned only the Tyneside area.

The Commission reported its findings towards the end of 1883 and recommended immediate capital expenditure of £74,400 on the creation of twelve new parishes[2] and the building of fourteen mission rooms. Annual expenditure of a further £2,000 to assist in the appointment of seventeen additional curates was also recommended as an immediate objective. Further capital expenditure of £23,720 was also proposed to increase the provision of facilities in certain parishes and while it was acknowledged that this expenditure was not so pressing as that on the new parishes and mission rooms, it was the view of the Commission that the need for the proposed facilities would become urgent in the very near future.

In December 1883 a committee was formed to provide funds for the implementation of the Commission's report. The intention was to complete the programme recommended by the Commissioners within five years. The priorities of the fund committee, as expressed in the first annual report were to provide funds for:-

(i) Mission clergy to be employed in the new
conventional districts

(ii) Lay agents

(iii) New church building

(iv) Mission buildings

The target for the appeal was £100,000 to be raised either centrally (by the Committee of the Bishop of Newcastle's Fund) or locally (by committees formed in parishes and districts where expenditure was proposed).

Bishop of Newcastle's Fund
Amounts received during the 5 year period to 31 December 1888

		Total £	Central Fund £	Local Funds £
Year to 31st December	1884	23,214	9,683	13,531
Year to 31st December	1885	15,718	4,056	11,662
Year to 31st December	1886	11,274	4,468	6,806
Year to 31st December	1887	5,495	2,962	2,533
Year to 31st December	1888	5,800	2,455	3,345
		£61,501	£23,624	£37,877

(See also Table I.)

When the fund started there seemed to be reasonable grounds for hoping that, before the end of the five-year period, several of the churches which it was proposed to build would be in a position to claim endowment from the Ecclesiastical Commissioners and their maintenance would cease to be a drain on diocesan funds. The proposed mission buildings would not qualify for endowment, but it was hoped that, after a few years they might prove self-supporting. However, the prolonged and severe depression of trade and agriculture in the country during the mid-1880s so affected the resources of the Ecclesiastical Commissioners that it became apparent towards the end of 1886 that they would not be in a position to endow any new parishes for some time.

TABLE I

The Bishop of Newcastle's Fund
Summary of Receipts and Payments for the ten years ending 31 December, 1893.

Receipts

Year	Subscriptions and Donations	Newcastle Diocesan Ladies Association	Church Offertories	Bank Interest	Local Funds	Total
	£	£	£	£	£	£
1884	9,126		444	113	13,531	23,214
1885	3,718		142	196	11,662	15,718
1886	4,003		286	179	6,806	11,274
1887	2,489	128	239	106	2,533	5,495
1888	2,008	246	135	66	3,345	5,800
1889	4,003	352	111	60	2,451	6,977
1890	2,511	209	107	69	4,105	7,001
1891	2,383	215	265	48	11,531	14,442
1892	886	218	92	31	3,166	4,393
1893	1,448	201	185	20	7,924	9,778
	£32,575	£1,569	£2,006	£888	£67,054	£104,092

Payments

Year	Sites and Buildings	Stipends	Local Objects	Expenses	Total
	£	£	£	£	£
1884	955	767	10,197	*334	12,253
1885	1,837	1,597	10,844	175	14,453
1886	5,119	1,661	11,454	162	18,396
1887	3,101	1,739	3,477	152	8,469
1888	1,180	1,626	3,307	167	6,280
1889	2,313	1,610	752	151	4,826
1890	1,550	1,491	4,317	142	7,500
1891	1,304	1,288	10,701	139	13,432
1892	2,348	1,091	2,570	131	6,140
1893	593	924	8,074	162	9,753
Balances remaining (taken over by the Diocesan Society)					2,590
	£20,300	£13,794	£65,693	£1,715	£104,092

*Including £77 expenses of Bishop's Commission

The effect of those same causes locally militated against the new mission churches becoming self-supporting within the originally proposed life of the fund.

In the light of these circumstances it was proposed to keep the fund open for a further five years. The main objectives were the continued support of those new parishes which had not been endowed by the

166

Ecclesiastical Commissioners, the completion of three churches and two mission rooms. A new parish in Heaton (St. Gabriel's) was also added to the original proposals at this stage. The total cost of the revised proposals was estimated at £30,000.

Bishop of Newcastles Fund
Amounts received during the five year period to 31 December, 1893.

		Total £	Central Fund £	Local Fund £
Year to 31st December	1889	6,977	4,526	2,451
Year to 31st December	1890	7,001	2,896	4,105
Year to 31st December	1891	14,442	2,911	11,531
Year to 31st December	1892	4,393	1,227	3,166
Year to 31st December	1893	9,778	1,854	7,924
		£42,591	£13,414	£29,177

(See also Table I.)

Whereas in the first five years the adverse economic conditions had prevented the fund from achieving its target, the improved conditions locally during the second period allowed the appeal to exceed expectations. Thus in ten years more than £100,000 had been raised.

While most of the efforts on Tyneside were directed towards the carrying out of the proposals of the Bishop's Commissioners for that area, in the rest of the Diocese, fund raising and new building was also taking place. The Diocesan Society and various local appeal committees were trying to do for the rest of the Diocese what the Bishop's Fund was doing on Tyneside. In the first five years of the life of the bishopric of Newcastle £244,189 was raised for ecclesiastical purposes, and after 1893 the Diocesan Society assumed responsibility for raising the necessary funds, not only for building and augmentation of stipends, but also for the provision of various social and moral welfare services.

Alongside the efforts to provide funds for the expansion of church facilities in the Diocese ran the final legislative procedures to complete the establishment of the new see. In 1884 the Newcastle Chapter Act was passed to make provision for a dean and chapter for the bishopric of Newcastle. Among other provisions came the financial requirement for a Newcastle Chapter Endowment Fund, which was to provide an income of £1,000 per annum for the dean and £300 per annum for each of four residentiary canons. Actually the 'dean' remained vicar of Newcastle until the early 1930s when he was designated 'provost' and the appointment was in the hands of the Bishop.

In the years following the winding up of the Bishop of Newcastle's Fund, the Diocesan Society widened its responsibility and undertook the task of fund raising both for recurrent expenditure within the Diocese and for the building programme which was by no means completed. In particular the new parishes of St. Gabriel's Heaton, St. Margaret's Scotswood and St. Faith's North Shields, required financial support to enable the building of their churches to be undertaken.

The next financial milestone was the creation of the Church Board of Finance for the Diocese of Newcastle, which held its first meeting on 23 January, 1917. The budget which the Board prepared for 1918 pointed to the necessity of an annual income of £14,000. It was decided that one half of the total sum should be raised by quotas, with the balance coming from subscriptions. The quota system has, of course, remained an important part of the internal financing of the Diocese to the present time (Table II). (In 1978 the deanery quotas provided almost 37 per cent of the total costs for that year and are likely to remain central to the future financial stability of the Diocese.)

In June 1926, under Bishop Wild the Diocese found it necessary to persist in the work of church extension, it set up a Commission and a fund was launched in 1930 and called The Bishop's Church Extension Fund. It helped with building of seven churches, four parsonages, nine church halls and seven schools. A covenant scheme like that used today, was employed.

TABLE II

Deanery Quotas 1918 to 1978

Deanery	1918	1938	1958	1978
	£	£	£	£
Bedlington	530	444	1,841	27,849
Bellingham	137	167	428	8,228
Corbridge	358	421	978	20,164
Hexham	516	550	1,252	18,777
Newcastle	2,830	2,150	6,422	110,222
Tynemouth	862	740	2,782	45,421
Alnwick	440	460	1,056	21,008
Bamburgh	163	171	401	12,116
Morpeth	480	434	1,584	24,504
Norham	314	310	835	13,111
Rothbury	212	180	423	–
Glendale	158	173	373	–
	£7,000	£6,200	£18,375	£301,400

As a result of reorganisations between 1958 and 1978, the Deaneries of Rothbury and Glendale have ceased to exist. The Deanery of Glendale was amalgamated with Bamburgh and Rothbury was divided between Alnwick and Bellingham.

NOTES
1. Terms of reference published in the report of the Commissioners.
2. The additional parishes were to be formed out of the following parishes: Benwell; Byker (2 parishes); Earsdon and Blyth; Gosforth; Newburn (2 parishes); Newcastle, St. Andrew's, St. Philip's and Shieldfield; Tynemouth, Christchurch and Holy Trinity.

Chapter X

THE UPSURGE OF BUILDING IN THE EARLY DAYS OF THE DIOCESE AND THE POSITION TODAY

W.S.F. Pickering

ONE OF THE strongly marked contrasts between life in the Diocese at the time of its emergence in the early 1880s and life a hundred years on is the great activity in church building that occurred shortly after the Diocese was constituted. Some contemporary critics with the advantage of observing the decline in congregations over the years might, with justice, castigate our Victorian forebears for erecting so many churches or building such large ones, which have subsequently proved so expensive to maintain and difficult to dismantle. A cooler look at the social and religious situation in the latter half of the nineteenth century might have tempered the enthusiasm of the authorities, for there were indicators that an erosion of the loyalty of members to the Church was beginning to occur. But to the outward eye at least, the building and renovating of so many churches was a clear sign that the Church was very much in business and on the move. Decline might be knocking at the door but the Church had its house sufficiently in order to resist any wholesale entry of forces hostile or indifferent to its cause. The response to the situation was to go out and attack it. Available to the Established Church, and to other denominations to a lesser degree, were land, money, initiative, and a determination to try to ensure that the ecclesiastical institutions kept abreast with the steep rises in population centred on towns and cities. The upsurge of church building in the Diocese was in no way unique — the whole of the nineteenth century had witnessed a veritable spate of church building and renovation, not least between 1830-50, which also included vicarages, church halls and schools, along with mission churches. The activity was to be seen throughout all England (see Chadwick 1966:84ff.; and 1970:239ff.). The First World War locally, and one suspects elsewhere, heralded the slowing down of such activity, and today it has virtually ground to a halt. The very idea of building a new church, or creating a new parish which involves building a church, is almost completely out of the question. No

170

Anglican authority, certainly in Newcastle, would speak today (1980) of erecting a church for Anglicans to worship in, despite the recognition of a growing population within a given area. The sentiments of our Victorian Church leaders have totally disappeared. Rocketing costs have made it prohibitive to build churches of the size and grandeur of previous generations. Could anyone imagine a church of the proportions of St. Michael's, Byker, being put in a new working-class district? All that can be done nowadays is to encourage a team ministry to embrace a new population area in conjunction with an adjoining parish. The other possibility is to co-operate with another denomination. A joint building for Anglicans and Methodists is a current possibility. Similar ventures may occur with Roman Catholics and this has happened in other parts of the country. Just before and after World War II one way of dealing with the problem of providing accommodation for Anglicans was to erect a church-cum-hall, in which the hall was the dominant structure: to this was added a bay which acted as a sanctuary and which could be used as such on Sundays but was screened off on weekdays. In the 1950s and 60s four such buildings were erected in the Newcastle Diocese (Table 1). With fewer requirements now for a church hall, the tendency is to create a church, part of which can be used as a smallish room for gatherings of parishioners and others (see Chapter XI). All these ventures, however, show a radical shift from the policy of the Church a hundred years ago, when the Diocese went ahead and built a large number of goodly sized churches. Nonetheless the Diocese has witnessed some limited building and extension to churches in the period 1960 to today (see Table 1).[1]

When the Diocese came into existence, considerable parish and church construction had recently taken place. In the first half of the nineteenth century the state of the churches was reported to be poor (Henderson 1900:60).[2] During the 1860s about 14 new parishes were established, 11 of them in Newcastle and along Tyneside and around Whitley Bay — 5 parishes were actually formed in the two years 1860 and 1861 (Table 2). Once the Diocese had become a fact, it was seen to be small and poor compared with the status and wealth of Durham, which in the early nineteenth century and before, was one of the best endowed dioceses in the country. The relative position between the two dioceses is to be seen in the different salaries paid for the same type of work. In the 1890s the salary of the Bishop of Durham was £7,000, that of Newcastle £3,500. Canons residentiary were paid £1,000 per annum in Durham and between £300 and £500 in Newcastle.

171

Bishop Wilberforce, the first bishop of Newcastle, saw as his immediate task the building of more churches in the Diocese (Atlay 1912:111). The work of the Commission in raising money for churches, church halls, vicarages, and so on, for the Tyneside area has already been described (see Chapter IX). The *Diocesan Calendar* for 1893 set out the achievements of the great campaign. Some of these have been summarised in the accompanying Table (Table 3). What was eventually achieved was considerably greater than what had been planned (see Atlay 1912:111). In the matter of 11 years, 16 new parishes were created, together with 9 conventional districts.

TABLE 1
Church building, 1882—1979, for the entire Diocese
(based on data kindly supplied by I. Curry)

	Parish churches (new and rebuilt)	Parish churches (extension & restoration)	Mission churches	Church cum hall	Total
1882-9	16	2	5	–	23
1890-9	9	4	3	–	16
1900-9	12	2	1	–	15
1910-9	2	–	–	–	2
1920-9	2	1	–	–	3
1930-9	7	–	1	1	9
1940-9	–	–	–	–	–
1950-9	9	–	–	3	12
1960-9	4	1	–	1	7
1970-9	3	–	–	–	3
Total	64	10	10	6	90

TABLE 2
Parishes established since 1860

	Newcastle Area	Tyneside/Whitley Bay	Rural Northumberland	Total
1860-9	7	4 (1 in 1859)	3	14
1870-9	1	1	3	5
1880-9	3	4	6	13
1890-9	6	–	4	10
1900-9	5	–	3	8
1910-9	1	–	–	1
1920-9	2	1	–	3
1930-9	2	1	–	3
1940-9	–	–	–	–
1950-9	1	1	1	3
1960-9	2	1	1	4
1970-9	2	–	–	2
Total	32	13	21	66

TABLE 3

Number of new parishes, conventional districts, churches
built, churches enlarged or restored between 1882 and 1892
in the Diocese of Newcastle.
(Source: *Diocesan Calendar* 1893)

	New Parishes	Conventional Districts	Churches Built	Churches enlarged or restored
1882	–	–	1	–
1883	2	–	–	3
1884	1	5	5	16
1885	1	1	4	10
1886	–	–	10	10
1887	3	–	5	8
1888	1	1	2	8
1889	1	–	1	4
1890	1	1	–	5
1891	2	1	(plus 1 purchase of a site)	6
1892	4	–	1	10
Total	16	9	30 Cost: £105,000 Seating: 11,000	80 Cost: £64,000

TABLE 4

Parishes closed in the Newcastle area

1891-9	1
1900-9	–
1910-9	1
1920-9	2
1930-9	3
1940-9	2
1950-9	–
1960-9	2
1970-9	3
Total	14

As many as 30 churches were built and 80 different sets of alterations and enlargements made to churches. In addition, 27 chapels or mission rooms were built, as well as 4 parish rooms, and 3 chapels were restored. New or additional burial grounds numbered 24. There were 33 new organs and 37 new harmoniums installed in churches or chapels. Schools were also given full attention — 52 were erected or enlarged. Finally, in the matter of buildings, 12 new vicarages and curates' houses were put up. The building of new churches provided an additional accommodation of 11,000 seats. Not surprisingly the

173

churches were the most expensive of any of the items — together they cost just over £100,000. St George's Cullercoats (1884) and St. George's Jesmond (1888) were the most costly to build — £20,000 each. And St. George's Jesmond had a church hall as well, amounting to £2,000. Set out below are other costs to the nearest thousand pounds of items *not* involved in the building of new churches.

Churches enlarged or restored	£ 64,000
Chapels or mission rooms built or enlarged	£ 15,000
Parish halls	£ 5,000
Chapels restored	£ 1,000
New or additional burial grounds	£ 2,000
New organs and harmoniums	£ 14,000
Schools erected or enlarged	£ 22,000
New vicarages and curates' houses	£ 13,000
Total	£136,000

If this sum is added to the £105,000 for the building of new churches, then the Diocese spent just under a quarter of a million pounds in a matter of about 10 years.

After this extraordinary outburst of building in the early years of the Diocese, what happened subsequently? A statistical 'picture' of the hundred years or so of the Diocese, but going back to the 1860s, is 'sketched' in Table 2. The criterion of measurement here is the legal establishment of a parish, not the erection of a church, although the building of a church is nearly always required in the setting up of a parish. It is to be seen that the active period was between 1880 and 1909 when 31 parishes were formed, but between 1910 and today only 16 new parishes emerged. If one goes back to 1860, which was a time of considerable building, then between 1860 and 1909, 50 new parishes came into existence in the matter of 50 years. An average of one every year is, by any criterion, a remarkable achievement. For the 50 years, the Newcastle area alone had 22 new parishes, Tyneside and Whitley Bay 9, and all other areas in the Diocese 19. As we have just observed, the watershed was the First World War or for a few years prior to it. From then on the increase in the number of parishes fell dramatically to what has become a period of virtual stagnation. A similar but not identical pattern emerges if one uses the criterion of the number of new church buildings and extensions to buildings (see Table 3).

174

Greater activity occurs in the period 1882-1909, after which a general decline sets in. However, just before and after World War II, including the period 1960-9, there was some sign of fresh development but buildings were seldom as grandiose as they were in the earlier period. (The differences in figures between the Tables 1 and 3 are, it is suggested, due to criteria in definition.)

Some parishes over the past years have ceased to exist, often due to the drifting away of population, particularly from the centre of large urban areas. We have tried to document this, with perhaps some omissions, using the closing of a church and not the amalgamation of a parish as the criterion (see Table 4). In the past ninety or so years, 14 churches have been closed in the Newcastle area. The numbers have been equitably distributed over the years. Local people may recall, for example, the closure of All Saints Newcastle, and also St. Cuthbert's, likewise in Newcastle. More recently (1979) St. Lawrence's, Byker, has closed.

Mission churches, within parishes, were usually built in working-class areas, where the support for them was often weak. They were nearly always under the authority of the vicar or rector of the parish and were often, in fact, run by the curate, deaconess, lay missioner, or some other 'inferior' church official. The buildings were usually of iron or wood and were seen by clergy and parishioners alike to be decidedly second-class (see Gray (ed.) 1911:93). If the mission areas were successful they graduated into parishes in their own right and were able to build churches. They constituted a popular way of dealing with working-class growth in the late nineteenth century. We have had occasion to note that local records state that 27 were erected in Newcastle between 1882 and 1892. Their history is difficult to trace with accuracy. Many disappeared within a short space of time and they seldom received the prominence in records that parish churches have held. Recently it was noted that along North Tyneside 14 mission churches had been closed with the passing of years and most of them forgotten. Five became parish churches (see *Team Review* of the Cullercoats Team Ministry, July, 1976, p. 14ff.). Today the notion of building a mission church in the sense employed here has been abandoned.

But to return to the beginning. The early years of the Diocese were quite outstanding in the attempt that was made to come to grips with what was to be seen to be a social situation challenging the Church. Tied to the parochial system, the Anglican Church, at first somewhat asleep, had to cope with the population explosion which arose out of the industrial revolution. A historian has recently written:

175

> The Church never caught up with the demographic and economic transforma-
> tion of the nineteenth-century world — though it was far from being unaware of
> the problems themselves, as some have liked to suppose (Norman 1976:5).

What went on in the past in the Newcastle area, before and after the
Diocese was formed, confirms what Norman suggests. The Anglican
Church in the North-East was in fact very much aware of what was
happening on its doorstep. But more to the point, it set about at very
considerable cost trying to rectify the situation. It can be argued, as
Norman hints, that the Church never got on top of the situation and
perhaps its tactics can now be seen to be wrong — its money and
resources should not have been spent on the creation of large buildings but on recruiting greater numbers of clergy to run more but
smaller parishes. However the fact remains that the Church did make
what at least could be called a valiant and heroic effort in the local
situation at the end of the nineteenth century. The report on the
Bishop of Newcastle's Fund for 1893 showed that between 1881 and
1891, along the north bank of the Tyne, the population had increased
by 25 per cent, whereas church accommodation had grown by 33 per
cent, and the number of clergy by 37 per cent. In absolute terms it
meant an increase of 10,000 more seats in churches and 27 more
clergy. But the effort was soon to run out of steam. A flagging interest
was in part due to the actual returns from the new churches by way of
unrewarding increases in church membership and practice (see Chapter VI).[3] Why pursue the task of erecting new buildings in the face of
such great cost when they bring in relatively so few members? The
First World War, with its carnage, gave rise to a period of decline as
numbers began to fall off.

The energies of Bishop Wilberforce constituted a noble attempt,
but it was to end all attemps by the Church to administer its services to
the population at large according to some kind of ideal situation. The
Church was thus forced to drop out of the race. But the generations
who followed found they had well-constructed buildings, adequate
for the level of church life and practice that was to emerge in the latter
half of the twentieth century, but then, in some cases, what was
inherited has turned out to be too commodious and very expensive to
keep in order.

And what of the future? In the light of what has just been said, and
the general trends in the following of the Church in the Diocese, it
seems most unlikely that there will be any extensive re-building of
churches, any great enlargement of churches, or the erection of new
buildings. Today there is the burdensome problem of redundant

churches: 50 years ago this was hardly a problem at all. For England it was estimated that in the years 1968 to 1974 the Church of England sanctioned the non-use of about 730 churches by redundancy, transference to other uses, and so forth. In 1976 one church was demolished every nine days. The rate will almost inevitably be accelerated in the immediate future. The causes of redundancy are not difficult to find although they spring from several sources. Mainly they turn on changes in the population surrounding a church so that it finds itself without a congregation or with a very small congregation because the potential population has moved away. The predicament is worsened by the general low level of church-going and the rising cost of the maintenance of buildings. As has just been noted, the closure of churches has been with the Diocese for all its history. But there was one difference in the past compared with now — the previous occasions of closure were offset by the opening of new churches and it was clear that the Church was trying to 'follow' the changes in population. Redundancy orders on churches today indicate only in a *negative* way that the Church is still doing the same thing, that is following the population trends in cases where the population has disappeared. No longer can it build churches in areas of population growth.

By and large the Newcastle Diocese has so far escaped the flood of redundancies that has occurred in other dioceses, such as Salisbury and Lincoln — basically rural dioceses. Between 1960 and 1976 only 13 churches in the Diocese came within the category of redundancy and some of them were in ruins before that date (Curry 1976:269). (The corresponding number for the Diocese of Durham was the same.) However, anticipating the years beyond 1976, it is possible that a further 26 churches could be made redundant, 6 in urban areas and 20 in rural areas (ibid). It is usually the inner area of cities where redundant urban churches are to be located — All Saints, Newcastle, for example. But now the tendency is that churches will close in the next concentric ring, that is in urban areas in transition. Of course, dioceses with many small villages, of which Newcastle is not one, suffer acutely from the problem of redundancy.

Seen against other dioceses, Newcastle should not be depressed: but within the overall picture of church life, what is happening, and what is likely to happen in the future, cannot but be sad in the eyes of local Anglicans.

NOTES
1. For details of what has happened during the last twenty years, see Appendix II.
2. Canon J. Henderson, rector of Wallsend, observed that in 1856 there were two ecclesiastical districts with over 10,000 people and no church, parsonage or school;

and there were three areas designated perpetual curacies with an average of over 16,000 people in each, and only one had a church. When later a church was built in one of the perpetual curacies, it had then to be auctioned because there was no money to pay off the debt (Henderson 1900:61).

3. None of the statistics available shows a comparable growth to the increase of 11,000 seats between 1882 and 1891. Confirmations in 1883 were 5,186, in 1884 2,140, in 1891 3,075, in 1901 3,204. Easter communicants in 1885 were 20,770, in 1891 21,216, in 1901 27,784. Admittedly the last figure is high but there was a general tendency for Easter communicants to increase throughout the country. There is no positive evidence to show that congregations as a whole increased in numbers.

178

A survival from the early days of Christianity in Northumbria, the crypt of St. Wilfrid's cathedral at Hexham, c. 675. In the seventh century it was said (by Eddius) to be the finest church this side of the Alps.

The remote moorland Church of St. Aidan at Thockrington. In the foreground are the graves of Lord and Lady Beveridge.

St. Andrew's, Bolam. Norman restoration of an Anglo-Saxon church; typical of the simple and crude character of Northumberland churches after the Conquest.

PLATE II

Hexham Abbey. The east end was designed by John Dobson in 1858 and the nave by Temple Moore in 1907. The medieval parts of the church date from c. 1180 to 1250.

The seventh century bishop's throne at Hexham.

PLATE III

Ernest Roland
Wilberforce, 1st Bishop
of Newcastle from 1882
to 1896.
Later Bishop of Chichester.

Edgar Jacob,
2nd Bishop of Newcastle
from 1896 to 1903.
Later Bishop of St. Albans

PLATE IV

*Noel Baring Hudson, 7th
Bishop of Newcastle
from 1941 to 1957.
Later Bishop of Ely.*

*Ronald Oliver Bowlby,
9th Bishop of Newcastle
from 1973 to 1980.
Later Bishop of Southwark.*

PLATE V

The Church of St. Nicholas, now the Cathedral, Newcastle. A photograph taken c. 1890.

The Church of All Saints, Newcastle designed by David Stephenson, 1786.
A photograph taken in 1974, see Plate VII

PLATE VI

All Saints', Newcastle. Altar and mosaic. The church, built in 1786, has been closed since 1956.

PLATE VII

Marble statue of and mural paintings by Louisa, Marchioness of Waterford, at Ford, see Chapter VIII.

PLATE VIII

Fish market in Sandgate, Newcastle, c. 1890.

Byker, Newcastle, in 1975.

PLATE IX

St. George's, Jesmond, Newcastle, with its vicarage, 1888.

St. Matthew's, Westgate Hill, Newcastle. A Sunday school group, 1972.

PLATE X

St. George's, Jesmond, 1888. The mosaics, made by James Brown, were probably designed by the patron and donor of the church, C. W. Mitchell, Lord Armstrong's partner, who was considered one of the best painters of his time.

PLATE XI

St. George's, Cullercoats, c. 1890

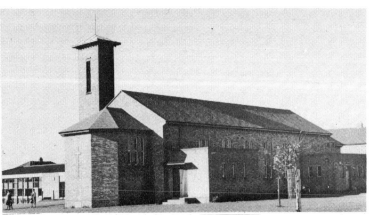

St. Aidan's, Brunton Park, Newcastle, 1966.

PLATE XII

St. Mary's, Rye Hill, Newcastle, 1966. A vandalized church, built in 1858, closed in 1964, and now pulled down.

PLATE XIII

Newcastle upon Tyne in 1967. The swing bridge is on the site of the first bridge built by the Emperor Hadrian. The Cathedral tower is in the centre of the picture.

Photo, Aerofilms

PLATE XIV

St. Nicholas', Gosforth, Newcastle. Young people at worship, 1978.

PLATE XV

St. Michael's, Byker, Newcastle upon Tyne. Administering communion, 1978.

PLATE XVI

Chapter XI

SOME ASPECTS OF CHURCH BUILDING IN NORTHUMBERLAND

Ian Curry

W HEN THE Diocese of Newcastle was created it naturally inherited all the existing churches and other parochial and benefice buildings within its borders previously pertaining to the Diocese of Durham. To what was inherited have been added new churches, referred to in statistical terms in the previous chapter. In what lies ahead, the intention is to comment briefly on the older churches and to say something about the churches built within the past century.

That otherwise admirable basic handbook *The Parish Churches of England* by J. Charles Fox and C.B. Ford, published in 1935, tends to dismiss churches north of Yorkshire as of little interest. Those of us familiar with the parish churches of the North-East of England can happily reject such a dismissal in the knowledge that we possess a heritage of fine churches from the seventh to the twentieth centuries, many of them humble, but some very grand and of the highest architectural quality. The arts, including architecture, should and usually do reflect the social conditions and attitudes of their age. Both for those resident in the Diocese, and others, attention will be drawn to aspects of church buildings which have particular Northumbrian qualities.

The Seventh to Seventeenth Centuries.
Through the influence of the early episcopal and monastic Celtic community of Lindisfarne (later transferred to Chester-le-Street, then to Durham), Hexham and the twin Benedictine establishments at Monkwearmouth and Jarrow, a wealth of Saxon work survives in the Diocese, most memorable being the groups of Tyne Valley towers. These include Warden; Corbridge; St. Andrew's, Bywell and Ovingham; even though some must be post-Conquest. Other important Saxon features survive at St. Peter's, Bywell; Bolam; Whitting-

ham and St. Mary's, Holy Island. There is very little Early Norman work, as such, and fully developed Norman on the grand scale is reserved for the refounded Lindisfarne Priory, Tynemouth Priory, and Norham and Warkworth churches, with smaller scale work at Old Bewick, Bolam and Heddon.

The end of the twelfth century and the first half of the thirteenth century was the most important period of church building in Northumberland, led by Hexham, Brinkburn and Tynemouth priories, and with a fine series of new or partly rebuilt parish churches. The long Early English chancels are striking features of Bamburgh, Holy Island and the Bywells, and the grouped chancels and transepts providing space for mass-altars at Corbridge, Whittingham, Rothbury and the stately Ovingham.

But the onset of the Scottish wars under Edward I ended the comparative prosperity of Northumberland and started a long period of retrenchment. Where churches were concerned, a defensive pele tower was built over the west end of the nave in Ancroft. Newbiggin and Ingram lost their aisles, and fire-resistant vaults were provided at Kirknewton, Elsdon and Bellingham. Only where the churches could be adequately defended — and there were feudal or merchant donors — was there much work in the fourteenth and fifteenth centuries, such as St. Nicholas', Newcastle; St. John's, Newcastle; Warkworth; and St. Michael's, Alnwick. As one of the largest parish churches in England, St. Nicholas', Newcastle preserves magnificently austere fourteenth century arcades internally, and a splendid fifteenth century tower and crown-like steeple, almost predestined for cathedral status, as first had been proposed in a Bill before Parliament in 1553. Though the continued unsettled state of the Border from the fourteenth to the seventeenth centuries restricted extensive church building in Northumberland, it did have the effect of preserving many Saxon, Norman and Early English features of our churches, which would have been lost in the later mediaeval church rebuildings of more prosperous parts of the country. It also must have given impetus to that unusual feature of Northumbrian churches, the series of western bell turrets surmounting large buttresses, for example Felton, Holy Island, Ford, Elsdon, Bothal and Longframlington.

In the seventeenth century the only major new churches to be built were in the garrison towns and ports of Berwick and North Shields. Holy Trinity, Berwick, 1642-1652 by John Young of London is in early Renaissance form though it retained Gothic east and west window designs (as did Bishop Cosin's chapel reconstruction at Auckland 1662), and Christ Church, North Shields, 1658-1668, designed by

Robert Trollope of York, who also built Newcastle Guildhall. These incidentally have been the first instances when the names of the designers are known. From such rare Gothic survivals in design in Northern England of the 1650s and 60s, it seems but a short step to the early Gothic Revival arriving at Alnwick castle, Auckland and Gibside in the 1760s, St. Helen's, Longhorsley in 1783, Carham in 1790 and Kyloe in 1792. But within this time, architectural design in Britain had run through its Renaissance, Baroque and Palladian phases, and the Romantic Movement was under way in literature and the arts, leading in architecture both to neo-classicism and the Gothic revival.

The Eighteenth and Early Nineteenth Centuries.

As in the seventeenth century, churches continued to be adapted and repaired during the eighteenth century, but not until the latter part of the century did social and economic conditions, and the increasing populations of towns and their vicinities, provide an opportunity for building churches. By this time a group of local architects were making their mark around Newcastle. William Newton (d.1797) designed the boldly classical St. Ann's, Newcastle, in 1768, David Stephenson (1756-1819) designed the strikingly original and superbly detailed oval church of All Saints, Newcastle in 1786, and John Dodds, as a replacement for the old chapel of St. Nicholas, Gosforth, in 1799. Trollope's Christ Church, North Shields, was altered and enlarged in 1792 and given its present plain classical form, and St. Peter's, Wallsend, was built as a simple classical preaching chapel with round headed windows in 1807, replacing the old church of Holy Cross. John Dobson added aisles to Dodd's church at Gosforth in 1818, setting its internal character of bold Tuscan columns and flat cambered arches, and he was later to design a neo-classical church for Grainger's housing developments in Elswick.

John Dobson (1787-1865), who had been a pupil of David Stephenson, continued his education at the Royal Academy in the classical tradition, but belonged to the new generation of architects who would design in a variety of styles to suit the occasion or their clients' whims. Grecian, Roman, Norman, Gothic and Tudor were styles that Dobson adopted during the course of his career, with his extensive practice which included country houses, urban developments, prisons, court houses and churches. In this last field his most striking essay is also one of his earliest churches, St. Thomas the Martyr, Newcastle, 1825-1830, with a highly individual use of Early English style, with externally soaring slender pinnacles and tower, and a light and open vaulted interior. Correct in its use of detailing, it is more akin in feeling to the Gothic of Adam and Wyatt than to the nineteenth century Ecclesiological Movement or Pugin. Dobson's later churches fell more easily into the accepted Victorian moulds of the period (Holy Trinity, Gateshead, 1837; St. Cuthbert's, Bensham, 1848; Otterburn, 1858; Jesmond Parish Church, 1858; East Front of Hexham, 1858), though by this time his work must have been influenced by his younger partner, Thomas Austin (1822-1867) (who did Brinkburn Priory restoration in 1858) and their pupil, R.J. Johnson. The Greenwich Hospital Estates in 1818 had provided simple Gothic churches at Greystead, Humshaugh, Thorneyburn and Wark, to the design of their surveyor, H. H. Steward, who was a pupil of Soane. Apart from these North Tyne churches, the predominance of local architects in church building in Northumberland is very marked. Ignatius Bonomi of Durham built the neo-Norman St. James at Duddo in 1832, and designed the major neo-Norman additions to Norham in 1836 (continued 1846 and 1852). The chancel (east end) of Doddington (1838), Scremerston (1842) and Nenthead (1845), all in simple lancet gothic, were also his. John Green (1787 - 1852) of Newcastle was favoured by the Duke of Northumberland and with his nephew, Benjamin Green, built aisleless churches, often with galleries, in a straightforward lancet style at Earsdon (1836); Holy Trinity, North Shields (1836); Sugley (1837), Holy Saviour, Tynemouth (1841); Cambo (1842) and Seghill (1849). Benjamin Green had considerable design abilities in his own right, and apart from the exterior of the Theatre Royal, Newcastle, should be best remembered for his High Victorian Decorated St. Mary's, Rye Hill, of 1858, now demolished. Next in the Duke's favour came Anthony Salvin (1799 - 1881) of a Durham family, but a pupil of Nash and with a London based practice and aristocratic clients throughout the county. He undertook extensive alterations to Alnwick castle, including building the polygonal apsed and vaulted Chapel in the 1850s. In 1834 he designed the neo-Norman church for North Sunderland and in 1846 St. Paul's, Alnwick, large and steeply roofed, but he returned to a simpler mid-Victorian style for St. Paul's, Cullercoats, and St. John's, Percy Main, both built on Ducal land in 1864.

The well-known High Victorian church architects left few marks on Northumberland, and we have nothing of Bodley, Burgess or Street. Sir George Gilbert Scott restored the tower and corona of St. Nicholas', Newcastle. (Dobson and Benjamin Green had been responsible for the earlier restorations); William Butterfield gave us the tiny church at Etal in 1858; Blomfield, Longhirst in 1876; Samuel

IAN CURRY

Teulon, Hunstanworth in 1863; whilst Benjamin Ferrey built the neo-Norman St. James, Morpeth, in 1843, and over-restored Stamfordham in 1848.

In the years preceding the founding of the Diocese of Newcastle, a very considerable mark was left on many churches in the northern part of the county by the otherwise little-known architect, F. R. Wilson, who had been a pupil of Cottingham, and worked from Alnwick. His book *An Architectural Survey of the Churches in the Archdeaconry of Lindisfarne* published in 1870 gives little hint of the extensive restorations for which he was responsible, but his style is distinctive and easily recognisable. He built the new chancel at Whittingham in 1871, he gothicised the naves at Lowick and Kyloe, and added their chancels, but his only new church was All Saints, Duddo, where he practically repeated the Holy Island gable buttress treatment. Wherever one goes in Northumberland one can recognise his work in pitch pine roofs, corbels, but more particularly in his leaded windows, with their delightful pattern making, as in Whittingham, Bolam, Elsdon, Ponteland and Wooler.

A. B. Higham designed Christ Church, Shieldfield, in 1859, and Holy Trinity, Whitfield, in 1860, the latter in creamy stone and with central tower and spire rising from clustered roofs — a surprising import into the verdant Whitfield glen. A. R. Gibson's St. Cuthbert's, Newcastle, 1871, (now demolished) with its big apse and open interior, owed its inspiration to North Italian gothic churches. It was built in a dark red brick both internally and externally, with moulded brickwork to window and door openings, though stone was retained for the nave arcades. St. Jude's, Shieldfield (no longer in use as a church), turned to Italian Proto-Romanesque forms for its design, red brick externally, with apses at both ends, and fine Corinthian colonnades inside of dark red sandstone.

Such essays in eclectic design were to reach their high point with T. E. Spence's St. George's, Jesmond in 1888, under the direction of the patron and donor, Charles W. Mitchell. Again, North Italian gothic in its overall forms with its free-standing campanile, and this time all in local sandstone, giving an opportunity for the most elaborate carved work. Its painted roofs, sanctuary mosaics, marble paving, fittings and furnishings combine to produce an extremely rich and impressive interior, and influenced by the most advanced Art Nouveau thinking of that date. It was practically the only church in the area to acknowledge the existence of the Arts and Crafts Movement so deeply influencing many secular buildings in Newcastle at this time.

183

The last and most important church built under the patronage of the Dukes of Northumberland is St. George's, Cullercoats, of 1878 to 1884, and was designed by John L. Pearson (1817-1898) who by coincidence also came of a Durham family, and began his pupilage under Bonomi, then moved to London and worked for Salvin, before beginning independent practice in 1843. Pearson had not become involved in the mid-nineteenth century conflicts of the Camdenians, and Cullercoats belongs to his long series of noble churches, thirteenth century in inspiration, vaulted and apsed, and with soaring spire. According to Bishop Lightfoot, it 'set an ideal of something better in the way of church building than that to which we are commonly accustomed'. It was built as a memorial to the fourth Duke, and its grandeur and purity of line and detail represents one of the high points of the Gothic Revival in the north, even if such perfection is more than any real mediaeval church would have attempted. It is one of the very few nineteenth century churches in the country vaulted throughout in stone and the only one in Northumberland.

Churches of the New Diocese : Nineteenth Century.
When St. George's, Cullercoats, was begun in 1878 it lay within the old Durham Diocese, but by the time it came to be consecrated it adorned the new Diocese of Newcastle. St. George's, Jesmond, also takes us forward into the first years of the Diocese, but the dates and numbers of churches built both prior to and after 1882 are clear indicators of the need to split off from the old historic diocese an area facing the pressing needs of the age.

Amongst architects, Dobson and the Greens had been the principal figures in church building in the county from early in the century, and were responsible for a long series of church restorations, often 'gothicising' otherwise plain churches built in the eighteenth and early nineteenth centuries.

Robert James Johnson (1832-1892) had been pupil and partner of Dobson and Austin, and continued the practice in the name of Austin and Johnson. He carried on their church building tradition, gradually developing a distinctive style based on fifteenth century Perpendicular models, despite his authorship of *Specimens of Early French Architecture*. His St. Stephen's, Newcastle, 1868, St. Silas', Byker, 1868 and St. Cuthbert's, Amble, 1870, follow in the Dobson and Austin pattern, and Stannington, 1871, shows a fine appreciation of the design of a tower silhouette, as of course does the tower and spire of St. Stephen, which was a later addition to that church. Of his later works, All Saints, Gosforth, 1887, is his most imposing exterior, its west tower completed in 1897, though inside the nave arcades are severe in effect. St Augustine's, Newcastle, 1892 is better internally, but perhaps his finest church interior is St. Matthew's, Newcastle, started in 1877 in mature Perpendicular (W. S. Hicks was his partner by this date and the big west tower was completed by Hicks). Inside, with the tall slender columns and fully developed fifteenth century detailing, we have come full circle in nineteenth century taste, and to an appreciation of the values of late Gothic, denied to the more doctrinaire Victorians. Together with his carver, Ralph Hedley, Johnson was responsible for providing the rood screen and choir stalls in St. Nicholas's Cathedral, Newcastle.

Stylistically similar to some of Johnson's work, as well as to St. Cuthbert's, Newcastle, are St. Luke's, Newcastle and St. Luke's, Wallsend, 1885, and 1886 respectively, the first in brick and the second in stone, large, competent, and with good spatial qualities internally, designed by the Newcastle firm of architects, Thomas Oliver and Leeson.

The most fruitful architectural partnership for the new diocese was that of Hicks and Charlewood. William Searle Hicks (1849-1902) came of a Devonshire family and was a relative of Charles Barry, but was articled to Austin and Johnson in 1866 and established his own practice in Newcastle in 1882, being joined by his brother-in-law, Henry Clement Charlewood in 1888. Hicks was the son of a parson and his views on churchmanship coincided closely with the aims and ideals of the newly founded Diocese of Newcastle, and until his death at the age of 53, he produced a flood of brilliant designs for reredoses and altars, screens and church furnishings. The 'In Memoriam Notes' of an issue of the *Newcastle Diocesan Gazette* after W. S. Hicks' death in November 1902, says of him that

> ....upon the northern Church he leaves an indelible impress. To him was given to realise in wood and stone the spirit of the Lindisfarne Church, and it is no matter of small importance that he was given to the Diocese at the period of activity in building and restoration. With future generations, as with the present, he will rank high in the list of Benefactors, Founders, and Worthies of the Diocese, while the reverence and spirituality of his art will unconsciously influence them in their worship of Almighty God. We who knew him, knew that the reverence and spirituality was but the reflection of his own personality, and that his one aim in all he did was to set before men the glory of God and the beauty of holiness. With a rugged solidarity of exterior befitting our northern climate, and an artistic spirituality of interior befitting the land of the Lindisfarne saints, his churches stand true types of the Christianity of Northumberland. To the Church of this Diocese he was a true son: hers is the loss.

The list of his works are spread over twelve English dioceses from Carlisle to Canterbury and Wells, and for Newcastle his new churches include St. James, Shilbotel; St. Cuthbert's, Blyth; and St. Mary's, Lambley; started in 1884; and St. John's, Ashington two years later. His best tower is St. Matthew's, Newcastle, added to Johnson's nave in 1894, and extensive 'restoration' or gothicising of existing churches occurred at St. John Lee, 1885; St. Peter's, Wallsend, 1891; Longframlington, 1895; St. Mary's, Horton, 1902, and a host of chancel reorderings, with distinctive and characteristic furnishings, and the symbolic seven steps up from nave to altar. Hicks' most important new churches lie outside the diocese (e.g. St. Hilda's, Bishopwearmouth, 1892 (now demolished); St. Oswald's, Hartlepool, 1902 and St. Chad's, Bensham, in course of erection at the time of his death, and where every detail, piece of furniture and altar silver was to his design, the results of a magnificently beneficent donor). His partner, H. C. Charlewood, continued with a further group of new churches in Newcastle, indicating the continuing development of the city in economic terms and social needs — St. Aidan's, Low Elswick, the best of Hicks and Charlewood interiors in Newcastle and where H. C. Charlewood was churchwarden, St. Barnabas', Jesmond, 1901 (now redundant); St. Hilda's, Jesmond, 1905; the chancel of Holy Trinity, Jesmond, 1905; St. Lawrence, Byker, 1908 (also redundant) and St. Margaret's, Scotswood, 1915. The needs of the mining and industrial areas of the new diocese were not overlooked, and between 1885 and the end of the century, Hicks and his firm provided mission churches at Burradon, 1893; Cambois, 1898; New Hartley, 1891; Dudley, 1895; Backworth, 1886; Holywell, 1885; West Woodburn, 1901; Shiremoor, 1888; Throckley, 1886 and Walbottle, 1892, though not all of these survive as churches. The practice was joined by the sons of the two partners, H. L. Hicks, soon after his father's death, and G. E. Charlewood, after war service in 1918. They carried out the extensive restoration work on Newcastle Cathedral in the 1920s and H. L. Hicks survived until 1947, while George Charlewood continued in practice until his death in 1962.

The Twentieth Century.
In the years before the 1914-1918 war the tremendous impetus in church building which accompanied the foundation of the Diocese was drawing to a close, and the last great undertaking, often overlooked, was the construction in 1907-9 of the nave of Hexham Priory. The Priory's nave had never been built in mediaeval times, though its west and south walls had been started, and also the eastern bay of the

nave arcade. The twentieth century designer, Temple Moore, had an exacting task to provide a nave worthy of the superb Early English chancel and transepts and he showed some sensitivity in choosing a version of the slightly later Decorated style for completing the nave.

Between 1918 and 1939 few churches were built in the Diocese. The nave, aisles and western tower and spire of Holy Trinity, Jesmond, were built as a war memorial (1920) and designed by Hoare and Wheeler in a form of modern gothic; St. James and St. Basil at Fenham, 1928, by Lofting in a quite fanciful un-English gothic. More significant and showing an awareness of modern design trends, was the Venerable Bede, Benwell (1936) by Professor W. B. Edwards, with tiled roofs and carefully detailed brickwork. The continued housing developments before and after the 1939-45 war around Newcastle itself and between Newcastle and the coast, produced new churches at Monkseaton (St. Mary, 1931 and St. Peter, 1938) which are typical of their period.

After 1945 building controls and restrictions had a direct influence on church design, and structures that were economical in materials as well as cost had to be devised. Amongst such churches might be mentioned St. Peter's, Cowgate, and St. Francis, High Heaton (both 1958 by W. B. Edwards); The Ascension, Kenton and Holy Spirit, Denton, 1955 (both by P. C. Newcomb); St. John, Wallsend, 1955 and St. Bede, Newsham, 1956 (both by G. E. Charlewood); St. Hilda, Marden, 1964 St. Mark's, Shiremoor, 1965 (both by I. Curry) showing a continuing development of current trends in church design, though only the later churches were influenced in their planning by the liturgical movement. Initially this had shown itself in the provision of adequate space in front of the altar and planning the communion rails to be as long as possible. Experiments were also made in banishing choirs to western galleries, though without much success. Subsequent developments in the liturgy required that the main altar be freestanding, away from the east wall, and with the congregation (and choir) grouped around it.

Most of the churches mentioned were provided with church halls, or were intended to have church halls associated with them, and the more recent have large meeting rooms which open off the church and can be used for overflow congregations. In addition, a number of church-cum-halls were built in the late 1950s and early 1960s — St. Hugh's, Regent Farm; St. Mary's, Fawdon; The Holy Family, Stakeford; and St. Wilfred's, Newbiggin Hall, as daughter churches within established parishes, and continuing to serve the large numbers who have been rehoused from the inner centres of population.

The post-war migration trends and the replanning of inner urban areas have played their part in changing completely the pattern of parochial life within these areas of the Diocese. Some of the town centre churches retain their active congregations, but others have become redundant, the fine nineteenth century churches of St. Mary's, Rye Hill, and St. Cuthbert's, Newcastle, have been demolished and St. Jude's, Newcastle, has found a new use in light industry. The superb All Saints, Newcastle, after extensive repairs by public subscription, was gratefully accepted by the city fathers 'for cultural purposes' in 1965, and one is saddened that at the time of writing no worthy use has been found for it by its present custodians and that it is inaccessible to the public. No one expects great works of art in the form of paintings or sculpture to be 'useful', yet society has not come to terms with the concept of a great building being regarded as large-scale open air sculpture. Surely All Saints falls into this category, without any need to insist that its marvellously open interior with floating domed ceiling be put to some utilitarian purpose.

Within Newcastle and the adjacent urban areas a second series or outer ring of churches, built within the past century, struggle on or search for new roles in modern society. Many are too large for their present congregations, and increasingly difficult to heat or repair adequately. Some have abandoned or sold the large church halls that were built in the latter part of the last century and originally intended as social centres and for youth activities. These services are now being provided elsewhere in the community. An increasing number of churches will seek to adapt to changing conditions, re-ordering their liturgical arrangements, and dividing off parts of their interiors as meeting rooms. Such drastic schemes can lead to much heart-searching within the parish and diocese, especially when a fine church is involved, of whatever period.

In the more isolated country areas, where the permanent resident and basically farming communities have declined in population continuously since the seventeenth century, a number of churches are potentially redundant and some already are redundant. St. Cuthbert's, Corsenside, and St. John's, Whitfield, survive only because their churchyards remain in use. Carrshield has disappeared entirely and St. Helen's, Longhorsley, is unused and likely to be demolished. Sparty Lee will probably become used as a barn. At least two of these redundant churches in the Diocese, St. Andrew's, Bywell, and St. Andrew's, Shotley, with its remarkable Hopper Mausoleum, have been considered of sufficient historic and architectural importance to be held in permanent trust for the Church of England, and the

Nation. A comparable historic church, St. Mary's, Woodhorn, has been accepted by a far-sighted district council and imaginatively adapted for exhibitions, meetings, concerts and permanent display of museum objects, without interfering with the overall spatial qualities of the church, or preventing its use for occasional services.

The Diocese was founded a century ago with a view to overcoming some of the problems facing the Church in the North. In terms of church buildings the Diocese had largely solved its immediate problems by 1910. It already possessed a legacy of fine mediaeval and later churches, including some real gems in a national context (for example Hexham, Bolam, Warkworth, Berwick, All Saints and St. Thomas the Martyr, both in Newcastle, already mentioned). To these the Diocese added more splendid creations, the refurbishing and furnishing of its Cathedral, and such churches as St. George's, Cullercoats, St. George's Jesmond, All Saints, Gosforth and St. Matthew's, Newcastle, which are as fine as any built in the rest of the country in the same period. By 1900 the new churches were less ambitious, and some were meanly furnished or were never finished — St. Lawrence, Byker, did not receive its north aisle, nor St. Aidan's, Elswick and St. Barnabas, Jesmond, their towers. At least Holy Trinity, Jesmond, of which only the chancel had been built, received its nave and spire as a war memorial. Those churches built between 1930 and the present day have been much less ambitious, neither striving for nor achieving any greatness as works of art or architecture to compare with the best modern churches in this country or abroad. But they have been utilitarian and functional and have usually succeeded in providing for the needs of their congregations and the Diocese.

PART TWO

ITS CONCERN FOR SOCIETY

Chapter XII

THE SOCIAL SITUATION: AWARENESS AND RESPONSE

Katharine Lloyd

> The rich man in his castle
> The poor man at his gate,
> God made them high or lowly
> And ordered their estate.
> *Chorus:* All things bright and beautiful etc.

THE ABOVE verse of Mrs. Alexander's well-known hymn was left out of the 1933 edition of the *English Hymnal*, but most people who were brought up on *Hymns Ancient and Modern* will remember singing it, at least in their childhood. Even now we carol cheerfully at Christmastide in *Good King Wenceslas* about ourselves finding blessing if we bless the poor without thinking much about what we mean or whom. The new Diocese began in a very structured society — there were still in Disraeli's phrase, 'Two Nations, the Rich and the Poor' and the rich were expected to give of their wealth and the poor to receive gratefully what was given. Children continued to learn by rote in their catechism that they should 'order themselves lowly and reverently to all their betters', and in the arrangements for confirmation in 1877 at St. Paul's, High Elswick, there were classes for 'young men' and 'young women' in the schoolroom on Mondays and Wednesdays respectively, and a third class for 'young ladies of good education' at the vicarage on Thursday afternoons. Masters and mistresses were urged to inquire of all their servants aged 16 or thereabouts whether they had been confirmed and if not to induce them to attend one of the first two classes (Henderson 1978:126).

However, as Beatrice Webb remarks (1926:176ff.), referring to the 1880s, 'the world of politics, philanthropy and statistical investigation were subjected to the working of a new ferment of thought and feeling ... to be discovered in a new consciousness of sin among men of intellect and men of property: a consciousness at first philanthropic and practical — Oastler, Shaftesbury and Chadwick: then literary and artistic — Dickens, Carlyle, Ruskin and William Morris: analytic, historical and explanatory — in his latter days John Stuart Mill; Karl Marx and his English interpreters: ... Henry George: Arnold Toynbee and the Fabians ... and a theological category — Charles Kingsley, F. D. Maurice, General Booth and Cardinal Manning.' It was also

193

a decade of publicity for social evils, especially when W. T. Stead previously editor of the Darlington *Northern Echo* became editor of the *Pall Mall Gazette* in 1883 and began his experiment in the 'new journalism' of sensation in connection with the publication of the *Bitter Cry of Outcast London*. This was a pamphlet on the horrors of the London slums based on a survey by the London Congregational Union and it led in 1884 to the setting up by Parliament of the Royal Commission on the Housing of the Working Classes (see Gilbert 1966:30ff.). In the same year Canon Barnett, vicar of St. Jude's, Whitechapel, held the meeting in St. John's College, Oxford (attended among others by Cosmo Gordon Lang), in which he invited his privileged student audience to come and see for themselves the extent of poverty and social injustice in the East End of London. That meeting led to the foundation of Toynbee Hall in Whitechapel and indirectly also to that of Oxford House in Bethnal Green where Hensley Henson, William Temple and 'Dick' Sheppard all served for short periods early in their respective ministries.

Other events in the decade contributing to public concern about social evils were the Trafalgar Square riots of 1886 which, according to the *Times* caused something 'little short of panic' because of the ferocity and boldness of the mob — the 'Two Nations' seem to have been momentarily at least in confrontation in a way not seen even in the Chartist demonstrations (ibid:35). There was also a new kind of industrial action in the successful strikes by the London match girls in 1888 and the London dockers in 1889. Meanwhile the electoral reforms of 1884 had given the vote to many agricultural labourers and thus established the principle of manhood suffrage, though women were to wait till 1918 for the first instalment of their voting rights. In spite of this however two famous women among many others were pursuing their respective campaigns for social reform — Octavia Hill in the sphere of housing management and Josephine Butler in her crusade to repeal the Contagious Diseases Acts — which was also an assertion of the rights of all women to be treated as individuals rather than branded as of inferior status because of their sex.

Against this national background there is evidence from the early volumes of the *St. Nicholas Church Chronicle*, the *Newcastle Diocesan Gazette* and the *Newcastle Diocesan Calendar* that in Northumberland, too, there was considerable and developing social awareness (see Ch.I). The new bishop, Ernest Wilberforce, had immediately started a great campaign to build and staff more churches but his concern extended also to arousing public opinion about social conditions and developing philanthropic action both within the Church and outside it in co-operation with Nonconformists and others. Thus at the Diocesan Conference held in 1885 there was a long session devoted to the 'Housing of the Poor' with several speakers (see *N.D.C.* 1885:272ff.). In discussion the vicar of St. John's, Newcastle, said that in his parish 'people were living under such miserable conditions that when you spoke to them of decency you were speaking in a foreign language ... no real steps had been taken — in Newcastle at any rate — by the municipal authorities to provide for those poor people who had been unhoused by the town improvements and overcrowding had been intensified because the men would not, if possible, go far away from their work and remained in the already densely populated courts and streets of the city'. The vicar said he had given evidence to the Royal Commission on the Housing of the Working Classes, just mentioned, and some of his facts were said by a member of the Commission to be as bad as anything in London. In one street, 62 houses had 310 families, (containing 1500 persons), living in them; in another, 23 houses held 115 families: i.e., about 5 families per house. A family rarely had more than a single room and nearly every cellar kitchen had a family in it. He advocated restriction of overcrowding, complete and separate sanitary arrangements for each family and inspection of all tenemented properties by an official independent of municipal authorities, *'many of whom are often interested persons'*. (my italics). There should be provision for the erection of workmen's houses in blocks and habits of thrift, temperance and decency should be encouraged by all possible means. In a session on rural housing Albert Grey M.P. said farm cottages in Northumberland had been greatly improved since 1841 when Dr. Gilly described miserable conditions in his pamphlet *The Peasantry of the Border*. Some of the village cottages were still very bad however (in North Sunderland most had only one room) as were some of the mining cottages, for instance in Seghill. Other subjects dealt with in the early Diocesan Conferences were *The Church and the Press, The Duty of the Church with reference to intending emigrants, The Duty of the Church in connection with the claims and social position of the Working Classes* and *Social Purity*. Fifteen years later in the *Newcastle Diocesan Gazette* for 1900 there is an account from Berwick of 'Winter Shelters for Poor Children', referring to the silent suffering of poor, shivering shoeless children for whom derelict rooms were rented as clubrooms, one at 6d per week so that they might warm themselves by a cheerful fire having done much of the cleaning and decorating themselves. And still today in Newcastle, as a permanent reminder of these kinds of conditions, stands a dark building close to the main bridge across the Tyne which has set high in one of its walls in letters of stone 'General Soup Kitchen 1880'.

Those indefatigable social researchers and historians, Beatrice and Sidney Webb spent five weeks at St. Philip's vicarage, Newcastle, in 1901, described in Beatrice's diary as 'the home of a high church Anglican priest, who is also a socialist, up on the high ground in a working-class quarter. The house was badly built and designed, but pleasantly appointed with a good library of theological and devotional books. Our impressions of Newcastle local government, not flattering — even worse than Leeds or Liverpool — are given fully in our notes' (see Webb 1948:169). The following is worth quoting:

> In contrast with the Birmingham Town Council, and in the last decade of the century also with the London County Council, the capitalists who dominated the Newcastle Town Council were honestly devoted to the doctrine of 'laissez-faire' which yielded conclusive arguments against undertaking improvements in the housing, education and sanitation of the poorer inhabitants of their city as matters of public concern and common well-being. It was this naive synthesis between their economic creed and their pecuniary self-interest which enabled them to carry out the policy of exploitation of the corporate wealth for private profit without self-condemnation and even without public blame from their fellow citizens (ibid).

This was Beatrice Webb's judgment and some of the discussion in the Diocesan Conference of 1885 could be said to support it. In addition, in the Diocesan Conference of 1893 Dr. Clark Newton said in a paper on the *Housing of the Working Classes*: 'It is my deliberate opinion that the intention of the law and the admonitions of Medical Officers of Health are defeated from the fact that so many members of Health Committees are interested in slum properties — nay that some owners get themselves elected on Sanitary Boards for the purpose of protecting their own interests'. A resolution was proposed urging the Corporation of the City to put into force all the powers they possess under the Artisans' Dwellings Act and the Housing of the Working Classes Act but in the event it was after discussion not put and a milder motion was passed instead. But it is only fair to add that recent research into local government records shows that Newcastle was in fact increasing its expenditure in this field quite considerably in the closing years of the nineteenth century (see McCord 1979:170-3).

There is much evidence then of the bad conditions and also that efforts were being made to overcome them, though with little effect. William Edmund Moll, the third vicar of St. Philip's with whom the Webbs stayed, must have impressed them with his theological knowledge, for they took away a lot of books on holiday to Bamburgh and

196

Beatrice expounds in her diary on the traditional wisdom of Catholic discipline in the training of character and the discipline of the emotions, almost lamenting the Protestant Reformation. He was a member of the Fabian Society and a friend of Ramsay MacDonald and was at St. Philip's for thirty-two years.

> In a day when religion was not supposed to impinge on the practicalities of workaday life, he engaged in battles with authority over pensions, relief and housing conditions . . . He was not to be daunted by officialdom or bumbledom when there was an injustice to be righted and his help was sought from far beyond the confines of his parish. That the church in the 1970s arranges public meetings on housing and cares for the elderly would have seemed entirely proper to Moll (Campbell 1973:14).

Here then was at least one priest who did not take the social order for granted or as ordained from on high. Another, curate at St. Philip's at the turn of the century, was Conrad Noel (afterwards to become famous in the 1920s as the Christian Communist vicar of Thaxted). Noel was a 'Pro-Boer', a very unpopular cause in the prevailing jingoistic atmosphere of the period, which later saw the almost hysterical celebration of the relief of Mafeking. He spoke as a Pro-Boer at public meetings; thereby earning a threat from munition workers to blow up the church, but Moll was unperturbed, saying that it would be no loss as it was the ugliest structure in Newcastle and they could build a new one with the insurance money! Noel mentions Canon Osborne of Wallsend in his *Autobiography* as a leader of Christian Socialist thought, who had been influenced by the famous Anglo-Catholic priest, Father Dolling of Portsmouth. There was felt to be a need for a more organised Christian Socialist movement and W. E. Moll and Conrad Noel called a conference at Morecambe which led to the formation of a society called the Church Socialist League joined later by George Lansbury, and supported among others by James Adderley and Arnold Pinchard in Birmingham (see Noel 1945:51-60).

No doubt attracted by the challenge of the appalling social and economic conditions of the area, a number of priests came to the Diocese in the period up to the 1930s, who were socialist in politics and Anglo-Catholic in churchmanship. Amongst them, mention should be made of John Groser, who was ordained in Newcastle and served as curate at All Saints' church during World War I. He recalled the following incident whilst he was there:

> I was astonished when one day the Bishop (Straton) sent for me, and, after giving me a proper dressing-down, said quite angrily; 'I sent you down there

to save the souls of those people, not to look after their bodies. Go back and do the work you were ordained to do.' I had of course no intention of doing anything else, and I had no idea that I was being political (Brill 1971:9).

After he left Newcastle Groser worked for many years in the east end of London and became well known as a preacher of the social Gospel and for his crusading work against all forms of injustice. He was a handsome man, always dressed in a black cassock but without dog-collar, and was an outstanding church leader (see Brill 1971).

Another priest of this outlook was Alec Vidler. In 1922 he came newly ordained to St. Philip's (where Moll was still vicar) to work at the Mission of the Holy Spirit in the poorest part of the parish (see Chapter III). He was appalled by the housing conditions and the extreme poverty he encountered on Tyneside. The houses in the mission district were for the most part occupied by two, three or four families, often with little more than one room each and many of the children had no shoes or stockings and were dressed in rags (see Vidler 1977: 41 *seq*). A vivid account of the conditions of the time has also recently been given by a former Police Court Missionary, who has written as follows (Cottam 1979):

When I first came into this area half a century ago (1927), social conditions were bad. I remember visiting in dangerous property where one had to go warily up rickety stairs which had an odd stair missing. One never knew whether a stair would give, or the handrail, if there was one, would hold if one had to grab it. Stairways were dark even in the daytime . . . even an electric torch was a poor aid if one came in out of the daylight. From the landing several doors led into several rooms which were barely furnished with old furniture, had unwashed windows with dirty curtains, or an old tablecloth in place of a curtain. The darkness of the rooms on winter days or in the evening was relieved by a spluttering candle and firelight, if any. In fact I remember a baby being delivered in such a room in those conditions, the gas supply having been cut off because the gas bill could not be paid. For fuel men took a sack and picked up very small bits of coal from the slag of the pit heaps, or dropped from coal wagons on to the railway tracks. Wood was obtained where possible and sometimes a piece of furniture was used. Children were ill clad and ill fed. I remember one room which had no upstairs, the door of which opened straight on to the street. Twelve persons ate, lived and slept in it. The atmosphere when the door was opened to one's knock took some withstanding. I remember places where one lavatory had to serve a dozen families and one tap on waste ground had to serve several houses. Fleas were common and the advent of D.D.T. was a boon to social workers. I remember when police went to certain areas in pairs and the missionary probation officer went alone. There was much poverty, begging on the street and from door to door, drawing crude pictures in coloured chalk on the pavement and sitting beside them with an upturned cap.

Vidler found his support for the Labour Party enforced because it seemed to be the only party that gave priority to improving such conditions. He spoke at political meetings during two general elections (as a citizen and not as a priest) and also became much involved outside politics in preparations for the Northern Copec conference held in Newcastle in 1924. Copec (Conference on Christian Politics, Economics and Citizenship) was the name given to a large interdenominational conference held in Birmingham in April, 1924. Since 1920 there had been intense preparations and William Temple who presided felt that its origins went back to a notable Student Christian Movement Conference at Matlock in 1909, at which students had considered the relation of social problems to Christian discipleship. Both the Birmingham and the Northern Copec's — the Newcastle Copec was held in October, 1924 — bore witness to the intense social idealism current amongst churchpeople in the 1920s, and manifested also in the 'Crusades' of the Industrial Christian Fellowship. To quote Vidler, they 'registered the acceptance by the Churches in Britain, of the idea that the Christian faith had social implications' (1977:53). Leslie Hunter, then a canon of Newcastle Cathedral, was secretary of the Northern Copec, with Vidler as assistant secretary, and to look at the programme today is to wonder at the depth of vision which it implied and the audacity it took to accomplish it (see Chapter XVI). A day was spent on: 'God and the World', with speakers on 'God in Christ', 'God and Human Society', 'God and the Individual' and 'the Ethics of Compromise'. The Conference then divided to look during the next two days at: 'The Home and Its Environment' and 'Industry and Property'. The last included papers on 'Christian principles in relation to Industry and Commerce', 'Moral Standards in Commercial Life', 'Insecurity of Livelihood and the problem of Casual Labour', and 'the Responsibility of the Consumer'. To attend all this cost 2/6! Suddenly the Church in Newcastle had come of age in its determination to wrestle with social and industrial problems.

Among the many lecturers of national repute at that conference was Henry Mess, Social Study Secretary of the Student Christian Movement, and a Congregationalist. As author of *Casual Labour at the Docks* he was a obvious speaker on unemployment. Also, he was the person to whom Leslie Hunter turned after the Conference to set up the Bureau of Social Research, in order to create on Tyneside, and especially within its churches, a healthy and well-informed opinion on social questions (see Chapter XVI). In the words of its first Annual Report, its particular purposes were: (1) to collect and supply accurate information as to conditions of life and work on Tyneside, (2) to encourage and to help especially by publication and lectures, the study of social conditions and the application of Christian principles to social life, (3) to co-operate with other societies which are pursuing similar objects. Sir Theodore Morison, Principal of Armstrong College, which was later to become the University of Newcastle upon Tyne, was the chairman. A number of courses of lectures were given by Henry Mess, particularly to clergy and religious groups, and he and his colleagues also lectured to various audiences on the information collected for the Social Survey of Tyneside, which covered Gateshead and the South Bank of the Tyne, as well as Newcastle and the North Bank.

The largest piece of work done by the Bureau was the making of a social survey of the area. The information on some of the subjects covered was first published in a series of pamphlets called, *Tyneside Papers*, published usually at 2d. each, between March 1926 and March 1928. Most of them, together with a good deal of other material, were incorporated in the final Survey Report published in the autumn of 1928, under the title, *Industrial Tyneside: a Social Survey*. It was undertaken not as a sample of the position of the country as a whole, but rather with the practical purpose of making the facts known in the hope that information published would suggest ways to improve social and industrial conditions in the area. To quote Constance Braithwaite, who worked closely with Mess from 1926-8:

> The method of the survey was the piecing together of information already existing in numbers of official and unofficial reports but never previously assembled, arranged and analysed. The impressions thus obtained were checked by information, mainly descriptive, supplied by persons with direct contact and experience. In many cases the significance of the facts was brought out by comparison — comparison with past conditions in the area itself, comparison between different parts of the area, and comparison of conditions in the area with those in England and Wales as a whole. The comparative method was of great value in throwing light on improving conditions. For example the figures showed that infant mortality rates on Tyneside, as in the rest of the country had fallen considerably . . . But (they) also showed that the rates in most of the Tyneside towns were considerably higher than the average for England and Wales, that there were large differences between the different towns in the area and that in some towns the rates were twice as high in some wards of the town as in other wards. The comparative method also showed up the very serious overcrowding on Tyneside. All but two of the Tyneside areas had more than 30% of the population living more than two to a room and this low standard of house-room of the two counties of Northumberland and Durham was lower than that of any other county in England and Wales (Braithwaite 1958).

Taken as a whole, '*Industrial Tyneside* is a measured, dispassionate and astonishingly full account of what it was like to live on Tyneside at that time. Crammed with facts and figures it is nevertheless written so that they are clear' (Lloyd 1950:196). William Temple, very shortly after his consecration as Archbishop of York, came to Newcastle on 22 January, 1929, to preach at the Cathedral and to present the Survey at the altar (ibid). He raised no false hopes of a speedy end to unemployment but emphasised that some aspects of the situation could be altered for the better, notably the shamefully low standard of housing on Tyneside.

Mess continued to work in Newcastle until 1935. Hensley Henson, Bishop of Durham from 1920-39, records in his journal for 30 December, 1927: 'Dr. Mess who presides over some kind of a social bureau in Newcastle and wanted to consult me about some developments of his work on Tyneside, came to lunch. I expressed myself benevolently, but urged that he must avoid two rocks, namely ignoring the social work already done by the clergy and others, and getting mixed up with party politics' (Henson 1943). However, the Bishop though apparently unimpressed at this first encounter, later commended the Survey to the clergy of Newcastle and Gateshead, saying that it poured on the social life of Tyneside maximum light with minimum heat (Lloyd 1950:196). Later, in 1935, he presided at a meeting at the Old Assembly Rooms in Newcastle to bid farewell to Henry Mess on his leaving to take up the post as Reader in Sociology at Bedford College, University of London. After some pungent reflections on current legislation that is 'ill-considered and unwise' he commented that, 'It is a very fortunate circumstance that we have had during these years an observer so keen and intelligent and a student so balanced and well-equipped as Dr. Mess.'

Industrial Tyneside became a classic among surveys and the blueprint for many subsequent developments and improvements. Mess had emphasised in the survey the lack of resources in the poorer parts of the area.

> Whereas a great city keeps the different classes, though widely separated geographically and psychically, within the unity of its borders, here the well-to-do leave the poor workers at the yard gate, and go home to another town and perhaps to another county ... Jesmond feels and discharges some duty towards Byker: they are bound together within the unity of the same city. But where is the Jesmond of Hebburn? Which are the well-to-do suburbs of Felling or Jarrow? The answer is that Monkseaton and Gosforth, Jesmond and Stocksfield and similar places, are the comfortable suburbs corresponding to miles of dreary streets along the river; but they do not realise their relationship nor in any way

do they discharge their responsibility . . . It seems desirable that there should be a council of social service for a wide area comprising rich towns and poor towns (Mess 1928:168).

Such was the argument put forward for the formation of the Tyneside Council of Social Service in the autumn of 1929 and Henry Mess was its first Director. Copec, the Tyneside Survey and this council were successful ecumenical ventures. The Council was at once concerned with schemes of unemployment centres and for personal service work and under different titles has survived major changes in local government boundaries. It was and has continued to be a most important inspirer and co-ordinator of voluntary social service in the region, and in 1979 it was re-constituted as the Newcastle Council for Voluntary Service. Throughout its entire history the Council has been supported by Christians of all denominations, many of them Anglicans.

This was not the only outcome of the Survey. It stimulated the formation of two public utility housing societies, one at North Shields and one the Newcastle Housing Improvement Trust, founded in 1928 by the Bureau for Social Research and the Newcastle Citizens' Society. The latter indeed, according to Roger Lloyd, was inspired by a sermon preached by Ronald Hall at St. Luke's, Newcastle, on Christmas Day, 1927, on the subject of 'Homes', using the work of Father Basil Jellicoe in the St. Pancras House Improvement Society as an example. After the service a man spoke to him and said: 'Something must be done about this' and something was, and the man (Col. A. D. S. Rogers) became the Chairman of the Trust and continued as such for many years. The Trust raised funds for the re-construction and conversion of old tenement houses, turning them into modern flats for families and individuals, and managing them on Octavia Hill lines. It was very strongly supported by church people who were well represented on its committee and among its subscribers, St. John's, Newcastle, in particular, raised enough money for the conversion of a house near the parish to be called 'St. John's House'. (Fortunately most of the worst slums within its own boundaries had been cleared.) The Trust has continued its work until the present day and now that many of its original properties have been demolished, it has taken a particular part in constructing and adapting properties for older people. Throughout the fifty years since its foundation in 1929, it has helped to arouse public opinion for housing reform and has also managed properties for other bodies, such as the Church Army Housing Ltd. and the Cathedral Nursing Charitable Trust.

This essay has attempted to give an outline of one or two kinds of response the Church made to the bad social conditions of the area, especially in the 1920s and 30s. The following chapters examine more systematically other approaches in the domains of physical illness, moral welfare, and the industrial world, but preceding them the endeavours of one parish priest are presented as a personal response to the situation in which he found himself half a century ago (for additional material on social and economic conditions, see Ch.I).

Chapter XIII

ONE MAN'S ANSWER

C. Ward Davis

CANON C. WARD DAVIS (1901-1978) was born of English parents in Edinburgh. Inspired by well-known Anglo-Catholic clergy, he was ordained and later became vicar of St. Lawrence's, Byker, situated along the north bank of the Tyne and just to the east of Newcastle. He was curate-in-charge and then vicar of the parish from 1927 until 1944. After he retired he wrote his memoirs and, with his widow's permission, we reproduce an edited form of what he said about his time in Byker. This constitutes the only such detailed first-hand account we have been able to find of the clergy working in what used to be known as a slum parish. St. Lawrence's was probably not the 'worst' parish in the Newcastle area but the memoirs show how one devoted priest responded to the bad social conditions of the day. The parish recently went through a period of decline and was merged with an adjoining parish. The church was closed about the time Canon Davis died. — Ed.

The vicar of St. John's, Newcastle, Father Noel Hudson (see Chapter III — Ed.) suggested me to the vicar of St. Anthony's, Newcastle, as a possible priest-in-charge of his mission district of St. Lawrence, South Byker. It was a mile away from the parish church, both being on the river-side, and it had a population of 10,000, most being unskilled shipyard workers, but there was a crowded slum population of several thousand down on the edge of the river, where great boiler and engineering works were situated.

The names of these industrialised parishes, situated along the river Tyne, are an intriguing relic of medieval days. St. Anthony's had been an isolated village on a bend of the river, so the timid villagers put themselves under the protection of St. Anthony, the hermit saint. A mile further up the river St. Peter's, now a slum, had been a fishing village under the patronage of St. Peter, the fisherman. Three miles further up the river, in Newcastle where the Cathedral Church of St. Nicholas now stands, sailors tied up at the end of their voyaging and thanked St. Nicholas, patron of sailors, for their safe landing.

In the municipal district of St. Lawrence's, within which St. Peter's slum was situated, still stood the ruined walls of the original St. Lawrence's, a chapel-of-ease on the edge of the river, built by the Dukes of Northumberland to maintain masses for the souls of the Percy family. This finally disappeared alas while I was there, and

Spillers' massive flour-mills were built upon the ruins. Nearby were Noddings the horse-slaughterers from whose premises a horrid smell of glue was emitted.

The church of St. Lawrence, beside a busy thoroughfare, was a considerable one, built with brick, and with a steep roof, and a flèche, after the Swiss style, so chosen by a former priest after a pleasant Swiss holiday, but rather incongruous above the long mean streets of New-castle flats, not one of which contained a bathroom or inside water-closet.

I went to see Fr. Royston, the vicar of St. Anthony's, about the job. The vicarage was built in the middle of a vast vacant swamp of clay soil and approached through piggeries, where I had one shoe sucked off! I had already looked at St. Lawrence's church and noticed that the boiler-house was flooded to street level. Fr. Royston, who amusingly always thought that he was fated to minister in the most difficult parish in England, explained all the snags, and when I, being young, said I thought it was a great challenge he said: 'you'll do!' and added that I should be left to look after St. Lawrence's ten thousand inde-pendently on my own. It was indeed a challenge, and seventeen thrilling years followed. The district of St. Lawrence's was made a parish after two or three years and I stayed on as its first vicar at the age of twenty-nine — such is the confidence of youth!

I soon discovered that only a hand-full of quarrelsome women and three or four men attended church. At first it was difficult to persuade the women to welcome others but as time went on it became easier and they took their place in the growing numbers who came along. The people of the St. Peter's slum did not come near the church, for the women, unlike the church attenders, wore shawls over their heads, the men were in rags, and the young men and children had bare feet. Unemployment in both parts of the parish was rife, and as the thirties went on there was practically no-one working for years on end. There was only one road down to the slum, which was on the lip of the polluted river; and where the road ended at the river, there was an enormous sewer, which ceaselessy poured polluted effluent into the Tyne from the domestic and public drains of Byker. It is hoped the tides washed it away! There the children played, and there the dead salmon, poisoned in their attempt to swim up the river, floated by on their backs. A favourite game for the young men was to hook them as they floated along!

During the industrial revolution four-roomed houses had been built in very narrow cobbled streets, but long ago they had all merged into one-roomed tenements with a family in each room. Often ten lived in one room and over forty in each set of four rooms. There was no inside sanitation or water. In each back yard was one ash-closet for the forty folk and one cold-water tap, which served all their needs and was liable to freeze in winter. In the streets the cobbles were awash with refuse and used water, thrown out of the windows to save taking it to the back-yard sink. Here, too, the half-naked children sat about and played while the ragged men and lads lounged against the house walls, and the women leaned out of the windows and talked to their neighbours opposite. The streets were so near the river and the sewer that rats ran everywhere, even across people sleeping in bed in the middle of the night. Most of the rooms contained two large double-beds for the ten or so members of the family living in each room. Five occupied each bed. At the head of one the father, mother and the baby would sleep, with two young children at the bottom. The other children, perhaps five in number, shared the head and the foot of the other bed! A rickety stair led to the two families upstairs. Usually the glass in the large landing window was shattered and the wind and the rain poured in. It seemed to be nobody's job to keep the stairs clean.

Both the birth-rate and the death-rate were high, and the nearest burial ground was at St. Anthony's church, a mile away along Walker Road. In order to save expense it was customary for newly born babies who died to be carried to St. Anthony's churchyard tucked under the arm of female neighbours. Usually two went the long walk, bearing in turn the tiny white coffin under their arm. Opposite St. Lawrence's was a popular pub. After my first week or two I discovered that the verger, having rung the bell for the Sunday eucharist, nipped across the road for 'a quick one' and was always back in time to ring the consecration bell, a habit I discouraged! This pub was conveniently half way between St. Peter's, where the babies died, and the church-yard, and my second startling discovery was that the two bearers by custom dropped in there en route, to get a rest and refreshment! They put the baby in the coffin under the pub seat and sat above it drinking the beer-money they had received in payment for their services! I discovered this because I noticed that they always arrived at the churchyard smelling of beer and in a rather garrulous mood. Quite often at closing time on Saturdays the street between our church and the pub was a battle-ground as all the men turned out in a quarrelsome condition. Some went home with black eyes or bloody noses but there was no bad feeling the next week.

The narrow cobbled streets of St. Peter's slum were in parallel rows, reaching down towards Hawthorn Leslie's great boiler-shops along the river frontage. Under the shadow of the boiler-shops, at the

206

bottom of the other streets, was Bottlehouse Street, a terribly mean street, not long but having four pubs. When one of them was condemned I was lucky enough to secure it for a nominal rent. It was called the William IV Inn and I quite believe it may have lasted from those days, but it was invaluable to us. There we gathered the teeming crowds of bare-footed young men, boys and girls, some at one time some at another. In time we were able to assemble a big mothers' meeting too. The floor of the bar was full of holes but the counter was still in position and there we had a very mini-canteen of cheap soft drinks, sweets and biscuits, and once a week, as a treat, ice-cream, which we trundled along in a yellow ice-cream container marked 'Toni', from half a mile away, through the mean Byker streets. In an emergency I took my turn and, still having the unselfconsciousness of youth, it never occurred to me, if it did to the passers-by, that a black suit and a 'dog-collar' were a bit odd behind an ice-cream barrow.

A favourite pastime among the older lads was to lie on their stomachs on the bar floor in a circle, and in turn to drop paper pellets into the cellar below where the rats swarmed. Every direct score on a rat counted for one. In time, as we got to know each other and they gained confidence, we were able to persuade some of them up to the parish church, where they began to join in the Sunday eucharist. This was a bit of a triumph because perforce they came among the rather better dressed congregation just as they were — ragged and with bare feet, even the young men, and the congregation accepted them. Ultimately some became faithful communicants. In time, besides many of the children, some of the women came too, at first with shawls over their heads, but these were gradually discarded for hats, even though these came from jumble sales! It interested me that in those days the Church of England willy-nilly raised people in the social scale whereas the Roman Church didn't seem to do so. I never know whether to be glad or sorry at this for I always feared that respectability might deter some from coming. So one Sunday morning, as I gave a ragged young man his communion, I wasn't unduly disturbed to see lice hurrying in and out of his matted hair.

For some years I lived in a tiny workman's house grandly called: 'St. Peter's Parsonage'. It was so small that my house-keeper and her two children had to live in a nearby street. My small study looked straight onto the pavement where hundreds of Hawthorn Leslie's men tramped up and down to work. So I became familiar with the 'Geordie' dialect and also gained a large vocabulary 'full of strange oaths'.

I furnished the little house from the Diocesan Deaconess's Home which, fortunately for me, though not for the Diocese, had to be closed just then. Head Deaconess, possibly out of pity for the impoverished young man, sold me lots of windsor chairs for 1/– each, and chests-of-drawers and iron 'hospital' beds for 5/– each, so I furnished cheaply!

On the Church's festivals, and in the summer, there were treats for the children. To pay for these I begged in the columns of the Newcastle press. In the summer we went for a day at the coast in our own special train. The return fare was 5½d, and the bags of buns we took cost 6d each, so a happy day for each child cost about 1/–! On Ascension Day we hired several double-decker cable tram-cars which took us all up to Paddy Freemans for a picnic. The mums and some of the dads went, with several hundred children. The tram-cars returned to fetch us all home at night and the charge for the double journey for each car was £1!

At the family eucharist on Christmas Day several hundred children, besides grown-ups, used to pack the church, most of the boys and girls with bare feet despite the winter weather, for many did not own a pair of shoes and stockings. The local social club gave the children a free breakfast on that morning. Those however were the days of fasting communion and Church discipline, so, by arrangement with the club, the children collected their bags of buns and then came to church. They piled up the buns at the west end of the church to wait until they went home, so the pleasant odour of incense and freshly baked buns filled the church. I always admired such loyalty on the part of the children, but people then expected to keep sacrificial rules.

One Sunday morning I arrived at church at 7.15 as usual, to find John, one of the choirboys from the slum, sitting on the vestry step. He always came for 9.30 a.m. but on enquiring he told me, in a matter-of-fact voice: 'My mother's had a baby in the night.' John lived with his parents, his two sisters and one small brother in one room and a scullery. In the scullery John (aged 12) always slept on two chairs covered with a sort of mattress. The others slept on two beds in the only other room. While some of the neighbouring mothers were delivering the baby others took the girls and the small brother to their homes. John, being older, was set adrift. When I said he should have come to the vicarage he said: 'I didn't want to waken you'. So he sat patiently waiting on the vestry step. I had the joy of seeing him grow up a sturdy Christian and become a churchwarden.

In Byker the wonder was that all through 'the hungry thirties', when practically the whole population was unemployed for years, and living on the means test, iniquitously applied, so many of the children grew up to be splendid, independent people. The church was not locked, night or day, for the seventeen years I was there, yet only once was an alms-box tampered with, and that by an outsider, a thief whom we caught. I never once in all those years needed to appear in court to speak for a young person in trouble. In rags, and often lice and flea-infested, they were more law-abiding, more contented and friendly, yes, and happier, than so many of the prosperous, well-fed and over-paid young people of to-day. They didn't covet other people's money or possessions, yet in later years, in Wallsend (where I became vicar when I left Byker), when prosperity, as high wages for adolescents, came along, then vicious violence by 'teddy boys' made no-one safe. One January a detective-sergeant told me that in that month there were over forty burglaries in the town. These included our church and rectory. As for our alms-boxes they were broken into several times each year, yet in the years of poverty in Byker not one of our ragged lads ever thought of such an act.

In the Byker days, too, there was little drunkenness except among those with jobs, for the out-of-work majority had little money to pay for it. One day, as I passed a door in a slum street, a woman lurched out against me singing, and with a bottle of beer stuck into the breast of her filthy blouse, while she waved another bottle in her hand. She took me by the arm and we went on our unsteady and noisy way up the street. She however was an alcoholic, ex-teacher who had come down to this through drink. The young men's worst vice was chuck-half-penny, which groups of them played at the street-corners every day and nearly all day, gambling for sometimes small, sometimes large sums. And what else had they to do? Having left school many of them had never worked for five or ten years. On one occasion I became 'an accessory after the fact'. Byker was a training ground for young constables, who annoyed me by their persistent attention to these lads, and one day, when passing the police-station, I found them gathering with bicycles for another raid. So I cycled ahead and warned the lads, who were all sitting innocently on the pavement when the young policemen arrived! Perhaps it was an unorthodox way of showing that Christ's Church cared for his people, but it paid dividends. The police always patrolled in twos but I was welcome anywhere night or day, and knew everyone by name. Of course the lads weren't perfect, and I remember one occasion when a gambling school led to a fight, but surprisingly finished with an out-door religious service!

We were having a caravan mission, with a visiting priest missioner. The caravan stood for ten days at likely street crossings, and services were conducted from the drop-end twice a day. The nightly services were well attended but one afternoon we couldn't persuade the women from their door-ways, where they stood gossiping. About forty lads were gambling in the gutter beside the caravan and suddenly, on some disagreement, two lads flew at each other. Their mates seized each of them like two battering-rams and pulled them apart amid much shouting. The mums ran up the street screaming, and this was the chance to hand round mission hymn-books, to lads and mums alike, and to start up a hymn. Quickly the hubbub ended to the strains of: 'Hold the fort for I am coming!' We had a crowded gathering!

During the time I was in Byker we managed to do a lot of building. After St. Lawrence's and its accompanying slum district of St. Peter's, were made into a parish, a vicarage was built with a hard tennis court, and later a parish hall. The hall was big enough for a badminton court. It had a stage with dressing rooms, a billiard room and a canteen.

We were helped in the great task of raising money by some professional friends and as well as by countless others. It was a great encouragement to know that, as one toiled day after day in our slum, one was supported by such a legion of wonderful fellow Christians in every walk of life. It did of course mean that one had a very large mail to deal with, after one's parish work was finished each day, and very often this kept one occupied until the early hours of the next morning: but one was young! Many gifts came anonymously, the most remarkable of which was a hundred separate £1 notes, enclosed in a tiny bit of bendable brown paper tied with a bit of string.

We had two days of celebrations at the opening of the hall, which was performed by our good friend Earl Grey. We put a very dogmatic Geordie at one door with instructions to see that everyone paid sixpence for admission. When I stepped aside to let Earl Grey go in before me he wasn't recognised, and, to my horror, I heard my tough elderly Geordie declare: 'Nay ye divent get in withoot paying yer tanner!' Happily Earl Grey was most amused, and forked up a very generous 'tanner'.

Both nights we had a crowded dance. The flat concrete ceiling was still slightly sweating onto the dancers (shades of the tin-shack roof!). One lad stole another lad's girl for one dance, but when a large drop of water fell down the back of his neck he thought the enraged lad had spat at him and began punching his nose. I had to step in quickly and explain, and the dance proceeded.

The ragged condition of our people and the poor clothes they shivered in during the winter were a constant anxiety. So was born the idea of running a full-sized clothing depot in the parish hall, if only one could get clothes for them. Then occurred the idea that better-off church people might respond, by sending their discarded clothing, and I appealed like other slum parishes in the *Church Times*. The result was most heart-warming. Every morning the parcel-post delivered a bag or more of parcels. These contained every variety of clothing, most of it of very good quality, from fur coats to socks and shirts. It at once became obvious that someone must be employed to run the depot. I was most lucky to have just the person. She was a keen church member who worked in a laundry, where she received 1d. for every shirt ironed. Voluntarily she washed and ironed our church linen and kept it immaculate. Her husband had gone to Canada to look for work several years earlier and finally had disappeared, leaving her with a small boy to bring up. She was very grateful to be given the job of manageress of the clothing depot, with a regular weekly wage. I decided to make a very small charge for all articles of clothing. This preserved the dignity of the recipients, and also paid the manageress's wages. She ran a savings-bank into which customers paid small sums with which to buy any articles they might want. Good shirts cost 1/–, suits 5/– to 10/–, fur-coats at least 10/– and so on. We begged for old wardrobes and cupboards. These we ranged round the walls of the room in the hall which we kept as the shop. Every morning parcels were unpacked, the addresses of donors were sent over to me to be acknowledged that night, all articles were sorted and priced and stored in the wardrobes. We put up a counter, and opened the shop for our mothers at 11 a.m. each day. News soon travelled, and poor people from all over Byker began to arrive, so we started a second session for them every afternoon. Our manageress was a genius at knowing the genuine mums from the imposters. Old-clothes dealers who came hadn't a chance to deceive her for they would have bought anything, whereas the needy mothers knew just what they needed, and shoes etc. of the required sizes were kept for them. Gradually one could see that the pitiful clothing of the people of Byker was being replaced. So a new hope and a decent pride returned to these splendid folk, who were the long-suffering victims of the economic disaster of the thirties.

Many families were living on 25/– or 30/– a week. Any older girls or lads who did get a job had to leave home because the means-test would deduct their wages from the family income. I discovered that lots of women would join with a friend to buy two tins of condensed milk for 5d, thus saving ½ each, because one tin cost 3d. How much nutrition could there be in a tin of milk at that price, after paying for the tin, the printed label, the carriage, and everyone's profits!

So, of course, tuberculosis was rife. In the district near the church the long rows of houses were all 'Newcastle flats' with one family upstairs and one down. In one upstairs flat I buried four members of the family in one month. They were all victims of tuberculosis. That was in Kirk Street, which had three hundred and fifty of these flats. In medical circles, as a medical journal pointed out, it was the most notorious street in the country for tuberculosis victims. No wonder that the mothers were pale and listless with sunken eyes, while the babies, as I knew when I baptized them, were like small wizened bundles, weighing almost nothing. How different from the healthy mothers and the often overweight babies one baptises to-day! Truly we've never had it so good! How pathetically poor they all were! One of our altar servers who was marrying one of our girls, as they so often did, came up to me one day and said: 'Father, I've just come from Woolworth's, where I've been buying something for our bottom-drawer! It doesn't half give you a thrill!' and he proudly showed me — a potato-peeler! He left me with a lump in my throat. Many of our young men owned neither a shirt, shoes, nor socks, but a ragged coat, trousers and waist-coat.

A few enterprising young men managed occasionally to earn a shilling or two. One was a stunted lad of eighteen, who would scarcely have got a job at the best of times, but to help his widowed mother he earned a few shillings each week. He collected bundles of clothes for the 'pop shop' (or pawn-broker's) from people too sensitive to go themselves, and on the day they got their dole money he redeemed them on their behalf. For this he got a few coppers from each customer. Then with the takings he bought small cheap oranges, soaked them in a bucket of water all night, and, when swollen, sold them 1d dearer on the street to gullible passers-by. His favouite stand was outside 'the coffin', the popular name for the local cinema, which, being at the foot of two converging streets, really was shaped like a coffin. Here the parish enjoyed itself: there were no bingo halls in those days. The price of admission was 3d and 2d or 1d and a rabbit-skin. Yes, this really was so! If Ascension Day was too wet for our outing I got the manager to put on a special show, which we filled with our children.

As the surplus proceeds of the clothing depot gradually grew I was able to satisfy a long cherished wish to open a holiday-house for our people out in the country.

This proved to be a very worth-while venture. It was made possible by the kindness of a new friend whom I met providentially at the right moment. Miss Waddilove was a Grey Lady whose uncle had recently died, leaving Brunton House empty. This was on Hadrian's Wall road, and halfway down the long Brunton Bank on the way to Choller-ford on the North Tyne, about twenty miles from Newcastle. Also empty was the chauffeur's house, and when we got to know each other, and she knew my idea, she persuaded her relatives, who were trustees of the estate, to let me lease the smaller house for a pepper-corn rent of 1/– a year.

My parents had both died recently, so I had enough furniture for the house. We put in three double beds and one single bed so that we could sleep seven, either two small families or one big one. There was also a bed-sitting room downstairs where a member of the staff could stay. The village school-master, of Wall nearby, and his wife, whom I knew, gave us a perambulator and a child's push-chair, which their children had outgrown. This enabled our parents to push their chil-dren round the glorious and bracing North Tyne countryside.

During the years I had the house, over a thousand jaded parishion-ers had a week's holiday there, and a very happy friendship grew up between the city dwellers and the village folk, which was good for both. The bus from Newcastle stopped at the door and cost 3/6. We charged another 3/6 rent for the house, if they could afford it, so for 7/–, apart from food, a family of seven could have a wonderful week's holiday. Moreover the gardener at the big house had instructions from Miss Waddilove to let people have all the vegetables, fruit, flowers, etc. they needed, and to load them up with more when they went home.

I remember one young boy looking over the top of a jug of milk when it arrived one day and saying: 'Ooh! I shan't like that: I like *real* milk!' by which he meant the cheap condensed milk he was used to at 3d a tin. He had never before seen fresh milk because literally no-one could afford it in our parish. The milkman called only at the vicarage. The cheapest variety of condensed milk was the only *real* milk to them!

Our folk enjoyed the country so much, and the new companion-ships they made, that the house was booked months ahead, even for Christmas week, and the fresh country air and the change of scene worked wonders for them. One of our mothers, who had two grown-up sons, had, like most of our women, never slept outside her own house for one night since she was married! On the first morning, in her enthusiasm, she arose early and went to pick mushrooms for the family breakfast, a novelty indeed for her! Fortunately Mr. Wardle, our farmer friend, was riding round his farm as she returned, and stopped for a friendly word. He noticed, on top of her basket a toad-stool, then another, and then another! The whole basket was full of poisonous toad-stools! She went back to breakfast sadder but safer!

Each summer, on different weeks, we took the Scouts, the choir, the altar servers, and the youth club to a camp near Brunton House. On St. Oswald's Eve (4 August) a special service was held in an historic little church nearby, dedicated to St. Oswald, King of Northumbria, and martyr. The service involved the choir, the servers, local people and members of St. Lawrence's church, the last came from home by bus for the day.

During the war years there was a new use for the holiday house. Our people, weary with constant air-raids and nightly warden's duties, were glad of rest and refreshment in a safe place for a week. We had many air-raid alarms and a few bad raids, because we were on the river-side among the shipping and the ship-yards which, by then, had spring to new life and were working feverishly for the war-effort. Enemy bombers often failed to find us because, besides a balloon-barrage and batteries of anti-aircraft guns, we had an efficient smoke-screen. This consisted of containers full of rags soaked in paraffin, placed every fifty yards along all our streets. These were ignited as soon as a raid began, so that a choking cloud of dense smoke hung like a pall over us, ensuring that we were safe but suffocating! One night, in the complete black-out, as I was returning home in my cloak and cotta from an emergency sick-call, I collided with one of these smoking containers and we rolled over together in the dark! I arrived at the vicarage somewhat shaken, my clean white cotta covered with oily soot, and blood streaming from my blackened and lacerated face. Such were the minor incidents of air-raids!

Another night when Manors goods station was partly destroyed, the mean streets scintillated in the search-lights like a fairy scene, with myriads of fragments of shattered glass. The irony, that it had taken an air-raid to produce this effect on our sombre streets, occurred to me as I made my way through them in my steel-helmet. When I got down to the slum I nearly fell over the small elderly watchman, lying outside the wood-yard gates, across the road, face downwards, and dead. The wood-yard was ablaze, and so was a fractured gas-main, lighting the whole district for the bombers overhead. The fire-brigade, to my surprise, were playing their hoses on the flaming gas-main! I very diffidently suggested that loads of soil would be more effective, and so it proved! Half of the familiar narrow streets were mountains of rubble. In the temporary mortuary we collected eighteen bodies, including one baby whose head we never found. The last man wasn't

214

found until two or three days later, when I smelt the odour of death in the rubble, and phoned the demolition squad to return.

Just before dawn, when the raid seemed to be over, my indomitable people said they wished to return later for the eucharist. So at an early hour I went to church and found quite a crowd assembled, red-eyed and jaded, but thankful to be alive. When, however, I opened the door there was an ominous, soft, shooshing sound! The whole church was inches deep in soot! During all the years since the church was built it had gathered on the roofbeams, and that night, as the bombs fell around, it had been violently dislodged. A eucharist was impossible: instead, our good weary folk spent the whole day with buckets and shovels and scrubbing-brushes. It was like shovelling black snow, and the soot had penetrated everywhere.

Eventually the authorities levelled the half of our slum streets that had not been bombed, and the good folk, whose lives I had shared for so many years, were dispersed for re-housing. During the demolition I remember finding two of the workmen, on a cold day, having their dinner in the street. 'Why don't you shelter in one of the empty houses?' I asked. 'Because the bugs are dropping off the ceiling into our bait' they replied. So the old place kept its character to the end!

Chapter XIV

THE CHURCH, CHARITY AND CHARITIES[1]

Ann Holohan

THE OPENING sentence in Charlotte Brontë's *Shirley* is a contemporary comment on the impact of the Church in mid-Victorian England:

> Of late years, an abundant shower of curates has fallen upon the North of England: they lie very thick on the hills; every parish has one or more of them; they are young enough to be very active, and ought to be doing a great deal of good.

Other accounts record the number of people attending church, the number of clergy, and also the location of the various denominations, as some measure of Christian belief. Newcastle upon Tyne, in the north of England, with a similar Victorian passion for recording the social and moral conditions in the great towns, was not neglected. Three reports written in 1850, 1854 and 1865 revealed a lack of churches and pastoral over sight, together with a general apathy in the clergy.[2] Yet the possibility of bias in these reports should not be overlooked; the authors of one report were members of a Temperance Society and the author of another was a James Street, anxious to make a case for a non-established church.

However there is one aspect of the Church in mid-Victorian England which is comparatively neglected in discussion of that period; the philanthropy of individuals, and in particular, the clergy. McCord (1976:90) makes a case for this approach and provides a definition of philanthropic activity: 'organised societies, extraordinary charitable exertions to meet some temporary need and the private charity extended by individual men and women'. It is hoped to explore some of these aspects of Victorian society in the lives of two clergy, working in widely contrasting areas: the Rev. J. Elphinstone Elliot Bates, Rector of Whalton (1843-1880), a rural parish about fifteen miles from Newcastle upon Tyne, and the Rev. Canon J. Lintott, the first vicar of St. Stephen's church (1868-1892), an urban parish in Low

Elswick in Newcastle upon Tyne. Elliot Bates provides evidence of a response to 'temporary need' following an outbreak of cholera in Whalton in 1852, and in the case of Lintott, it is principally his support of two medical charities, the Newcastle Dispensary and the Newcastle Infirmary for the Sick and Lame Poor, both founded in the late eighteenth century. As one aspect of social relationships, it is hoped that the lives of these two clergy and their families will illustrate the movement from private to public philanthropy, and from one organised charity to another. Indeed they built around themselves a complex network of giving, not only in monetary terms, but also in time and energy.

Edward Charlton, M.D., physician to the Newcastle upon Tyne Infirmary and Dispensary, published one of the most remarkable epidemiological accounts of the arrival and spread of cholera in Whalton in September 1853 (Charlton 1854). Cholera was raging in Newcastle upon Tyne; a newspaper report listed as many as 280 deaths from cholera between 31 August and 14 October, 1853. Charlton begins his account of the deaths in Whalton as follows:

> The first case of cholera in Whalton occurred in the person of William Womack aged 19, the carrier from that village to Newcastle. This young man was in Newcastle on Saturday September 10th on his usual business. He returned from Newcastle to Whalton on Saturday evening in his usual health, and, on the next day Sunday the 11th was seized with vomiting and diarrhoea. Previous to this date, diarrhoea had not been prevalent in Whalton; on the contrary few, if any, cases of autumnal diarrhoea had occurred. Womack continued to suffer from these symptoms until Wednesday the 14th September when they assumed the character of genuine Asiatic Cholera and he died on the 15th.
>
> On the day that Womack died, Thursday, September 15th, Mrs. Nicholson, the wife of a Mrs. Moore's manservant, was attacked with cholera. Mrs Nicholson had been in Womack's house when he was ill. Her own house is a single-roomed cottage, of good size, situated on the north side of the road, and about the same distance west of Mrs. Moore's house, as Womack's is to the east. McVardy (medical practitioner of the village) attended both Womack and Mrs. Nicholson, and the latter, who narrowly escaped with her life, was nursed by her husband, Mrs. Moore's manservant, who repeatedly passed from one house to the other. Neither Mrs. Moore, however, nor Mrs Vardy, who were the next two sufferers, ever visited either Womack or Mrs. Nicholson.

He continues to describe the social characteristics of the eight victims, their visiting patterns and the circumstances surrounding their deaths. Corroboration of Charlton's named fatalities can be found in the Parish Records for the parish of Whalton with added information on occupation, dates of burial, and the names of the officiating clergy.[3]

For some time before the 1853 cholera epidemic in Whalton, the clergy and people had donated money to at least two apparently remote disasters.[4] In 1822 £23 was forwarded to the Committee for the Relief of the Irish Famine. The Rev. Noel Ellison, rector of Whalton (1816-1824) headed the list of subscribers with a donation of two guineas followed by a further two guineas from his family. Three servants at the rectory also contributed 1/– each respectively. On 23 January 1827, in response to the King's Letter to the Rev. R. B. Hunter, rector (from 1824-1843 and succeeded by Rev. Elliot Bates), £11 was donated to the Poor Manufacturers (workers in industry).

The impact of cholera in Whalton cannot be underestimated; it was a local disaster. Charlton comments on its unexpectedness 'Whalton has been generally considered to be one of the healthiest villages in Northumberland'. The disease was known to thrive in areas of poverty and overcrowding, not conspicuous features in Whalton, according to Dr. Charlton, and moreover the occupations of the deceased clearly indicate that it struck rich and poor alike. The following extract from Dr. Charlton's account of the disease indicates a degree of social interaction between rich and poor, and compassionate concern for the sick which illuminates some aspects of village life in mid-Victorian Northumberland:

> Womack had communicated with Newcastle having visited the town while cholera prevailed there. He was visited by Mrs. Nicholson and by Crawford and by Lieutenant Meggison (previously noted for his extensive charities and kindness to the poor). All these were attacked by cholera. Ann Gibson had perhaps not visited any cholera sufferer, but her master Mr. Forster had seen Mrs. Vardy during her illness and was attacked himself twenty-four hours later but recovered. Mrs. Moore seems to have taken the disease from her servant Nicholson who was then in attendance on his wife, and himself died of cholera three days after his mistress. Mrs. Vardy could have received the disease through her husband, who himself remained unaffected.

The clergy officiating at the burials would not have been unaware of the possible risk of infection as a stream draining from Whalton churchyard was considered locally as a possible cause of the outbreak. It was against this background that the Rev. Elphinstone Elliot Bates organised a fund 'Subscriptions for the Cholera Fund and Drains 1854'.[5]

The two largest individual donations of three guineas, from a total subscribed of £30, were from the Rev. Elliot Bates and a Mr. T. Rochester. In 1871 Mr. T. Rochester of Whalton had also donated

£1,000 to the Newcastle Dispensary,[6] indicating that his, or his family's philanthropy embraced more than just a response to 'temporary need', but extended to alleviating the continuing distress of the urban sick and poor. If we consider the donation of one pound to the Cholera Fund from the Board of Guardians to represent 'official' sources, it is clear that this sum was greatly exceeded by 'unofficial' giving.

McCord makes the point that 'it is misleading to suppose that official Poor Law machinery and unofficial philanthropy existed in two different spheres in the nineteenth century, and in practice offical and unofficial activity for the care of the poor were controlled by much the same people' (1976:100). This was certainly true in the life of the Rev. Elliot Bates. He was also chairman of the Castle Ward Board of Guardians (Ponteland) for 38 years and on 29 September 1879, he was presented by the Guardians with an illuminated scroll for 'constant and valued services'.[7] Around the edges of the scroll are five miniature paintings; the Castle Ward workhouse, Milbourne church, Whalton church, Milbourne Hall and the Bates family crest, a constant reminder of the interlocking spheres of Church, official Poor Law and landed aristocracy.

This leads to a final and important aspect of the life of the Rev. Elliot Bates; his relationship, by marriage, to the Bates of Milbourne Hall, a village a few miles from Whalton. He was born James Elphinstone Elliot from a Border family, and he married Georgina Bates, a daughter of Ralph and Sarah Bates, and adopted their surname[8] (she was the only member of the family to marry). Through his marriage he inherited a tradition of philanthrophy stretching to the eighteenth century; his wife's maternal grandfather was the Rev. Nathaniel Ellison, vicar of Bolam (another village close to Whalton) and he appears as a subscriber to the Newcastle Infirmary for the Sick and Lame Poor in the years 1751-1753.[9] In 1878, on the death of the last surviving member of her family, Georgina Elliot Bates succeeded to the lands and property.

There is little doubt that in his contact with the Bates family the Rev. Elliot Bates would have been aware of the wide range of their philanthropic activities. They appear as subscribers to the Northern Counties Institution for the Deaf and Dumb, the Blind, the Orphaned Institution and the Newcastle Infirmary for the Sick and Lame Poor.

Finally in the 4th *Annual Report of the Newcastle Convalescent Society* (1863) a Miss Bates of Milbourne Hall donated two guineas and collected a further two pounds and the Rev. J. Lintott is named Chaplain and Secretary of the Society, with a Mrs. Lintott on the

Ladies Committee. It is here, in this mosaic of Victorian charities and charitable activities that the paths of the Rev. Elliot Bates and the Rev. J. Lintott cross and it is to his philanthropic endeavours that we now turn.

In the abstract of the accounts of the Newcastle Infirmary for the Sick and Lame Poor in the nineteenth century, the financing of the medical care of the poor by a system of subscribers and letters of recommendation is clearly described:[10]

> Every subscriber of one guinea per annum may each recommend one out-patient; and two such subscribers jointly, one in-patient. Every subscriber of two guineas per annum may recommend one in-patient or two out-patients and so on in proportion for larger subscriptions. Benefactors of £10 have the same privilege as subcribers of one guinea per annum and those who give larger sums proportionately.

The management was entirely in the hands of the Governors who were often clergy. They were either annual subscribers of two guineas or upwards or benefactors of £20 or more at one time, and *the sick had to provide these letters of recommendation* before treatment except 'persons who meet with sudden accidents requiring immediate help of surgery; they are received at any hour of the day or night without any recommendation'.

In the Rules and Regulations of the Newcastle Dispensary, a similar system of subscribers and conditions of eligibility for treatment are described:[11]

> That each subscriber of one guinea either to the general or to the Samaritan Fund* shall be entitled to recommend seven patients and each subscriber of two guineas fourteen patients annually, and in proportion for larger sums. Benefactors of ten guineas at one time to the Charity shall be entitled for life to recommend seven patients annually, and in proportion for larger sums.
>
> *A Fund for beef, mutton and wine for the sick.

That the sick faced considerable difficulty in procuring letters of recommendation cannot be denied. However it would be wrong to assume blind indifference to the sufferings of the poor, as the following remarks of the Resident Medical Officer of the Dispensary clearly indicate[12] (that he did not criticise the system of medical care is not a quality peculiar to Victorian England):

> I beg to call the attention of subscribers and non-subscribers to the constantly increasing demand for letters of recommendation owing to the increasing population of the town ... numerous applicants stating that they have spent days in fruitless search.

Bearing in mind that the rich in Victorian England could pay for private medical care, what was the financial outcome of a system of subscriptions in supporting these medical charities? Table I below lists the sources of income for the Newcastle Infirmary for the years April 1852-April 1854.[13]

Table I

Annual Income of the Newcastle Infirmary
(1852-1854)

Source of Income	1852	1853	1854
	£	£	£
Annual Subscriptions	2330	2262	2616
Interest on captial	524	635	560
Donations under £20 (no privileges)	41	28	59
Annual and other Sermons	44	36	51
Annual dinners	–	–	–
Benefit plays, concerts, lecturers etc.	–	–	21
Poor box, Sale of grains etc.	13	15	16
Apprentice Fees	54	24	206
Discounts for prompt payment	18	3	–
ordinary receipts	3042	3003	3529
Benefactions of £20 and upwards			
(Life Governors)	120	116	140
Legacies	834	45	993
Total receipts	3996	3164	4662

Source: Annual Report of the Newcastle Infirmary for the Sick and Lame Poor (1854).

Of particular interest is the contribution from sermons, and it can be seen that the annual contribution was small in relation to the total subscribed.

In 1868-9 the income for church collections was again small in relation to the total subscribed (Table II).

Table II

Church Collections in Aid of Newcastle Infirmary
(1868-69)

Source of Church Collections	Amount (£)		
St. Nicholas Anniversary Sermon	54	7	6
West Clayton Church	4	10	0
Ponteland Church Offertory	2	0	0
Corbridge Harvest Festival	2	2	0
Total	62	19	6

Source: Annual Report of the Newcastle Infirmary for the Sick and Lame Poor (1869).

In 1870 the Committee of the Infirmary faced by an increasing demand for in- and out-patient treatment from patients *without* letters of recommendation, thus increasing what was to be known as *'casuals'*, expressed its views on the apparent lack of altruism in the community:[14]

> The mass of the community has not been moved. There are multitudes of thriving merchants and tradesmen whose names are not seen on the roll of Governors. The easiest way of reaching the small givers is by having an annual collection in all churches and places of public worship.

St. Stephen's Parish, Low Elswick, Newcastle, came into being by an order in Council, 7 July, 1868 (Brion 1968:11). (The Holy Saviour church, Milbourne, was built by the Bates' family in 1869). The first vicar of St. Stephen's was the Rev. J. Lintott, and almost immediately his concern for the alleviation of suffering was acknowledged in the *Annual Report of the Newcastle Dispensary:*[15] 'The Committee gratefully acknowledge a donation of £9, from a collection at St. Stephen's Church, Scotswood Road'. In that same year the Committee of the Newcastle Dispensary expressed similar doubts about philanthropy in the town, and if forthcoming, its effect on reducing suffering:

> They would respectfully refer to the Donation from St. Stephen's church which leads them to remark, and a fact to be regretted, that in most of the places of public worship in the Town, a Collection on behalf of the Dispensary has never been made, and the Committee think the various congregations in the Town ought to have the opportunity afforded them of assisting, by their smaller contributions, such an Institution as the Dispensary, which is doing so large an amount of good among the poorer classes.

It was the Rev. J. Lintott who took up this challenge, and the result of his activities are well documented: he organised and became joint Honorary Secretary of the Hospital Sunday Fund, an organisation whereby various churches and chapels nominated a specific Sunday for collections for the sick.

The Newcastle Dispensary Annual Report for 1871 'gratefully acknowledged the sum of £224 from the Committee of the Hospital Sunday Fund'. In the following year they acknowledged a donation of £232 from the same fund and in 1873 it was resolved:

> ... that the best thanks of the Governors be given to the Committee of the Hospital Sunday Fund for the valuable aid afforded by them to this Charity and that the Rev. John Lintott and Mr. R. H. Holmes, the Honorary Secretaries to that Fund, be made Life Governors of this Institution.

222

The Hospital Sunday Fund was a common method of raising money for hospital charities[16] but apart from the obvious financial benefit to the institutions, it also 'centralised' the issue of letters of recommendation, thus reducing 'fruitless search' for individual patients.

In face of competition for funds from the Hospital Sunday Fund, not only by the Newcastle Dispensary, but by other medical charities, what impact had these organised Sunday collections on the financial position of the Newcastle Infirmary? In the 1870 Annual Report of the Infirmary, donations from church collections amounted to £121. In the following year there was an astonishing response; £1,245 was received from church collections and sermons, of which £1,093 was donated from the Hospital Sunday Fund. In the Infirmary Report for the year 1872 the Rev. J. Lintott was appointed an Honorary Governor, and his charitable organising efforts for both medical institutions was now publicly acknowledged.

It is clear that, in absolute terms, the financial gain to both medical charities from the Hospital Sunday Fund was considerable, but what is more difficult to assess is the relative advantage to the Institution. What, for example, was the relationship between subscriptions and church collections; did the introduction of the latter reduce the impact of the former? In Table III below, the total sum and proportions of annual subscriptions, church collections and Hospital Sunday Fund donations and 'other' (interest on capital and legacies etc.) are listed in relation to the total income of the Infirmary for the years 1875-1886.[17]

Table III

Subscriptions, Hospital Sunday Fund etc. to the Newcastle Infirmary (1875-1886)

| Year | Annual Subscriptions | | Church Collections and Hospital Sunday Fund | | Other |
	Total £	%	Total £	%	%
1875	2694	32	3280	39	28
1876	3094	43	1083	15	42
1877	2784	39	1217	17	44
1878	2893	40	1175	16	43
1879	2756	36	1702	22	42
1880	2881	43	525	8	49
1881	2981	40	1114	15	45
1882	2972	39	1337	18	43
1883	2988	37	1667	21	42
1884	2752	36	1775	24	40
1885	2942	36	1953	24	40
1886	3003	35	1881	22	42

Source: Annual Report of the Newcastle Infirmary for the Sick and Lame Poor (1890).

As can be seen in the above Table the total amount of annual subscriptions remained remarkably stable over the years 1875-86; fluctuations were however more marked in the Hospital Sunday Fund contributions. It is however clear that the Hospital Sunday Fund tapped a new source of philanthropy, and its contribution was not at the expense of subscriptions. It could be argued that subscribers represented a middle or upper class contribution, and the Hospital Sunday Fund the artisan and working class members of congregations. For this reason the Hospital Sunday Fund would tend to reflect prevailing economic conditions, and this is particularly marked in 1880 when the Fund reached a low of £525 per annum (Table III). The Infirmary Report for that year comments on 'the depressed state of commerce in the country'. The Newcastle Dispensary Annual Report for the same year also comments on 'the dullness of trade and the number of attendances was never even approached in the great epidemics of former times'. Thus, to some extent, the financial viability of these medical institutions was dependent on economic conditions outside their control, and in times of economic hardship increasing numbers of patients would require medical care, unsupported in many cases, by letters of recommendation, tied as they were to donations to the Hospital Sunday Fund. With a degree of understanding of 'market forces' the Rev. J. Lintott affected the 'supply' of letters of recommendation. In the *Annual Report of the Dispensary* in the year 1880 he moved that:

> It be an instruction to the Committee to issue to the Committee of the Hospital Sunday Fund, 12 instead of 10 Admission letters for each guinea received from the Fund for the purchase of letters during the ensuing year.

In the Infirmary Report of 1883 the Governors were under attack for the continuation of letters of recommendation as a prerequisite for medical care. They were in a dilemma — if the letters of recommendation were withdrawn (perhaps indirectly a measure of social status) would the annual subscription rate automatically fall? The matter was deferred, and the search for other sources of revenue continued. In that year an unprecedented step was taken to improve the financial position of the Newcastle Infirmary. In 1885 the number of 'casual attenders' (patients without letters of recommendation) reached an annual figure of 27,811 and a resolution was passed to levy a charge of 3d for each 'casual' visit.[18] It was also agreed that three workmen should be appointed Governors. In 1886 and 1887 the revenue raised by this attendance levy was £53 and £11 respectively, and the number of casuals fell dramatically from 27,811 to 19,624.

The scheme of charges was abandoned and the Governors (who included two clergymen as honorary governors; the Rev. J. Lintott and the Rev. Canon Lloyd M.A., vicar of Newcastle) reiterated the objectives of the Infirmary:[19]

> The resolution of the Governors expressly provides for the gratuitous treatment of the destitute, but at present they seem to be scared away. The famished, ill clad children of destitute or drunken parents are subject to a variety of diseases and they are a class of patients peculiarly deserving of sympathy.

The *Report* for the year ending 1888 was a milestone in the history of Newcastle Infirmary for the Sick and Lame Poor; admission was based on 'suffering, accompanied by the inability to provide medical assistance privately'. The long history of subscribers and letters of recommendation instituted in 1751 was ended. Winds of change were blowing through the old corridors and wards of the Infirmary at Forth Banks (besides Manors Railway Station) and to continue this process of change, nine working men were selected for the House Committee by the working-class governors. It was also decided that the philanthropic net should be cast even wider to include 'workmen's contributions'. What relative effect did this new class of contribution have on the revenue of the Newcastle Infirmary? Table IV, below, illustrates the impact of these contributions.[20]

Table IV

Newcastle Infirmary Revenue
(1887-1889)

Year	Annual Subscriptions		Church Collections and Hospital Sunday Fund		Workmen's Contributions		Other
	Total £	%	Total £	%	Total £	%	%
1887	2874	30	1617	17	1550	16	38
1888	3079	30	748	7	2503	25	38
1889	3180	28	1487	13	3150	28	31

Source: Annual Report of the Newcastle Infirmary for the Sick and Lame Poor (1890).

The fears of the Governors, as expressed in the Infirmary *Annual Report* of 1883, were groundless; the removal of letters of recommendation did not affect subscribers and many of the privileged continued to support the alleviation of suffering and distress. The Hospital

Sunday Fund was initially affected by the introduction of workmen's contributions but many working men would also be church attenders, and a choice of charity, with small incomes, would have to be made. In 1889 (Table IV) the Hospital Sunday Fund and workmen's contributions accounted for just over 40 per cent of the total subscribed; a remarkable example of community involvement.

The Rev. John Lintott served the parish of St. Stephen from 1868 to 1892 and he died on 16 November 1897. He gave his time and energy to many other charitable institutions; he was chaplain and Honorary Secretary to the Northern Counties Orphan Institution; he was Honorary Secretary and chaplain to the Convalescent Society, and Honorary Secretary and chaplain of the Prudhoe Memorial Convalescent Home at Whitley Bay.

Both the clergy mentioned are commemorated in their respective churches; the Rev. J. Elliot Bates retired in 1880 and died in 1890. In that year the Lord Bishop of Newcastle dedicated a Rood Screen in Whalton church with the following inscription:

> To the glory of God and to the memory of John Elphinstone Elliot Bates M.A. priest, rector of this parish 1843-1880 this screen was erected and the chancel restored by Georgina Elliot Bates of Milbourne Hall his widow.

The Rev. J. Lintott was an Honorary Canon of the Cathedral church of St. Nicholas, and the commemorative window in St. Stephen's church bears the following inscription:

> Besides their labours in this parish Canon Lintott was chiefly instrumental in founding the Northern Counties orphanage and took a leading part in establishing the Prudhoe Convalescent Home at Whitley Bay and the Hospital Sunday Fund in this city and district.

Both these clergy and their families in their philanthropic activities were involved in the organisation of charitable institutions, fund raising to meet temporary and permanent need, and private charity.[21] In an age, embryonic in its concept of state intervention, such endeavours are an important element in our understanding of Victorian society and the Poor Law. Their efforts, in a sense, blunted some of the rough edges of official Poor Law practices. In retrospect we know that individual efforts would not cope with the complexities of modern industrial society, but they laboured with compassion in the compass of their time. The Diocese of Newcastle can also be proud of the philanthropic contribution of church members to alleviate the suffering of the sick and poor in the past. The present situation is very

ANN HOLOHAN

different and charitable organisations organised by the Church are notably absent or of relatively little importance. This conclusion in principle is very close to that offered in the following chapter.

Notes and References

1. I should like to thank Mrs. Violet Anne Bates Porter and Mrs. Barbara Kathleen Bates Yorke, great grand-daughters of the late Rev. and Mrs. Elliot Bates for giving so much of their time and valuable information. I am also indebted to the Rev. Clifford Hedley, vicar of St. Stephen's church, for providing information on the life and works of the late Canon J. Lintott, and also the staff at the Northumberland Record Office and the Library, University of Newcastle upon Tyne.
2. *N.D.Ch.* 1850 ('Inquiry into Conditions of the Poor of Newcastle upon Tyne'); Newcastle upon Tyne Temperance Society 1854 (*Newcastle As It Is. Reviewed in its Moral Aspect, Social State and Sanitary Conditions*); Street 1865.
3. *Parish Records*, Northumberland Record Office, Gosforth, Newcastle upon Tyne.
4. ibid.
5. ibid.
6. *Account of the Newcastle upon Tyne Dispensary*, 1871, p.26.
7. Personal communication, Mrs. Violet Anne Bates Porter. See 1 above.
8. Personal communication, Mrs. Violet Anne Bates Porter and Mrs. Barbara Kathleen Bates Yorke. See 1 above.
9. *A Report of the State of the Infirmary for the Sick and Lame Poor*, April 13 1751 - April 3 1753.
10. *Annual Report of the Newcastle Infirmary for the Sick and Lame Poor*, 1851.
11. *Account of the Newcastle upon Tyne Dispensary*, 1865, pp.10-13.
12. ibid.
13. *Annual Reports of the Newcastle Infirmary for the Sick and Lame Poor*, 1854, p.6.
14. ibid, 1870:8.
15. *Account of the Newcastle upon Tyne Dispensary*, 1869, p.6.
16. Anning, S.T. 1963 *The General Infirmary at Leeds*, p.8.
17. *Annual Report of the Newcastle Infirmary for the Sick and Lame Poor*, 1890. p.8.
18. ibid, 1886:9
19. ibid, 1887:12
20. ibid, 1890:8
21. See *N.D.C.* 1893 (p.247 ff.) for a description of Lord Crewe's Charity at Bamburgh Castle and for a list of charitable insitutions in the area.

Chapter XV

SOCIAL WORK IN THE DIOCESE

Katharine Lloyd

J. B. ATLAY in his *Life of Ernest Wilberforce* (1912) refers to the 'courts and alleys of the swarming city' that lay at the foot of Benwell Tower, the new Bishop's Palace, donated to the Diocese by J. W. Pease, a leading member of the Society of Friends, as was also Dr. Thomas Hodgkin who lived at Benwelldene close by. Pease then lived at Pendower and the three were close friends. According to Atlay, Wilberforce was known as the 'Poor Man's Bishop' and he must have been well aware of the appalling Newcastle slums since it was his habit to stride up Westgate Hill on his way to and from his home whenever he could rather than take the tram (see Ch. III). Wilberforce, as well as striving indefatigably for the building of new churches and mission halls, also from the very beginning, identified himself with social causes, especially as will be seen those of 'Temperance' and 'Social Purity'. Social work in the Diocese went on at two levels — first, day-to-day work in the parishes; second, in special church associations or societies set up to deal with particular problems. And here straightaway there is the question of semantics, for the term 'social work' was traditionally — and still is — used to describe helping with any kind of social problem or personal problem which has a social component. Nowadays it is used also to describe the developing of the still rather self-conscious and inchoate profession of social work claiming to possess its own body of knowledge and skill.

In the late nineteenth century the Poor Law was still virtually the only statutory social service, operating partly through a comprehensive network of workhouses each serving its own defined area and mostly through a strictly administered system of outdoor-relief for the old and sick and widows with their orphaned children. The doctrine of 'less eligibility' was still widely accepted — namely that the terms of granting outdoor relief to the able-bodied poor should be so strict, even harsh, that even the lowest paid and hardest job would be preferable. Those in distress were expected to manage somehow, or, if

228

they did not want to 'go on the parish' to apply to one of the numerous charitable organisations. Only in the last resort would application be made to the Poor Law relieving officer.

In the early years of the Diocese, and indeed right up to the development of the Welfare State (a term said to have been used first by Archbishop Temple in 1942) after the Second World War, there must have been a vast amount of day-to-day 'social work' done by clergy and laity in the parishes, much of it in the very nature of things unrecorded and therefore unknown and immeasurable. The parish had been after all the original centre of almsgiving and when religious duties were crystallised during the late sixteenth century into civil obligations to pay poor rates, it became the administrative unit of the Elizabethan Poor Law. Unions of parishes had been formed after the Poor Law Amendment Act of 1834 to provide workhouses, the often hated and feared institution usually known as the 'union'. Even now some towns in Britain still have their 'Union Streets'. Towards the end of the nineteenth century however the rigours of the original work houses as satirised by Dickens in *Oliver Twist* were becoming much less severe. Workhouse infirmaries were being provided for the sick and poor, better arrangements made for children and women were beginning to serve as Guardians of the poor. Sometimes the clergy themselves might be Guardians and would, in the nature of things, be in touch with workhouses, infirmaries, voluntary hospitals, and relieving officers. Meanwhile, outside the Poor Law administration the parish church continued, and in the new Diocese the parochial system was strengthened as more and more churches were built and existing parishes divided. The incumbent and his curates, and possibly also Sisters from a religious order, normally lived within the parish boundaries and with few exceptions continued to do so until accelerating social change and widespread population movements due to re-housing, made some revision of the original territorial parochial system inevitable.

The very fact of the clergy being resident meant that they came up against all manner of personal and social problems. Whether in town or country they would be in touch with families who never otherwise came to church for christenings, churchings, weddings and funerals. In the earlier years of the Diocese people knowing the clergy were available twenty-four hours a day would send for them to visit the sick and the dying much more than now. Also they might need a sub-scriber's letter to obtain treatment at the Newcastle Dispensary or one of the hospitals and the vicar could pass parishioners on to various charities for help, or to the Newcastle Citizens Society which advertised itself in the Diocesan Gazette. During specially bad times many individual parishes would help by organising soup kitchens (St. John's, Newcastle). St. Luke's, Newcastle, ran a service of 'meals on wheels' pushing a trolley round the parish on Wednesdays and Thursdays, the hungriest days for the unemployed since the 'dole' was paid on Fridays (see Lloyd 1950:204). A great deal of help would be given in providing clothing (see Ch. XIII). In the parish of St. Peter's, Wallsend, the vicar's wife founded the Wallsend Nursing Association in 1894 and was President of the Wallsend Ladies Committee of the National Society for the Prevention of Cruelty to Children (see Richardson 1923:135). There was also the Cathedral Nurse and Hearse Society founded in 1883 of which the first Chairman was Canon A. T. Lloyd, later Bishop of Newcastle. This later became the Cathedral Nursing Society and finally after the work was taken over by the local authority, the Cathedral Nursing Society Charitable Trust. In the 1960s the vicar of St. Matthew's, Newcastle, concerned about the many problems facing children growing up in the Rye Hill district and the lack of local leadership for youth organisations, took the initiative in appealing to the local authorities for help in financing a full-time youth leader — an appeal which led to the foundation of the 'Big Lamp Youth Club'.

Especially in the days before cinemas, parish halls played a most important part. Some were very large and St. Philip's, Newcastle, had one next to the church which could seat 600 people — later it was used as a cinema. In a live parish these halls served as community centres — there could be all kinds of activities, Mothers' Union, Girls' Friendly Society, Church Lads Brigade, boys and girls clubs, later scouts and guides, cubs and brownies. Social work in its widest sense sets out to serve individuals, families, groups and communities and before the days of cinemas, radio and television the halls were much more used than they are today.

Apart from the helping of individuals, groups and communities in the parishes — and this day-to-day work was extensive and important — there were certain fields of work which were specially developed in the Diocese — namely moral welfare work, or as it was rather vaguely termed at first, 'Social Purity' — Temperance — through the Church of England Temperance Society in particular and work for the congenitally deaf and dumb. But these three probably represent only the tip of the iceberg — in that there really was a great deal of philanthropic endeavour among Victorians and Edwardians; and churchmen played a considerable part in it both in the parishes and in the various charitable organisations (see McCord 1976:105).

KATHARINE LLOYD

Historical Background of Local Welfare

An American social worker once defined an outstanding problem of social work as that of developing its service as a function of well organised community life without sacrificing its capacity to inspire in men enthusiasm for a cause. In other words quite frequently people doing social work become so involved in the ordinary, sometimes wearying and exhausting routine of helping individuals and families to cope with problems of poverty, bad housing, illness or disablement that they forget the enthusiasm for a cause which first made them decide to do this particular job. Sometimes, on the other hand, they become so disillusioned with their failure to help people that they feel the only thing to do is to work to change the whole social system and so they become involved in political action, arguing even that this is the only way to achieve any kind of progress. In the sphere of moral welfare work in the 1880s these two approaches — proclaiming a cause and carrying out the function of helping women in distress were illustrated very clearly in Josephine Butler, who is now to be commemorated in the Anglican calendar as a saint. She herself described her campaign to repeal the Contagious Diseases Acts as a 'great crusade'. Unlike many Victorian reformers in this field, she never condemned individuals as such, only the evils and injustice of the system. Born in 1829, the daughter of John Grey of Dilston, she began and ended her life in Northumberland and is buried at Kirknewton, though much of her married life was lived in Liverpool. Her 'crusade' had begun before the Diocese was formed and in 1870 she had spoken at a series of meetings including Newcastle, Berwick, Alnwick and Morpeth gaining support from workers in the shipyards, also from Dr. Spence Watson, the leader of Northumberland Liberalism, and from members of the Society of Friends.

In the very first issue of the *Newcastle Diocesan Calendar* (1883), there were already listed, though not specially connected with the Church of England, the 'Brandling Place Home for Penitent Women' and the 'Female Penitentiary' in Diana Street. This had been erected in 1837 and was described in 1844 as an 'institution for females who, having forsaken the paths of virtue, but now give evidence that they are penitent, and desirous to return from their wicked practices, may be prepared for a return to virtuous society'. In the early part of the nineteenth century the 'cause' had been mostly one of 'rescue' with the emphasis on the enormity of the 'fall' by the women — not the men — which necessitated the penitential institution to redeem it. 'There was a current widespread assumption that it was the woman's responsibility to resist temptation, not the man's to refrain from

231

offering it and that should she succumb the woman should suffer to the full the consequences of her fall' (see Hall and Howes 1965:17). Thus she often only had the choice either of being separated from her child and entering a strict penitentiary for a lengthy period of training or, if she wished to keep the baby of entering the workhouse where she could be detained indefinitely. In addition, if she lived near a military establishment, she could under the Contagious Diseases Act (1864), if believed by a corps of special police to be a common prostitute, be arrested, made to submit to compulsory medical examination and if she refused it, to imprisonment. Josephine Butler's particular concern was that the Acts deprived these women of their civil rights of freedom from arrest, except on a clearly defined charge, and freedom from imprisonment except by proper trial by jury.

In the 1885 *Newcastle Diocesan Calendar* there is already listed not only the Newcastle Diocesan Training Home and Receiving House for friendless girls, but also the Northumberland Association for the Protection of Women and Children and the Newcastle White Cross Association. The Bishop and Mrs. Wilberforce were joint presidents of the Diocesan Society and for the Northumberland Association the patron was the Duke of Northumberland and the presidents, the Lord Bishop of Newcastle and the Rt. Rev. the Bishop of Hexham and Newcastle (the Roman Catholic Bishop) — an early instance of ecumenical co-operation. Vice-Presidents were the Earl of Tankerville and Sir Charles Trevelyan and the committee included Thomas Pumphrey and H. E. Richardson, members of the Society of Friends. The objects of the Diocesan Society and the Northumberland Association were mostly identical and were as follows:-

> This Association is established for the Protection of Women and Children by the Promotion of Social Purity and the Diminution of Vice.
> Objects 1. To raise the standard of public opinion on moral questions.
> 2. To see that the Laws at present in existence for the suppression of immorality are put into force.
> 3. To obtain improved legislation both Imperial and Municipal.
> 4. To raise the condition of Women and Girls employed in Factories, Shops and Brickyards.
> 5. To prevent cruelty being practised on children.

The Newcastle White Cross Association was started by Ellice Hopkins in 1883 with similar objects but emphasising that the Law of Purity was *equally* (sic) binding on men and women.

Here in the objects of these three bodies there is evident widespread interest in a cause reflecting no doubt a variety of motives and interests but also a genuine concern to combat current social evils. Both the Diocesan Society and the Northumberland Association did however set out to perform a useful function as well — the Diocese with its training home and refuge for friendless girls, later to become the House of Mercy (afterwards St. Hilda's School), and the Northumberland Association with its Lodge for girls in difficulty in Ridley Place. Some *Reports of the Northumberland Association* survive and reflect the prevailing nineteenth century acceptance of a rigid class structure and strict moral code. Thus, 'nearly one-seventh of the cases dealt with since the commencement (of the Lodge) have belonged to the lowest class of girls . . . A condition, latterly more stringently insisted upon, that these wretched girls should go to Homes has caused a marked diminution in that class among visitors to the Lodge. Many object and it is not to be wondered at — to a prolonged probation with continuous work without wages' (1888). Hence the reluctance to apply for assistance. On the other hand 'It must, surely, be a comfort to those anxious for the welfare of young women and children to know that there exists in Newcastle an institution which receives them without payment at any hour of the day or night, if there be room; that there they are comfortably tended and that the best that is possible is done for them . . . Hardly an evening passes when former residents in the Lodge do not call and see the Matron. They repair thither for rest, especially on Sunday, have tea together, talk over their hopes and sorrows and then with Mrs. Spalding attend some evening service and return to their situations brighter and happier for the change, and the only little taste of home life which many, alas, have ever known' (1889).

The multiplicity of organisations relating to this particular 'cause' is at first very puzzling. The clue probably lies in the interest already existing locally before 1882 and the new bishop's enthusiasm and ability to co-operate with people not necessarily connected with the Established Church. There is quoted in Atlay's biography an undated letter to the Bishop from Ellice Hopkins, an enthusiastic worker against the evils of prostitution and the exploitation of young children in the white slave traffic, whom he had already met in his work in the slums of Portsmouth. There, to quote his biographer, 'the young soldiers and sailors, to say nothing of the civil population, moved in the midst of vice, flagrant and unashamed' (Atlay 1912:62).

Another explanation of the variety of organisations is apparent in the record of the Diocesan Conference in October 1885, when the last session was devoted to the topic of 'Social Purity'. There was an introductory address by the Bishop (not printed) and one by the vicar of Newcastle, Canon Lloyd, on 'The Problem as Affecting Men'. Canon Lloyd criticised the 'recent revelations of foul and devilish iniquity practised wholesale in our great metropolis' during the recent debates on the Criminal Law Amendment Act. A more factual address was that on 'Rescue and Preventive Work' by the Rev. S. E. Pennefather, secretary of the Diocesan Society for the Protection of Women and Children, who said that rescue work had three aspects: political, social and religious. He referred to the passing of the Criminal Law Amendment Act only two months before, which had raised the age of consent for sexual intercourse from 12 to 16 and had laid down rules for the regulation of brothels and the control of commercialised prostitution. He also stressed the need for action to raise the whole standard of social life by arousing public opinion and finally the religious aspect of rescuing girls from a life of sin. The Diocesan Society for the Protection of Women and Children had been originated by the Bishop shortly after his consecration at the same time as he suggested the formation of the Northumberland Association on as wide a basis as possible. In addition to the wider general Association a Diocesan Society was to provide homes for destitute and friendless girls, in which definite religious teaching according to the principles of the Church of England was to be given. Of the three houses in Ravensworth Terrace (off Westgate Hill), one was a receiving home, one a training home and one a lodging house for deaconesses and others, who were waited on by the girls in training for domestic service. 'While on the one hand there is love and brightness, on the other there is discipline, constant industry, no pandering to violence, no weak indulgence but a true representation of that living, loving Gospel which "raiseth up the poor out of the dust and lifteth the needy out of the dunghill".' There was a need for a House of Mercy for girls who had actually 'fallen into sin and had to be restrained from a life of vice, in some place removed from old scenes of temptation and haunts of vice, where in fresh air, surrounded by country scenes with plenty of occupation for mind and body these erring sisters might be gently but firmly brought back into the paths of virtue'. In fact a few years later one of the Ravensworth Terrace houses did become a 'Home of Mercy' and must have been the forerunner of the House of Mercy opened in Gosforth in 1897. There were further addresses by Major Coulson of Blenkinsop Castle (who was in favour of flogging for those who led children into vice), and by the Chief Constable of Newcastle who, responding to recent criticism of Newcastle, was at pains to point out the efforts made by the police to control prostitution in what must have been a difficult situation. There were, he said, 41 disorderly houses and 262 'unfortunates' known to the police.

The Bishop in conclusion attacked the dual standard for men and women, as had Josephine Butler and Ellice Hopkins. 'It was not at all true to say that horrible sin and vice they met together to consider was really caused by the gold of rich men ... it was a vice inherent in human nature. They were told this sin was a necessity, that they could not help it, but if they believed in the power of the Lord God was He not more powerful than any sin.'

So much for the 'cause' of 'Social Purity'. The way of proclaiming it may seem strange in the permissive society of today but to the Victorians there were no shades of grey — only black and white, and for many a very direct scriptural and simple faith — almost fundamentalist in its conviction.

The Diocesan Society continued at Ravensworth Terrace and by 1891 there was a refuge at No. 6 and a Home of Mercy at Nos. 7 and 8. Meanwhile the Northumberland Association had a separate Lodge at 23, Ridley Place. About 1897 the Home of Mercy moved to new premises at Salter's Road, Gosforth, remaining there till the Second World War when it became a school for girls (St. Hilda's), 'approved' and financed by the Home Office though still an Anglican organisation.

Eventually the Northumberland and Diocesan organisations seem to have merged but it is not clear how the work was organised in the early years of the new century. By 1920 there were 3 separate organisations: the Diocesan Homes for Women and Girls comprising the Lodge (a training home at 18, St. Thomas's Crescent closed in 1932) and the Refuge at 41, Jesmond Road (which fulfilled the function of providing a shelter for young women and girls in moral difficulties and dangers); the House of Mercy in Gosforth; and the Newcastle Diocesan Association for Rescue and Preventive Work which had outdoor workers at Alnwick, Berwick, Blyth, Hexham, Morpeth, Newcastle, Tynemouth, Wallsend and Willington Quay. In addition, Elswick Lodge Maternity Home was opened in 1920.

In summarising what has happened since the 1930s it is proposed to deal with Elswick Lodge, the home for unmarried mothers and their babies and St. Hilda's School separately before describing the last 37 years of the 'Outdoor Work'.

Newcastle Diocesan Maternity Home (Elswick Lodge)
Elswick Lodge, the Diocesan Maternity Home for unmarried mothers, was opened in 1920 and continued apart from brief periods of temporary closure until 1970 when the need for it apparently no

longer existed. But it was very much needed in 1920 when illegitimate pregnancy often meant that a girl was rejected by family and friends and was in desperate need of shelter and support through her confinement. To quote the *First Annual Report:* 'Elswick Lodge is a bright sunny house with a good garden and a terrace where the babies spend their days whenever the weather is suitable'. Its aims were later set out as being:

1. To maintain a home to help young unmarried women, of respectable character, who are expectant mothers or who have recently become mothers and to bring them under moral and spiritual influences.
2. To teach such women to be good wage-earners by careful training while in the Home, in order that they may support themselves and their children.
3. To give these children a healthy start in life.

At first the girls went to hospital for their confinements — later in 1934 a Maternity block was added so that normal confinements could take place in the Home. Girls were expected to stay in the Home for two months before and two months after the birth of the child (at the beginning the stay was for a total of six months).

It is difficult to generalise about life in Elswick Lodge, especially as this must have varied considerably according to staff and resources available at different times. A retired moral welfare worker of great experience told the writer how a particular superintendent in the 1960s had made the Lodge a real home for the girls because of her warmth and concern in caring for them. Such individualised concern is an essential part of any Home especially when it is remembered the anxieties and griefs the girls had to face — estrangement perhaps from their families, anxiety about their confinement heightened because in many instances they might be giving up the baby for adoption or would have to have him fostered so that they could work. There was a chapel in the Home (The Chapel of the Good Shepherd) — the chaplain would visit regularly — there would be daily prayers and instruction and church on Sundays and every year some girls would be confirmed. Mention is made in the *Annual Reports* of singing, sewing, cookery and country dancing classes. So for many years, especially in wartime, the Home fulfilled its function of providing a sanctuary for girls who wanted and needed it. But finance was always a problem — this evidently was not a popular cause in the twentieth century and there were also many difficulties in finding suitable staff which must have at times affected the quality of life. In 1969 there was talk of renovation and extension of the Home — then quite suddenly there was a drop in applications for admission which made it impossible to carry on on a viable basis. Wider use of contraception, the Abortion Act and even more, the rapid change in society's attitude to illegitimacy, meant the need for a safe retreat for unmarried mothers was diminishing. There were far fewer of them and of those many were normally able to stay with their families and keep their babies with them. It was wise for the Diocese to recognise this and to allow the house to be used instead as a home for the rehabilitation of alcoholics.

St. Hilda's School (formerly the House of Mercy)

St. Hilda's is now the only survivor of the work which came into being under the leadership of Bishop Wilberforce in the 1880s and even that is under the control of the Newcastle Social Services Department though with continued Anglican representation on the Board of Governors. As related earlier, it seems to have been started by the Diocesan Society for the Protection of Women and Girls in Ravensworth Terrace (off Westgate Hill) very close to St. Matthew's church. It moved to Salter's Road, Gosforth, in 1897 and it is indeed a far cry from the Statutes then passed to the activities of the School at the present day. The object in 1897 was to be 'the reception and protection of penitent women who have led unchaste lives with a view to their reformation and amendment of life'. No records have been traced for the period between 1897 and 1939 but in 1939 the general control was vested in a Council — the Bishop for the time being was Visitor — the Warden (nominated by the Bishop) was the Rev. Canon W. A. Studdert Kennedy, Vicar of All Saints, Gosforth, and the Sister-in-Charge, who was subject to his superintendence and had responsibility for the government of workers and inmates. There was also a Ladies Committee dealing with domestic affairs. There were about thirty girls, eight of whom were mental defectives subsidised by Northumberland County Council and training was given in laundry work and domestic duties and some girls worked in the gardens. There were financial and organisational difficulties and the whole constitution required revision, having apparently been drawn up for a Sisterhood and being too antiquated for present needs. The Home was taken over in 1942 as an Approved School under the Home Office and continued as such until the 1969 Children and Young Persons' Act set up a new system of Community Homes under the control of the Local Authority which took over the School in 1973.

Mention should be made of Miss Bird who became Headmistress of St. Hilda's School in 1943 and stayed until her death in 1959. She was of the older school of social workers who tended to stay in a job for many years and she gave the best part of her life to looking after the girls. There was a warm, relaxed atmosphere about the place which was immediately apparent. She once related to the writer how two girls who were supposed to be lighting a fire started reading the old newspaper instead and not understanding some phrase said to her, 'What's a frump?' She replied 'You're looking at one'! Apparently the girls then intimated they preferred to have someone like her who could give all her time to the school and to them.

Much more could be said about St. Hilda's if space permitted, for example, its custodial and punitive image seems to have disappeared. To quote Mr. Davidson the present Headmaster: 'Control in the school is generally maintained by good personal example, without resort to more restrictive punitive practice ... and the detention rooms which have been a part of the controlling characteristics of the school for some years, are under-used and a seemingly unnecessary addition'. What was started by the Church to serve a very different function a hundred years ago continues as part of the statutory social services to train girls for living in an even more challenging social situation but at least one where poverty, as the Victorians knew it, is a thing of the past. Church influence is still there in the Anglican tradition of the school and the church affiliation of some of the Managers. Four foundation member managers continued in 1973 together with the eight appointed by the local authority. Incidentally some girls who talked to one of the Managers said they preferred having a structured discipline and guidelines: 'you know where you are' and 'if we didn't have it we'd all be fighting'. Though two were for abolishing the Chapel, the other two were for keeping the Chapel services: 'Chapel was one place where you could get a bit of peace' and 'you could talk to the Chaplain'.

Moral Welfare Work in the Field (1939—76)
Problems in relation to family life and especially to illegitimacy always increase in wartime and the Newcastle Diocese was no exception. The Refuge which had moved to Clifton Road in the West End was extremely busy during World War II giving shelter to girls in moral danger, mostly aged 13–16, and many cases were sent on remand from the Juvenile Court. Girls could be sent to the Refuge not only by the Diocesan Outdoor Workers but also by the Local Education Authority, the Police, Probation Officers, N.S.P.C.C. etc. for shelter, temporary care and for observation.

The Refuge was also responsible for outdoor work in Newcastle during the war and there were many unmarried mothers needing help as well as a large number of married women with husbands serving abroad giving birth to illegitimate babies. After the war however, because of staffing and financial problems and the need for expensive fire precautions to the building, and also in view of the re-opening of Elswick Lodge, the Refuge was closed down. From then on the emphasis was on outdoor work and on the work at Elswick Lodge already described.

There was an Organising Secretary for the whole Diocese and outdoor workers in Hexham, Blyth, Berwick, Wallsend, Tynemouth and Ashington, and with much better co-operation and organisation the Diocesan Council was more able to fulfil its function of providing a social work service over the whole area. Many hundreds of girls and their families were helped during the period. For obvious reasons details of cases were never given in *Annual Reports* but to take a sample year (1963) in Newcastle alone there were 214 cases classified as follows:

Unmarried mothers	157
Married with illegitimate child	28
Divorced with illegitimate child	4
Matrimonial troubles	12
Seeking advice	5
Care and protection	2
Putative father	1
Unclassified	5
	214

The amount of care and concern needed for these many sided problems cannot be over-estimated. As in the case of girls coming to Elswick Lodge endless understanding and patience were needed especially when mothers had decided to give up their babies for adoption. Many local authorities preferred to use voluntary organisations for this particularly difficult work and this continued even after the creation of the new Children's Departments in 1948, specially charged with caring for children deprived of a normal home life. The workers themselves, who had usually been trained at Josephine Butler House in Liverpool, often wanted to work for a church organisation. Their training had strong devotional and theological components in contrast to university social work courses.

Finance was always a desperate problem. Each local Committee was largely responsible for raising its own funds and while some parishes helped through collections many did not and there had to be constant local money-raising efforts. Moreover, through the years, worker after worker retired — in the last years there were only three, all working from a central office in Newcastle — and when they too retired or resigned no more trained people were available to succeed them. (It is worth noting that Miss Margaret Tharp had been Organising Secretary from 1950 until she retired in 1976.) Josephine Butler House had closed for moral welfare work training in 1970 so the main source for new workers had ceased. Moreover the *Seebohm Report* on Local Authority and Allied Personal Social Services had recommended in 1968 that, while recognising the outstanding pioneering work done by religious organisations, 'there should be a realistic alternative source of assistance to those unmarried mothers who do not wish to approach religious bodies. There should in fact be a clear assignment of responsibility to the social service department for ensuring adequate social care and advice for both the unmarried mother and her child.' In other words, there was developing a unified though still rather tentative professional approach to social problems.

In 1976 the Diocesan Board for Moral and Social Welfare closed down its work and handed over to the Diocesan Board for Social Responsibility.

Temperance Work

An interesting entry in the *Newcastle Diocesan Gazette* for 1886–7 giving evidence of one of the Bishop's particular concerns is: *The Bishop of Newcastle's Navvy Mission to the Men on the Alnwick and Cornhill Railways*. This provided a chapel in Alnwick, a Club every evening at 6 p.m. with a concert and entertainment on Saturdays and a temperance meeting on Fridays. There was also a mission hut and reading room at Wooler. It must have fulfilled a very necessary function in that wild and remote stretch of Northumberland — even more remote then before the motor age.

To quote the Bishop's biographer, 'Intemperance is the twin sister of impurity and drunkenness with all its train of misery and sin was only too prevalent in certain parts of the Newcastle Diocese' (Atlay 1912:158). The Bishop had already campaigned for the Church of England Temperance Society (C.E.T.S.) when he was working in Lancashire and had found that this provided the readiest means of campaigning against the evil and helping to rescue the 'drunkards'. 'It also provided a platform on which Churchman and Dissenter could meet in a common cause without any sacrifice of principle on either side' (ibid:159). A local branch had been founded in 1874 and its object was to promote habits of temperance, reform the intemperate, and remove causes which lead to intemperance. The Bishop carried his support to the extent of becoming a total abstainer himself though he did not exclude wine when dispensing hospitality at Benwell Tower and is reported to have made the half-regretful admission, 'What a good thing in itself is a glass of old sherry!' (ibid). In 1883 there was a meeting at Berwick with a vast audience including many Nonconformists in order to found a branch of the C.E.T.S. and the Bishop held its attention for over an hour in a memorable speech. About the same time he wrote an explanatory letter about the society to Early Percy explaining its aims and methods and saying: 'I see thousands and thousands living miserably and dying impenitently on account of their misuse of alcohol' (ibid:161).

The C.E.T.S. continued to flourish in the Diocese, judging from the frequent references to its work in the *Newcastle Diocesan Gazette*, and its many appeals for funds. One particular activity and a very important one was that of the Diocesan Police Court Mission which seems to have begun in 1898 when, at the instigation of the Bishop and the C.E.T.S. council, an agent was placed in the Police Court in Newcastle because it was estimated that 90 per cent of the total appearing were charged as a result of drink. In 1898 the C.E.T.S. Police Court Mission began its work. The Missionary would be at the prison gates a little before 7 a.m. (males were discharged at 7 and females at 7.30 a.m.). Every discharged prisoner *really deserving help* (my italics) was given breakfast by a warm fire and many prisoners were passed on to the Discharged Prisoners' Aid Society. The difficulty was to 'place these men and women out of reach of their old associations and to give them something to replace the longings for drink and sin' *(Diocesan Gazette,* vol. 136). The Missionary's work included visiting courts, home visiting, raising money and keeping in touch with institutions such as the Lodge in Ridley Place and House of Mercy in Gosforth. Here was a good example of the Church undertaking voluntary work which later developed into a statutory service i.e. the Probation Service which was first established in 1909. It is interesting to note that in 1905 the vicar of Bolam undertook to attend at the Police Court at Wallsend, which was without Missionary help, and that in 1925 Miss Teresa Merz (a member of the distinguished Merz family who later moved from Quakerism to Anglicanism) and a well known volunteer social worker, was apparently acting as a probation officer. She was mentioned in the *Newcastle Diocesan Gazette* in connection with the 'After Care of Boys' asking for people to befriend them. There were numerous references in the *Diocesan Gazette* over the years to the work of the C.E.T.S., thus in 1907 the

Missionary had attended courts at Morpeth, Blyth, Bedlington, Bellingham, Rothbury, Alnwick, Amble, Belford and Berwick. A former Police Court Missionary, later a probation officer, long since retired, writes as follows (Cottam 1979):

> The work of the Police Court Mission ... covered much 'out of court' work. Many persons approached the missionary directly, clergy, doctors or members of other social organisations. This work included conciliation in matrimonial disputes, enquiries requested by the Court regarding home surroundings, means, etc., supervision of payment of fines and supervision of children released from approved schools, youths from Borstal and men from prison. After these became statutory duties much voluntary work remained. Missionaries carried on this work in addition to probation duties and it included parents with children out of control, disputes with neighbours and landlords, finding accommodation, mainly for youths and arrangements for access to children of parents who had separated. The social work of the Church through the Court Missionary ... was not confined to Church members and included people of all ages, in all circumstances, rich and poor, regardless of colour or creed.

Much more could be said about the origins of probation in the work of the Police Court Missionary — undoubtedly it was their religious conviction that made much of their work possible and convinced the courts of the necessity for a full-time probation service.

Today, although alcoholism remains a most serious increasing problem, much more is understood about it from the medical angle and treatment is available through the National Health Service. However, there is still a great need for residential care for alcoholics, who are in the process of controlling their drink problems; and in 1970 Elswick Lodge, formerly the home for unmarried mothers already described, was re-opened as a therapeutic hostel for male alcoholics. Basic funding of the property was made possible by the Bridgehead Housing Association and the day-to-day expenses of the house are met by contributions from the men, voluntary subscriptions and a Home Office grant.

The terms of the grant were such that the Lodge had to restrict its admissions to ex-offenders with alcoholic problems. However, this proviso has now been dropped and the funding taken over by the Department of Health and Social Security. Many referrals do still come however through the courts and the prison and probation services. The Lodge normally accepts as residents men who have already undergone some medical treatment and show themselves well motivated to overcome their problem. No alcohol is allowed in the house and the staff are available for counselling. Appropriate men are encouraged and helped to find employment. There is still a link with the Church, largely in the person of the chaplain (the vicar of St. Philip's church) who visits regularly, conducts services in the chapel and is an ex-officio member of the management committee.

Concern for Deaf and Dumb

In 1876 there was founded as a result of a meeting at the Alliance Hotel, Newcastle, the Northumberland and Durham Religious Mission to the Deaf and Dumb. 'This was at the earnest solicitation of many of the well disposed Deaf and Dumb residents in and near Newcastle' (First Annual Report). It was to be a 'purely Religious Mission to the Adults of this sadly afflicted class of our fellow-men of whom more than 300 reside in the districts over which it extends'.

The first President was the Principal of the Deaf and Dumb Institute (already existing since 1886 to look after the education of deaf children). Later in 1889–91 he was Thomas Hodgkin, a Quaker also banker and historian, whose name appears constantly in lists of committees and subscribers to the early causes of the Diocese. By 1903 there were centres at Newcastle, South Shields, Jarrow, Blyth and Consett and the number of Deaf and Dumb was estimated at 630. In regard to finding employment there were problems because of the Workmen's Compensation Act (1897), which deterred employers from giving employment to the deaf. A stern warning was given in the report against assisting tramps and beggars, whose problems needed to be dealt with through a labour colony or the workhouse. They 'eat the bread of idleness at the expense of misguided exponents of sentimental "charity" whose gifts are more of a curse than a blessing to the recipients, while the truly poor, the aged, sick and infirm are left unhelped'. (A good illustration of Charity Organisation social work theory at its most extreme!) Several reports at this period draw attention to the fact that the Mission was quite separate from the Deaf Children's Institution and that while the state provided for children's education, it did nothing to help in finding employment for them.

The work of the Mission continued to develop on the lines originally laid down. For many years the main centre of its work was at 182, Westgate Road, Newcastle but in 1933 it moved to its present headquarters at South Ashfield, a large, stonebuilt private residence (another 'rich man's castle', complete with large stables), which had been a Home for Deaconesses when given up as a family house. There was increasing co-operation with statutory bodies, e.g. an After Care Committee was formed in 1933 to co-operate with special schools for the deaf and the Public Assistance Committee. By 1939 there was a staff of a chaplain and 6 men and 4 women. By 1952 five Centres had been established each with a chapel, a room or rooms for social activities and an office for the worker. Much time was given to finding jobs and 67 were placed in industry including 9 school leavers. (Sometimes 20–30 employers had to be approached in order to find one job.) The work centred of course mainly on keeping in touch with the deaf and providing classes and clubs for them with the church services as the centre — much better attended then than now when the little church at South Ashfield probably has far too many seats for its diminished congregation. The voluntary organisation has now, as regards much of its social work, been taken over by the statutory Social Service Departments.

The Club premises at Newcastle are still open every night though now attended mostly only by elderly folk. The Mission continues to provide church services, social centres, visiting in home, hospital and at place of employment, and, a very important function, Interpretation for the Deaf and Dumb, and Deaf Blind (which may be suddenly and urgently needed in hospital, police-station or courts).

Conclusion

> Still the weary folk are pining
> For the hour, that brings release
> And the city's crowded clamour
> Cries aloud for sin to cease.
> And the homesteads and the woodlands
> Plead in silence for their peace.

This seems an appropriate ending to chapters that began with a hymn illustrating the structured society of the Victorian age. Written by Henry Scott Holland, Canon of St. Paul's, one of the founders of the Christian Social Union in 1889, it is even more relevant to the closing decades of the twentieth century. We have seen how the Newcastle Diocese in addition to the day-to-day work in the parishes sponsored various kinds of social work, often linking them with a crusade for social justice and social reform. Such was the work for the unmarried mother and her child (following on Josephine Butler), and the temperance work which placed missionaries in the courts, who became the pioneers of the probation service. Less spectacular but no less important was the work for the congenitally deaf and dumb, a particularly lone and isolated group. A century ago and indeed right up to the Second World War there was little or no grant-aid from statutory authorities and heroic efforts were necessary to raise funds in order to keep church social work in existence. However, as has been found again and again in the history of the social services, where a need is recognised and met to some extent by voluntary effort, it becomes more obvious, and statutory provision follows covering the ground more completely. So now the Social Service Departments have taken over much of the work for mothers and children, (though voluntary children's homes run by the Church of England Children's Society continue), and the work for the deaf and dumb, while the probation service has long ago replaced the court missionary work. Since 1970 there has been a Diocesan Board for Social Responsibility to keep in touch with the many kinds of voluntary caring work still undertaken by the Church, especially new ventures and sponsoring them where appropriate. For instance a Social Responsibility Officer was appointed in 1978 to concentrate in the first instance on problems arising out of unemployment but also with a wider remit.

Meanwhile the day-to-day work of parish priest and parishioners, both much fewer in numbers than a century ago, continues. Material poverty thankfully is much less but there are other kinds of poverty and deprivation, and both in urban and rural areas people are still all too often bewildered, lonely and despairing in the new anonymous society of tower blocks, outlying housing estates, bleak new towns, and sometimes near-deserted villages, which have replaced the crowded slums of the past. The new full-time professional social worker may talk of 'crisis intervention' but he does not usually live in his neighbourhood. The family doctor is often replaced at night by a deputising service, police patrol in cars. Even the parish priest may have several parishes to look after and some or most of his congregation scattered or non-resident. So we end with a question mark which this chapter cannot answer. What is the role of the Church in relation to social work and social change in the closing decades of the twentieth century?

It is widely recognised now that the Victorian method of encapsulating problems in institutions (workhouses, prisons, mental hospitals, orphanages, homes of all kinds), has to be replaced as far as possible by helping people in their own families and in their own neighbourhoods. The greatest challenge is perhaps still in the parishes with churchpeople playing their part in such ventures as Age Concern, Telephone Samaritans, Christian Aid, W.R.V.S., and many other bodies. Only a few church folk nowadays may be full-time professional social workers, in contrast to Henry Mess's observation that most social workers were members of the Christian churches. There is however a continuing and increasing need for voluntary workers and they are needed to work with professionals, especially in work for children, for refugees, and in the probation service. Increasingly there will also be new kinds of parishes as in the ecumenical centre at Killingworth where the church centre is used by all denominations and the Anglican warden works closely with his non-Anglican colleagues. In a gaunt new town, which inevitably lacks tradition and roots, this centre radiates warmth and friendship, and takes in strangers.

Sadly, after a hundred years of social work and social change, most church people would agree that we are very far from discovering the things which belong to our peace and are much less certain of our function than the determined Victorians, or the fervent crusaders who sponsored the Copec conference and the housing reforms of the 1920s and 30s. Perhaps in view of the unanswered question, it is time once again for a 'new ferment' in the Church and society, for as Canon Barnett was wont to remark in the 1880s 'the sense of sin is the starting point of progress.' There needs to be a continual re-thinking of the implications of the parable of the Good Samaritan for the Church in a society which while professing a more equal social structure, and despite its great achievements in the past which have been described here, seems to have lost its way.

Chapter XVI

THE CHURCH IN ITS INDUSTRIAL SETTING

Peter Dodd

THE DIOCESE of Newcastle was born of the industrial revolution. In the eighteenth century that revolution had shifted the balance of population and of wealth from the south to the north, and the old conditions of society had passed away. Yet the Church of England had been slow to respond in its administration to these new conditions, and the year before Queen Victoria came to the throne saw the same number of English dioceses as did Queen Elizabeth. When eventually it was proposed to create new dioceses in the 1870s there was strong opposition. One critic in Parliament, Joseph Cowen, speaking about the possibility of a diocese in Newcastle rejected the idea on the gounds that the Anglican clergy did not have the troubles and needs of their parishioners at heart (see Chapter II). He looked back in his speech to the golden age of the Lindisfarne prelates who had really been pastors to their flock, but in the present proposed appointments he merely saw state officials 'swaggering in the foretop of the State', rather than providing 'a place of refuge for the weary, of shelter for the poor, of solace for the sick, of help for the desolate and of tribuneship for the oppressed.' His outburst is significant in that he claimed with some justification to speak for the mass of working people who saw bishops in this light, and he drew attention to the way in which reform in the Church of England seemed to revolve so much around the individual persons of the diocesans. This latter point emerges also in the attempts to raise sufficient money for the endowment of the bishop and here again Newcastle was in a difficult position. Northumberland and Durham were in the throes of a great coal strike; there was economic depression; 1879 was a particularly bitter winter, and it was not until 1881 that sufficient monies came in to launch the Diocese finally in the spring of 1882 (see Chs. II and IX).

The creation of the new Diocese was an administrative response to the shift in population; but a far greater response was needed to the very different world which industry was creating. The purpose of this essay is to show something of the variety — and limitations — of the Church's response over the century; in its thinking, its action and its style of ministry, and thus to indicate the degree to which the Church was open to the profound changes in society taking place around it, and open to any necessary change within itself. What stage then had been reached in 1882, in the process of industrialisation in the north east of England, to which the Church could respond?

It is easy to assume that the progress of industrialisation in the eighteenth and nineteenth centuries was a gradual, inexorable one with its own logic of development. In fact it was, as it is today, full of trauma, hardship and failure. Nevertheless by 1882 much had been achieved, although much had also failed or passed away (see Ch. I). Attempts at effective trade unions within the mining industry had been thwarted in several strikes, but in 1864 Thomas Burt proposed that the Northumberland miners should form a separate organisation of their own. By 1872 through a combination of moderation, integrity and skillful leadership he had established a strong union in Northumberland, and had obtained a better position for his men than any other coalfield in England. In Durham the wages were considerably lower, but the unions there also survived the bad times in the later seventies and by 1882 'were unrivalled' in the country 'in financial strength, organisation, stability and firm purpose.' After the Reform Act of 1867 the pitmen-householders of Morpeth returned Burt as a Radical member of Parliament, and in 1884 three more miners' representatives were elected, who, like Burt, were Radicals supporting the Liberal party. It was only later, about the time of the great dock strike of 1889, that socialism began to take the place of Methodism as the chief influence on the miners views and outlook.

Other industries had contracted or lost the initiative to companies elsewhere. In the early industrial revolution it had been iron that had set the pace; for bridges, locomotives, rails and all types of machines. The Bedlington ironworks which had been established about 1740 had attained a position of considerable importance by the early nineteenth century, but the competition from Cleveland was fierce, and in 1856 it stopped production of pig iron and closed down altogether in 1860. A similar fate was suffered by the Wylam furnaces which went out of blast for the last time in 1865. By 1882 nostalgia and envy of the Tees were already features of industrial attitudes in Northumberland.

Smaller industries had also contracted. Soap, glass, pottery, alkali and wrought iron industries had all flourished up to the 1850s and even 1870s, but then became minor industries or faded out altogether. The most significant contraction however was the end of the railway boom. In 1848 only 256 miles of the pre-1914 North Eastern Railway system had been opened. From then until 1889, 1,335 miles of new line were constructed, but in the following 25 years only 164. Significantly for our time we may note the construction in 1880 of the riverside branch from Newcastle to North Shields which carried the 'workmen's train', previous to which a river steamboat had been the order of the day.

Beside this contraction there was of course enormous growth, particularly in shipbuilding and engineering. 1852 had seen the building of the John Bowes, the first sea-goir.g iron screw collier, by Charles Mark Palmer. She made the journey to and from London in five days, compared with the previous month, and a great demand for Tyne-built ships ensued. The 1860s and 1870s saw the small beginnings of some of the companies which were later to dominate Tyneside. In 1860 John Wigham Richardson bought the shipyard at Low Walker. Swan and Hunter Ltd., was founded at Wallsend in 1872. These were later to merge into Swan Hunter and Wigham Richardson, and later still be the major partner in the Swan Hunter Group. William George Armstrong was perhaps the greatest inventor and entrepreneur of that generation. As early as 1844 he gave a lecture to the Literary and Philosophical Society on a 'hydro electric machine' which he had invented for the generation of electricity. In 1855 he invented a new type of field artillery, and by 1863 was taking orders from all over the world. In 1868 he launched the first gunboat for the Admiralty in C. W. Mitchell's yard at Walker, and in 1882 the two firms merged to form Sir W. G. Armstrong, Mitchell & Co. By 1900, after a further amalgamation with Sir Joseph Whitworth of Openshaw, the sites occupied by Armstrong's various works covered 230 acres and employed 25,000 men.

By 1882 therefore Tyneside industry was being passed on to a second generation of outstanding entrepreneurs and inventors, who during the period up to the first world war were to consolidate and build upon the previous generation. Other household names belong to this period, such as Charles Parsons with his invention of the steam turbine in 1884, and ten years later his laying down of the Turbinia, which attracted the world's attention at the Spithead Review of 1897. The thirty years up to 1914 saw many triumphs, but by 1882 the course had been set and the direction of progress charted.

It is perhaps not surprising that the earliest debates in the Diocesan Conferences of the newly formed Newcastle Diocese concentrate almost wholly on the affairs of the Church rather than the State. When they do occasionally turn to the impact of industrialisation on people's lives, it is the negative side of the impact which is their concern. Thus, in a debate on the Housing of the Poor in 1884, Mr. Daglish of Tynemouth refers to the fearful evils of over-crowding — 'the terrible misery and crime which result are constantly before our eyes (*N.D.C.* 1884:272). He goes on to recite the failure of Newcastle to respond to the opportunities provided by the various Acts concerned with the 'Artizans and Labourers Dwellings.' A paper from Mr. J. Price of Newcastle reveals the work ethic of the time. 'The poor may be divided into two great sections, the deserving and the undeserving. Whilst the former are entitled to our warmest sympathy and support, as being placed in their unfortunate position through no fault of their own; the latter are poor, and probably always will be poor, on account of their own vicious habits which seem as difficult to get rid of as for the Ethiopian to change his skin.' He goes on to identify the cause. 'I have no hesitation in expressing my opinion that the primary cause of much of the poverty and wretchedness to be met with in the slums of Newcastle arises from a constant craving for drink by the inhabitants, which destroys all regard for the best affections of human nature,' but later adds, 'the principal cause of poverty amongst the deserving class is the want of employment, now unhappily so prevalent.'

In contrast to those two papers Mr. Albert Grey M.P., speaking of housing in rural areas of Northumberland reveals a remarkable improvement which had taken place in the previous fifty years and he goes on to state the responsibilities of land owners and coal owners to provide not only 'the blessings of a comfortable home,' but also 'provision in the shape of reading rooms, libraries and recreation grounds.' 'I trust that we are approaching the time when the action of employers in cooperating with their employees to provide them with adequate facilities for purposes of instruction, mental refreshment and recreation, will be hurried on by the demand of the labourers and by the presence of public opinion.' He mentions certain black spots such as Seghill, 'where there are many of these deplorable unimproved cottages,' but the picture he paints is a bright one in comparision with the slums of Tyneside.

The attitudes of the Church to the contemporary scene emerge even more clearly in a debate in 1885 on the Duty of the Church in connection with the Claims and Social Position of the Working Classes (*N.D.C.* 1885:269). Rev. S. Beal, Rector of Wark who opened the debate had this to say: 'The duty of the Church in connection with the condition of the poor is to teach the dignity of work and honest independence. There is no position we may assert so honourable and enviable as that of the man who by his skill and labour is able to support his household, wife and children in comfort. The rich have their bread found them; they inherit their substance; and in using their wealth wisely and charitably, they may be instrumental in doing much good. But what position so truly honourable as that of the daily bread winner?' When he turned to the question of the claims of the working class, his political stance became clearer. 'These "claims" must be, at any rate, equitable ones. The Church cannot support any others; the theories which are put forward by agitators for equality, for confiscation for a division of land as a right inherent in human society, these claims, although they are made sometimes in the name of justice and even of religion, the Church cannot countenance or support' (ibid).

It was left to Mr. G. B. Hunter, the shipbuilding magnate of Swan and Hunter, to present a more balanced picture of workers' claims which 'must be considered as having one common aim and object in view, and that was the elevation, well-being and comfort of their class.' He detected two serious omissions by the previous speaker. One concerned the widespread temptation to drink, and the other the claims of trade unions. 'It was the duty of the Church to recognise the absolute equality of all classes, and it should be its work to break the barriers between class and class. The sympathy which the Church felt with the working men and women was not so deep as it might be, and he thought he knew one reason, and that was that our bishops, most of the clergy and many of the members were drawn from the higher and middle classes, and very few of the clergy were drawn from the working classes. He pointed to the Primitive Methodists and other Methodist churches with pastors drawn from the working classes, and said that the Church of England had at times occupied a position of opposition to the claims of the working classes which was due to the want of that sympathy and full knowledge of the claims and feelings of the class.' At the end of his address he moved the motion; 'That it is the duty of the Church to support the just claims and rights of all classes, and especially to aid and support all just and reasonable measures which will promote the wellbeing and comfort of the working classes.'

Mr. Hunter's comments are significant in that they admit the serious social imbalance within the Church of England at that time, but also indicate that an informed, liberal approach to the claims of trade unions can be heard although unionists themselves were not present at the Conference. Another industrialist, Mr. John Philipson of Newcastle, spoke of cooperation, and the possibility which he favoured of having workmen share in both the profits and the losses. Mr. C. B. P. Bosanquet of Rock Hall pointed out that the meeting was exclusively upper class, and hoped that that would not be so ten years later.

It was five years later, in 1891, that the Conference debated the Unequal Distribution of Wealth and its Responsibilities, and here also the conscience of the Church about its own life style emerged (*N.D.C.* 1891:xxxii). Sir Benjamin Browne was the main speaker. An aphorism neatly summarised his paper; 'Wages are payment for *work done*. Inherited wealth is payment for *work to be done*, and a strict conscience ought to see that this return is paid to the uttermost.' He went on; 'many who wish to see wealth more equally divided fall into the mistake, so common among Socialists, of speaking as though they thought the existing wealth of men should be redivided. Now for one person who would listen to this, hundreds can be found who wish the wealth that will be created in future years to be more evenly divided. The first would simply make all property insecure, and all history shows that where property is insecure the first to suffer are the weak and the poor. The possession of riches is the greatest force for getting more.'

It was the Bishop at the end of the debate who summed up the Church's stance and the understanding of the majority of Christians of their role. He did not think it was for the Church of England in any way to take up these politic-economic questions; but her work was to stand before the nation and to make it quite plain that nothing was politically right that was morally wrong. Justice was not always on the side of the weak, any more than always on the side of the strong, but bring the teaching of our Lord Jesus Christ to bear in practical life on all classes of men, rich and poor, high and low, and there would naturally come a way to settle this question of the redistribution of wealth' (ibid).

This series of debates at the Diocesan Conference came to a climax in 1893 when the subject of socialism was debated. 'How far may the Church control, oppose or support it?' (*N.D.C.* 1893:lxxvii). The first speaker was Rev. W. Richmond who saw socialism as an appeal to principles and two in particular — that morality and justice ought to be dominant in economic life, and that the law has the right to control economic conduct in the interest of morality. 'In maintaining and emphasising these principles the Socialists are doing what we ought to have done long ago.' In an aside he goes on to describe a reason why men do not come to Holy Communion, 'I am compelled in my business to do things which make it impossible for me to come to Communion,' and urges the Conference to ponder what that means.

The second, invited, speaker, Rev. W. D. Ground, took a very different line and at one point provoked uproar in the Conference. His theme was the Spirit of Christ, and in accordance with that Spirit he argued that 'we ought always to look on the best side of every movement or system such as Socialism. Our endeavour should be to find out what is the measure of truth and right in its claims. A sense of injustice, a sense that something is wrong in the constitution and working of society, is its real motive force. That very injustice then may have rankled, and the seeming impossibility of securing redress may have led to crime. But that very crime is little more than an appeal to the Judge of all the earth. Dynamite and dagger may be but the unhallowed clothing of an impassioned prayer.' When this remark was later challenged Mr. Ground refused to amend it, in spite of shouts of 'Withdraw'. The scene was so memorable that the Diocesan secretary in editing the debate feels obliged to comment that the same idea runs through Carlyle's 'French Revolution' and Hood's 'Bridge of Sighs,' and he even adds a clause to soften it, so that there is recourse to dynamite and the dagger only 'in a crushing and cruel despotism where other redress is denied.'

This outburst by the Conference clearly shows the limits to which the Church felt it could go in welcoming socialism. It was leading society in the direction that Christianity ought to have led it, and yet property must remain inviolate. In summing up, the Bishop wished that the word socialism had been a little more explained. He wanted as little government interference as possible, and looked to profit sharing and cooperative production as the way forward. 'Our Lord dealt with individuals, so must we. There could be no real regeneration of society in which the religious idea was not held up before the eyes of the people of this land.'

In the period leading up to the First World War it is clear that the Church is a victim of the class structure. It is not therefore surprising that when the nation goes to war in 1914, the Church should try to make the most of the nation's unity. The *Corbridge Parish Magazine* of October 1914 is quoted by the *Diocesan Gazette* (1914:109) for catching the spirit of the time. 'There is absolute unanimity between all parties and classes in this country. We see the Government and the Opposition standing shoulder to shoulder in taking measures for the defence of our homes and our native land. We find Labour members counselling their constituents to lay aside all disputes in the present emergency. We find the rich giving up their hunting and shooting engagements and in many cases offering their horses as a free gift to their country. We see ladies out of every social clique, meeting together to form plans and to do hard work for the benefit of their fellow creatures, who may be sufferers through the war.' The style of these comments clearly reveals their social base in the upper middle class, yet they are not wholly wishful thinking. As the war proceeds and the appalling wastage of men's lives becomes apparent, deeper and more realistic notes are struck.

A church magazine from December 1915 (*N.D.G.* 1915:126) speaks of God's judgement. The war is a judgement of God, striking us in chastisement for manifest sins. The present great industrial epoch, with its conspicuous material prosperity is founded upon the gross and erroneous principle of 'Individualism' which is nothing more than flagrant selfishness, every man for himself. 'And whilst this policy has produced great wealth to the clever, who have accordingly been able to take advantage of opportunity, those unfortunate ones who are not clever, but come into life physically and mentally hand-icapped, it has meant to them slums, poverty, disease, sweated labour, child death rate and widespread sense of injustice and discon-tent ... The terrible trenches in Flanders and Gallipoli have in them men from every grade of society, who have lost count of class, and are joining in the new fellowship with others less fortunate than them-selves in self sacrifice for the nation and God. A better England and a better world will be the outcome of it all. But it will have to be on the clear, revealed principle written deep in every heart, the brotherhood of humanity and self-sacrifice for others' good.'

Judged from that perspective the First World War was not in vain. At a national level the traumatic experience of the trenches produced Toc H and the Industrial Christian Fellowship, and the latter made constant appeals throughout the 1920s for the church to understand the world of labour (*N.D.G.* 1921:39). In 1921 May Day fell on a Sunday and the I.C.F. used the opportunity 'to make of Labour's festival a national dedication to the service of God.' The appeal goes on: 'It will be said no doubt, that it is a vain delusion for the Church to coquet with Labour or to win Trade Unionism to her side merely because it is likely to be victorious. Nevertheless — though the Church may deserve such sneers — she cannot turn aside from her mission without betraying her sacred trust. For the Church holds that deposit of faith without which every movement — moral, social or political — must come to irremediable ruin. Nay more, in the Indus-trial Christian Fellowship there stands among us an agency which has won the goodwill of both parties. By its very name it suggests the

Christianisation of Industry through Fellowship' (ibid).

In fact the response to the situation along those lines was already occurring. The vicar of Newcastle writes in December 1920 of the establishment of a Labour Branch of the District Federation of Church Councils (*N.D.G.* 1921:5). 'Weekly meetings are held at the Y.W.C.A. Westgate Road on Fridays at 7.30 p.m. A band of clergy and labour men meet for common council, deputations are sent to Friendly Societies, branches of Trade Unions, C.E.M.S. groups etc., wherever there is a chance of urging the need of a spiritual basis for Labour, and the need of greater attention on the part of the Church to the great ideals of the Labour Movement.' Earlier that month Mr. George Edwards M.P. had addressed a meeting on the relations of Church and Labour, and had spoken at a service — 'the first Labour leader to preach in our Cathedral.' Later the vicar of Newcastle, Rev. G. E. Newsom, records two years of 'quiet work' achieved by the Church and Labour Fellowship, and reports that new branches are being established at Benwell and St. Mark's, with more to follow soon (*N.D.G.* 1922:33).

It is in fact events outside the factory gates that give the clues to people's attitudes to work and Christianity in this period. It was the era of great ecclesiastical occasions. The Newcastle Deanery Notes for June 1923 record, for instance, a service for the London and North Eastern Railway. 'In the afternoon the Cathedral was very closely filled with a great concourse of staff and men belonging to the London and North Eastern Railway. Arrangements had been most carefully made by a committee of men and a Lesson was read by a signalman. The Lord Bishop led the prayer. The Archbishop of York preached a memorable sermon about which much has been heard since from members of the congregation.' It would surely be too cynical to dismiss the value of that occasion because those who attended it did so out of duty or obligation. For many railway workers it must have spoken of both the dignity — and difficulties — of labour.

The other — sadly all too frequent — occasion was an industrial disaster. At about 10.30 on the morning of 30 March 1925 there was a sudden inrush of water into one of the seams of Montagu Colliery, Scotswood. Thirty-eight men and boys were trapped, and later overcome by the 'black damp'. Pumping operations were in vain and it became slowly apparent that the men were doomed. In fact it was several weeks before the bodies were brought to the surface, and that after the most exhausting efforts.

In their long description of the pithead scene on the day of the disaster *The Journal and North Star* had this to say.

It is at time like these, when the elementals are reached, that class and creed are merged in a common desire to show sympathy and render service. One of the most impressive demonstrations of this unity in the face of stark tragedy was given spontaneously yesterday afternoon. Gathered at the pit-head, amidst a scene of great activity were representatives of almost all Christian denominations ... To someone came a moving inspiration — 'Let us pray', and forthwith representatives of the Churches gathered round and in a corner of the pithead shed a bare headed congregation joined reverently in a prayer meeting of intercession.

The description of the role of the parish priest on a occasion like this is telling. *The Journal* continues:

A good deal could be written of the real influence of the parish priest at such moments. For generations the men of Scotswood village have gone straight to the Scotswood pit from school, and grandfathers have worked there with grandsons. Hence it comes that the vicar of Scotswood knows and is known by the families of nearly everyone of the poor men and lads trapped by the waters. He told a Journal and North Star representative how he visited a home where a death occurred yesterday. He tendered his sympathy and gave words of comfort to the bereaved. He was answered straightly. 'Well, Vicar, there are others worse off than ourselves. There seems to be death all round us. Take this pound note and give it where it is most needed amongst the families concerned in this great disaster'. 'I told them' added Mr. Hudson, 'That I would add it to the relief fund and they told me', 'No. Give it where you know personally it will be most needed'. No doubt the ministers of other denominations can relate similar stories which reflect a true spirit of brotherly sympathy and kindness.

There can be little doubt that this story reflects the closeness of the parish priest to his people which was general at this time (see Chs. XII and XIII) — a closeness which sprang not just from a particular tragedy, but from the hardness of the time and from the resources of the Christian religion which could speak to suffering and bereavement. In the mass funerals which took place months later — funerals dictated by the fact that very few bodies could be identified — fifty thousand people lined the route to pay their respects and acknowledge the tragedy that the community had suffered.

In Newcastle in 1922 a man arrived who was to exercise the greatest influence on the Church in its attitudes to the changing industrial world, both within the Diocese, and later within the Church at large. Leslie Hunter was born in 1890, son of the distinguished Church of Scotland minister, Rev. John Hunter D.D., minister of Trinity Church, Glasgow. On leaving Oxford in 1912 he became deeply committed to the Student Christian Movement which he served as assistant secretary from 1913 to 1920. He served with the British Expeditionary Force in 1916, and from then on until 1919 was a member of the Army and Religion Inquiry Commission. From 1921 to 1922 he was curate at S. Martin's-in-the-Fields. Such experience both with students and with the B.E.F. clearly equipped him for the task ahead at Newcastle. He was appointed a canon at the Cathedral early in 1922, and his first article to the *Diocesan Gazette* contains this sentence: 'Laymen thirst for knowledge, especially for knowledge which can be applied to life and work, more than those of us who preach usually suppose.' For the next four years, until he went to Barking, this was to be Leslie Hunter's great theme, and he worked it out in two major projects — the Northern 'Copec' conference of September 1924 and the founding of the Bureau of Social Research in 1925 (see Chapter XII).

In his book commissioned by Leslie Hunter for the Bureau of Social Research, Henry Mess vividly describes the precariousness of industrial life. The economic life of Tyneside was precarious before the First World War because it was based on a few great industries, because it was dependent largely on the demands of foreign countries which might begin to manufacture the required goods themselves, and because so much of the industry was due to the race in armaments which could not continue indefinitely. 'When the War came, Tyneside became a huge arsenal and dockyard. In the couple of years of trade boom after the Armistice there was a further delirious expansion of shipbuilding ... Then came the steepest slump on record, with heavy losses and appalling unemployment' (Mess 1928:41).

Henry Mess analyses the unemployment situation with reference to the Census returns of 1921, and is particularly concerned about those who put themselves down as 'Labourer or General Labourer or Unskilled Worker' with no indication of any special occupation. 'In all they were rather more than 23,000 on Tyneside and they formed about one in fourteen or fifteen of all occupied persons ... The largeness of this group must be regarded as a danger signal, since it almost certainly includes a number of men ill-equipped to earn a living, and probably with a very precarious hold on work at all times' (ibid).

Two chapters follow on the particular problems of shipbuilding and coal, and each chapter ends with prophetic judgements on the future of those industries.

> It may be objected that this is the wrong time to worry about unemployment in the shipyards. Things have been bad, but they are on the mend; good times are

257

coming, let us be optimists! But that is not optimism: it is blindness to realities. If a really busy time should come in the shipyards it would be followed (unless all previous experience were suddenly reversed) by bad times once more. The good times should be used to prepare for the bad times ... Perhaps the best hope for the coal industry is that it may be found possible to recapture some of the markets lost by it to oil. But no-one believes that all those who are now unemployed will be absorbed; indeed their number may be further increased as less efficient or exhausted pits close. It is clear that there are more men in the industry than the industry can support. A problem has been created for which there is no easy solution, and it is likely to work itself out slowly and with much suffering.

Mess's book is a most comprehensive survey, and it is significant that it covers every aspect of industrial Tyneside except one. As Leslie Hunter was to remark forty years later, 'we never thought to look beyond the factory gates'. It was an omission he was to rectify in his own subsequent ministry, but at that time the Church's vision was limited to the effects that industry had on society, particularly in unemployment, rather than looking at the life of industry itself.

The Church's response to unemployment, although slow, was not unimpressive. An appeal in the Bishop's letter of January 1926 shows a practical awareness and concern (*N.D.G.* 1926:1). 'I would call attention once again to the appeal of the churches for warm clothing and boots for the children of the unemployed. The appeal in the first instance is for good clothing suitable for boys and girls under 16; in the second place for donations for the purchase of boots etc.' He goes on to describe how these will be distributed and continues: 'In the week ending November 21st, 1925, there were 15,797 men and women registered as unemployed at the Newcastle Labour Exchange. The relief given keeps them from starvation, but does not enable them to buy boots or clothing when these wear out. School teachers report that many children are coming to school shockingly ill clad for these cold days with wretched footwear, and in some cases bare-footed, while some of the older boys and girls are not able to come except on fine days. Experience has shown that the best way to help these children is through the benevolent committee of the education authority' (ibid).

Many local churches had their own relief funds, and the problem, contrary to what the Bishop hinted, was at times a matter of food as well as clothes. A plea from Lynemouth at the end of 1926 is typical. 'It is a struggle to keep the Kitchen going. It is feared that unless more money comes soon we must stop feeding the children.'

The general strike of 1926, but even more the long Coal Dispute, indicate where the Church stood in relation to these great political and social questions (*N.D.G.* 1926:33). The Bishop again: 'At such a moment the most that we can do is to endeavour to kindle in the hearts of all men the true love of peace and to promote an atmosphere in which reconciliation may be possible; to endeavour to repress outrage and violence and to implore all men to bear themselves as members of a Christian commonwealth.' And referring to the incident at Cramlington he adds, 'There are certain things that we can unhesitatingly denounce such as the outrage which led to the wrecking of the Scotch Express, which was in intention murder pure and simple and contrary to the laws of God and man.'

Later in the year he writes: 'The past month has been marked by the attempted intervention of certain bishops and religious leaders who have been eagerly claimed as allies by one of the parties to the dispute, but the fact is that no outside intervention, however well-meaning, can be a substitute for the spirit of goodwill and common-sense within the industry which shall bring the main disputants together to face facts which they understand better than any outsider. Until both parties agree to face the facts and to work the coal industry without outside help as a business concern, nothing can be done.' The Bishop is at least consistent in his message which is repeated month after month in different words during the long progress of the dispute.

As the period of unemployment extended well beyond the traumatic months of 1926 the Church began to search more deeply for its proper role in such a crisis. The affair of the Prayer Hut in the grounds of the North East Coast Exhibition — although a trifling incident in itself — may throw light on both the Church's desire to serve and its lack of vision. The hopes of that exhibition were that it would bring work and employment to the area, and as such the Church wished to back it, but all that could be thought of was the erection of a Prayer Hut in the grounds so that people of all denominations could use it for private prayer while at the exhibition. From all accounts, however, it appears to have been very well used.

It was not in fact until the return of Leslie Hunter to the Diocese in 1931 as Archdeacon of Northumberland that the Church began to make fresh initiatives in relation to unemployment and see its role in a wider context. In October 1932 a threefold policy is urged upon the Diocese (*N.D.G.* 1932:170ff.). '(1) In parishes where there are many out of work, a room or two rooms, cheerful and warm, might be open during the day for the use of unemployed men and youths — for women and girls too where there are many of them out of work. It should be easy to get responsible members of the Church who are out

259

of work to act as stewards of such rooms: clergy in more happily circumstanced parishes might get their people to supply books, papers and games for such rooms and perhaps even wireless sets. (2) There remains the vast number of unemployed whom the churches cannot touch directly. Following the Prince of Wales' visit the Tyneside Council of Social Service is appealing for special funds to finance recreational and occupational work among the unemployed and to make possible a development of the work started in Newcastle and elsewhere last winter. The Archdeacon of Northumberland, who is chairman of the appeal committee, has sent a special letter to the clergy asking them to urge Church people to respond. (3) When however we have done even as much as we can along the channels of social service, there remains a mass of human need and suffering which we seem powerless to alleviate directly. Let us therefore constantly sustain the unemployed in our prayers, praying also that a solution of the world-wide evils and maladjustments, which are the causes of unemployment, may be found' (ibid).

People may be encouraged to pray that a solution may be found, but any discussion of the causes and remedies for unemployment is excluded from the Diocesan Conference in December 1932. 'This is a matter for our statesmen.' In debating unemployment the conference did however consider 'Our Pastoral Responsibility to the Unemployed.' Rev. P. D. Robins of St. George's, Leeds described how food and shelter for hundreds of people was provided in his crypt. Mr. C. E. Wilkins of the Industrial Christian Fellowship in South Shields spoke about occupational centres, and there were contributions on both the rural and urban problems of unemployment within the Diocese. Typical of the initiatives which received encouragement from this Conference was the work of Church people at Wallsend St. Peter's. They were using a large building in Neptune Road as a centre of 'cultural training and recreation for the unemployed.'

By the end of 1934 it was reported in the *Diocesan News Sheet* that 'Tyneside is now moderately well supplied with centres where unemployed men and women can occupy some of their enforced leisure usefully to themselves and the community. Through the work of the unemployed themselves some of the centres have become excellently equipped clubs, where under competent supervision, handicrafts, drama, music, education classes, poultry keeping, and in the vicinity, allotments are carried on. More recently centres have been started in other parts of the county, and last month a County Advisory Committee was set up under the chairmanship of the Archdeacon of Northumberland. We ask the prayers, practical help and continued financial support of Church people for this work.' (*B.L.D.N.* 1935:3).

William Temple, who was then Archbishop of York, had a great effect upon the Diocese when he spoke to the Diocesan Conference at the end of 1934 on the subject of unemployment. 'His address and our applause were carried as far as the wireless waves of Droitwich can carry.' The significance of his speech was that he dared to enter the field of political economy, with the obvious implication that it was a Christian duty to do so, and not to leave it to the statesmen. That was an important thing to do for it encouraged those who had been hesitant in their criticism to emerge and be open about it.

It is not surprising therefore to find at the beginning of 1935 comments in the *Diocesan News Sheet* about the administration of relief by the Unemployment Assistance Board. 'We cannot refrain from pointing out that these new and carefully considered regulations confirm the diagnosis made by a group of our clergy nearly three years ago and embody their recommendations, which at the time were sharply criticised — namely a distinction between the rates of standard benefit for short time unemployment and the rates of relief adequate to the needs of those who have been out of work for long periods; an allowance for high rents; greater uniformity in the rates of relief — three years ago the variations on Tyneside caused much vexation; larger allowances for children; a more humane and discriminating administration of the Means Test under control of a permanent Central Board.'

Later that year Leslie Hunter appealed for evidence from clergy and others about the effect of making relatives responsible for unemployed members of the family. Evidence was accumulating that this system was putting an intolerable strain on family relationships and causing a great deal of unhappiness and bad feeling. As a member of the Archbishop's Committee on Unemployment he wished to set this right.

Undoubtedly the main theme of the Church's concern with the industrial world in the inter-war years was unemployment, and Leslie Hunter was the catalyst who broadened and deepened the Church's understanding of its role in his two periods of ministry in the Diocese. In 1939 he left to be Bishop of Sheffield. In his letter of August 1939 paying tribute to Leslie Hunter, the Bishop writes of his work which led to the formation of the Tyneside Council of Social Service, but adds sadly that Yorkshire dioceses have taken three Newcastle clergy to be bishops in the course of eighteen months, and their behaviour has an unpleasant resemblance to the Scots raids into Northumberland in former centuries (*B.L.D.N.* 1939:1). The comment is in fact an interesting one from a sociological point of view, for the comparative strength of the Church in Northumberland and its closeness to the working class is in marked contrast to that of Yorkshire, and particularly Sheffield, in which Leslie Hunter was called to work out over twenty-five years his strategy for the Church's mission to the industrial world.

Leslie Hunter was not a prolific writer — his great contribution was to stimulate others to action based on sound theological judgement — but his importance as a thinker can be gauged from occasional lectures, as well as the programmes he initiated. He gave a course of lectures in Glasgow University in 1950 on Christian Morality and the Standards of Today, and the following year at McGill University, Montreal. These lectures were later expanded and published as *The Seed and The Fruit* (1953) and they cover a wide range of current issues forced upon the Church by the development of industrial society. What is significant about the book is that almost for the first time a theologian is taking the impact of industry on the lives and attitudes of ordinary people seriously.

In a section of the book on 'Responsibility and Freedom' Leslie Hunter describes the state of mind produced by contemporary patterns of work. 'The industrial revolution brought into existence an industrial society in which, for five or six generations now, the majority of the population has been denied responsibility and has thereby been made irresponsible. They do not want responsibility. They want security; shorter hours; better wages' (1953:54). Citing his experience of meeting shop stewards in the steel industry, he goes on to conclude that 'it will take more than a few years to change the psychological consequences and a mental attitude which has become endemic' (ibid). The same thoughts, but from a different perspective, emerge in a section on the use and abuse of power. 'What is true of individuals is even more true of groups. The impersonal exercise of power by a group of men will become more callous and cruel than the individual member of such a group might be if he were on his own. The member of such a group can excuse to himself the ruthlessness of their corporate decisions by his loyalty to the group ... Industrial history and modern politics — to look no further afield — will supply many examples of this corruption' (ibid:59).

It is within a section on work itself that Leslie Hunter shows the most contempt for the current theology. He wrote:

Nor does it take us far beyond platitude ... to be told by Canon Richardson, in a (then) recent article on the biblical doctrine of work, that the 'consequence of man's disobedience to God's law is that work, which ought to have become a

262

congenial and salutary human activity, has become a discipline and a task to be endured under the sanctions of fate or fear, or under the stimuli of profit or reward'. If he means that all the difficulties and problems of industrial society are due to the imperfections of human nature, and would be solved if all mankind were in a state of grace, that seems to me just theological baloney. The complex, world-wide, economic and political structure of modern society is quite beyond the horizon of the biblical writers. The Bible is not a text book for the solution of such problems — though it may provide apposite texts — only the Holy Spirit can lead men to their solving (ibid:71).

Three problems in particular are cited by Leslie Hunter in relation to work. The first concerns the rhythm and tempo of industrial work which is dictated by the machine.

The industrial worker today, enslaved to the machine, is doing violence to his nature. It is, therefore, not surprising that he does not find in his work a reminder of his Creator, and that, on the contrary, it inclines him, when he reflects, to ruthless and materialistic ideologies. I am disposed to think that an element in the small, sporadic strikes of recent times, and in absenteeism, is a subconscious protest of human beings against the inhumanity of the machine and against their enslavement to it (ibid:74).

The second problem concerns the gap between the producer and the consumer.

May one whose relations to industry is only that of a consumer be allowed to ask if those in indsutry are sufficiently conscious of those for whom they are producing? The knowledge that they are producing things necessary to a wholesome and full life might help to reconcile them to the inevitable dullness of much daily work — a housewife's and the clerk's as well as the work of the man and the woman in the factory. Here the Christian might set a pattern and the ministry of the Church an example. Unfortunately the Church has been incurably middle-class in its deliverances upon work. Before we can talk to the manual workers at all we must get within talking distance and have more of them within the Christian community (ibid:75).

The third area Leslie Hunter comments upon is industrial relations, pleading for a 'closer, more intelligent and unsuspicious co-operation between all groups in industry, leading to a better quality and quantity of output. That means forgetting some bad memories and old prejudices and acquiring a new outlook. Some bad habits have been created by Trade Union restrictions which were a direct consequence of insecurity and bad conditions of employment. It will take a generation or more to work that particular poison out of the system of industrial society' (ibid:76). He goes on to cite examples of competition between Trade Unions and their need for rationalisation and ends with a very positive assertion: 'every time I visit a Works I am impressed with how much men do, not how little — men quite as much as management' (ibid).

Although these comments of Leslie Hunter stem from a period after he had left Newcastle, he had clearly learnt much from his experience in Newcastle, and it is significant that he comments upon every major issue which was to concern Industrial Mission during the fifties, sixties and seventies. The alienation of factory workers from the life of the Church; apathy and irresponsibility; lack of job satisfaction; the nature of power; and appropriate doctrine of work; the divisions of society; industrial relations and the role of Trade Unions — all these have been key topics for industrial chaplains to explore at all levels of industry; and the concern of Leslie Hunter for such topics thus acts as a bridge between the pre-war and post-war periods in understanding the Church's response.

While the experience of the trenches in the First World War led to an erosion of traditional class attitudes and a broadening of the life of the Church, so the experience of the Second World War enabled the Church to see the necessity of manufacturing in terms of the war effort and the national good. Not only were chaplains called to minister to the Armed Forces, but also to certain factories concerned with essential war production. This happened to the Rev. Ted Wickham, a young curate at Shieldfield, who was called to the Royal Ordnance Factory at Swynnerton in Staffordshire, from where in 1944, Bishop Hunter asked him to come to Sheffield and start an industrial mission in the steel industry under his guidance. The Sheffield Industrial Mission was later to become the pace-setter for industrial missions throughout the English-speaking world. Many years were to elapse before dioceses generally were to see the need for such a policy of mission towards the industrial world, but the South London Industrial Mission also dates from this period, and it was from that Diocese that Hugh Ashdown came to be Bishop of Newcastle in 1957.

The previous episcopate of Bishop Noel Hudson had lacked Christian vision in relation to society (see Ch. III). The remarkable ministry which he exercised as bishop was primarily as a pastor of clergy in order to build up the local 'Body of Christ'. To this extent it had grave limitations in relation to the industrial world, and the Church exerted little or no influence on economic life after the Second World War. This lack of vision coincided with the establishment of the welfare state, which pre-empted many of the Church's traditional social concerns, and was another reason for the fallow period in the Church's understanding of its role in society.

As Provost of Southwark, Bishop Ashdown had seen something of the work of Industrial Mission in South London and was anxious to find ways for the Church in its ministry to come close to the working lives of ordinary people in factories and pits. His sermons contained many allusions to industry and he frequently spoke of 'industrial man', almost as if a new species had arrived on earth. In the early years of his episcopate he undoubtedly inspired a number of clergy to visit works canteens, and even on occasions the shop floor, in an attempt to extend their pastoral work and the outreach of the Church. Thus for instance the vicar of Wallsend regularly visited the works canteen of the shipyard of Swan Hunter at Wallsend.

It was not only at clergy however that Bishop Ashdown preached his message about the importance of industrial life. Laymen also were urged to see their involvement and responsibility in industry as an essential part of their Christian commitment. The Church of England Men's Society was for instance encouraged to concern itself with industrial issues. In neither case however, either with clergy or with laymen was there enough theological reflection to sustain the initiatives, or to give real depth to the conversations that took place. Furthermore, the objectives were seen to be imparting some Christian 'message' or else finding a new sphere for the Church's pastoral work, rather than discovering a new area of God's activity and human growth in which to explore new responsibilities. Sadly the Rev. Gordon Hopkins' pioneering work in the 1950s and 1960s at Pallion on Wearside, where he worked out a very comprehensive and creative relationship between the Church and the shipbuilding and engineering works in that parish, had no parallel on Tyneside.

It was not until 1967 that an industrial chaplain was appointed to the Diocese, who had previously been a chaplain with the Sheffield Industrial Mission. Newcastle was in fact the last major industrial centre in England to be without such an appointment. From the point of view of the ecumenical and regional strategy of the Church in the region, that appointment was the last piece in the jigsaw, which thus allowed the broad picture to be seen. The Durham Diocese had appointed a chaplain to work with the Coal Board in Durham in the late fifties; the Methodist Church had a number of chaplains associated with various small works; the Presbyterian Church had a minister who visited the Walker Naval Yard. It was therefore relatively easy to draw these initiatives together to form an ecumenical industrial mission which could look at the region as a whole, and work out a strategy on behalf of the whole Church. The Bishop of Durham as the natural *primus inter pares* was asked to make the first move, and he in turn asked Dr. Reid, later Sir William Reid, Chairman of the Durham Coal Board, to bring the various parties together. Thus the Northumberland and North Durham Industrial Mission, as it was first called, came into being, and curiously it was the first body to build a bridge back across the Tyne to the mother Diocese of Durham.

Three years after the appointment of the first industrial chaplain in the Diocese a second was appointed, and the two main spheres of Industrial Mission work were shipbuilding within the Swan Hunter Group, and light engineering within the Fluid Seal Division of George Angus and Co. at Wallsend. What was attempted in the first instance was a deepened understanding, shared between chaplains and those with whom they talked, of the nature of industry and its effect on human life. Only with such a deepened understanding could groups and individuals within industry begin to relate the Christian faith to the many industrial issues in front of them. Many groups of people, on the shop floor, in offices, among foremen and managers, had regular 'debates' with chaplains on a great variety of industrial and economic issues. In particular a group of managers at George Angus and Co. were enabled with the chaplain's aid to work out their relationships and responsibilities more clearly, and a series of conferences for people at all levels within Swan Hunter Shipbuilding was held to look into the future of that industry. In both these instances the Industrial Mission was discovering, by no means for the first time but in a new significant way, the role of the Church as a catalyst in bringing people together from the different pressure groups or disciplines of an industry, to share their humanity, their aspirations and their vision, and relate them to the often harsh economic constraints which they were under.

At the same time the Industrial Mission was anxious to encourage the Church at large to be properly involved and concerned with the industrial world. A series of conferences was held each year for clergy to inform them about the broad aspects of the industrial scene, and to allow them to consider how best to respond within their own churches and locality. Conferences with lay people from churches were less successful. For so long had the preaching and teaching of the Church been centred on the individual and the Church itself, that it was hard for many lay people to gain a vision of a role for themselves as Christians in the working world.

It was in 1969 that this work was strengthened by the imaginative appointment of a theological consultant in industrial and social affairs. Margaret Kane was appointed by the Bishop of Durham in consultation with church leaders ecumenically, to work not only within that Diocese, but in York and Newcastle as well. She brought with her much experience, from a mining parish in Yorkshire and from the Sheffield Industrial Mission where she had been a chaplain, and that experience proved invaluable in her task of helping different people and groups throughout the region to find meaning in life and faith.

In 1975 she published a book *Theology in an Industrial Society*, setting out, by a thorough sociological analysis, what the Church's task ought to be. For Margaret Kane the primary task is to help the community 'reach that reflective understanding of Christian truth which is demanded for the full and fruitful living of the Christian life at a particular time'. For this to take place nothing less than 'the Revolution of the Laity' is required, whom Margaret Kane sees as either lost in the world or trapped in the Church. The many questions that are thrown up by technological development — structural unemployment, participation, the use of the behavioural sciences in industry — are questions, that profoundly affect masses of people, and yet they cannot be examined without raising such fundamental issues as what men and women are for, what the possibilities of life are, and what human and material resources are available. Margaret Kane argues that it is these fundamental issues that Christian faith is all about, and it is therefore in the context of the big questions which society faces that theology must be done. This is the style of ministry — 'doing theology' — which is undoubtedly of fundamental importance if the immense resources among Christian lay people are to be developed and a proper stance taken by the Church in relation to the social issues today.

Two examples of this style may be cited from the early 1970s. One was the great 'think-in' at Newcastle City Hall in 1972 on Unemployment in the Northern Region. The national unemployment level was at that time approaching one million people (a figure which now appears comparatively modest, but caused great disquiet at the time), and a number of industrial chaplains meeting with the Regional T.U.C. felt the occasion prompted a big public meeting of representatives from all over the North, to study the implications of what was happening, and suggest possible ways forward. The two industrial missions in the region — Teesside as well as Northumberland and North Durham — were involved along with the Regional Advisory Committee of the T.U.C. in organising it, and some six hundred people attended the day, from industry and commerce, local government, education and various professions including the clergy. What was remarkable was the way that the Church was seen still to possess the authority and contacts to draw in such a wide cross-section of concerned and influential people. In the event the debate may be seen to mark a turning point in the traditional approach of many people in the region who look for help from outside the region as the main source of employment. While it achieved much on the actual day in terms of allowing real public debate and participation, the event was not followed up and impetus may well have been lost through that failure.

The other event was the debate in Diocesan Synod in 1974 on 'The Current Crisis — what can Christians do?' Like the occasion in the City Hall it was an attempt to respond to outside events; only this time within the life of the Church. The oil crisis of autumn 1973 had thrown the economy into confusion and had raised many questions in people's minds about current values and assumptions. It was the Church's understanding of God's purpose within those events, and therefore the Christian's attitude to material resources and the world's use of them, which was the heart of the debate, but behind those questions — confusing enough in themselves — was even more confusion about the nature of the Christian response to such issues. One speaker, who had proposed that the debate should not take place at all, thought the subject too complex for Christians to tackle, that disagreement would prevent clear action, that the political implications would cause dissension, and synod's time should not be spent on education. Another speaker from the trade union movement said that he confronted all problems with the statement, 'I am a Christian', implying that this absolved him from the need to think further. Although many useful insights emerged — both environmental and theological — this underlying confusion prevented the debate achieving any major breakthrough in understanding.

These two events of the early seventies foreshadowed the main social issue of the late seventies — increasing, and seemingly permanent, unemployment. The issue again confirms the necessity to 'do theology' — in this instance around the area of work and 'non-work'. This has in fact been one aspect of the Church's response in the new attitudes about work, and within the Industrial Mission a lot of theology has been 'done' around it. In particular a conference on 'Employment and its Alternatives' in 1977 with a demand for a new 'life ethic' to replace what has been called the Protestant work ethic, was a step forward. Also in 1977 the Social Responsibility Board of the Diocese undertook a major study of the nature and problems of work, and at the time of writing is still engaged in investigating the main issues. Another aspect of the Church's response has been in the field of job creation, and its use of the government's Job Creation scheme. A limited number of parishes have cooperated with the scheme, but it has been seen primarily in terms of getting jobs done rather than developing the potential gifts and skills of the young people involved. An example of how the scheme can be used by the Church for the benefit of the community has been seen in Killingworth Township where many young people have been involved through Job Creation in different aspects of the Communicare project within the new town.

From all that has gone before it is clear that the Church in the Diocese of Newcastle has been sadly inconsistent in its witness to the importance of the industrial world — sadly, because the various industries described earlier at the point of their development in the 1880s have had an incalculable effect upon the lives of all within the Diocese. Certain questions must be asked about this inconsistency and failure of vision. Why was it that in the 1880s and 1890s the Diocese seemed scarcely aware of the work of F. D. Maurice, or the Christian Social Union under Gore? Why was it that in the 1920s and 1930s the Church was so slow to respond to the economic traumas of the time, and seemed to depend so much upon the vision and energy of one man? Why was it in the 1960s that Newcastle was the last major industrial centre to set up Industrial Mission? Why is it that for the mass of Church people today a person's occupation is not seen as a prime concern in the working out of his faith?

A number of answers may be given. The Diocese has a high proportion of native clergy, many of whom have little, if any, experience of the Church or the world outside the North-East. The Church thus shares the isolation which is a characteristic of the area as a whole. There is, or has been, a natural deference in the character of the people of Northumberland, stemming from relationships on the land, but subsequently reinforced in the larger traditional industries. That deference can be seen in the relations of laymen to clergy, and clergy to their bishop. Such deference is an obstacle to 'the Revolution of the Laity' which is so crucial for the development of the Church.

Profounder answers to these questions must come from a broader study of the people of the Diocese and the assumptions within their faith. Suffice it to say that there is a clear historical thread running through the failures and limitations upon the vision of successive generations. Amid the richness and vitality of much of the Church's life there is here a curious flaw.

Chapter XVII

THE CHURCH AND SCHOOL EDUCATION

J. C. Tyson

1. UP TO 1981

EDUCATION of its very nature is a fundamental concern of the Church, for it is through teaching that the Christian Gospel is disseminated and passed on to future generations. In this process, the education of the young is of especial importance. Not without point a speaker at the Diocesan Conference in Newcastle in 1890 referred to schools as 'the backbone of the Church' (*N.D.C.* 1891:lvii). Over the centuries the provision by the Church of education for the young has taken many different forms, appropriate to the needs and circumstances of any particular period. Provision could be exclusively religious in character or (increasingly since the seventeenth century) could combine with religious education instruction in secular subjects. Attention in this and the following chapter will be focussed entirely upon provision of education for the young which combined religious and secular instruction — in short, upon the Church day-schools.

It is important to emphasize that in the sphere of education — as, indeed, in any other — the Church must not be thought of only in a formal, institutional sense. A great part of the educational provision associated with the Church of England originally came from the piety and private benefaction of individual men and women. When in the late seventeenth and early eighteenth centuries the first attempt was made to supply popular education on a national scale through the establishment of parochial schools the initiative came not from the Church of England as a central institution, but from the Society for Promoting Christian Knowledge (S.P.C.K.), a society founded in 1699 by five individuals, of whom four were laymen. The charity school movement of this period was sustained by the enterprise and zeal of very many persons, who individually or collectively, founded and supported schools. Within the next hundred years, when acute social problems came in the wake of the great agrarian and industrial changes which were transforming this country, the Church as a national organisation began to take an increasing part in the provision of education, but the initiative of individual men and women still had an important role to play.

An Anglican school system was already well-established in the Diocese of Durham when the northern part of the see became the separate Diocese of Newcastle in 1882. At the end of 1881 there were some 286 Church schools in the undivided Diocese of Durham. This remarkable number of schools is eloquent testimony to the zeal of diocesans, clergy and lay people during the two preceding centuries.

Not a few of the schools had started life as charity schools in association with the S.P.C.K. The credit for the development of charity schools in the Durham Diocese must largely go to the parish clergy who were active in promoting and maintaining schools and acting as correspondents for the S.P.C.K. With the exception of Joseph Butler, the eighteenth-century bishops of Durham were not in fact themselves notable for their advocacy of charity schools. Nathaniel Lord Crewe, the first bishop in the eighteenth century (1674–1721) did however make up for want of interest during his own lifetime, for under the terms of his will a charity was established which in future years gave substantial support to education. Lord Crewe's Charity maintained, supported or assisted schools for the education of the poor in any of the parishes or places where any of the property of the charity was situated. During the eighteenth century alone it gave help to schools or teachers in no less than 47 places within the Diocese. The parishes of Bamburgh, Lucker, North Sunderland and Beadnell in north Northumberland, of Blanchland, Shotley and St. Andrew's Auckland in the south, received the especial attention of the charity. In 1882 all but the last of these parishes came within the newly-established see of Newcastle. Though its work was by no means exclusively confined to education, Lord Crewe's Charity none the less represented the largest single educational charity in the Diocese of Newcastle.

By the early nineteenth century agrarian and industrial changes had already brought pressing social problems. There was a desperate need for an increase in the provision of education for the children of the poor. The Church of England responded with the establishment in 1811 of the National Society 'for promoting the Education of the Poor in the Principles of the Established Church throughout England and Wales'. At a time when no state provision of education existed, this quickly became by far the largest agency for the establishment and support of schools. It was fortunate that the Diocese of Durham

271

during this period was presided over by a bishop for whom the dissemination of education mattered very deeply. The leadership and dedication of Shute Barrington, bishop from 1791–1826, triggered off a real expansion of education provision in the Diocese. Barrington himself founded schools in the Upper Weardale area; more importantly, he gave strong encouragement to the work of the National Society throughout the Diocese. A school established by Barrington at Bishop Auckland in 1810 became the first 'model school' of the National Society in England, where training of masters in the monitorial system of schooling advocated by the Society was carried out. Dr. Bell, the pioneer of this system, was offered and accepted an appointment in the Diocese to encourage him to remain in the North-East. Barrington's influence upon the development of education continued long after his death through the Barrington School Trust which assisted schools in the Diocese of Durham and, later, that of Newcastle also.

Prior to 1833 the state had played no part whatever in either the establishment or support of schools. In that year, however, Parliament made a grant of £20,000 'in aid of Private Subscriptions for the Erection of School Houses, for the Education of the Children of the Poorer Classes in Great Britain'. Though the sum itself was pitifully small, a precedent of the utmost importance had been set, for after that date Parliament continued to make an annual grant in aid of education which, as the years passed, became substantial; in 1859, for example, it stood at £836,920. At first no machinery existed for the disbursement of the grant, which in practice was handed over to the two voluntary societies, the National Society and the British and Foreign School Society. Then in 1839 a Committee of the Privy Council was set up 'for the consideration of all matters affecting the education of the people', including superintendence of Parliamentary grants in aid of education. In 1856, as recognition of the growing importance of education in the affairs of Government, the Education Department was established. The first state provision of schools did not come until the Elementary Education Act of 1870. But long before that date the influence of the state upon educational development had become very strong. Though the schools belonged to the voluntary bodies the steadily-increasing scale of the Parliamentary grant led inevitably to increasing state direction and it was a *sine qua non* that all schools in receipt of grant should be open to Her Majesty's inspectors of schools. The Church of England, which was by far the largest provider of schools during the period, viewed the encroachment of the state in educational affairs with an admixture of alarm and dismay. It had maintained that the education of the nation's children was a matter for the nation's Church, and the influence of the Oxford Movement in the 1830s served to stiffen its attitude on that matter. It goes without saying that Nonconformists and advocates of unsectarian religious education stoutly resisted any claims advanced by the Church to a monopoly of education. Herein lay the cause of the so-called 'religious difficulty' in English education during the nineteenth century which led many in despair to advocate provision of purely secular education by the state.

There can be no doubt that the growing influence of the state in educational matters seriously eroded that of the Church. In 1839, when the newly-established Committee of Council on Education proposed to institute a system of inspection of schools, the Church was sufficiently powerful to insist that only inspectors approved by the archbishops should have right of entry to Anglican schools. By the 1860s the struggle between church and state for control of education had ended in a significant victory for the latter, which now recognized only secular subjects for grant-earning purposes.

After the passing of the Elementary Education Act in 1870 the state at last entered into competition with voluntary bodies in the matter of school provision. It was abundantly clear that over the country as a whole there was a serious deficiency in the number of schools. The Liberal government of the day decided to 'fill up the gaps' wherever these existed. Under the Act of 1870 England was divided up into school districts, which were the municipal boroughs or civil parishes. The Education Department was empowered to investigate the school accommodation in each district. Where deficiencies were found to exist, the voluntary bodies were given a period of grace in which to make good the accommodation required, and could apply for Parliamentary grant for that purpose. If they failed to do so, school boards were then to be set up, elected by the ratepayers, and charged with the responsibility of building schools to supply the extra places required. Ratepayers in any district could also, if they so wished, petition the Education Department for the establishment of a school board before the latter instituted its own enquiries.

Religious education in board schools if it was given at all, was not to be distinctive of any denomination. Historically, the importance of the legislation of 1870 is that it introduced into English education a dual system which survives — though in a much altered form — to the present day. On the one hand there were voluntary schools, most of them owned by the Church of England, on the other schools set up by the state, completely undenominational in character.

273

Thus after 1870 the Church of England, together with other churches, particularly the Roman Catholic Church, found itself in direct competition with the new school boards. To make matters worse, the board schools, unlike the voluntary schools, were able to receive rate aid. The Act of 1870 did not make elementary education either compulsory or free. In 1880 and 1891 Acts were passed which, respectively, brought in compulsion and allowed any parent the right to claim free education for his child.

It is against this background of ever-increasing state intervention in educational matters that we have to see the development of education in the northern Diocese after the time of Shute Barrington. Thanks to vigorous local initiative and the unremitting support of the National Society in the years ahead, the Church was able to advance its provision of day schools, and, as reference to the Report of the Royal Commission on the State of Popular Education in England (1858–1861) clearly shows, its Sunday schools also played a not unimportant part in the supply of secular as well as religious instruction at this time. The work of the day schools could be assisted by Parliamentary grant, but, as we have seen, it was an indispensable condition that any schools so assisted should be open to inspection by H.M. inspectors of schools. It is likely that most of the Church schools chose to take advantage of the grant system. The Minutes of the Committee of Council on Education, issued annually, list all the schools which received aid from Parliamentary sources, and it is from these that the commitment and extent of the Church's work in education can be discerned. A substantial majority of the schools in the area of the Diocese of Durham listed annually in the Minutes were in fact Church schools.

The Minutes also reveal the great part played by the Church of England's central agency for educational work, the National Society. In 1856–57 for example, 45 out of a total of 84 schools in the area which was later to form the Diocese of Newcastle were National Schools. There were only 6 Roman Catholic schools and 16 British Schools in the area at that date; the remaining 17 schools were mostly Anglican. The National Schools owed their existence to a happy combination of local initiative and central support. Stated simply, what the clergy and lay people in any locality had to do was find half the cost of building a school; the other half would be found by the National Society. Once built, the school continued to receive financial support from the Society, and was known as a National School. The Society was also prepared to take over existing charity or parochial schools which found themselves unable to continue because of lack of

274

financial resources.

After the Elementary Education Act of 1870 made possible an alternative, entirely secular, provision of schools the position of the Church in educational matters was inevitably weakened. To many Churchmen it now seemed that the Church's historic role in education was under siege, and that the proliferation of school boards must be resisted. Unfortunately, the financial resources of the Church were not strong enough to cater for the growing educational needs, which were most pressing in the large towns and rapidly-expanding industrial areas. It is an interesting point that whereas in the eighteenth century the charity school movement was most successful in the urban areas, during the nineteenth century the Church was less and less able to meet the ever-increasing needs of the new industrial conurbations. Looking at the situation in the Diocese of Durham, it is precisely in such areas that during 1870–1 the first school boards were established. In all, twelve boards were set up; of these, three fell in the area which later became the separate Diocese of Newcastle, in Newcastle itself, at Tynemouth and Haltwhistle. The smaller number of school boards north of the Tyne in 1871 can however be only partly explained by the fact that much of Northumberland was rural in character. There was, after all, a substantial concentration of industry in the south-east of Northumberland. The conclusion must be that here the Church had made greater headway in answering local needs than had been the case in the industrial areas of County Durham. Of the twelve school boards established in 1870–1 all but one were situated in heavily industrial areas; the exception was Haltwhistle in Northumberland.

During the twelve years between the passing of the 1870 Elementary Education Act and the creation of the Diocese of Newcastle, the area which was to form the new see witnessed a substantial effort on the part of the Church to improve its provision of education. At the beginning of 1870 there were some 95 Church schools in receipt of Parliamentary grant; by 1882 the figure had risen to 143. This increase had not, however, been able to keep pace with the educational needs of the area as identified by the Education Department. In 1873, for example, there were 122 Church schools in receipt of Parliamentary grant — an increase of 28 per cent since 1870 — yet that year saw the creation of another four school boards. During the years 1874–6, no less than fourteen school boards were established, two more in 1877 and another in 1880. By 1882 there were in all 24 school boards in the area of the new Diocese. Most of these boards were in urban or industrial areas, but at least one third were in areas which were entirely rural in character.

So far as education is concerned, it must be said that, looking at the wider situation, the Diocese of Newcastle was instituted at a far from propitious time. In the dual system established by the Act of 1870 the voluntary bodies did not start off on equal terms with the school boards, and as the years passed, voluntary schools found themselves in an increasingly disadvantageous position. The board schools, unlike the voluntary schools, were able to receive rate aid as well as Parliamentary grant. In the inevitable competition between the voluntary bodies and the school boards which ensued after 1870, the boards gained a great advantage. Moreover, as educational standards rose and the Education Department demanded more and more of the schools, the cost of maintaining schools at a level of efficiency which would satisfy inspectors and guarantee the continuance of grants rose appreciably. The financial difficulties of the voluntary bodies thus grew ever greater. Over the country as a whole, many voluntary schools were obliged to close or were handed over to the school boards. In school districts where voluntary schools had previously been the only source of education closure was inevitably followed by the setting up of school boards. Just two years before the Diocese of Newcastle was formed, the Education Act of 1880 made elementary education compulsory for all children between the ages of five and ten, and this led to an influx of children into the schools. Then in 1882 the Education Department introduced a new Code which brought changes in the grant system. These clearly favoured well-supported and well-staffed schools. The school boards, supported as they were by rate aid, were in a stronger position to attract teachers, for they could offer better pay and better facilities. Again the voluntary bodies found themselves under severe strain. Not without point the first subject to come before the Newcastle Diocesan Conference of 1884 was that of the influence of the new Code on voluntary schools. Speakers complained bitterly that the Code 'pressed with undue severity' on the voluntary schools (*N.D.C* 1885:211).

It is a tribute to the determination and enterprise of the new Diocese that when, in 1902, another Education Act brought an end to the school-board system, the number of Church schools in receipt of Parliamentary grant, so far from diminishing, had actually increased to some 159, a net gain of some 11 per cent. Only two schools which appear on the 1882 list were missing from that of 1902. The increase was almost exclusively in Church schools as distinct from those supported by the National Society. Nor do these figures tell the whole story. Throughout the period 1882-1902 existing schools were enlarged to provide additional accommodation and facilities in them were improved, such as better heating, addition of cloakrooms and outbuildings. From 1882 onwards the number of new school boards set up in the Diocese levelled off appreciably. In all, twelve boards were established between that date and 1902, as follows: Corsenside (1882), Cramlington (1883), Eltringham (1884), Netherton (1884), Benwell (1889), Alston (1892), Burradon (1893), Ancroft (1897), Kyloe (1898), Broomley (1899), Lucker (1899), Berwick-on-Tweed (1900). Most of these were rural boards, which suggests that the Church was finding increasing difficulty in the country areas. What can be said is that, bearing in mind the problems which beset voluntary bodies after 1870, the new Diocese had started surprisingly well: it successfully maintained the school system which it inherited in 1882 and had managed to contain the inexorable march of the school boards.

The central agency in the Diocese for educational matters was instituted in 1885. This took over the work carried out in the days of the undivided Durham Diocese by the Durham Diocesan Schools Society and the Diocesan Board of Inspection of Schools, and was in fact a Committee of the Newcastle Diocesan Society which itself was established in that year to focus and oversee all activities of the Church in the Diocese. The proposal to set up the Diocesan Society was made at the first Diocesan Conference held in Newcastle in September, 1883. Four main areas of Church work were identified at the conference, among which education came second only to church extension in importance. When the Society was formally incorporated in 1885 a committee was established for each of the four main areas of work. The Education Committee, which one of its later secretaries was to describe as 'filling the place of a Diocesan Board of Education' was to oversee the maintenance and inspection of both day and Sunday schools, the building or enlargement of schools and teachers' houses; and the provision of teacher-training (*N.D.C.* 1897:xx). Among these responsibilities considerable importance was attached to inspection, for which there was to be a separate Inspection Fund with its own committee, one half elected by school managers and other subscribers, the other half by the Diocesan Society.

Arrangements made for inspection mirrored closely and, indeed, grew out of those which existed in the undivided Diocese of Durham. The Durham Diocesan Board of Inspection, elected by school managers and contributors to a diocesan inspection fund, was launched in 1871. The date is not without significance. Coming on the heels of the Elementary Education Act, it emphasized the anxiety of the Church to safeguard its own religious teaching at a time of substantial inroads by the state in the field of education. So seriously did the Church in Durham regard the situation that an appeal to the laity was promulgated in the Diocese to raise monies for an inspection fund; donations — including £100 from the S.P.C.K. — and annual subscriptions quickly came in, and the financial stability of the enterprise was firmly secured by asking the managers of schools to pay annually a sum calculated on the number of children in their schools. A scale for such payments was adopted in July 1871. In the first year of operation some 360 schools in the Diocese of Durham with about 33,000 pupils and 350 pupil-teachers were placed under inspection in religious subjects. Comparable figures for 1882 were 498 schools, 57,997 pupils, 606 pupil-teachers. After 1882 the Diocesan Board of Inspection in Religious Subjects continued to function for the two Dioceses of Durham and Newcastle. Its work in the latter was taken over by the Education Committee of the Newcastle Diocesan Society in November, 1885. The change was merely a constitutional one, for all the Northumberland members of the old Diocesan Board of Inspection served in the Education Committee, and the same two diocesan inspectors continued in office. Looking at the annual returns for the next 15 years, an average of some 225 schools in the Diocese came under inspection. The numbers of schools given in the returns exceed those which appear on the Education Department's lists of schools in receipt of Parliamentary grant. The explanation lies in the fact that from the very beginning of the diocesan system of inspection any department of a school under a separate teacher was counted as a separate school. (This underlines a particular problem which arises for the historian, attempting to determine the number of schools which existed in any given period.) A school which had separate boys, girls and infants departments may, in some cases, be counted as one school or in others as three. Moreover, one extremely interesting point which arises from a study of the returns relating to diocesan inspection is that the diocesan inspectors did not confine their attention exclusively to Church schools. Any school, the managers of which subscribed to the Diocesan Inspection Fund, could be visited by the inspector. The extraordinary thing is that several board schools in the area of the Diocese came under diocesan inspection for religious subjects!

It would be a mistake to imagine that the Diocesan Education Committee was the only agency in the Diocese which was concerned with the furtherance of the Church's work in education. The National Society, which made grants towards the building and enlarging of schools, the supply of books and fittings, was strongly represented in the Diocese. In 1882 more than half of the Anglican Schools in receipt of Parliamentary grant were National Schools, and the proportion was only slightly less in 1902. The parish clergy undertook the task of furthering the Society's work at the local level, for in each deanery of the two archdeaconries of the Diocese there was a clergy representative of the National Society. Another national organization which operated in the Diocese was the Church of England Sunday School Institute to which many of the Sunday schools were affiliated. Apart from Lord Crewe's Charity there were, however, no charities of any significance in the Diocese which supported educational work. Thus, apart from Parliamentary grant earned by the schools, grants made by the National Society to its own schools and school pence brought in by pupils, the Church had to rely on donations and subscriptions to maintain its educational work.

By 1890 it had become clear that much might be gained if a federation of schools in the Diocese were to be established. The grant system operated by the Education Department was a complicated one and the introduction of a new Code in that year left many school managers in doubt as to where they stood. Moreover, another Education Act was in the offing and the expectancy was that this would bring in free education, thereby creating further problems for school managers to tackle. The benefit of pooling ideas, perhaps even resources, was obvious. At the Diocesan Conference in October 1890 it was decided that the Education Committee should take steps to form a general federation of Church schools throughout the Diocese and that £1,000 at least should be raised to give assistance to managers of schools in carrying out whatever requirements the government might make upon them. When the next conference met in 1892 the Education Committee was able to report that a diocesan association of schools was in process of formation, and that in each deanery an education secretary had been appointed with a view to establishing deanery associations also. Five years later some fifty schools had come together and a school management sub-committee of the new association had notified the Education Department that all correspondence relating to these schools should in future be sent in its direction. It was in fact intended that the sub-committee should act as a clearing-house for Church schools in the Diocese. The advantages of such an arrangement, particularly for managers of isolated rural schools, were obvious. Similar developments were taking place in other English dioceses at this time, and the idea of establishing a central clearing-house for all Church schools in the country was at least under discussion. The Education Department itself gladly fell in with the new arrangements. Changes in administration at the centre were also being mooted during this same period, and in 1899 the Education Department was succeeded by the Board of Education.

The evolution of a diocesan association of schools during the 1890s was brought about because of the need to find united strength in a period of much hardship and difficulty. By now the position of the voluntary bodies had worsened substantially. The Education Act passed in 1891 offered a fee-grant to achieve abolition of school pence altogether or at least to bring about a great reduction in the amount paid, and parents were given the right to demand free education for their children. In practice managers of schools found they had to raise a larger amount by way of subscriptions than before. This led some parents to become subscribers, but there was still a loss of income to make good. Apart from the financial problems which came in the wake of the Act of 1891, the Diocese found in 1892 that H.M. inspectors had ordered improvements in no less than thirty schools. The minimum cost was estimated to be £3,400 of which £1,500 could be raised locally, leaving a deficiency of £1,900. To make matters worse, some 42 more schools were expected to require improvements in the immediate future. The demands of the Code of 1890 were now biting hard. Tremendous effort was needed by the Diocese to save its schools during the 1890s. Its Education Committee directed that effort from the centre and the diocesan association of schools worked with dedication in the field.

As to the nature of the education given in the Church schools, it goes without saying that the greatest importance was always attached to religious instruction. This was denominational in character in accordance with the principles of the Church of England. In those schools which received Parliamentary grant — as most of the Church schools did — the content of secular subjects was determined entirely by the state. This situation came about in 1862 when, with the introduction of the so-called Revised Code, grants to schools were made dependent on annual attendance and the performance of pupils in annual examinations conducted by H.M. inspectors. At first only reading, writing and arithmetic were examined and this in effect led to an extremely narrow curriculum, for an inevitable result of the system of 'payment by results' was that teachers concentrated on the grant-earning subjects, to the exclusion of others. In course of time, however, the list of subjects which could earn grant was extended very substantially and successive Codes not only broadened and liberalized the curriculum but also changed the conditions under which grants were assessed. The system of payment by results was not finally extinguished until 1897, though its most harmful effects had been eliminated long before that date. One important consequence of the broadening of the elementary school curriculum in the later nineteenth century was that more and more equipment and better facilities were required in the schools. It was now that the lack of rate aid particularly placed the voluntary schools at a serious disadvantage in comparison with the board schools.

Though the Church had to meet steadily-increasing competition from the state in the supply of schools, there was one area of educational work in which, at any rate until 1890, it had a complete monopoly - this was provision for the training of teachers. The Diocese of Durham had established a training college for masters in 1841 and a similar institution for mistresses in 1858. These colleges enjoyed the support of the Church north of the Tyne no less after 1882 than they had before. The fact that in the two North-East dioceses, as indeed throughout the country, teacher-training was monopolized by the Church of England incensed Nonconformists and school boards alike and it led to demands for non-denominational, non-residential colleges. With respect to the area of the Newcastle Diocese, the first significant breach in the Anglican monopoly came in 1890 with the establishment of a day-training department at the Durham College of Science in Newcastle, the forerunner of what is now the School of Education in the University of Newcastle upon Tyne.

It has to be said that during the period under review provision of education was a source of mounting bitterness, in which Anglicans, Roman Catholics, Nonconformists and Secularists were all embroiled. After the Elementary Education Act was passed in 1870 many Churchmen believed that the Church's position in education was now in danger and they viewed with alarm the establishment of the godless school boards. The Roman Catholic Church, which was adamant in maintaining that the children of Roman Catholics must be educated in Roman Catholic schools, equally disapproved of the school boards. Nonconformists, whose own stake in education provision was a relatively small one, and whose financial resources were slender in comparison with those of the Church, generally supported the extension of the school board system — for them the only alternative might be to send their children to Anglican schools. Those who had no religion at all opposed the role of the churches in education as a matter of principle.

School boards could be established in any school district either at the request of ratepayers or compulsorily if the Education Department had ascertained there was a deficiency of provision. In districts where boards were set up elections for a new board were held every three years. Especially in industrial and heavily-populated areas, where the influence of the Church was always weaker than it was in the countryside, demands for the setting up of school boards were strong, and elections were conducted in an atmosphere of much excitement, not uncommonly with a great deal of acrimony. Newcastle and Tynemouth, the two most heavily-populated school districts in the Diocese, each exhibit strong manifestations of this sectional bitterness. At both places school boards were set up as early as January, 1871, in response to powerful local demands. Not that involvement in school-board politics was officially organized by the Church as a body, but individuals, both clergy and lay people, entered the arena and actively campaigned either to keep out the boards, or, if that failed, to gain representation on the boards in order to exercise some influence on their decisions. Candidates known to support the interests of the Church appeared at each election. This same line was followed by the Roman Catholics. At the time there were many Churchmen who looked upon such activity as a crusade against the forces of Secularism and irreligion. By gaining seats on the boards they might at least try to curb the worst excesses of the enemy, give the Church some voice in the decision-making of the boards and watch over the interests of the voluntary schools. Needless to say, the appearance of Church candidates in the elections inflamed both the Nonconformists and Secularists. Churchmen were almost automatically accused of attempting to sabotage the work of the boards.

Though the presence of Church candidates undoubtedly worsened relations between the Church of England and some sections of the community, it is equally certain that their activities did give the Church of England a not insignificant voice in the affairs of the boards. There was at least one Anglican priest on almost all of the eleven Tynemouth boards. The Roman Catholic Church secured representation also. On the seventh Tynemouth board (1889-91) a Roman Catholic priest was chairman and an Anglican priest was vice-chairman. Perhaps the most interesting case is that of Rev. H. S. Hicks, the Vicar of St. Peter's, Tynemouth, who sat on the first and third boards, and who later became secretary both of the Diocesan Education Committee and the Diocesan Inspection Fund. Similarly, Church of England and Roman Catholic candidates were returned at each school board election in Newcastle. Here it was laymen rather than clergy who represented the interest of the Church of England on the boards, and they were returned in sufficient numbers to form a powerful lobby.

282

During the 1890s it had become increasingly obvious that the arrangements made in the Act of 1870 were placing an intolerable strain upon the voluntary bodies — they were, after all, not able to compete with the school boards on equal terms. The two political parties now entered the arena, and the main issue centred on whether or not voluntary bodies should receive additional financial help in carrying out their educational work. At the end of 1902 the Conservative government of A.J. Balfour passed an Education Act which achieved just that and at the same time swept away the school boards. Legislation in 1888 had provided the country with a new system of local government, and it was on this system that the Act of 1902 secured the provision of education, with the establishment of Local Education Authorities. County councils and county borough councils became L.E.A.s which were given responsibility for the provision of both elementary and secondary education (Part II Authorities). Boroughs with a population of over 10,000 and urban districts with a population exceeding 20,000 became L.E.A.s with responsibility for elementary education only (Part III Authorities).

Under the new arrangements the board schools were simply taken over by the L.E.A.s and were now called 'provided' schools. Voluntary schools were brought under the control of the L.E.A.s in the matter of secular instruction, and one-third of the managers of such schools had to be appointed by the authority. The cost of capital expenditure on buildings, as well as of alterations and structural repairs, was to be met by the religious bodies to which the schools belonged — hence these schools became known as 'non-provided' schools. But they were now eligible to receive rate aid. Managers of non-provided schools retained the right of appointing and dismissing teachers, subject to the approval of the L.E.A. on educational grounds. Religious instruction in the schools remained under the control of the managers.

The Education Act of 1902 represents a real landmark in the development of English education. Though it did not establish a national system of education, certainly it provided the base upon which such a system could be built during the present century. The dual system, introduced by the Act of 1870, was retained and the extension of rate aid to voluntary schools assisted the continuance of their contribution to national education. At the time, however, the Act was violently opposed by the Nonconformists, some of whom flatly refused to pay the rate intended for the voluntary schools. The Liberal party saw a golden opportunity to embarrass the government by making common cause with those who opposed the Act.

L*

During 1903 the new Local Education Authorities were set up in accordance with the terms of the Education Act and began their work. In the area of the Diocese of Newcastle there were six L.E.A.s all told; of these Northumberland, Cumberland and Newcastle were Part II authorities, Berwick, Wallsend and Tynemouth were Part III. In 1910 Tynemouth became a county borough and therefore a Part II authority; Berwick on the other hand ceased to be a Part III authority in 1921. With respect to the Church schools of the Diocese, obviously by far the greatest number of them (some 85 per cent) came under the jurisdiction of the Northumberland L.E.A. The 1902 Act required each L.E.A. to set up an education committee, to which all educational matters should be referred, except the power of raising a rate or borrowing money. It was stipulated that whilst the majority of members of an education committee were to be members of the council other persons were to be added who had educational or relevant experience, and in practice the L.E.A.s numbered among these the representatives of voluntary bodies. Thus, once the new L.E.A.s were established the Newcastle Diocese obtained representation on their education committees, and it is interesting to note that the constitution of the Northumberland committee drawn up in March 1903, specifically designated a member from the Diocesan Association of Schools.

There were other indications of the growing importance of the Association. Under section 11 of the Education Act the owners, trustees or managers of schools were required to apply to the Board of Education for an order appointing them foundation managers. Where trust deeds were not available, or were in any respect inconsistent with the provisions of the Act, the Board was empowered to make orders which would regularize the position in each individual case. All this involved a great deal of business, both locally and at the centre. Between April and August, 1903, the Board issued interim orders which embraced the Church schools in the Diocese. At local level it was the Diocesan Association of Schools rather than the Education Committee in the Diocese which bore the brunt of the work. Moreover, partly to expedite payment of outstanding grant due to the schools, the Board of Education suggested in 1903 that a trust deed should be executed for the administration of the common funds of the Association.

Thus the logic of events imposed on the Diocese a need to re-examine existing arrangements for the oversight of its educational work. The Education Committee of the Diocesan Society had had this responsibility for some eighteen years; now clearly the Diocesan

Association of Schools, which had evolved gradually during the 1890s, was deeply committed too, and through its functions acquired increasing status with outside bodies. Some overlap of business inevitably occurred, and this led the Diocese to discuss a proposal to devolve on the Association, at least for the time being, the main duties of the Education Committee. Meanwhile, a constitution for the Association had been brought into operation as from 1 April, 1903; this provided for the election of a governing body every three years. Each deanery in the Diocese was represented on the governing body and there was generous provision for co-opted members. In the years ahead the Association received funds which came in by way of donations and subscriptions and in answer to appeals, such as the urgent appeal for £10,000 launched by the bishop in aid of the Church schools. It was the Association which normally represented the Diocese on the education committees of the L.E.A.s. Diocesan calendars still carried references to the Education Committee of the Diocesan Society until as late as 1917, but *de facto* the Newcastle Diocesan Association of Schools had long since taken over its work as the effective body concerned with education.

Little more than a decade existed between the setting up of the L.E.A.s and the outbreak of the First World War. During that period implementation of the Education Act was carried through, in the course of which various issues were identified. Chief among these was the continuing difficulty experienced by the voluntary schools. The Education Act of 1902 had no doubt removed the grievous disadvantages under which the Church of England and other voluntary providers of education had laboured during the school-board period. But the new administrative arrangements and the introduction of rate aid did not usher in a golden age, and before long the voluntary bodies were again struggling. The real cause was that the Board of Education, anxious to improve both the physical conditions and the quality of work in elementary schools, made increasing demands upon the schools. L.E.A.s, which were responsible for secular instruction in all the schools in their areas, non-provided no less than provided schools, had to see to it that these demands were met. With regard to voluntary schools, capital expenditure on buildings, the cost of alterations and repairs, fell entirely upon the managers, not the L.E.A.s. The most which the managers could recover from an L.E.A. was expenditure due to reasonable 'wear and tear', and the Board of Education seems to have watched this closely. When for example the Newcastle L.E.A. in 1904 offered an allowance of 1/- per head per annum, this arrangement was disallowed by the Board a year later, after which managers were to see that repairs were done and render claims to the L.E.A.

The extent of the task which faced both L.E.A.s and voluntary bodies after 1902 was clearly revealed as soon as the new L.E.A.s had undertaken surveys of all the school buildings in their areas. Reports of H.M. inspectors added to what indeed was a daunting picture. Of all the six L.E.A.s within the Diocese, the Newcastle L.E.A. inevitably had the most acute and pressing problems. Here school accommodation could not keep pace with the steadily-increasing population and there was serious overcrowding, which led in some cases to double banking of desks and classes working back to back. The Board of Education threatened lack of recognition unless improvements were made. These conditions obtained in provided schools as well as those of the voluntary bodies; for the latter there was great strain, as they alone had to foot the bill. Even in rural areas there was a great deal for the Church to find. In 1905 for example, the Northumberland L.E.A. asked for repairs and improvements to no less than 79 Church of England schools. The managers of the schools undertook to carry these out, but the cost was a heavy one.

Looking at the period between 1903 and the outbreak of war in 1914 it is obvious that a real weakening occurred in the position of the voluntary schools. The Northumberland Education Committee reported in 1913 that during the previous ten years some 53 voluntary schools had been taken over by the local authority. Of these 14 were Church of England schools. The relative position of non-provided and provided schools had in fact been reversed. Whereas in 1904 the former educated 61 per cent of the school population and the latter 39 per cent, in 1913 the non-provided schools educated 38 per cent and the provided schools 62 per cent. In Newcastle, the next largest authority in the area of the Diocese, voluntary schools provided 16,030 places in 1903; by 1914 the figure had dropped to 9,127. The Church of England perhaps suffered less losses than other voluntary providers of education, but this was cold comfort, for it was undoubtedly losing ground.

At least one happy feature of the period was that the relations between the L.E.A.s and the Diocese were in general very good. During the later years of the school board period there had been great bitterness, and it says much for the legislation of 1902 that a cordial relationship soon developed between L.E.A.s and voluntary bodies. This good working partnership came despite the noisy and rather silly opposition of the more extreme Nonconformists aided and abetted for a time by their Liberal allies. The noise was greatest in Newcastle and Tynemouth, both areas of large population, where local newspapers were able to disseminate — and exacerbate — popular prejudices. Nationally the so-called Passive Resistance League had been established by Nonconformists to galvanize opposition to the 'iniquitous' Act, and its members, fired by the leadership of Dr. John Clifford, pledged themselves not to pay that part of the rate for the support of education in voluntary schools. This led to distraint of property and the risk of imprisonment. The League had its adherents among the Free Churches in the Diocese and court appearances of passive resisters certainly continued until as late as 1914. Apart from the religious scrupulosity of the more bigoted Nonconformists, Liberals and Secularists attacked the Education Act of 1902 for placing unfair burdens on the ratepayers. In 1903 the Newcastle *Daily Leader* roundly accused the Church, in spite of its rich endowments and many state privileges, of not scrupling to throw the whole cost of educating its own children, in its own religion, on public rates and taxes. This was of course, palpable distortion of the facts. The substantial expenditure which the Diocese was called upon to find after 1902 in support of its schools is itself sufficient testimony of the mischievous nature of such a comment. Moreover — and this is a point which its critics too easily ignored — the Church of England through its schools did in fact save the ratepayers a very great deal. If these schools had ceased to exist, the burden of a heavy compulsory rate would have fallen upon the ratepayers. As it was, the L.E.A.s and the ratepayers got a substantial number of schools on the cheap.

In the matter of establishing schools, the piety and private benefaction of individual men and women and the organized effort of the Church as a body were directed almost exclusively towards provision of elementary education, and it is therefore education of this kind which engages most attention in a study of the Church's part in school education. The connection of the Diocese with grammar-school education is much more tenuous. In 1882 there were seven schools in the new Diocese which had started life as grammar schools. Of these by far the most important were at Berwick, Hexham, Morpeth and Newcastle. Berwick essentially began as a corporation school and the other three were founded under royal charters. None had any organic connection with the Church. The remaining three schools, at Haydon Bridge, Rothbury and Stamfordham, were by 1882 grammar schools in name only. Haydon Bridge had been founded by Rev. John Shafto in 1685, and Rothbury under the will of Rev. John Tomlinson in 1722. Both schools therefore had been founded through the benefaction of individual clergy.

Some five years before the new Diocese was instituted, the reconstitution of an existing educational charity led to the foundation of two schools which in future years were to add substantially to the provision of grammar-school education in Newcastle. These were the Dame Allan's Endowed Schools, the opening of which came within a year of the setting up of the new see. The Dame Allan's Schools for Boys and Girls certainly had their roots in Anglican piety, for they sprang out of the charity school of St. Nicholas, founded by Dame Eleanor Allan of Newcastle early in the eighteenth century. When Dame Allan's Charity was re-organized in 1877 the strong connection with the Church of England was retained. The vicars of each of the four ancient parishes of Newcastle became *ex-officio* governors of the new Dame Allan's Schools, and one half of the scholarships awarded on the results of the examination for admission to the schools was restricted in the first instance to boys and girls who had been educated for at least three years at elementary schools in Newcastle where religious instruction was given in accordance with the doctrines of the Church of England. Religious instruction in the Dame Allan's Schools was specifically Anglican in character.

During this period there was a pronounced national demand for the admission of girls to the benefits of a grammar-school type of education, enjoyed hitherto almost exclusively by boys. In 1872 a proprietary body, the Girls Public Day Schools Company, had been founded for the purpose of establishing day schools for girls, and the conspicuous success of this venture was to lead to the development of other companies with similar objects. Many Church people, both lay and clerical, were convinced of the need to promote the establishment of schools which united secular education with definite religious teaching in accordance with the principles of the Church of England. Thus in 1883 a Church Schools Company was launched. Two years later, in 1885, the Company opened a school for girls in Newcastle, the Church High School. From the first, the school established a very close association with the Diocese, and indeed, the Bishop of Newcastle became its patron. At the prize-giving in 1900, the Archbishop of Canterbury himself came to address the school. By this time it had established a good academic reputation and a number of its pupils had gone on to study at Cambridge and other Universities.

The schools of the Church Schools Company were each managed by a local committee, all members of which were shareholders. With the passage of time, most of the schools were handed over to the local committees, and devolution of this kind happened in the case of the Newcastle school in 1909. The local committee now became the governing body of an independent girls school. There was, however, no change of policy, and the school retained its close connection with the Church of England. The Bishop of Newcastle continued to act as patron, and it was staunchly supported by clergy and lay people in the Diocese as before.

Thus in the early years of the new Diocese the provision of second-ary education in Newcastle had been enhanced by the opening of three schools which had a very real connection with the Church of England. Two resulted from the re-organization of an educational charity, and the third was established by a proprietary company of which the shareholders were individual men and women in the Church. Interest-ingly enough two of the schools were for girls, the first schools of their kind in Newcastle – or the Diocese. Here certainly the Church was attuned to one of the most pressing educational needs of the time.

The First World War inevitably brought much disturbance to the education service. Well before hostilities ended the government began to think of the transition from war to peace and to lay plans for the building of a better land which returning warriors would so richly deserve. Education figured prominently in the plans for post-war reconstruction, and in August, 1918, before the War actually ended, an Education Act was passed which gave practical expression to the optimism of the time.

This Act provides the starting point for the next chapter, for it marks the threshold of a new period in the history of school education in the Diocese. Looking at the hundred years since the Diocese was first instituted, the sad but inescapable fact is that so far as school education is concerned the over-all picture is one of decline. That decline does not, however, occur evenly. There are two main periods, one before, the other after, the Education Act of 1918. The later period, for which much greater documentation exists, witnesses a rapid decline; the earlier is a more heroic period, marked by a valiant and largely successful struggle on the part of the Church to retain a significant presence in the educational field. Before 1902 it had to compete with the secular school boards, which possessed financial advantages denied to voluntary bodies, notably rate aid. The Educa-tion Act of 1902 brought only temporary respite, for although the Church schools were now able to receive aid from the rates, the demands made upon schools by the Board of Education increased steadily and this led to financial difficulties for the Church no less severe than before. In the circumstances decline was inevitable, but it says much for the resolution and enterprise of the men and women of the Diocese that the inroads which were made into the Church's position were substantially contained. Some loss there was, yet even as late as 1918, the Church still maintained a very sizeable and influential presence in educational affairs.

Chapter XVIII

THE CHURCH AND SCHOOL EDUCATION

G. W. Hogg

2. FROM 1981 TO THE PRESENT

THE 1918 Education Act concentrated on providing some form of post-elementary education for all pupils. It finally ended the half-time system (whereby older children had been able to attend school half-time and spend the other half in paid employment), raised the leaving age to fourteen, advocated day-continuation schools, central and senior schools, and called for the inclusion of courses of advanced and practical instruction in the curriculum of the elementary school. The post-war economic crisis, quickly followed by the Geddes Axe, inevitably put paid to most of these schemes, but even before 1921 it was evident that the dual system was a major stumbling block to any reorganization of post-elementary education.

The debates leading to the 1918 Act had been surprisingly free of religious acrimony. The President of the Board of Education, the distinguished academic H.A.L. Fisher, fully intended to avoid the repetition of the earlier religious strife but clearly the churches would experience great difficulty in promoting school reorganization. Central schools were beyond their financial capacities; with poor endowments and declining subscriptions, even the extension of existing premises to provide advanced and practical instruction for senior pupils would be difficult as most Anglican schools, for example, were small, rural and housed in old buildings. In 1921 there were 124 Church of England schools in the Northumberland L.E.A. area which was mainly rural. The average accommodation was for just over 100 pupils, and 17 of these schools had under 30 on their books. So from the summer of 1919, Fisher held conferences with Anglican and Free Church representatives where the compromise solution that non-provided schools would be transferred to the L.E.As. with special provision being made for religious instruction received favourable Anglican support. This was in essence the so-called 'Scottish System' of 1918 which guaranteed efficient denominational teaching in transferred schools by stipulating that teachers must be approved for their religious beliefs and character by church representatives. However, there was much opposition to such a solution. Bishop Knox of Manchester led the Anglican lobby for separate church schools and the veteran Free Church leader, Dr. John Clifford, true to form, opposed any plan that might in any way rescue Anglican schools in particular. Obviously the old wounds were still open but the Scottish solution was not really on as it would prove too expensive south of the border. In 1918 only a tenth of Scottish schools were non-provided schools, whereas in England and Wales the number was almost half the total. It would also prove political dynamite, for teachers' organisations, especially the influential National Union of Teachers, strongly opposed any forms of religious tests for the appointment and promotion of their members. Despite Fisher's efforts the dual system remained and so did the attendant problems.

The problems of church schools were further exacerbated in the mid-1920s. A series of Board of Education circulars called for reduced class sizes and improved standards of accommodation. The Board surveyed schools in 1924-5 and informed L.E.A.s of deficiences. The so-called 'black list' schools were in three categories: 'A', those with buildings unsuitable for continued recognition; 'B', those that might be made suitable but only by substantial expenditure; 'C', those not unsuitable but for much lower numbers of pupils. Non-provided schools on the list numbered 2,113, almost three times the number of provided ones. In the Newcastle Diocese out of some 120 church schools 5 were in category A, 16 in B, and 8 in C — 24 per cent of the total. The Diocese made efforts to improve its black list schools and the 1929 annual report of the Diocesan Association of Schools announced that the church schools at Choppington and St. Anthony's, Newcastle had completed the work required by the Board and would be removed from the list. But much more needed to be done as there were a number of schools in the Diocese where all the children were being taught in one room. For example, a 1928 H.M.I.'s report on Kenton school complained that 98 children were being taught side by side in one room by three teachers! Even by 1939 there were still some 572 non-provided schools in the country on the black list out of a total of 797; twelve of these were in the Newcastle Diocese. The financial dilemma of Church authorities was well brought out in a debate in the Commons in July 1926 when the remark was made: 'Who knows the Board's inspectors may not make a new set of demands two or three years hence? Then we shall have spent all this money, and we shall be no further forward'. This sums up perfectly the Church's difficulties in the rapidly changing educational scene since the 1920s. New demands, whether they have been re-organization in the 20s or 30s, or the provision of secondary moderns after 1944, or the comprehensive re-organization in recent years, all entail increasing financial outlay for an uncertain future. Church leaders could well sympathise with nineteenth century British ministers who, when they thought they had solved the seemingly intractable Irish question, found the Irish had changed the question!

In the 1920s very few Anglican schools were built. In the decade only 33 new schools for the whole of the country appeared on the Board's grant list, not one of these being in the Newcastle Diocese. This number compared unfavourably with 769 new provided schools and 76 Roman Catholic schools. Indeed, the Church was stretched to maintain its existing schools with closure and transfer to the L.E.A. being not uncommon. In Northumberland by 1930, 77 non-provided schools had been transferred to the authority since it had begun to operate in 1903, and the bulk of these schools were Anglican. In the same period the numbers of places in non-provided schools in the county had halved (from 43,043 to 21,571) whereas those in 'council' schools had more than doubled from 23,020 to 48,164. A not atypical closure was that of Dinnington Church of England school where, in a letter to the Northumberland Director of Education, the managers' correspondent wrote in June 1920:

> I have to inform you that the Managers find they are unable to increase the accommodation of the school and that in view of the new housing scheme it would be advisable for the Education Committee to take steps for the erection of a Council School and they recommend that it should be in the vicinity of the existing school. (Dinnington Church School Logbook, letter dated 9 June 1920).

Even where there were good prospects for a church school the financial support was not there. Dinnington closed as a church school in 1923 and the buildings were then transferred to the L.E.A.

Typical of the conditions of transfer of a church school to the local authority was that of Herdley Bank in April 1929. This school was

> reported by the Board of Education as defective in various respects, and the managers were not in a position to carry out the works required to render the buildings satisfactory. The owners of the school have offered to sell the premises to the Local Education Authority at the price of £250, subject to arrangements for the use of the premises for Church purposes on Sundays and occasionally on evenings during the week, rent free. (Northumberland Education Committee Minutes XXV, p. 529).

293

Main problems of closure, then as now, concerned small rural schools in the Diocese. In 1932, following Board of Education insistence on economies, Northumberland L.E.A. reported that 49 schools under its administration had each under 31 pupils and most of these were Anglican Schools, two of which had under eleven scholars. The managers of Meldon church school voluntarily agreed to closure in that year, the thirty pupils being transferred to Hartburn council school some four miles away. But closure was not always an economic proposition. For instance, West Lilburn Church of England school with 27 pupils cost the authority £468 in 1932, made up of a government grant of £210 (almost 50 per cent) and £258 from the rates. Conveyance of pupils to a nearby school would cost £225 for which only a 20 per cent grant was available (£45), the remaining £180 to be met from the rates which would also have to bear another £100, half the cost of the additional member of staff necessary at the school to which the pupils would be transferred. Clearly it would not pay the authority to transfer the West Lilburn scholars and the church school remained open. (It may be that in the 1980s and beyond, increasing transport costs will be the important factor in deciding to keep small rural schools open.)

The publication in 1926 of the Report of the Consultative Committee on the Education of the Adolescent heralded increased problems for church schools. The Hadow Report, as it is popularly known, recommended some form of post-primary (post-II as they suggested) education for all up to the age of fifteen. What came to be termed the Hadow re-organization of elementary education would involve the churches in considerable expense either to re-equip existing schools for the education of 'senior' pupils or to build new 'modern' schools, and this at a time of increasing building costs and shifting population patterns. It became evident that one church senior-school, if it could be afforded, would have to serve a number of parishes and many clergy considered this would sever the intimate connexion the parish priest had with his children. In November 1926 the Church Assembly gave its defiant but wholly unrealistic reply to the Hadow Report when it called for the provision by local authorities of more denominational schools, the right of entry to any newly provided 'secondary' schools to give denominational instruction and the setting up of local committees to supervise the religious instruction given in provided schools. However, wiser counsels prevailed and in the following year the National Society accepted the Hadow re-organization in principle and agreed that in most areas children would have to proceed from the church school at eleven to the provided senior school, subject to the

Anson bye-law of 1902 which gave parents the right to withdraw children from provided schools during a period of religious instruction.

With some hesitation Eustace Percy at the Board of Education accepted the Hadow proposals and re-organization was officially launched with the publication of the Board's pamphlet 'The New Prospect in Education' in 1928. As was not uncommon, local initiative in educational experiment pre-dated official policy. Unfortunately, the economic crisis meant the Exchequer grant to L.E.A.s for the purpose of re-organizing post-primary education was withdrawn in 1931. Before that date Sir Charles Trevelyan who had succeeded his fellow Northumbrian, Percy, as President of the Board of Education in 1929, had made a number of attempts to raise the leaving age to fifteen with a promise of some form of aid to church schools to help them re-organize. All proved abortive.

Re-organization of schools on the Hadow lines was actually taking place some years before the publication of the Report in 1926. As early as 1920, L.E.A.s to fulfil obligations under the 1918 Education Act, began to draft schemes for the re-organization of elementary schools, including the provision of senior schools and divisions and possible central schools. In that year the Diocesan Association of Schools reported that schemes to meet the situation raised by the creation of central schools had been prepared. The Church was mainly concerned with the loss of senior pupils to council schools and with the consequent problems that would befall their numerous decapitated rural schools. In 1921 Northumberland L.E.A. proposed re-organization in the Wooler district where a council school would cater for the older pupils and the church school would remain for 5 to 12 year olds. The managers objected and the scheme fell through. Bishop Bilbrough in his presidential address to the Diocesan Conference in 1923 counselled a wiser approach. He remarked:

> There are talks of a large general appeal for a fund which will enable us to keep our church schools. Personally I have no trust in such an appeal, but I would have us keep our eyes open to the fact that we seem to be moving slowly and inevitably towards a unified system. It is our duty to ask ourselves frequently whether the duty of the church may not be, even at some sacrifice, to secure for every Christian child as efficient a religious education as can be secured under a state system. ... at the same time I do not doubt that it is our duty to keep every school that we can and to maintain it in a state of efficiency. For this object it is necessary we agree to strengthen our Board of Finance (*N.D.G.* XVII:119).

At the request of the Board of Education local authorities began to produce three-year development plans from 1927. No new church schools in the Diocese or additions to existing ones were included in the first plans, though the Diocese's first 'modern' school for seniors finally opened its doors in October 1930. This was Thomlinson's School, Rothbury, which had been formed in 1921 by the amalgamation of the declining Sharpe's secondary school and Thomlinson's elementary school, but which the Board did not give its approval for development as a school for 148 seniors till 1928. It was not till the publication of a government White Paper in 1930 asking L.E.A.s to enter into agreements with managers of non-provided schools for purposes of the Hadow re-organization that the Diocese became more concerned with the formulation of development plans. In that year a conference of church school managers met at Hexham specially to discuss the problems of senior schools and the Diocesan Association of Schools set up a special sub-committee to prepare for talks with the various L.E.A.s on their 1930–3 development programmes. Bishop Bilbrough and Canon Harding, Secretary of the Diocesan Association of Schools, were two of the five church representatives who met members of the Northumberland Education Committee on 19 March, 1930, to discuss re-organization. The authority was not keen on re-modelling old church schools for senior pupils having regard in particular to the provision of halls, libraries, practical instruction rooms and dining facilities. There was some agreement however about the provision of small central senior departments in existing church schools to serve feeder primary schools in rural areas and such an experiment at Eglingham church school was proposed though it never came about. The idea was revived in 1934 when the managers of Shilbottle church school proposed an ingenious solution to the problem of re-organization of rural schools. This entailed building a new church school for 160 seniors, making use of existing buildings for an assembly hall, practical rooms and dining facilities. The authority would have to provide a council school in the village for infants and juniors. The scheme was not finally abandoned until 1939.

In July 1930 a meeting took place between diocesan representatives and those from Newcastle L.E.A. and a new senior department at St. Anthony's, Byker, was included in the 1930–3 development programme. The provision of nursery education was also discussed. Provision of a new church central-senior school in the city never got past the talking stage.

Diocesan schools actually fared much better in the early 1930s and this despite the failure of Trevelyan's proposals which would have afforded financial aid and the economic depression. This was a period when funds for provided-schools building almost dried up, yet by parochial effort and with the help of the newly-established Bishop's Church Extension Fund church schools were improved and extended and provision made for advanced and practical instruction for seniors at Whitley Memorial, Bedlington; St. Peter's, Wallsend; Newbiggin; Newbrough (re-opened 1935); Ponteland; St. Paul's Elswick (re-opened 1934); and Christ Church, Newcastle.

In spite of these efforts, the annual report of the Diocesan Association of Schools of 1935 was not at all optimistic about the future. An improving financial situation meant that L.E.A.s were now able to proceed with their schemes of re-organization which had been frozen because of the economy measures begun in 1931. The report noted:

> Each of these schemes involves the removal of children from a number of Church Schools to a provided senior department. As it has been impossible for the Church herself to reorganize on a sufficiently large basis to allow for the development of the Hadow Scheme, it will be impossible for her to resist these efforts in the march of our educational system (*B.L.D.N.* 1935:17).

It went on to advise bodies of managers to inform parents of their rights under the Anson bye-law. However, a rescue operation to help church schools provide for senior pupils was at hand.

After much preliminary negotiation particularly with the churches and teachers' organisations, the National Government introduced a Bill which was in part based on Trevelyan's earlier proposals and which became the 1936 Education Act. Its two main proposals were to raise the school-leaving age to fifteen on 1 September, 1939, and to empower L.E.A.s to make building grants of between 50 per cent and 75 per cent towards the cost of providing new church schools or enlarging existing ones for senior pupils. This was an acceptable compromise but with important limitations. The grants would only be available for three years and any proposals had to be made by 1 September, 1938; teachers in what later came to be called 'special agreement schools' would be appointed by the L.E.A., though there would be 'reserved' teachers for religious instruction; schools in single-school areas would provide R.I. according to an agreed syllabus if parents demanded it; denominational instruction was to be available for children transferred from a non-provided to a provided school — the Anson bye-law became universal. The National Society had proposed important amendments such as that grants should be available for all church schools, as in the future a large number of these would be for juniors only and that R.I. for church children in provided schools should be at the expense of the authority and be held on the premises. However, none of these was acceptable.

In December 1936 a special sub-committee of the Northumberland Education Committee was set up to discuss the schemes and plans submitted by the managers of non-provided schools under section 8 of the new Act. Archdeacon Hunter (see Chs. XII and XVI) representing the Diocesan Schools Association and two other church representatives attended one of its meetings by invitation in May 1937 and Colonel A.D.S. Rogers, the newly-appointed secretary of the Board of Finance representing the Diocesan Association of Schools, another in October. The sub-committee recommended to the Northumberland Education Committee that three new church senior schools be built with the aid of a 75 per cent grant from the authority — Humshaugh (for 120 pupils at a total cost of £11,750); Ponteland consequent upon the closure of the Coates Endowed School (160, £15,000); and Bellingham (100, £11,700). The last was conditional upon the church authorities providing a new infant and junior school. The sub-committee also recommended that extensions consisting of a hall/gym, domestic science room and canteen/kitchen at a cost of £8,025 be approved for Thomlinson's School, Rothbury.[2] The Diocese had put forward more ambitious proposals for eight senior schools.

In July 1938 Northumberland's special sub-committee on schemes and building plans for new senior non-provided schools met, with Canon O.F. Granlund, who had succeeded Canon Harding as Secretary of the Diocesan Association of Schools as the diocesan representative. This approved the scheme for a senior church school at Shilbottle for 120 pupils which the managers had first mooted in 1934, but deferred a decision on a proposed church senior school at Whitley Chapel. It agreed to provide equipment for practical instruction at Blanchland church school where the numbers were insufficient for a scheme for recognition under the 1936 Act.

Though the projects at Humshaugh, Ponteland, Rothbury and Shilbottle were included in Northumberland's programme of capital works for 1938–43, none was actually begun because of the outbreak of hostilities in September 1939. The only building under the terms of the 1936 Act that actually took place before that date was the remodelling of Christ Church school, Newcastle, for senior pupils at a cost of £6,635 to the Newcastle authority. The national picture was not dissimilar. Up to the outbreak of war 519 proposals, of which 230 were Anglican, for new senior schools under the terms of the 1936 Act were registered but only 37 were realised. By that date the cost of a senior school place had risen to £100 and the Anglican Church found it difficult to provide even 25 per cent of this. Most dioceses concentrated more on providing senior departments in all-age schools though even here the record was not notable. By March 1939, 62 per cent of the senior pupils in provided schools were being educated in senior schools or departments but only 16 per cent of non-provided school pupils.

Between the wars secular instruction in church schools was the responsibility of the L.E.A. and differed hardly at all from that given in provided elementary schools. In the 1920s in a 24-hour school week, the bulk of time was spent on the 3R's. In all standards, at least four hours would be devoted to arithmetic, five to reading and recitation and four to composition. Geography and history took up two hours, observation and singing an hour each, physical exercises up to two hours. The rest of the time was given to practical subjects such as needlework, handwork and drawing. The 1918 Education Act had made it the duty of authorities to provide facilities for practical work for seniors but there were difficulties, especially for rural schools, over suitable accommodation, equipment and the provision of specialist teachers. To some extent such problems were overcome by pupils during the warmer months proceeding by bicycle and bus to centres (usually other schools) for instruction in practical subjects and by L.E.A organisers holding classes for teachers, especially in physical education and handicrafts, to make them more competent. However, organisational difficulties especially in a rural area like Northumberland were tremendous and the authority could report as late as 1935 that barely one third of its senior pupils were receiving practical instruction.

Teaching methods changed slowly and, to some extent, the scholarship examination for entrance to secondary schools had a harmful effect.[3] Formal teaching predominated. An H.M.I. in his report on St. Nicholas' school, Newcastle in October 1927, remarked: 'There might at times be a little less direct "teaching" and a little more self-expression and initiative on the part of the children. Much of the work might be made more interesting if brought into some direct relation with the children's own surroundings'. However, the publication of the Hadow Report on the Primary School in 1931 which, while emphasising the importance of the 3R's, recommended that the curriculum should be thought of in terms of activity and experience rather than of knowledge to be acquired and facts to be stored, brought about a change in attitudes and methods. These latter were now more paedocentric, more concerned with the all-round development of the child, and began to concentrate on the need for more creative and expressive activity. One interesting experiment in teaching method was carried out by the headmistress of Kirknewton church school who in 1932 was granted by the L.E.A. an initial outlay of £37. 7s. 6d. and an annual sum of £8 9s. 0d. towards adopting the methods of the Parents' National Education Union in her school. These incorporated the ideas of Charlotte Mason about the importance for six to twelve-year olds of the atmosphere of environment (of a home, of a large family), of the discipline of habit (especially the habit of reading books that were worthwhile), and of the presentation of living ideas.

Diocesan inspectors, two in number, carried out frequent inspections of religious knowledge in church schools. These were formal oral examinations, though as early as 1919 Rev. A.F.S. Harding was wise enough to ask teachers to conduct the questioning. What follows is a not untypical inspector's report, that for Kenton church school in December 1924.

> The school is now producing work well up to the best traditions of Church Schools in the Diocese. The infants offered well-balanced knowledge in which quotations bearing upon the Biblical subjects forming part of their syllabus were much to the point and accurately rendered. The middle group also was consistently good, and the outstanding feature of the work of the eldest scholars was their reciting of the Public Baptism of Infants. The Prayer Book subject appointed in the Diocesan Syllabus was taken last year for the first time and the progress made on this occasion was very remarkable. The singing of the whole school is much improved (I would suggest that the children should stand while singing hymns) and the general mark 'Excellent' was fully earned this year. (Kenton Church School Logbook, 15 December 1924).

By 1937 less emphasis was being placed on the oral examination and inspectors were concentrating more on giving help and advice to teachers.

Section 13 of the 1936 Education Act gave parents the right of withdrawal of children from provided schools during R.I. periods and some advantage seems to have been taken of this 'parents' charter' as William Temple called it. For example, in 1937 the vicar of Spittal took some ninety children from the council school for R.I. in St. John's church for half an hour each Monday and Wednesday. In the same year ten Roman Catholic children were withdrawn from Wooler church school each morning to attend instruction in St. Ninian's church. Much depended on the initiative of the local incumbent and Berwick and district seem to have been most active over withdrawal.

From 1941 the vicar of Berwick taught R.I. in St. Mary's church to senior Anglican children from all the provided schools in the town.

Teachers in church schools were appointed by the managers (only one third of whom were local authority appointees) subject to approval by the L.E.A. who could only withold appointment on educational grounds. Relations between teachers and managers were usually good though Northumberland Education Committee received a resolution from the managers of Cornhill church school in 1921 expressing the opinion that teachers' salaries should, as in other appointments, be reduced owing to the fall in the cost of living and so offer relief to ratepayers. The headmistress at Beltingham church school was asked by the authority to terminate her duties at the end of March 1927 because she had recently married. She wrote in the school logbook: 'A request to resign I ignored as I feel it is most unjust to be dismissed because I am married'. The school managers upheld the ruling of the authority and she was dismissed. In 1942 Northumberland Education Committee held an inquiry into the affairs of church schools at Longhorsley and Wingates. There had been irregularities in the appointments of trustees and the vicar of Longhorsley had gained almost complete control of both schools' managing bodies and had manipulated them according to his own views which appear to have been very eccentric. Relations between the vicar and the two headteachers were very strained. Salaries were withheld, there was disagreement over religious matters and the vicar was alleged to have acted in a most high-handed manner in raising the rent of a teacher's house. At Wingates the headmistress resigned but the feud between vicar and headmaster at Longhorsley persisted. In May 1945 the vicar unsuccessfully requested the L.E.A. transfer the headmaster and on Mondays regularly withdrew pupils for a corporate act of worship in the parish hall.

Under the terms of the 1902 Education Act managers of non-provided schools were responsible for 'provison', that is new building, structural repairs and exteriors. The L.E.A. was responsible for 'maintenance' — salaries, equipment, heating, 'fair wear and tear'. Lack of cash was a perpetual problem and though church school managers could call upon certain diocesan funds (these never paid out more than £1,500 in any one year between the wars and then the total included payments for Sunday schools), in the main they had to rely on donations, voluntary contributions and the like to survive. For example, in 1927 the managers of St. Mary's Berwick church schools had only £6. 5s. 0d. regular income for their annual upkeep and a letter of appeal was sent out to parents which brought in some £14. At

Beadnell two years later a house-to-house collection realised £10 towards the £25 needed to pay for a new playground, the other £25 being provided by the authority.[4] Cordial relations usually existed between managers and the local authorities. From time to time the Newcastle L.E.A. complained that church school managers gave insufficient notice of the dates of their meetings. In the 1920s church school managers somewhat reluctantly agreed to a Northumberland L.E.A. ruling on the appointment of headmistresses (on salaries of abour £270 a year) rather than headmasters (£350) to schools of under 40 pupils. Managers relied on the officers of the Diocesan Association of Schools to represent their views to the three L.E.A.s in the Diocese on whose education committee they sat as selected or recommended members.

Wartime brought new problems and experiences for church schools. Some urban schools such as Kenton and St. Anthony's, Byker, closed on the outbreak of hostilities never to re-open; others like Christ Church, North Shields, were commandeered by the military authorities for the duration. A number of schools suffered damage through enemy action. By 1941 952 non-provided schools throughout the country had been hit, 233 seriously. Only Tritlington church school was hit in the first wave of bombing in September 1940 and it was not till near the end of the war that further damage occurred. In 1945 Radcliffe school (though the premises were no longer being used as a church school) was completely destroyed and Christ Church and Byker schools in Newcastle received minor damage. Bomb damage presented problems, for any considerable sum spent on repair work on a poor or old building would hamper post-war educational re-organization. School air raid shelters had been built before the war but it was as late as 1943 before the the local authority provided those at Christ Church Newcastle though it refused to provide shelters at St. John's because of the redundancy of the premises. As late as 1967 shelters were still being demolished at Whitley Memorial Bedlington and, no doubt, many still remain serving multifarious functions.

Church schools played their part in evacuation schemes, particularly of schoolchildren from the Newcastle, Tynemouth and Wallsend areas. For example, in September 1939, Beltingham church school received 37 evacuees from Willington Quay together with eight private ones. As elsewhere a double-shift system was worked — local children attending during the mornings one week, the afternoons the next and the evacuees at the other times. This was not to last long. At the end of September 1939 there were almost 9,500 evacuated children in the county of Northumberland; by the end of the year the number had fallen to just over 4,000.

Church schools 'did their bit' in other ways. The closed church school at Lillswood was used as a dwelling house by an evacuated family. In Northumberland six church schools were designated emergency feeding and shelter stations under the County Public Assistance Committee to be used in the event of any of the local population being rendered homeless through enemy action. School playing fields at Humshaugh and Whitley Chapel were ploughed up to sow potatoes and swedes.

Discussion about the building of a new society after the war accelerated from 1941. Education would play a dominant role in such a society and the nation's educational system would require a major overhaul. The churches still provided a half of the country's schools and, though prewar these had been a major obstacle to reorganisation, nevertheless their contribution would be essential. It would prove too costly to get rid of them and it was hoped that in return for some closer integration within the system they would obtain the greater financial assistance needed. Just before R.A. Butler became President of the Board of Education in July 1941 the so-called Green Book ('Education After the War') was issued to interested parties as a discussion document. Chapter Nine dealt with the dual system and allied problems, and elicited much opposition to its continuance. The Association of Directors and Secretaries of Education whilst not opposed to the retention of R.I. in the curriculum of state schools, referred to 'administrative dualism with all its harmful consequences', and Free Churchmen, though no longer the force they had once been, were anxious about the 4,000 single school areas that still existed. Two possible lines of policy for voluntary schools began to emerge and these were both eventually incorporated in the Government's 1943 White Paper ('Educational Reconstruction') outlining its proposals for an education bill. One policy suggested complete financial support with authority control and limited R.I. facilities; the other unlimited facilities for R.I. but with limited financial support and authority control. Some Anglicans, such as the Bishop of Chichester, favoured the former for they could not contemplate the Church being able to build and maintain schools to the standards expected. Besides, they argued that R.I. in council schools appeared to satisfy most parents. As the Bishop of Durham pointed out in a letter of January 1943: 'The R.C.s have the great advantage that they are absolutely clear that undenominational teaching is wrong. We cannot speak so clearly because many of us think it *may* be very good, and certainly many Anglican parents could not clearly distinguish it from Anglican teaching'.[5] Roman Catholics would have no solution but the second; any state control was anathema and rather than accept it they would pay for their schools twice over. This view was shared by some Anglicans like the high churchman, Bishop Kirk of Oxford. The Newcastle Diocese adopted a very sensible attitude. A general survey of some 110 church schools had recently been carried out and a report in 1941 called for the retention of 47 key schools and the establishment of a diocesan maintenance fund. In his report on church schools in 1941 Canon Granlund, after affirming that the diocese could not possibly take responsibility for all church schools, wrote:

> A few first-class schools will do more for the cause of the Church on the whole matter of religious education than a larger number which includes poor schools. Money doled out in driblets by the Diocese for the temporary needs of Church Schools has often been found to have been wasted, either because the satisfaction of these temporary needs has not enabled the school to catch up with the general standard required by the L.E.A., or because in the end a new school is what is really required. In the experience of some Vicars it does not follow that because the school is the Church School it brings the support to the Church which is imagined it will bring (*B.L.D.N.* 1941:91).

William Temple, the new Archbishop of Canterbury, initally declared he was against the 'wholesale surrender or transfer of Church Schools', but he quickly changed his tack after a frank interview with Butler who quoted him revealing statistics of Anglican schools. Of the 753 schools still remaining on the Black List, 399 were Anglican; over 90 per cent of Church schools had been built before 1900 and most of these were small and uneconomical. In November 1942 the Church Assembly debated the National Society's report calling for acceptance of modification of the dual system. Temple's plea for a 'wise adjustment to the situation in which we find ourselves' won the day, and there was a virtual end to any obstruction to compromise on the part of the Church of England. Indeed, compared with earlier education bills there was little religious bitterness in the debates which led to the passing of the 1944 Education Act in August. No doubt the fact that it was a measure introduced by a coalition government helped but due praise must be given to the diplomacy and tact of Butler and of his Parliamentary Secretary, Chuter Ede, and to the common sense shown by most church leaders.

The 1944 Education Act provided among other things for secondary education for all, the raising of the school age to fifteen at an early date (it actually came about in 1947), and for compulsory R.I. and corporate acts of worship in state schools. More importantly from the churches' point of view it saved their schools. Henceforth non-provided schools would be called voluntary, as distinct from county schools, and would be of three types. Aided schools were where the Church appointed two-thirds of the managers who were to have control over teaching appointments and where the state provided half of approved expenditure on external repairs and improvements and half of the cost of any alterations that might prove necessary to ensure secondary education for all up to 15. There was the possibility of a 50 per cent grant for new church schools for 'displaced' children due to slum clearance or town planning but there was much debate over this. Special Agreement schools were very like aided ones in matters of management and maintenance and church authorities would be able to revive pre-war proposals for new and re-organised schools under the 1936 Act which attracted a 75 per cent grant. Voluntary controlled schools had only a third of their managers appointed by the churches but the state assumed complete financial responsibility. R.I. was to be given in accordance with an agreed syllabus but denominational instruction could be given by 'reserved teachers' under certain conditions and on not more than two occasions each week if parents so desired.

All L.E.A.s had to submit development plans to the new Ministry of Education by 1 April 1946. Even before the Act was passed the Bishop of Newcastle had written to the Chairman of the Northumberland Education Committee saying he was anxious to co-operate in matters relating to the new education act and suggesting an *ad hoc* sub-committee of authority and Church representatives to discuss future plans. Alderman Bell considered this premature but promised no decisive steps would be taken without previous discussion. All three local authorities were late in submitting their plans and Newcastle's was not given Ministry approval until February 1949. Under these plans 43 out of the 89 church schools in Northumberland were scheduled for closure, 4 of the 7 Newcastle schools, while the two Tynemouth church schools were to be retained. In Northumberland four church secondary modern schools were proposed at Rothbury, Ponteland, Wallsend and Humshaugh with an option on another at Embleton. Only one new primary school at Wallsend was planned. The successor to the Diocesan Association of Schools, the Diocesan Education Committee (D.E.C.)[6] proposed two secondary modern schools using the existing buildings at Chist Church and St. Paul's, Newcastle, together with two new 'transferred' primary schools at St. Anthony's and Kenton. The L.E.A. disagreed with the plan for the two modern schools on the grounds that their sites could not be extended, that they fell far short of standards prescribed by new building regulations and, most importantly, that they would serve areas of declining population in the centre of the city. They could not agree to the opening of two new primary schools either. Diocesan objections were made to the various plans and some alterations achieved. For example, Northumberland agreed rather reluctantly to the retention of Acklington church school and, after strong protest by the D.E.C., Alnwick junior school was reprieved.

Within six months of the approval of a development plan by the Ministry those designated voluntary schools had to apply to the Minister for an order directing that they be granted aided or special agreement status, otherwise they became automatically voluntary controlled schools. In effect it was not until 1953 that aided status was finally accorded to 18 church schools, by which time 58 of the schools in the Diocese were either aided or special agreement, almost two-thirds of the total. Despite the Church Assembly's resolution in June 1951 that 'as many Church Schools as possible should obtain aided status', few other dioceses could match the Newcastle figure, a testament to its concern for its schools and to the magnificent work of Canon P. M. Martin, Secretary of the D.E.C. from 1948 to 1961, in persuading school managers of the advantages of aided status. Aided schools were assisted by the introduction in 1952 of the diocesan Maintenance of School Buildings Scheme which, in return for annual per capita contributions, paid all repair bills and helped finance improvements such as heating, lighting and sanitation. It was later extended to include wider insurance cover and a quinquennial inspection of schools.

A full afternoon session of the June 1956 Diocesan Conference was devoted to aided schools and the following year it was finally agreed that the Diocese should go ahead with the D.E.C's 1950 plan which called for the retention of 39 key aided-schools, over twenty of which would require extensive remodelling and three to be built on new sites. Also four new schools were planned, three of them secondary at Rothbury, Ponteland and Humshaugh. Unfortunately, by this date the implementation of this programme was likely to prove beyond the Diocese's financial capacity particularly as building costs had risen and interest rates on Ministry loans had more than doubled since 1945. Great hopes had been laid on the 'Call to Churchman' begun in 1946 with a target of £400,000, but it reached only over half this total, of which a capital sum of £35,000 for schools was agreed, affording an annual income of only £1,400. This together with funds from other sources including the sale of disused schools under section 86 of the 1944 Act would over the next twenty years produce some £140,000 just over half the £270,000 required.

Diocesan education policy was not without its critics. At the October session of the 1963 Conference the Reverend A.K. Hamilton, vicar of St. John's Newcastle and later Bishop of Jarrow, complained that not enough finance had been made available for the building of new churches and that it was a grave mistake to spend a very large sum on church schools. In the December session he moved £10,000 should be cut from the budgets for 1965 and 1966 for schools but his motion was defeated.

As in 1936 help was at hand for church schools. Roman Catholics in particular had for some time been demanding grants out of public funds for all approved voluntary school building. The Government was pressing for the full implementation of the policy of secondary education for all. In Northumberland for example, more than one senior child in nine was still attending an all-age school and most of these were church rural schools. But higher building costs, an increasing birth-rate and shifts of population made church schools difficult to maintain, let alone re-organise. By 1958 the annual cost to the Church of England for providing, altering and repairing its schools was £850,000: for the Roman Catholics £1,900,000. The 1959 Education Act increased maintenance and improvement grants from 50 per cent to 75 per cent for church schools and provided for 75 per cent grants for the building of new secondary schools for children from primary schools of the same denomination which existed in that year. Schemes for new schools had to be notified to the local authority within a twelve-month. The Act was generally welcomed by the churches though some Roman Catholics complained that they were still three-quarter citizens.

September 1959 saw the opening of the first diocesan secondary modern school at Ponteland. Northumberland L.E.A. had agreed to the proposal for a three-form entry special agreement school as early as March 1955 and the Ministry had approved but only for a two-form entry school. Spurred on no doubt by this and by the opportunities opened up by the new Act, numbers of schemes for church secondary modern schools were put forward. Some of these like those at Roth-bury and Humshaugh were revived proposals and were included in the county's revised development plan for 1959; some were new such as those at Wallsend, Newcastle and Tynemouth. Only that at Roth-bury materialised. The Humshaugh proposal was abandoned in 1965 as not being a viable scheme; the L.E.A. considered a one-form entry school at Wallsend 'in an urban area educationally unsound' and the Ministry turned down the proposal in 1960; a 1959 scheme for a three-form entry secondary modern/technical school in Freeman Road, Newcastle, was finally abandoned largely on the grounds of insufficient primary feeder schools and besides the authority was in the process of re-organising its secondary education on comprehensive lines. In Tynemouth, where in the 1950s a number of new housing estates were built, the local clergy were keen to provide new church schools, but in a letter to the vicar of St. Peter's, Balkwell, North Shields, Canon Martin wrote: 'We share your great desire that the Church of England should have new schools in the new districts but we have to be guided by the practicalities of finance'. In 1959 the vicar of St. George's, Cullercoats, proposed a secondary school on the new Marden Estate but the D.E.C. decided it could not finance the project and the L.E.A. provided a four-form entry school instead. The project for a church secondary school serving Tynemouth and the surrounding area was revived in 1963 when local government boundary changes were being discussed which might have led to Wallsend and Longbenton being incorporated in Tynemouth county borough thus providing four feeder church primary schools. However, nothing came of the project and, though similar boundary changes actually came about in 1974, by that time radically different patterns of secondary education existed in the new metropolitan borough of North Tyneside.

After 1945 there were a number of proposals for a church secondary grammar school. One of these actually got off the ground when in 1947 the Cathedral Choir School opened with 21 pupils on its books. It had diocesan support and the help of a substantial legacy. The Minister of Education recognised the school as efficient in July 1951 but it got into increasing financial difficulties and its numbers declined. In 1972 the Department of Education and Science insisted on significant improvements for continued recognition but, despite the setting up of an appeal fund, the school closed in 1977. In 1956 Canon Ward Davis of Wallsend (see Chapter XIII) approached the D.E.C. about the possibility of acquiring an independent grammar school as a church school. This was Tynemouth School and the asking price was £10,000. The committee had the property viewed and the report to its executive committee concluded that the state of the buildings left much to be desired and that a further £10,000 would be required to bring them up to a satisfactory standard. Its purchase was not recommended, Bishop Ashdown summing up the whole project as being 'entirely unrealistic'. As late as 1960 the D.E.C. executive committee discussed a proposal for a church grammar school but declared the suggestion impracticable. Grammar school education was, it remarked, already well provided for in the city's independent and direct grant schools and besides was under serious attack from the supporters of comprehensive schools.

Though these Newcastle grammar schools, now all in the independent sector, are beyond the scope of the present survey (see previous chapter), nevertheless some have very special links with the Church, notably the Dame Allan's Schools and the Church High School. Unfortunately, these schools have a limited number of places and are fee-paying which, despite a few scholarships and bursaries, means they are beyond the pockets of many Anglican parents.

In 1965 it was reported that £400,000 had been spent since 1962 on the provision and support of schools in the Diocese. The Rothbury secondary modern school had finally been completed in 1964 and new primary schools opened at St. Anthony's, Newcastle, and Christ Church, North Shields. Advantage had been taken of emergency government aid to the area for schemes costing under £20,000 and of industrialised building methods to re-build or modernise schools at Kirknewton, Longhorsley and Tritlington. However, the early 60s had not been without difficulties for voluntary schools. Teacher shortage had led to strict Ministry quotas and small rural primary schools in particular suffered. Between 1959 and 1962 twelve church schools in Northumberland, five of them aided, had been closed.

Also the Church was once again to suffer from the perpetual reorganisation which has been so prominent a feature of the educational scene. Newcastle Education Committee decided in September 1958 to work towards an eventual re-organisation of their secondary schools on comprehensive lines. Its first comprehensive school at Kenton was opened in 1960. Discussions took place between the authority and the D.E.C. who in 1962 agreed to the transfer of senior pupils from the three church primary schools to the authority's 11–18 comprehensive schools. It was to be a temporary measure pending the provision of a church secondary school which, though proposed in 1965 to be included in the 1972–73 building programme, never materialised. The Labour government's Circular 10/65 called for the end of selection for secondary education and its re-organisation on comprehensive lines. Tynemouth chose an 11–16 high school/sixth-form college pattern and this, like the Newcastle 11–18 all-through scheme, would not seriously affect church primary schools which would be able to retain their pupils till eleven. Northumberland, however, were naturally slower to re-organise. They chose a three-tier system (first schools from age five to nine, middle schools from nine to thirteen, high schools thirteen to eighteen) largely for economic reasons, and this would mean the truncation of all church primary schools in the county as they would lose their two top junior years. In October 1966 the Diocesan Conference considered the Northumberland plan — it would take well over ten years to realise — and decided to retain its primary schools as first schools and to establish new middle schools in key areas. The possibility of a church comprehensive high school was mooted. The 1968 Diocesan Conference agreed in principle to participate in the county's plan. In order to assist the churches in the re-organisation of their schools the 1967 Education Act raised to 80 per cent the grant to church schools and, more importantly, provided 80 per cent of the cost of establishing completely new schools or enlargements of existing ones. This would apply to primary as well as secondary schools.

Many influences over the past twenty years have combined to broaden and humanise church primary education. The retreat of the eleven-plus examination, the work of the Schools Council, the influence of official reports such as that on Children and their Primary Schools (*Plowden Report*, 1967) and, following Priority for Primaries policies of the early seventies, increased resources and better staffing ratios have all aided change. The modern church primary school like its state counterpart is characterised by the integrated day, unstreamed classes, the project approach and individualised learning techniques. Emphasis is still laid on the basics — the 3R's — but other subjects, especially creative activities, play an increasingly important role alongside that of socialisation in the primary child's education. Religion still plays an important part in the life and work of church schools. The morning assembly for the whole school is now generally a weekly occurrence with class assemblies held more frequently, and though the Bible no longer holds the central place it once did in it, religious education is taken seriously. The Diocese recently adopted the 1977 Durham Syllabus of R.E. for Church Primary Schools. The teaching of Church doctrine depends very much on the enthusiasm of the local clergy and in many schools an energetic incumbent will instruct top classes weekly and ensure children attend church on the major festivals.

In November 1970 the successor to the D.E.C., the Diocesan Education Board produced its discussion document 'Diocesan Education Policy in the 1970's.'[7] This closely followed the alternative future policies for church schools set out in the Durham Report published in the same year. The document advanced four alternatives — radical disengagement; large-scale development; retention and improvement; gradual phasing-out of commitments to schools and transfer of effort to the employment of specialised personnel for religious education. The Diocesan Synod of June 1971 passed motions adopting the retention and improvement alternative and proposed the development of middle schools at Ponteland, Rothbury and Wallsend. In April 1977 Canon David Ogden, Diocesan Director of Education, presented a discussion paper 'Education Policy and the Church' to the Diocesan Synod in which he mentioned that since the end of the war 34 church schools had been re-built or re-modelled at a cost of just over £2 million of which the Diocese contributed some £350,000. Of this £144,000 had come from parochial contributions via the Quota; proceeds of the sale of disused schools amounted to £145,546; the remainder was made up from grants and the interest from investments. The Synod in its discussion of educational policy for the 1980's agreed that the Diocese could no longer hope to expand its present provision of fifty church schools — 40 aided of which three are special agreement, and 10 controlled.

If the period between the foundation of the Newcastle Diocese and the end of the First World War was one in which Anglican schools, at least in numbers, were in decline, that from 1918 to the present was one in which this decline accelerated rapidly to the point where on a number of occasions the very wisdom of keeping any church schools at all in the Diocese was seriously doubted. In 1918 there were 129 Church of England schools with over 22,000 pupils, just under 20 per cent of all schoolchildren in the Newcastle Diocese. Today only some 4,000 schoolchildren, about 3 per cent of all those in the Diocese, are educated in 50 church schools. Forty-seven of these are primaries, three middle schools and not one, it should be noted, is a secondary school which means that for most children an 'Anglican' education ceases effectively at the age of eleven.

As has already been discussed, a number of factors exacerbated the problems facing the voluntary schools after 1918, not least of which have been the increased financial demands and organisational changes (especially in the secondary field) brought about by legislation. Rapid decline there has been since that date but due credit must be given to the work of the various diocesan organisations in providing finance and advice, to the enthusiasm of local clergy and to the labours and devotion of the teaching staffs for the fact that fifty church schools have survived in the Diocese. This is not an unproud record when one remembers, that unlike in most other dioceses, the bulk of these are aided schools which have entailed considerable sacrifices on the part of the Church.

Today one hardly hears mention of the dual system which could generate so much sectarian strife, even as late as 1959, and which educational administrators tolerated somewhat reluctantly. New problems face education such as the declining birth-rate leading to falling school rolls, ever-continuing inflation and, more recently, serious financial cut-backs in local government spending. Doubtless, in the near future more church schools in the Diocese will close as many of them are small rural schools. Quality, more especially in the instruction given in schools which in turn depends on a well-qualified, dedicated teaching staff, will count for more in education in the future. There are clear signs that the church schools in the Newcastle Diocese can respond to this and other challenges, adapt, and more than survive.

NOTES

1. The talks referred to were those originating from a meeting of the Standing Committee of the National Society of 10 October 1923.
2. Bishop Bilbrough inaugurated an Appeal Fund in July 1937 asking for £60,000 which would include the £11,000 needed for the four schools — some 25 per cent of the estimated costs.
3. Elementary school-teachers on a sub-committee set up by the Northumberland Education Committee in 1938 to look into homework referred especially to the harmful effect on scholars in junior schools of special preparation for the admission examination for secondary schools. Church schools seem to have gained more than a fair share of 'scholarship' places. In February 1925 standardised tests drawn up by Professor Cyril Burt were used for the first time for the examination of all children between ten and twelve in Northumberland authority schools.
4. A recent High Court decision had made local education authorities responsible for half the cost of playgrounds for non-provided schools.
5. Bishop Williams was replying to a communication from a local incumbent who had referred to the Roman Catholic Bishop of Hexham and Newcastle's pastoral letter for Advent 1942. Hensley Henson, the bishop's predecessor, was more forthright in his views. Writing in his autobiography of the national debate at the time of the abortive Liberal education bills 1906–08, he noted: 'Much emphasis was placed on the injury inflicted on parents by the type of religious teaching provided in the State schools, but it was not true that the parents themselves were conscious of any hardship'.
6. The Diocesan Education Committee, a statutory body, was established under the Diocesan Education Committee Measure 1943, with, among other tasks, 'the right, power, duty and obligation from time to time' to watch the interests of church schools, to secure the provision of new schools and to give advice to school managers. It seems to have functioned in the Newcastle Diocese from 1945 and was incorporated under the Companies Act 1950. Its chief officer was the Director of Education aided by an executive committee with a clergy majority.
7. The Diocesan Education Board was established in 1970 in accordance with the Synodical Government Measure. Its membership includes the Bishop, the two archdeacons, the Director of Education (now known as the Director of Education and Training), twelve elected members (six clergy, six laity) and co-opted and nominated members. The Board's Schools' Committee which meets about ten times a year deals with the business of Church schools.

EPILOGUE

Ronald Bowlby, Bishop of Newcastle (1973-1980)

WHEN I suggested the outline of this book to its editor, there were at least three aims in my mind.

The first was to help people appreciate more of the history of the Diocese, and to see how closely it has been entwined with local society at many points.

The second was to convey an accurate picture of what has been happening to church life during this past century, and the extent to which the local story confirms what has been happening nationally (see especially Chapters VI and VII).

The third was to provide material on which we might reflect with care, to see what are the relevant issues to be faced as the next century in the life of the Diocese begins.

These purposes have been amply fulfilled by Dr Pickering and his contributors in a rich and fascinating set of essays. As he himself says, 'The material that has come to light in taking a close look at the Diocese over the past century does not in itself make a great contribution to a fresh understanding of the complex process or processes of church decline. The trends merely confirm what has been occurring in the country as a whole' (page 129).

The overall picture is one of rapid change in society, which both affects the Church as an institution and makes heavy demands on its ability to communicate the Gospel in new and appropriate ways.

The concluding chapters on education, for instance (Chapters XVII and XVIII), illustrate the process precisely. The nineteenth century was characterised at first by a widespread and generous response to the need for basic education, and many church or parish schools were founded — nearly all of them in rural areas. Towards the end of the century, the population rose dramatically, and much of the increase was to be found in industrial Tyneside. At the same time, more and better schools were demanded. Aging buildings needed maintenance and often enlarging. The Diocese and parishes were no longer able to meet this growing need, though for a while valiant

313

efforts were made to maintain what had been begun. The twentieth century witnessed steady decline, especially in the decades just before and after the First World War. Finally, a small number of church schools were retained and improved, almost all of them still in rural areas and catering for the youngest age-groups.

Certain points may be observed.

i. The institutional involvement of the Church in education declined dramatically. There remained a Christian presence in many other schools through the teachers, pupils and governors: but it is much harder to assess its influence.

ii. Lack of finance is the instrument which forced decision and may also reveal a decline in living faith and commitment. Taking the century as a whole, and despite the particular hardships of the North-East, it was a period of economic growth and improved living standards. But the will to continue and expand what has been begun is not there; or at least not in the same way.

iii. The story of the schools illustrates the rural emphasis which still characterises the Diocese in many ways. Not only has this meant an imbalance in the distribution of clergy which is hard to correct (see pages 111-2), but it has given the rural parishes and deaneries a dominance in Diocesan leadership and affairs which is still noticeable in certain ways.

iv. The story of the schools is almost totally devoid of an ecumenical dimension — in fact much of it records intense conflict between the Church of England and the Free Churches, with the Roman Catholic Church pursuing its own independent line. When real co-operation comes, it is — by and large — too little and too late. Reading these essays, it is significant that the first century of Diocesan life emerges as a period of infrequent co-operation with other Churches, except towards the end.

Looking into the future, it is already clear that further major challenges await the Diocese.

The first and most obvious is that of inflation. The figures on page 168 about deanery quotas conceal the true impact of what has already happened by 1980. Since 1973, when I first came to the Diocese, the quota has risen from £83,850 to £491,900 in 1980-81, a staggering increase of 486.64%! Four-fifths of this sum is required to pay the clergy and other full-time workers of the Diocese. The rate by which the quota has been increasing is actually greater than that of national inflation, since the Church Commissioners are unable to keep pace with inflation through investment, and in addition spend a larger proportion of their income on such things as pensions, which must be kept in line with the rate of inflation as far as possible.

So far almost every parish in the Diocese has responded to the challenge in full, and that is cause for great encouragement. But for how much longer can this be maintained? There is a difference between raising large sums for an appeal (e.g. to endow the Diocese, see Chapter II; or to build new churches and halls, see Chapter X), and raising larger and larger sums every year for running costs; particularly if the average congregation contains relatively few of those whose salaries or wages keep pace with inflation.

A second challenge concerns those parishes which are situated in predominantly or entirely working-class areas. Over the past century, it is clear that strong congregations have existed in some of these areas, and the churches have often been at the hub of social life as well. No one can fail to be moved by the deep faith and self-sacrifice of individual ministries described in Chapters IV and XIII. But as Katharine Lloyd and Peter Dodd in particular make clear, the Churches now face a different situation, in which many social needs are met by other agencies, and industrial work has caused much hardness, division and bitterness over the years. There is a marked resistance to the Gospel, perhaps accentuated by some of the institutional forms of church life.

If this process continues much further, large parts of urban Tyneside will soon be left without any obvious Church presence. The remarkable and far-reaching influence of the Parish Communion in this Diocese (see especially pages 59-60) needs to be balanced and extended by an equally theological and passionate commitment to Parish Mission and Ministry. This will require new forms of evangelism; a determination to make new Christians and to use the gifts and abilities of the laity or laos ('people of God'); and to understand the culture and aspirations of those who live in the inner city or the great housing estates of the post-war era. It will require sacrificial giving on the part of many Church of England members who have never had to give very much before. It could mean — and here I venture beyond what the facts of this book allow — that the whole fabric of our Diocese will undergo severe disruption and change, as many existing buildings are abandoned and a more flexible pattern of church life and ministry emerges once more.

This issue was discussed in a debate at the Diocesan Synod in March 1979, at which a motion was passed establishing an inner city Commission to develop a programme of positive action with regard to the causes of disaffection, the mission of the Church, the deployment of manpower, and financial and administrative support in such areas.

This Commission began work in 1980. Similar concern is being expressed about rural ministry and society.

It is evident from several of the chapters, that the Diocese has been served by many clergy who have been deeply committed in their ministry and have laboured to the point of being local heroes. No matter how much their work may seem as a whole to have been unsuccessful, judged at least by the criteria employed by social historians, nevertheless their ministry as local leaders of the people of God has kept the Church going in many places where it might otherwise have disappeared. While a more flexible pattern of ministry must evolve in the future, and will include not only part-time auxiliary clergy but a much wider use of lay people, nevertheless a full-time professional ministry will undoubtedly continue to be at the centre of much local church life.

A third challenge lies in the area of social work and social change. Katharine Lloyd poses the question, 'What is the role of the Church in relation to social work and social change in the closing decades of the twentieth century?' (page 245). She underlines the shift from institutional to community care, and hence the possibility of parishes coming into their own again as centres of compassionate concern and involvement.

The Holy Family Church at Killingworth is an example of churches working closely together to 'minister' in their community in many different ways; the Diocesan Board for Social Responsibility, through the Adviser, supports a variety of projects which include an 'advice shop' on a housing estate, set up in close collaboration with local churches and the social services. I have no doubt that many parishes will increasingly train their members for some kind of community service as a normal part of Christian living and working together.

But there is a deeper issue within. What is to be the motivation for such work? And at what point does concern for those in some kind of need (physcial, emotional, spiritual) pass on to consider the causes of such need in society? Recent years have witnessed a considerable interest in prayer and the spiritual life (non-Christian as well as Christian), which suggests a search for deeper purpose and meaning. Alongside this, there is a widespread concern for the future of a world which is threatened by natural and nuclear disasters of a horrible kind. (The Brandt report, *North-South*, highlights the disparity between the rich and poor nations of the world, and the decisions which need to be made if disaster is to be averted.) As the Diocese responds to the challenges of the second century of its life, it must give absolute priority to the quality of its worship and its teaching about prayer; but it must increasingly help its members to understand their interdependence with one another and with the peoples of the world, and sustain them in working for justice and compassion in society.

The perennial temptation of our first century has been to turn aside from the struggle to hold together a commitment to Christ and a commitment to the world for which He died. Yet this volume of essays shows how much has been achieved, and is a fitting tribute to those who did so much to extend God's Kingdom at a time of rapid and unprecedented change. The struggle must continue.

APPENDIX 1

NOTES ON THE CONTRIBUTORS

MARTIN BASS studied economics at King's College, Newcastle, in the University of Durham, graduating in 1960. The next three years were spent in obtaining a professional qualification in accounting and he then returned to the University of Newcastle upon Tyne (as it had then become) as lecturer in accounting in the Department of Economics.

RONALD BOWLBY read history at Oxford after serving in the Army. Following theological training, he served as a curate in a shipyard parish in Sunderland, and then became vicar of a new housing area in Billingham on Teesside for ten years. In 1966 he became vicar of Croydon, and then returned to the North-East as Bishop of Newcastle in 1973. In December 1980 he left Newcastle to become Bishop of Southwark.

IAN CURRY studied architecture at King's College, Newcastle, University of Durham (Dip. Arch. with distinction; A.R.I.B.A. 1956; F.R.I.B.A. 1968). He has been Diocesan Surveyor in the Diocese of Newcastle since 1963, and was President of the Ecclesiastical Architects' and Surveyors' Association, 1969-70. He works as an architect in private practice, specializing in historic buildings and is Consultant Architect for Durham Cathedral. He is a member of the Advisory Committees for the Care of Churches, Dioceses of Newcastle and Durham.

PETER DODD studied theology at St. John's College, Cambridge, and prior to attending a theological college, spent a year on the shop floor in the steel industry in Sheffield. Ordained in 1960, he joined the Sheffield Industrial Mission in 1963 and came as the first industrial chaplain to the Newcastle Diocese in 1967. For nine years he was associated with ship building. He was made rural dean of the Newcastle East Deanery in 1978.

ROBIN GILL is a lecturer in the Department of Christian Ethics and Practical Theology at Edinburgh University and the non-stipendiary priest-in-charge of Ford with Etal, Northumberland. He was awarded a Ph.D. in theology from London University and an M.Soc.Sc. in sociology from Birmingham University. He has written several books including *The Social Context of Theology* and *Theology and Social Structure*.

GORDON HOGG is a graduate of the universities of London and

318

Durham. At present he is a lecturer in the School of Education in the University of Newcastle upon Tyne where he specializes in the history of education.

ANN HOLOHAN studied social sciences at Glasgow University and from 1971-8 worked as a medical sociologist in the Medical Care Research Unit of the University of Newcastle upon Tyne. In 1978 she joined the Department of Social Studies in the same university and lectures on current issues in medical care.

PETER J. JAGGER (M.A., M.Phil., F.R. Hist.) is Warden and Chief Librarian at St. Deiniol's Library, Hawarden. He studied at Wesley College, Leeds, College of the Ressurection, Mirfield, and the University of Leeds. He was ordained in 1969 and is now a member of the Principal's Conference. His particular interests are in history and liturgy.

KATHARINE LLOYD (O.B.E., M.A., J.P.) was at Oxford University (1925-8) and Birmingham University (1928-9) and also the University of Chicago (1948-9, 1955-6). She has had varied experience in social work. She has served on numerous committees including Central Training Council in Child Care, Regional Hospital Board, Community Health Council, Probation Committee, Newcastle Council of Social Service. Until she retired in 1967, she taught social work courses in the University of Newcastle upon Tyne.

GEOFFREY MILBURN took a degree in history at Manchester University and later an M.A. He worked for the Student Christian Movement and has taught in schools. Since 1970 he has been lecturer in history at Sunderland Polytechnic, specializing in the Reformation, and the social and religious history of eighteenth and nineteenth century England. He is a Methodist and a lay-preacher.

MALCOLM NICHOLSON was at King's College, Cambridge as an Exhibitioner and then at Cuddesdon theological college. Ordained in 1932, he served at St. John's, Newcastle; Monkseaton; Sugley; and Cullercoats. He was examining chaplain and secretary of the Ordination Committee from 1946-55. Afterwards he was archdeacon and examining chaplain in Sheffield. He was also Select Preacher, Cambridge, 1955; Woodard Fellow, 1955-9; Leader of the Friendship Mission from English Churches to Berlin, 1957; and Headmaster, King's School Tynemouth (1959-70); and finally a country rector in Berkshire from 1970-77. He is now retired and lives in Hexham.

WILLIAM PICKERING studied theology at King's College, London, and received a Ph.D. from the University of London in 1958. For eight years until 1966 he taught sociology in the University of Manitoba and is at present lecturing in that subject in the Department of Social Studies, University of Newcastle upon Tyne. He was ordained in 1950 and is a non-stipendiary curate in a Tyneside parish.

D. J. ROWE is a lecturer in economics in the University of Newcastle upon Tyne, specializing in the economic history of the North-East. He graduated from the University of Southampton and later was awarded an M.A. from the same university.

COLIN TYSON graduated in history at the University of Sheffield and in 1960 received an M.A. in history at the University of Birmingham. After being a schoolmaster for some fourteen years, he was appointed lecturer in education at the University of Newcastle upon Tyne in 1963. He is now head of the higher degrees and research division of the University School of Education.

APPENDIX II

Churches Built in the Diocese of Newcastle since 1882

Ian Curry

Date of Construction or Consecration	Church & Dedication	Designer where known
1877	Newcastle St. Matthew (consecrated 1904) (New church)	R. J. Johnson & W. S. Hicks
1878–1884	Cullercoats St. George (New church)	J. L. Pearson
1881–1884	Tynemouth St. Augustin	—
1882–1885	Shilbotel St. James (former church replaced)	W. S. Hicks
1884	Blyth St. Cuthbert (New church) (continued 1893)	W. S. Hicks
1885	Wallsend St. Luke	Oliver & Leeson
1885	Dudley St. Paul (Killingworth) (Mission church)	W. S. Hicks
1885	St. John Lee (Reconstruction)	W. S. Hicks
1885	Seghill St. Mary Holywell (Mission church)	W. S. Hicks
1886	Ashington Holy Sepulchre	—
1886	Ashington St. John (continued 1896–8)	W. S. Hicks
1886	Byker St. Silas	R. J. Johnson
1886	Dissington St. Matthew	—
1886	Mickley St. George (Restoration)	W. S. Hicks
1886	Bingfield St. Mary (Mission Church)	W. S. Hicks
1886	Lambley St. Mary & St. Patrick (New church)	W. S. Hicks
1886	Earsdon St. John Backworth (Mission church)	W. S. Hicks

Date of Construction or Consecration	Church & Dedication	Designer where known
1883–1887	Gosforth All Saints	R. J. Johnson
1887	Throckley St. Mary	W. S. Hicks
1888	Jesmond St. George	T. R. Spence
1888	Shiremoor St. Mark (Mission church) (to 1967)	Hicks & Charlewood
1889	Henshaw All Hallows	—
1886–1890	Newcastle St. Luke	Oliver & Leeson
1887–1896	Newcastle St. Aidan	Hicks & Charlewood
1891	Newcastle St. Jude (Shieldfield) (Site conveyed 1879)	—
1891	Wallsend St. Peter, (Reconstruction & Gothicisation)	Hicks & Charlewood
1892	Newcastle St. Augustine	R. J. Johnson & W. S. Hicks
1892	Walbottle (Mission church)	Hicks & Charlewood
1893	Burradon (Mission church)	Hicks & Charlewood
1889–1893	Bywell St. Margaret Hindley	Hicks & Charlewood
1894–1897	Hepple Christ Church	Hodgson Fowler
1894	Benwell St. James, Steeple, porch and N. Aisle added to Dobson's church	Hicks & Charlewood
1896	Newbiggin St. Bartholomew, new vestries and in 1908–10 North Aisle.	Hicks & Charlewood
1896	Hexham St. Mary Lowgate	—
1896	Haydon Bridge St. Cuthbert, new chancel etc.	Hicks & Charlewood
1896	Wall St. George	Hicks & Charlewood
1897	Seaton Hirst St. John	—
1898	Cambois St. Andrew (Mission church)	Hicks & Charlewood
1899	Heaton St. Gabriel	F. W. Rich
1899	Whorlton St. John (Site Conveyed 1867)	—

Date of Construction or Consecration	Church & Dedication	Designer where known
1900	Gunnerton St. Christopher	Rev. Mr. Hall
1900	Wallsend St. Aidan (site conveyed)	—
1900	Wallsend St. Patrick (site conveyed)	—
1900–1901	Greenhead St. Cuthbert — Chancel, Organ Chamber & Steeple added.	Hicks & Charlewood
1900–1905	Jesmond St. Hilda	Hicks & Charlewood
1901–1907	Allendale — Catton Mission	Hicks & Charlewood
1902	Wylam St. Oswin (New church)	R. J. Johnson
1902	Horton St. Mary (complete restoration)	Hicks & Charlewood
1901–1904	Jesmond St. Barnabas (New church)	Hicks & Charlewood
1906	Sleekburn St. John	—
1906	Byker St. Mark	—
1907	Corsenside All Saints (New church) (West Woodburn)	Hicks & Charlewood
1908	Byker St. Lawrence (New church)	Hicks & Charlewood
1908	Jesmond Holy Trinity (Chancel) (Nave completed 1922)	Hicks & Charlewood
1909	Hexham Abbey — completion of Nave	Temple Moore
1915	Delaval St. Paul (Seaton Sluice)	—
1915–1917	Scotswood St. Margaret (New church)	Hicks & Charlewood
1920–1922	Jesmond Holy Trinity (Nave etc. completed)	Hoare & Wheeler
1927	Stocksfield St. John the Divine	—
1928–1931	Fenham St. James & St. Basil	E. E. Lofting
1931	Monkseaton St. Mary (site conveyed 1914)	—
1932	Byker St. Martin	—
1932	Cambois St. Andrews (Mission church)	See H & C 1898
1932	Seaton Hirst St. Andrew	—
1936	Newcastle Holy Cross, Fenham	—

Date of Construction or Consecration	Church & Dedication	Designer where known
1937	Benwell, Venerable Bede	W. B. Edwards
1938	Balkwell St. Peter	—
1938	Monkseaton St. Peter	—
1938	Widdrington St. Mary (Church-cum-Hall)	C. Franklin Murphy
1953	Newcastle St. Peter (Cowgate)	Edwards & Partners
1953	Newcastle St. Francis (High Heaton)	Edwards & Partners
1956	Wallsend St. John (New church) (Site in use since 1935)	G. E. Charlewood
1956	Kenton, Church of the Ascension (New church)	P. C. Newcombe
1956	Denton Holy Spirit (New church)	P. C. Newcombe
1957	North Gosforth St. Chad (Woodland Park)	—
1957	Longbenton St. Mary Magdalene	P. C. Newcombe
1957	Newsham St. Bede (New church) (Site conveyed 1930)	G. E. Charlewood
1958	Rothbury St. Andrew (Thropton)	—
1959	Gosforth St. Hugh, Regent Farm	P. C. Newcombe
1959	Gosforth St. Mary Fawdon (Church-cum-hall)	P. C. Newcombe
1959	Morpeth St. Aidan (Stobhill) (Church/Hall)	Edwards & Partners
1960	Horton St. Benedict (Cowpen) (Church-cum-hall)	P. C. Newcombe
1961	Lynemouth St. Aidan (consecrated) (Built as Church Hall 1924)	G. E. Charlewood
1962	Choppington Church of the Holy Family (Stakeford) (Church-cum-hall)	P. C. Newcombe
1962	Linton St. Aidan	—
1963	North Gosforth St. Aidan (Brunton Park)	F. Heron

324

Date of Construction or Consecration	Church & Dedication	Designer where known
1966	Cullercoats St Hilda (Marden) (New church)	I. Curry
1967	Shiremoor St. Mark (New church)	I. Curry
1965–1972	Whorlton Church of the Holy Nativity (Church/Hall) (Chapel House)	R. N. Mackellar & Partners
1966–1972	Whorlton St. Wilfrid (Newbiggin Hall Estate) (Church/Hall)	P. G. Elphick
1972	Walkergate St Oswald (consecrated) (Built as Church Hall 1932).	G. E. Charlewood

APPENDIX III

BIBLIOGRAPHY

As well as books, articles, pamphlets, and so on, which are mentioned in the chapters of the book, there are also included below references to other books and articles which refer to the Diocese of Newcastle and the area it covers (see Bibliography and References, p.x). In the case of Chapters II and XIV the reports, documents and books are stated in detail at the end of those chapters. Items given below, which relate directly to the Diocese and its area are marked with an asterisk*. The bibliography is not intended to provide a comprehensive list of source-material for a historical study of the Diocese.

*ARMSTONG, H. E. 1878, 1879, 1880, 1882 *Reports of the Medical Officer of Health for Newcastle upon Tyne*, City and County of Newcastle upon Tyne.
*ATLAY, J. B. 1912 *The Life of the Right Reverend Ernest Roland Wilberforce, First Bishop of Newcastle upon Tyne and afterwards Bishop of Chichester*, Smith, Elder, London.
*BARING, C. *Charge Delivered to the Clergy of the Diocese of Durham*. (Charges for 1870, 1874, 1878).
BATEMAN, J. 1883 *The Great Landowners of Great Britain and Ireland*, Harrison, London.
*BELL, E. M. 1962 *Josephine Butler*, Constable, London.
BERGER, P. L. 1967 *The Sacred Canopy*, Doubleday, New York; and as *The Social Reality of Religion*, Faber and Faber, London 1969.
Bishop's Letter and the Diocesan Newsheet (B.L.D.N.) (see Newcastle Diocesan Gazette)
BRADLEY, I. 1976 *The Call to Seriousness: The Evangelical Impact on the Victorians*, Jonathan Cape, London.
*BRILL, K. (ed.) 1971 *John Groser, East London Priest*, Mowbrays, London and Oxford.
*BRAITHWAITE, C. 1958 *The Bureau of Social Research for Tyneside*, privately published.
*BRION, M. 1968 *One Hundred Years at St. Stephen's, Low Elswick*, privately circulated.
*BRUCE, J. C. 1889 *Handbook to Newcastle-on-Tyne and District*, Andrew Reid, Newcastle.
BRYMAN, A. (ed.) 1976 *Religion in the Birmingham Area*, University of Birmingham.
*Bureau of Social Research for Tyneside, *Annual Reports*, 1926-1930.
*BURN, W. L. 1956 'Newcastle upon Tyne in the early nineteenth century', *Archaeologia Aeliana*, 4th series, Vol. XXXIV, pp. 1-13.
*BUTLER, J. E. 1869 *Memoir of John Grey of Dilston*, Edmonston and Douglas, Edinburgh.
BUTLER, J. E. 1898 *Personal Reminiscences of a Great Crusade*, Marshall, London.
*CAMPBELL, W. A. 1973 'High Elswick a Hundred Years Ago. Centenary of St. Philip's Church', privately circulated.
Census 1851: Education in England and Wales, Report and Tables, Parliamentary Paper, 1854.

*Census of Worship 1851: Reports and Tables, Parliamentary Paper, 1853. Re-printed by the Irish University Press, 1970.

*CHADWICK, O. 1966 The Victorian Church, Part I, A. and C. Black, London.

*CHADWICK, O. 1970 The Victorian Church, Part II, A. and C. Black, London.

*CHADWICK, O. 1975 The Secularization of the European Mind in the Nineteenth Century, C.U.P., London.

*CHARLTON, E. 1854 'Illustrations of the Propagation of Asiatic Cholera by Human Intercourse' in Report of the Pathological Society of Newcastle and Gateshead, Newcastle upon Tyne, pp. 31-46.

*Church of England Yearbook, Church Information Office, London.

Commission on Religious Education in Schools 1970 The fourth R, The Durham Report on Religious Education, S.P.C.K., London.

*COTTAM, J. C. H. 1979 'The Church and Social Service', privately circulated.

*COXE, R. C. 1860 A Cursory Survey of the Churches and Church Buildings within the Archdeaconry of Lindisfarne. A Charge founded on the Reports of the Rural Deans, Francis and John Rivington, London.

CRUICKSHANK, M. 1963 Church and State in English Education 1870 to the Present Day, Macmillan, London.

CURRIE, R. and others 1977 Churches and Churchgoers: Patterns of Church Growth in the British Isles since 1700, Clarendon, Oxford.

*CURRY, I. 1976 'Anglican Church Redundancies in the North of England', in P.A.G. Clack and P.F. Gosling (ed.s) Archaeology in the North, H.M.S.O., pp. 265-71.

*DAVIES, C. Ward 1978 'One Man's Furrow', privately circulated.

DAVIES, R., GEORGE, A. R., RUPP, G. (ed.s) 1978 A History of the Methodist Church in Great Britain, Epworth, London.

*DIXON, D. D. 1895 Whittingham Vale, Redpath, Newcastle.

*DIXON, D. D. 1903 Upper Coquetdale, Redpath, Newcastle.

*DUNKLEY, C. (ed.) 1900 The Official Report of the Church Congress held at Newcastle upon Tyne on September 25th, 26th, 27th and 28th (1900), Bemrose, London and Derby.

*The Durham Diocesan Calendar, Clergy List and Church Almanack, Durham.

*FAWCETT, M. G. and TURNER, E. M. 1927 Josephine Butler, Association for Moral and Social Hygiene, London.

GAY, J. D. 1971 The Geography of Religion in England, Duckworth, London.

GILBERT, A. D. 1976 Religion and Society in Industrial England: Church, Chapel and Social Change, 1740-1914, Longman, London.

GILBERT, B. B. 1966 The Evolution of National Insurance in Britain, Joseph, London.

GILL, R. 1975 The Social Context of Theology, Mowbrays, Oxford.

*GILLY, W. S. 1841 The Peasantry of the Border: An Appeal in their Behalf, Berwick on Tweed.

*GOODFELLOW, D. M. 1940 Tyneside, The Social Facts, Introduction by R. H. Tawney, Co-operative Printing Press, Newcastle upon Tyne.

*GRACE, R. 1977 'Tyneside Housing in the Nineteenth Century', in N. McCord (ed.), Essays in Tyneside Labour History, Newcastle upon Tyne Polytechnic, Newcastle.

GRAY, W. F. (ed.) 1911 Non-Church-Going. Its Reasons and Remedies, Oliphant, Anderson, and Ferrier, Edinburgh and London.

HALL, M. P. 1960 Social Services of Modern England, Routledge and Kegan Paul, London and Boston.

HALL, M. P. and HOWES, I. V. 1965 The Church in Social Work, Routledge and Kegan Paul, London and Boston.

*HARE, J. C. 1893 The Story of Two Noble Lives, Vol.s 1-3, George Allen, London.

*HELLEN, J. A. 1972 'Agricultural Innovation and Detectable Landscape Margins: the Case of Wheelhouses in Northumberland', Agricultural History Review, 20, 2, pp. 140-54.

*HENDERSON, J. 1900 'Home Work: In the Diocese of Newcastle', in C. Dunkley (ed.) 1900 (see above).

*HENDERSON, P. 1978 *St. Paul's Parish, Elswick,* Dissertation, Newcastle upon Tyne Polytechnic.
*HENSON, H. H. 1943 *Retrospect of an Unimportant Life,* 2 vol.s, O.U.P., Oxford.
*HERBERT, A. 1923 *Northumberland,* Black, London.
 HOGG, G. W. and TYSON, J. C. 1976 *Popular Education 1700-1870,* University of Newcastle upon Tyne.
*HORNER, J. P. 1971 *The Influence of Methodism on the Social Structure and Culture of Rural Northumberland, 1820-1914,* unpublished M.A. thesis, University of Newcastle upon Tyne.
 HUNTER, L. 1953 *The Seed and the Fruit,* S.C.M. Press, London.
 HUNTER, L. (ed.) 1966 *The English Church — a New Look,* Pelican, Harmondsworth.
 INGLIS, K. S. 1960 'Patterns of Religious Worship in 1851', *Journal of Ecclesiastical History,* XI.
*INSKIP, J. T. 1948 *A Man's Job. Reminiscences,* Skeffington, London. (see Ch.s XIII and XIV).
*JACOB, E., Rt. Revd. 1900 'Inaugural Address' in C. Dunkley (ed.) 1900 (see above).
*JAGGER, P. J. 1975 *Bishop Henry de Candole. His Life and Times. 1895-1971,* Faith Press, Leighton Buzzard.
*JAGGER, P. J. 1978 *A History of the Parish and People Movement,* Faith Press, Leighton Buzzard.
*JONES, E. R. 1886 *The Life and Speeches of Joseph Cowen,* Marston, Searle and Rivington, London.
 KANE, M. 1975 *Theology in an Industrial Society,* S.C.M. Press, London.
*LAWS, W. G. 1890 *Report of the City Engineer relative to the Memorial on the Death Rate,* Newcastle City Council, Newcastle.
*LIGHTFOOT, J. B. 1882 *Primary Charge, Two Addresses Delivered to the Clergy of the Diocese of Durham in December, 1882,* Macmillan, London.
*LLOYD, R. 1946 *The Church of England in the Twentieth Century,* Vol. I., Longmans Green, London, New York, Toronto.
*LLOYD, R. 1950 *The Church of England in the Twentieth Century,* Vol. 2, Longmans Green, London, New York, Toronto.
*LLOYD, R. 1966 *The Church of England 1919-1939,* S.C.M. Press, London.
*McCORD, N. 1976 'The New Poor Law and Philanthropy' in D. Fraser (ed.) *The New Poor Law in the Nineteenth Century,* Macmillan, London.
*McCORD, N. 1979 *North East England: the region's development 1760-1960,* Batsford, London.
*McCORD, N. and ROWE, D. J. 1971 *Northumberland and Durham: an industrial miscellany,* Frank Graham, Newcastle upon Tyne.
*McCORD, N. and ROWE, D. J. 1977 'Industrialisation and Urban Growth in North-East England', *International Review of Social History,* XXII,1, pp. 30-64.
*MACDONALD, S. 1979 'The Role of the Individual in Agricultural Change: the example of George Culley of Fenton, Northumberland', in H. S. A. Fox and R. A. Butlin (eds.), *Change in the Countryside,* Institute of British Geographers, London.
 McLEOD, H. 1973 'Class, Community and Religion: The Religious Geography of Nineteenth Century England', in M. Hill (ed.) *Sociological Yearbook of Religion,* No. 6, S.C.M. Press, London, pp. 29-72.
*MESS, H. A. 1928 *Industrial Tyneside: A Social Survey,* Benn, London.
*MIDDLEBROOK, S. 1950 *Newcastle upon Tyne: its Growth and Achievement,* Newcastle Journal, Newcastle upon Tyne. Republished 1968, S.R. Publishers, Wakefield
*MIDDLEBROOK, S. (ed.) 1969 *Pictures of Tyneside or Life and Scenery on the River Tyne circa 1830,* Oriel Press, Newcastle.
 MILBURN, G. E. 1977 'The Census of Worship of 1851 and its value to the Local Historian', *Tyne 'n' Tweed Journal of the Northumberland Local History Society,* 29, pp. 3-13.

328

MURPHY, J. 1971 *Church, State and Schools in Britain, 1800-1970*, Routledge and Kegan Paul, London and Boston.

*National Sunday School Union, Annual convention, Newcastle upon Tyne 1932.

*National Sunday School Union and Christian Youth Service, Autumnal Convention, Newcastle 1949.

*NEVILLE, Hastings M. 1897 *Under a Border Tower*, Mawson, Swan and Morgan, Newcastle upon Tyne.

*Newcastle Church of England Institute, Annual Reports, 1862-1972.

*Newcastle Corporation, Schedule of Places of Worship (1967), Newcastle Corporation, Town Planning Commission.

*Newcastle Daily Chronicle (N.D. Ch.), after various changes of name, becoming incorporated into *The Newcastle Journal*, which itself had various earlier names. See also *The Evening Chronicle*, Newcastle.

*Newcastle Diocesan Association of Schools, Interim Orders and Trust Deeds, Minute Book 1937-48.

*Newcastle Diocesan Calendar (N.D.C.), 1882-1927; becoming *Newcastle Diocesan Year Book (N.D.Y.B.)*, 1928 to date.

*Newcastle Diocesan Gazette (N.D.G.), 1897-1933, becoming *Bishop's Letter and the Diocesan Newsheet (B.L.D.N.)*, 1934-1960; becoming *The Link*, 1961 to present.

*Newcastle upon Tyne Diocesan Education Board. Diocesan Educational Policy in the 1970s.

*Newcastle Diocesan Education Committee, Minute Book 1947-50, Executive Committee Minute Book 1956-60.

*Newcastle Diocesan Year Book (N.D.Y.B.), (see *Newcastle Diocesan Calendar*.)

*Newcastle Diocese *The Bishop of Newcastle's Fund. Annual Reports* (1-10), 1884-1893, published by *The Daily Journal*, Newcastle upon Tyne.

*Newcastle Diocese *The Consecration and Enthronement of the First Bishop of Newcastle, the Right Reverend Ernest Roland Wilberforce, D. D. on July 25th and August 3rd 1882*, Mawson, Swan and Morgan, Newcastle upon Tyne and Parker, London.

*Newcastle Diocese *Bishop of Newcastle's Commission 1926-7.*

*Newcastle Diocese *The Report of the Commissioners appointed by the Right Reverend The Lord Bishop of Newcastle to eaxmine into The Spiritual Wants and Requirements of certain parishes in the Diocese of Newcastle on the North Side of the River Ttyne, 1883.*

*NICHOLSON, M. 1970 *Noel Baring Hudson, 1893-1970*, Northern Press, Alnwick.

*NOEL, C. 1945 *Autobiography*, Dent, London.

NORMAN, E. R. 1976 *Church and Society in England 1770-1970. A Historical Study*, Clarendon, Oxford.

*The North Mail.

*The Northern Echo.

*PERRY, P. J. 1972 'Where was the "Great Agricultural Depression"? A Geography of Agricultural Bankruptcy in late Victorian England and Wales', *Agricultural History Review*, XX, pp. 30-45.

PICKERING, W. S. F. 1967 'The 1851 religious census — a useless experiment?', *British Journal of Sociology*, 18, pp. 382-407.

PICKERING, W. S. F. 1968 'Religion, a leisure-time pursuit?', in D. Martin (ed.), *A Sociological Yearbook of Religion in Britain*, No. 1, S.C.M. Press, London, pp. 77-93.

PICKERING, W. S. F. 1974 'The persistence of rites of passage: towards an explanation', *British Journal of Sociology*, 25, pp. 63-78.

*POWER, W. S. 1970 *The Real Thing*, Thomas Dixon, London. (see Ch.s V and VI).

*RENNISON, R. W. 1979 *Water to Tyneside: A History of the Newcastle and Gateshead Water Co.*, Newcastle and Gateshead Water Co., Newcastle.

*Reports of Her Majesty's Commissioners for enquiry into the Housing of the Working Classes 1884-5, Eyre and Spottiswoode, London 1885.

*RICHARDSON, W. 1923 History of the Parish of Wallsend, Northumberland Press, Newcastle upon Tyne.

*ROBERTS, J. S. 1887 *The Jubilee Handbook of Newcastle upon Tyne*, Newcastle.

*ROWE, D. J. 1971 'The Culleys, Northumberland farmers, 1767-1813', *Agricultural History Review*, 19, 2, pp. 156-74.

*ROWE, D. J. 1971 'The Economy of the North East in the Nineteenth century: a Survey with a Bibliography of works published since 1945', *Northern History*, VI, pp. 117-47.

*ROWE, D. J. 1973 'Occupations in Northumberland and Durham, 1851-1911', *Northern History*, VIII, pp. 119-31.

*ROWE, D. J. 1977a 'The Chronology of the Onset of Industrialisation in North East England', in M. Palmer (ed.), *The Onset of Industrialisation*, University of Nottingham.

*ROWE, D. J. 1977b 'The population of nineteenth century Tyneside', in N. McCord (ed.), *Essays in Tyneside Labour History*, Newcastle upon Tyne Polytechnic, Newcastle.

*SHULER, J. C. 1975 *The Pastoral and Ecclesiastical Administration of the Diocese of Durham 1721-1771*, (with particular reference to the archdeaconry of Northumberland), unpublished Ph.D. Thesis, Durham University.

*SMITH, J. 1977 'Public Health on Tyneside, 1850-80', in N. McCord (ed.), *Essays in Tyneside Labour History*, Newcastle upon Tyne Polytechnic, Newcastle.

*SNELL, B. J. 1884 *The Illustrated Guide to Newcastle-on-Tyne*, Thomas J. Scott, Newcastle.

*STREET, J. C. 1865 'The Night Side of Newcastle', *Medical Pamphlets*, 27, Newcastle.

*SURTEES, V. (ed.) 1972 *Sublime and Instructive: Letters from John Ruskin to Louisa Marchioness of Waterford, Anna Blunden and Ellen Heaton*, Michael Joseph, London.

*SWABY, W. P. (ed.) 1882 *The Official Report of the Church Congress held at Newcastle upon Tyne on October 4, 5, 6, 7, 1881*, Hodges, London.

*THOMPSON, F. M. L. 1963 *English Landed Society in the Nineteenth Century*, Routledge and Kegan Paul, London and Boston.

THOMPSON, D. M. 1967 'The 1851 Census of Worship: Problems and Possibilities', *Victorian Studies*, XI, pp. 87-97.

Tyneside Council of Social Service, Annual Reports, from 1929.

*WAINWRIGHT, R. C. (ed.) 1922 *Anglo-Catholic Congress in Newcastle upon Tyne, October 10, 11, 12, 13, 1922*, Richard Maynes Press, Newcastle upon Tyne.

*WALTERS, W. (ed.) 1869(?) *The History of the Newcastle upon Tyne Sunday School Union: From Its Formation to the Close of Its Fiftieth Year*, Sunday School Union, London.

*WARN, C. R. 1975 *Rural Branch Lines of Northumberland*, Frank Graham, Newcastle.

*WEBB, B. 1926 *My Apprenticeship*, Longmans Green, London.

*WEBB, B. 1948 *Our Partnership*, Longmans Green, London.

*VICKERS, H. 1922 *A History of Northumberland*, Vol. 11, Andrew Reid, Newcastle upon Tyne.

*VIDLER, A. 1977 *Scenes from a Clerical Life*, Collins, London.

*WAND, W. 1965 *Changeful Page*, Hodder and Stoughton, London.

WICKHAM, E. R. 1957 *Church and People in an Industrial City*, Lutterworth, London.

*YATES, N. 1975 *Anglican Parish Records*, Occasional Papers No. 1, North Tyneside Libraries.

INDEX

This index is of authors, churches, people and places. There are no entries under City or County of Durham, City or County of Newcastle upon Tyne, County of Northumberland, Diocese of Durham, Diocese of Newcastle, the North-East, Tyneside. Subjects are not indexed and there are no entries under the names of the denominations; nor have items in the Appendix been indexed. Some churches or parishes may be under the name of the church, or town or village, etc.: both possibilities should be checked. — Ed.

INDEX

Wilberforce, William W., 50
Wild, Bp. H. L., 55–7, 71, 168, 258–9
Wilkins, C. E., 260
Williams, Bp. A.T.P., 303–4, 312 n.5
Williamson, Hedworth, 20
Willington Quay, 12, 235, 302
Wilson, F. R., 183
Wingates, 301

Woodhorn, 72
Wooler, 183, 240, 295, 300
Wordsworth, Bp. Christopher, 33
Wylam, 10, 19, 248

York, 5; Diocese of, 80, 106
Young, John,180

NOTTINGHAM UNIVERSITY LIBRARY